HOMER AND HIS CRITICS

HOMER
AND
HIS CRITICS

by the late
SIR JOHN L. MYRES
O.B.E., D.Sc., F.B.A.

EDITED BY DOROTHEA GRAY
Fellow of St. Hugh's College, Oxford

ROUTLEDGE & KEGAN PAUL
London

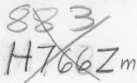
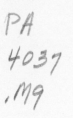
*First published 1958
by Routledge & Kegan Paul Ltd.
Broadway House, Carter Lane, E.C.4
Made and printed in Great Britain
by William Clowes and Sons, Limited
London and Beccles*

CONTENTS

ILLUSTRATIONS

Between pages 96–97

Plate

    (c) The Death of Achilles, West Greek (?), sixth century. (*MuZ* 163.)

6 Soldiers in formation

    (a) The Warrior Vase, Mycenae.
       (H. Bossert, *Altkreta*³ 135.)

    (b) (i) and (ii) The army of Rameses III engaging the Peoples of the Sea.
       (*OIP*, *Medinet Habu* I, Pl. 32.)

    (c) Athenians, eighth century.
       (*Ath. Mitt.*, 1892, p. 215.)

    (d) Assyrians, *c.* 700, from the Palace of Sennacherib.
       (A. H. Layard, *The Monuments of Nineveh*, I, Pl. 69.)

7 Siege scenes

    (a) Capture of an Hittite city by Rameses II.
       (Drawing from Wreszinski, *Atlas* II, 108, and H. Bossert, *Altanatolien* 758.)

    (b) Silver bowl from Amathus, Cyprus, seventh century.
       (*JHS* LIII (1933), Pl. 1, by permission of the Council of the Hellenic Society.)

8 Vases from eighth-century graves at Pithekussai, Ischia

    (a) Cup with inscription:

       Νέστορος: ε[---]ι: εὔποτ[ον]: ποτέριο[ν]·
       hὸς δ᾽ ἂ[ν] τôδε π[ίε]σι: ποτερί[ο]:, αὐτίκα κêνον
       hίμερ[ος: hαιρ]έσει: καλλιστε[φά]νο: ᾽Αφροδίτες.
       (*Rend. Linc.* X (1955), Pl. 111.)

    (b) Shipwreck (of Odysseus?).
       (*Röm. Mitt.* 60/61, p. 42, fig. 1. Photographs by the Deutsches Archäologisches Institut; the editor is much indebted to the generosity of Dr. G. Buchner.)

PREFACE

T HE first half of this essay took shape in 1931 as a course of six Ballard Mathews lectures in University College, Bangor. They should have been published forthwith; but other interests and duties intervened, and though I continued to lecture at Oxford on "Homeric Archaeology" till 1943 and gave the Charles Eliot Norton lectures in America for the Archaeological Institute in 1937–8, I published nothing in this field except a few reviews, the substance of which is incorporated here, and a study of *Homeric Art* in the *Annual of the British School at Athens* XLV (1950). Meanwhile the course of Homeric criticism has been rapid and many sided, stimulated chiefly, as heretofore, by literary comparisons and archaeological discoveries, but also by cross-lights from the most unlikely sources. Consequently it has not been so easy as before to detect and formulate main lines of progress. It has taken a really epoch-making achievement, like the interpretation of the Minoan Script, anticipated in Evans' address to the Hellenic Society in 1912, to force all scholars to take stock of their methods and achievements, and to fall back on fundamental studies in epic poetry.

It is deliberately, then, at this stage of Homeric Criticism, that I offer this retrospect of the remoter as well as the newer past. It is something to be able to close a few blind alleys and to show why other lines of enquiry have been as fruitful as they have.

J. L. M.

Oxford, January 1954.

Sir John was not able to complete or revise his lectures before his death in March 1954, and I was glad to agree to Mr. J. N. L. Myres'

suggestion that I should put them into a form suitable for publication. Though I have tried to avoid the "insidious peril of devout
editorship", much recasting of the form was inevitable, including a
little writing up of jottings left as notes. In the content, when I knew
that fresh material had caused Sir John to change his opinion, I
altered his text; otherwise I omitted the passage or rephrased it to
show that the conclusion was reached on the evidence available a
quarter of a century ago. The result is less a systematic history than a
series of essays differing in scale; the chapter on Gladstone, for
example, taken from his inaugural lecture at Liverpool, is fuller than
the rest. They bear, however, the stamp of a very individual approach,
and since much in them was fresh to me, I hope that others also will
find something which is not in the many other books about Homeric
criticism. Sir John liked people who took their Homer actively;
Virgil because he wrote the *Aeneid* and Chapman because he made
Homer an Englishman, Gladstone because he used him as a living
force in Oxford education, Wood because he went to look for the
places and Schliemann because he dug for the kings. The emphasis
is less on the academic critic than on the traveller, the poet and the
gifted amateur. He had a good eye for the permanently important.
He saw that, although questions and answers seem to chase each
other on a treadmill, they emerge from each cycle with a slightly
greater air of verisimilitude. He was a hopeful traveller, and that is no
small merit in an Homerologist.

Sir John drew his allusions from a wide field, and I am grateful to
more people than I can name individually, and especially to my
colleagues at St. Hugh's, for help in tracing references which ranged
from Christian allegory to twentieth-century films. I have added the
footnotes, and two concluding chapters which take the main themes
of the essays down to September 1957.

D. H. G.

ABBREVIATIONS

AA	*Archäologischer Anzeiger.*
AJA	*American Journal of Archaeology.*
AS	*Anatolian Studies.*
Ath. Mitt.	*Mitteilungen* des deutschen archäologischen Instituts, Athenische Abteilung.
BCH	*Bulletin de correspondance hellénique.*
BICS	*Bulletin of the Institute of Classical Studies,* London University.
BSA	*Annual* of the British School at Athens.
BSR	*Papers* of the British School at Rome.
CAH	Cambridge Ancient History.
Class. Phil.	*Classical Philology,* Chicago.
Class. Rev.	*Classical Review.*
CQ	*Classical Quarterly.*
Δελτ.	Ἀρχαιολογικὸν Δελτίον τοῦ Ὑπουργείου τῶν Θρησκευμάτων καὶ Παιδείας.
Documents	Michael Ventris and John Chadwick, *Documents in Mycenaean Greek,* 1956.
EA	Ἐφημερὶς Ἀρχαιολογική.
Ergon	Τὸ Ἔργον τῆς Ἀρχαιολογικῆς Ἑταιρείας
Goldman	*The Aegean and the Near East: Studies presented to Hetty Goldman,* 1956.
ILN	*Illustrated London News.*
JdI	*Jahrbuch* des deutschen archäologischen Instituts.
JHS	*Journal of Hellenic Studies.*
JRAI	*Journal* of the Royal Anthropological Institute.
Karo	G. Karo, *Die Schachtgräber von Mykenai,* 1930–33.
Monuments	H. L. Lorimer, *Homer and the Monuments,* 1950.

Mus. Helv.	*Museum Helveticum.*
MuZ	E. Pfuhl, *Malerei und Zeichnung der Griechen*, 1923.
Myres	J. L. Myres, *Who were the Greeks?* 1930.
OIP	*Oriental Institute Publications*, University of Chicago.
Op. Arch.	*Opuscula Archaeologica.*
Palace	Sir Arthur Evans, *The Palace of Minos*, 1921–36.
PPS	*Proceedings* of the Prehistoric Society.
RE	Pauly-Wissowa-Kroll, *Realencyclopädie der Altertums-wissenschaft.*
Rend. Linc.	Atti della Accademia Nazionale dei Lincei: *Rendiconti.*
Rev. Arch.	*Revue archéologique.*
Rhein. Mus.	*Rheinisches Museum.*
Röm. Mitt.	*Mitteilungen* des deutschen archäologischen Instituts, *Römische Abteilung.*
Trans. Phil. Soc.	*Transactions* of the Philological Society.

Chapter One

HOMERIC CRITICISM: THE MEANS
AND THE END

IT is not easy to say anything new about Homer. In Greek antiquity he was studied and annotated as no other ancient author was, or deserved to be; for however implicitly each generation of Greeks accepted the authority of Homer, as a source of inspiration and a standard of achievement, as literature, as history, as instruction and guide in matters of belief and conduct, they recognized in his work something distinctive and apart from themselves; and while the fact of this aloofness was accepted and did not need to be explained, the consequences of it—certain unique merits, and not a few difficulties in the use and enjoyment of his work—challenged enquiry, and evoked what may justly rank as *criticism*; in the sense (which I hope I may take as agreed) that a "critic" is one who not only is affected in a certain way by that which he criticizes, but is moved to ask why he is so affected, and to seek by analysis and comparison to determine exactly what it is that so affects him, and how this influence is produced. We shall (I hope I may assume) agree also that it is but the beginning of wisdom to know what it is that we know or feel, and how it comes about that we know *this* or feel *so*: by which I mean that literary and artistic criticism has this in common with the parallel enquiries into the nature of things around us, and into human nature —the nature, that is, of ourselves—namely, that experience is providentially linked with experiment; the need to *know*, with the need also to *do*. We seek first to discover how Homer (or Shakespeare, or Michelangelo, or Beethoven, or Rodin) achieves his dominion over us; how he has himself attained to his own art and mystery of craftsmanship, to that outlook over things which he communicates to us, to that mastery of what lies under his hand which makes all things new when that hand has passed over them. Yet to discover this is but the revenue side of the critic's account with him. On the opposite page of that account is the use which we may make of that analysis, that reasoned account of our experience, for the enlargement, disentanglement and articulation of our own experience and the training of our own native ability. So we may begin to see things as Homer or Shakespeare saw them, and be, in our own outlook and our rendering of it in expression, ourselves more Homeric, more Shakespearean, more nearly master-craftsmen in the supreme art of living well, in the twentieth century.

Homer must be, of course, for every one of us, his own interpreter. That is, I hope, presupposed; we either know our Homer passably well, or are trying to know him and to see things as he sees them. But in this pursuit of the Homeric outlook on things, with the double objective of recreating that which Homer was, and of becoming that which Homer in our time can, if we will, guide us to be, no recorded experience of what other people in the past have known and felt about Homer can be without significance or without value to us. All criticism has some value, but the criticism that goes beyond reasoned analysis has most to give. Consider the best of what the Greek critics of Homer have to offer us as the conclusion of their experience. Compare this with what Virgil, for example, found in Homer and learned from Homer how to do, with what Chapman or Pope or Madame Dacier found in him, with what Robert Wood or Goethe or Wolf or Schliemann saw in Homer and (in the light of that revelation) went on to *do* for themselves. You will realize then that the significance—let us call it frankly the inspiration—of a great poet *lives* evergreen and like the tree of life "yieldeth her fruit every month". All that any critic of Homer can do is to bring his knowledge and interpretation up to date, abreast of his generation's outlook— perhaps in some particular a little ahead of it, as a few great critics have done.

Now it may happen that someone coming quite fresh to a study of this kind, like our own Keats "on first looking into Chapman's Homer", may have the good fortune to bring some natural gift or store of experience, competent to reveal great poetry in a quite fresh light and in original perspective. So aircraft has given us a quite fresh revelation of the meaning of landscape and architecture, and of the organic make-up of cities like Florence and Oxford which we knew before, from maps and sketches and pedestrian excursions in Flatland, to be beautiful and full of meaning, but not yet *how* great in these respects. But commonly there is a third element in criticism; over and above the work of art and the native genius of the critic, there is the whole world of associations which the critic brings by way of traditional preconceptions; and there is the special halo—or is it sometimes a haze?—of traditional interpretation, which clings round an artist and his works, in whatever form the critic first encounters them. Keats, for example, first encountered Homer in Chapman's Elizabethan English; most German boys meet him first in the megalithic hexameters of Voss. But how many people, for example, first read Homer or Homeric matters in Greek? How few, even of these, first encounter Homer, not on a printed page, but recited under a clear Greek sky, or even read aloud by an old Jew in an attic, as happened to Heinrich Schliemann?

The true object of Homeric Criticism is to understand and appreciate the Homeric poems both as masterpieces of literature and as documents in the history of early Greek culture. As poetry they are independent of place and date, for their appeal is to human nature. Yet they were composed (every line of them) *somewhere* and *somewhen*, and, since both poems are long and complex, they were composed in some order of their parts and in accordance with some design. Indeed, they are so long, and so complex, as to suggest some change of design, perhaps even *re*composition, and this forces us to ask whether the divergencies are such that they require a longer period of composition than a single lifetime and show a greater diversity of outlook and technique than is compatible with single authorship. This further question has come to be treated as if it were in some sense *the* Homeric Question, whereas it is, at most, only a special phase of it. As documents in the history of early Greek culture, the poems stand in reciprocal relation to the culture to which they belong. They contribute, by their content as well as by their form as works of a particular school of craftsmanship, to our knowledge of that period and country and people, or, if their origin be composite, of the various periods, districts and communities within which one or another section originated. For they describe types of armour and

3

modes of fighting, houses, furniture and way of living, political situations and religious customs and beliefs, which are all liable to change from time to time and from place to place. They are only appreciated in their full meaning if, by comparing what they do describe with other data, we can assign them to their time-context and study them against their proper background, including aspects of life not specifically mentioned in the poems themselves. Thus anything we may learn about pre-Hellenic and early Hellenic civilization contributes, or may contribute, to our appreciation of the poems as history and as literature. To this end, the methods to which we must turn are those supplied by philology, including metrology, and history, including archaeology, sociology and literary history.

Philology comes first, because the primary condition of appreciating or understanding the poems is an accurate knowledge of their language. Not only is the vehicle of information and ideas the prime condition of the growth of any literature at all, but the language of the poems is of unique importance as evidence for a specific stage, or stages, in the growth of the Greek language. It certainly influenced later phases, such as the diction of tragedians and historians, and it was itself influenced by the idiom of later phases; the so-called "Atticisms" in Homer have been recognized as such since the fourth century B.C., and may be the reason for the belief in a "Peisistratid" recension. Here again it is a further question whether the Homeric idiom is itself homogeneous, and, if it is not, whether the variations are to be explained by development from early to late within the tradition, or by the combination of elements from contemporary but different dialects; and it is a further question still whether these processes of development and conflation are too long and complicated to have occurred within one man's lifetime. With philology goes metrology. Presumably Homeric audiences, not to mention Homeric poets off duty, normally talked in prose; like Monsieur Jourdain, they did not know that they did so, but none the less it was merely prose. But the poems are in verse, and verse of a high order of construction and flexibility as a literary form. The determination of the place of this verse form among Greek metres and in relation to other early metres and rhythms is a separate enquiry, to be made on similar scientific lines. If the flexibility and handling of the Homeric hexameter are found to vary, the limits of this variability must be established quite independently of the grammatical enquiry into the

4

homogeneity of the dialect and are a distinct criterion of the relative age of parts of the poems. These achievements in linguistic and metrical form are all that has been preserved to us directly of the arts and crafts of the Homeric Age. In the long process of transmission, for a while perhaps mainly by word of mouth but for a much longer period in written copies, they have certainly been exposed to the risk of careless handling and to the more insidious peril of devout editorship; and it is a preliminary question, which every critic of Homer must face and answer for himself, how far what came down to the first printers of the poems may be trusted to represent even what the first copyist had before him in early Hellenic times. Of this by no means negligible contrast we may perhaps form some idea if we compare the spelling and punctuation of any modern pocket Bible with the first edition of the same "Authorized Version", or an "Everyman" Shakespeare with a First Folio. It is only one step backward from this, though it may be quite a long one, to enquire how closely the verses dictated to the earliest writer of an Homeric text conformed to those which first delighted an audience attuned to pre-Homeric entertainment:

$$\tau\grave{\eta}\nu \ \gamma\grave{\alpha}\rho \ \dot{\alpha}o\iota\delta\grave{\eta}\nu \ \mu\hat{\alpha}\lambda\lambda o\nu \ \dot{\epsilon}\pi\iota\kappa\lambda\epsilon\acute{\iota}o\upsilon\sigma' \ \ddot{\alpha}\nu\theta\rho\omega\pi o\iota,$$
$$\ddot{\eta} \ \tau\iota\varsigma \ \dot{\alpha}\kappa o\upsilon\acute{o}\nu\tau\epsilon\sigma\sigma\iota \ \nu\epsilon\omega\tau\acute{\alpha}\tau\eta \ \dot{\alpha}\mu\phi\iota\pi\acute{\epsilon}\lambda\eta\tau\alpha\iota^{1}.$$

For those alone were authentic, and the voice which uttered them perished at the end of each line. All extemporized recitation, however carefully prepared within the creative mind, is immortalized, like the masterpieces of oratory and much of the finest bronze work, by a *cire perdue* process. Homer himself, like Pericles and Demosthenes, we shall never hear, any more than Aristarchus heard him, or than Aeschylus was present at the "great banquet" of old song, from which Homer, he thought, had carried away so much and he himself so little.[2] Thanks, however, mainly to the metrical form, the epic hexameter, which in its Homeric form we must, I think, regard as the outcome of some experimental process; thanks also to the probability, which in view of recent discoveries we must, I think, regard as increasing, that alphabetic writing had a longer and more widely distributed vogue than examples of it on intractable materials such as stone or bronze would indicate, we may regard extant epic as being at least as well transmitted as lyric or elegiac poetry.

[1] α 351–2.   [2] Athenaeus, *Deipnosophistai* VIII, 347 e.

Of the historical evidence, the archaeological deserves to be considered first. The material contents of the poems, like the daily life of the people among whom and for whom they were composed, include two quite distinct kinds of facts, both made known either by direct statement or by allusion. Warriors of all periods fight with weapons of some kind; men and women of all periods wear some kind of clothing, live in some kind of homes, fashion and enjoy works of decorative art, and usually also of representative art. From one period to another, fashion changes in the form and use of these; and if such changes are reflected in descriptions embodied in the poems, it is a fresh and independent question what the significance of these changes may be. Now, the equipment consists of material objects which, if they are of durable material, sometimes outlast their makers and users and are preserved to our own time. Partly by comparison between similar but slightly varied forms, leading to technological conclusions as to development of type and style, partly by the more stringent test of stratigraphical superposition of later above earlier forms in excavated sites, leading to archaeological conclusions in the more special sense of the word, it is possible to determine not merely the relative antiquity of different phases of style and usage but, within certain well-defined limits, the chronological age of some or all of them, in terms of documentary history. Not dissimilar are the methods of sociology, which may be called the archaeology of immaterial things. Side by side with descriptions of material works of art or craftsmanship which outlast the acts that create them, the poems contain descriptions of manners and customs—marriages and funerals, for example, acts of worship, beliefs and principles of conduct in private or public life, all, in fact, that we describe as a people's civilization. And these too change as time passes and differ from place to place. At one period, for example, a whole nation faces destruction rather than surrender a prince's stolen bride; at another, a writer like Herodotus can think it historically impossible that they would not have given up Helen if they could.[1] Now, since social structures and usages leave no such "deposits" behind them as manufactured equipment does, the precise nature of the changes, their causes and their effects, cannot be verified archaeologically except in so far as they determine the plan and construction of buildings or the lay-out of towns. Yet by comparative study of insti-

[1] II, 120; cf. the "Persian account", I, 4, 2–4.

6

tutions, a high degree of probability is attainable as to the order in which such changes of observance occur; and just because none of the changes leaves any tangible remains, descriptions of them can hardly be other than contemporary. Consequently it is possible to recognize as earlier or later passages in the Homeric poems those which describe earlier or later customs, for example as to the endowment of a bride or the expiation of blood guilt. Once again, to be of critical value at all this investigation must reach its conclusions by its own appropriate method, and independently of any considerations derived from those other enquiries which have been outlined already.

A special category of such sociological or cultural facts, liable like the rest to vary from place to place and to change from time to time, is the place occupied, in what we may perhaps anticipate the argument by calling "Homeric Society", by poets and their poetry. Here, too, we find traces of different social conditions, not necessarily incompatible, but distinct. On the one hand there is the wandering minstrel, friend or devotee of the muses or recalcitrant against them,[1] on the other the court poet, established in a particular palace-society, and an honoured member of it for his personal skill.[2] A third category covers the accomplished amateurs, Achilles consoling his solitary leisure with κλέα ἀνδρῶν, or Odysseus entertaining his Phaeacian hosts with five whole books of his own *Odyssey* and anticipating the Hesiodic *Eoiai* by his *Vision of Great Women* in the *Nekyia*.[3] Now, since the days of wars and wanderings, of heroes and palace-society, belong to the traditional past of the Greek world and are only perpetuated into the classical period in outlands such as Cyprus and Cyrene, and since wandering minstrels like Thamyris are difficult to distinguish from those who congregated, like the "blind old man from Chios", at the Delian Festival and on similar occasions, the same question arises in regard to the literary antiquities which the poems contain; are these different customs also to be conceived as having coexisted within the lifetime of one poet or as evidence of earlier or later date of composition for the sections which mention them?

While fashions of equipment and social observances, and even the status and function of the poet in society, change as a rule gradually and uniformly over the whole area of a civilization, those changes

---

[1] B 594–600.   [2] α 153–55, etc.; θ 62–70.
[3] I 189; λ 225–330.

7

which we call historical events result in the main from the over-mastering action of individuals or of closely knit communities and lead to consequences which were usually unforeseen. They are there-fore never repeatable at will, in the sense that you may repeat an order for armour or clothing, or marry off a whole generation of brides with similar ceremonies. Now, both Homeric poems have as their main theme events of this kind, and in each poem the action is projected upon a coherent background of other events. The situation they describe was familiar to the Greeks of the classical age as a period in their own not very distant past, and the Trojan War and its sequel of perilous *Returns* stood in a clearly conceived perspective among the most important events of that period. The War was not only a consequence of outrageous conduct under the conditions of a precisely defined type of society, it was also the cause of other histori-cal events, and especially of the disintegration of the Achaean *régime*, the effects of which were propagated into fully historical times. The Peisistratids in Athens, for instance, were believed to be Neleids from Nestor's Pylos, and Evagoras was king of Salamis in direct descent from Teucer, the brother of Ajax.[1] Among the historical events, unforeseen, irrevocable and unrepeatable, of that Heroic Age and of the Dark Ages into which its survivors fell, one fact, or rather one series of achievements, stands out as undisputed and unparalleled— the creation of the Homeric Poems themselves; poems which are among the supreme masterpieces of literature, of human mind and tongue. Somehow, somewhere, somewhen, from a repertory of traditions, legends, folklore and myth, someone was moved to choose two tales. Each belonged to a popular and numerous class, the *Iliad* to the cycle of Μῆνιες or *Quarrels of the Chiefs*, the *Odyssey* to that of Νόστοι or *Homeward Wanderings*; but whoever chose them, retold them in his own way. How much more than this we must suppose to have happened is a matter for speculation. After this creative genius had passed away, did his poems fall for centuries into the destructive custody of careless, reckless, unimaginative "editors", "expanders" and "interpolators"? Before he set to work, had others practised the same minstrel's art with varying degrees of success? Before he began to plan his *Iliad*, for example, did there already exist many shorter poems, of diverse authorship, with various idioms, intonations,

[1] Hdt. IX, 97 and Paus. II, xviii. 9; Isocrates IX, 14–18, and Paus. I, iii. 2.

styles of composition and ways of telling the story, so that his work was less creative than editorial? Or again, did both processes occur, and if so, in what proportion of previous and of subsequent stages? Or finally, did both these processes, however protracted, effect little change in comparison with the work of the great poet, so that through and among sources and supplements we may still detect, in something more than outline, his poems reverently conserved through after-time? All these hypotheses about sources and transmission provide us ultimately with the commentary on those masterpieces, the setting for those jewels; and we are left, in the phrasing of Robert Wood's essay, with "The original genius of Homer" as the central problem of the Homeric Question. To this object of enquiry, all examination of language and metre, material resources, social observances, historical periods and crises, is supplementary and subordinate. They may narrow the issues, close attractive bypaths, and exclude tempting alternatives; but they are the signposts and the hedges, not the road that leads each seeker after Homer to the Homer he deserves.

That is why the Homeric Question stands, with the other great questions of literature and of history, and with the greater questions of the other sciences, outside the limit of finality. There is always something new to be learned about Homer; like the leaves of the trees, critic falls after critic, theory after theory, and school after school; of one achievement of scholarship after another we may say, as the poet of his own verses, "that song ever is sweetest which most newly assails men's ears". But it is we, and our tools and methods, that change, not the genius of Homer nor the perennial humanity of the poems. And such enquiry is cumulative in its results; "as iron sharpeneth iron", so doubts and conjectures challenge new study of these originals, reveal new points of view and establish new positions by new methods of reasoning. It is in the conviction that criticism, in spite of popular misapprehension, is a progressive and constructive study, tending not only to the discipline of a liberal education but in the strictest sense to the advancement of science, that I have ventured upon the retrospect of Homeric studies which follows; tracing within the large main divisions of them which I have outlined, the transmission of whatever seems to me permanently valuable in what has been contributed (so far as I have been able to ascertain it), and the gradual, though by no means uniformly rapid, elimination of one source of error or illusion after another. In such

9

a survey, much useful work unavoidably goes unnoticed, not because it is uninstructive but because it happens not to be so typical of its kind, nor so effectual, through the accidents of date and place, as that which finds mention. Most of all, among the more recent literature, contributions of which the full bearing is not yet apparent are probably discussed less prominently than they deserve. That is the retribution on all compilers and most historians; only the Nestors of our craft "look alike before and after".

What, on the other hand, I most hope that I shall have succeeded in doing, is to illustrate that interdependence of distinct lines of research on each other's results; history and archaeology, for example, afford to the philologist and literary critic vistas of time for the production of effects within their special department, which earlier workers were not justified in postulating in the stage of historical or archaeological discovery during which they worked.

Chapter Two

HOMER AND HIS CRITICS
IN ANTIQUITY

⎯⎯⎯⎯⎯⎯⎯⎯

Before we can safely discuss the significance or the value of a
work of art, we must be certain, if that is possible, what it is that we
are discussing. Even with a picture or a piece of sculpture, this is
not always certain. There are, of course, deliberate falsifications,
sometimes easy, sometimes almost impossible to detect, until (as in
recent instances which are notorious) modern chemistry or X-ray
brings devastating disillusionment; but sometimes, quite apart from
these, we find ourselves confronted with school-pieces, the work of
pupils and understudies, where the master's conceptions and
technique are rendered, not quite as he might have rendered them
himself, but so conscientiously and closely that it is only by scrupulous comparison with authentic masterpieces, or by the flair of a born
expert, that the vital distinction is made. In material works of art,
however, we are at all events dealing with originals, which we see
and handle for ourselves; and everyone who has had to order goods
from a catalogue, instead of selecting them over the counter, knows
how much that means. But in literary criticism we are dealing with
texts; and a text, as its very name implies, is itself a fabric, a tissue,
constructed by the subsidiary craftsmanship of printer and scribe,
editor and amanuensis, who are intermediary between the author and
ourselves. How different our own writings, still more even our most
formal utterances, look when presented to us again in "cold print"!
Sometimes we are so fortunate as to have access to an author's auto-
graph copy; and by comparison of this with the so-called "first

11

edition" we realize how much editing has gone to the making even of that; for while the printer's devil lies in wait on the one side, the publisher's reader lurks meticulous and remorseless on the other; nor are the writer's second thoughts always like those of the Creator when "God saw every thing that he had made, and, behold, it was very good". Sometimes we are in a position to know that what has been transmitted is only the rough copy for oral discourse or for a master-piece of which only parts ever received the last revision. Most of the works of Aristotle, and the fifth and eighth books of Thucydides, we read as we study a print from an etching of Rembrandt while it was in its "first state", or it may be in its "second" or "third"; at all events not in any sense a "perfect work". We know that there were two such "states" of the *Clouds* of Aristophanes; how does our text of the play stand to either of them? What "purple patches" from the first found their way into the published edition of what purports to be the second? On the other hand, how much of the long geographical exposition in the *Prometheus* as Aeschylus produced it, for a fifth-century audience eager to go in and possess the good land that was slipping from the grasp of the King of Kings, was cut by the manager of a fourth-century revival, leaving Io and the gadfly between them to stage that flying leap from Transcaucasia to the Far West?[1] But these masterpieces had at all events a "first night" performance, however little we may be able to learn of what then occurred. We know at all events what we are looking for.

To answer analogous questions about the *Iliad* and the *Odyssey*, however, we have first to frame the questions themselves. It is use-less, for example, to enquire into an original state of the text, if we do not even know within centuries when the text was written down, or how much of it was written by any one hand or in any one generation of men. It is premature to criticize the merits or the defects of the plot and construction of these admitted masterpieces, until we have either laid the ghost, or resurrected the personality, of the Peisistratid Editor, the contriver of the *Wrath of Achilles*, and those other ἀμενηνὰ κάρηνα who flitter round every one of us when we leave the light of the sun about the time of the Persian Wars, and go down into the Dark Ages to take counsel with the shade of Homer.

---

[1] 791–2; but in *Class. Rev.* LX (1946), pp. 2–4, Myres proposed an interpretation of the passage which makes it unnecessary to assume extensive cuts by later stage-managers.

Sometimes, like the soul of Anticleia, he whom we seek is within speaking distance; but when we seem nearest to it,

> ἐκ χειρῶν σκιῇ εἴκελον ἢ καὶ ὀνείρῳ
> ἔπτατ',

"like a shadow, yea, or a dream, it flies from our hands"; and we hear a voice, surely not Homer's but the mockery of modern analysts:

> ἀλλ' αὕτη δίκη ἐστὶ βροτῶν, ὅτε τίς κε θάνῃσιν.
> οὐ γὰρ ἔτι σάρκας τε καὶ ὀστέα ἶνες ἔχουσιν,
> ἀλλὰ τὰ μέν τε πυρὸς κρατερὸν μένος αἰθομένοιο
> δαμνᾷ, ἐπεί κε πρῶτα λίπῃ λεύκ' ὀστέα θυμός,
> ψυχὴ δ' ἠΰτ' ὄνειρος ἀποπταμένη πεπότηται.
> ἀλλὰ φόωσδε τάχιστα λιλαίεο.

"Yet this is the way of mortals when they die; no longer do sinews hold flesh and bones together, but then the strong force of blazing fire conquers, when the life first leaves the white bones; but the soul like a dream flutters and flies away. Turn, then, and quickly set thy face towards the light."[1] The Homeric Question, indeed, is harder to put than to answer.

The *Iliad*, as we have it, has been transmitted in no less than 188 manuscripts and the *Odyssey* in 76, an unusually large number, testifying to the popularity of Homeric poetry after the middle of the fifteenth century, and to a smaller vogue in the thirteenth. They have essentially the same tradition, and may be regarded as establishing the vulgate text of Hellenistic times. In addition there are some 500 fragments of papyrus copies, mostly of the third and second centuries A.D. with a few which go back to before 200 B.C.[2] They exhibit a text very close to that of our manuscripts, but they are embellished with additional lines which are a little surprising until we turn to the record of the great Alexandrian editors; for a large part of their work consisted in signalling (though fortunately not in ejecting) such lines, mainly on the ground that they did not appear in texts then current in various parts of the Greek world, which they

[1] λ 207–8, 218–23.
[2] MSS. of the *Iliad* from P. Mazon, *Introduction à l'Iliade*, 1942, and G. M. Bolling, *Ilias Atheniensium*, 1950; of the *Odyssey*, from T. W. Allen, *O.C.T.*; R. A. Pack, *The Greek and Latin Literary Texts from Greco-Roman Egypt*, 1952, lists 1233 Greek texts identified by author, of which 488 are Homeric texts and 62 Homeric commentary, and other fragments have been published since.

had reason to believe to be trustworthy. On the other hand, though occasionally lines contained in the received text can be shown to have been missing from careless copies, we have obviously no means of knowing how much had already been omitted, in this way, before Alexandrian times; and instances of such early loss are known, when pre-Aristarchian papyri or passages quoted by fifth and fourth-century writers have lines which do not occur in the vulgate or in the critical notes. The fact that the Alexandrian editors did leave in the text the lines which they disallowed, while marking them with an obelos, is strong testimony to the popularity of the vulgate; and the very small number of their amendments which is transmitted in extant manuscripts is further proof of the general confidence in its authenticity.

There had been critical attempts to improve the received text at least as far back as the generation of Alcibiades;[1] but they seem to have been private ventures, without vogue or authority. Moreover, not only were the Homeric poems taught to boys as an essential element in the normal programme of education, but the great majority of people could, and did, "keep up their classics" so far as Homer was concerned, by attending public performances, some of them official, by professional reciters such as Plato has described in the dialogue between Socrates and a stranger named Ion, who is represented as one of them. These performances were competitive, under rules of procedure which were believed to be Solonian, and designed to ensure the presentation of the poems as consecutive wholes and the acquaintance of the performers with them as such, not merely with favourite passages. With a public which had at least the familiar acquaintance which a churchgoer has with the Bible; with a professional class of reciters, free in their interpretation but restricted as to their subjects; with state regulation of customary public performances; and with the public respect for Homeric authority which is attested even by those who disapproved of Homeric doctrine and morals; the circumstances would appear to have been on the whole favourable to careful if not flawlessly accurate transmission, so long as these conditions held good.

But how long did this system exist? On the educational side, attesting general acquaintance with Homeric literature—in an age when *all* literature was produced for oral performance, either publicly, or (as with lyric) within social groups of some magnitude—

[1] Plutarch, *Alcibiades* 7; Aelian, *V.H.* XIII, 38.

there are the protests of the educational reformers, Xenophanes and Heracleitus, against the Homeric presentation of the gods; protest as eloquent for the sixth century as those of Plato are for the fourth.[1] For general popularity, there are the numerous vase paintings, Athenian, Aeginetan, Corinthian, Chalcidian, of Homeric scenes, sometimes authenticated by the written names of the personages, more commonly not and all the more significant for that reason. They go back (some of them a good way) beyond the beginning of the sixth century; the "Euphorbos-plate", of Asiatic fabric, with Argive-Dorian lettering, and therefore probably Rhodian, the Aeginetan jug showing Odysseus and the Ram, and the Cretan plate with Peleus and Thetis, take representations of the stories well back into the seventh century.[2]

Ancient critics certainly knew that at Athens the Ionian alphabet had replaced the older Attic alphabet at the close of the fifth century, and it has been suggested that they used this knowledge to explain and correct what they regarded as errors in their texts of Homer. But this notion, though in antiquity Galen thought that it explained corrupt passages in the text of Hippocrates,[3] does not seem to have been at all widely employed by the Alexandrian critics; at most it is applied to a few vowel sounds of which the pronunciation and, still more, the metrical value were variable. The principal modern exponents of this theory either wrote, like Cobet,[4] before modern epigraphy came into being, or, like Wm. Christ,[5] in a surprising

[1] Diels, *Vorsokr.*[6], Xenophanes fr. 11, Herakleitos fr. 42; Plat., *Rep.* 377d–388d.

[2] *MuZ.* 117, 64–5, 57.

[3] *In Hippocratis epidemiarum libr. VI comm.* III, 44, III, (*C.M.G.*, 1940). γραφόντων γὰρ τῶν παλαιῶν τόν τε τοῦ η φθόγγον καὶ τὸν τοῦ ε δι' ἑνὸς χαρακτῆρος, ὃς νῦν μόνος σημαίνει τὸν ἕτερον φθόγγον τὸν τοῦ ε, πολλὰ γέγονεν ἁμαρτήματα τῶν ἐκγραφομένων. . . . ὁμοίως δὲ κἀπὶ τοῦ ο καὶ ω ποιητέον, ἐπειδὴ καὶ τούτων ἀμφοτέρων οἱ φθόγγοι δι' ἑνὸς χαρακτῆρος ἐγράφοντο. cf. *in Hipp.* κατ' ἰητρεῖον II 23, XVIII, b 778 K (Kühn). κατὰ τὸν ὀνομασθέντα μεταγραμματισμόν.

[4] *Miscellanea critica* (1876), pp. 289–98, οἱ μεταχαρακτηρίσαντες.

[5] *Geschichte d. gr. Literatur* (1884), pp. 105–6. *IG* (Attica) I was published in 1873 and A. Kirchhoff, *Studien zur Geschichte des gr. Alphabets* in 1863, but much work was published between 1876 and 1884, e.g. *IG* I (suppl.)–III, G. Dittenberger, *Sylloge inscr. Graec.*, H. Roehl, *Imagines insc. Graec. antiquiss.* On the alphabets, see P. Chantraine, *Grammaire Homérique* I (1948), pp. 5 ff.

ignorance of the epigraphical material. It is worth considering whether poems commonly believed to be of Ionian origin were written out in the old Attic alphabet at all. Even supposing that the poems were arranged and edited for Peisistratus, which is quite a different matter, there is no reason to believe that they were then written down for the first time; and if these old Ionic poems already existed in manuscript, it is reasonable to suppose that they were written in the Ionian alphabet; and also as unreasonable to suppose that they were then transliterated into the old Attic alphabet, as to suppose that Solon's poems or his letter to Mimnermos of Chios were written in any other script than that appropriate to the dialect in which they were composed. For there is ample evidence that it was mainly, if not only, for official purposes that the old Attic alphabet was conserved at Athens until the official adoption of the Ionian alphabet at the end of the fifth century. For literary works and every-day purposes, the Ionian alphabet had long been in general use. There is consequently no reason to suppose any sudden or systematic modification of the outward appearance of the poems between the fifth and the fourth centuries. Athenian copyists, doubtless, during both centuries, played a large part in the dissemination of a text more liable to accidental intrusion of Attic forms than the texts transmitted in other regions of Greece; and analogy with other literary masterpieces suggests that it was in the fourth century in particular that the texts of Greek classics were established, which were the material for Alexandrian criticism.

Can we go further back than this? On the one hand the metrical form was some safeguard for the verbal phrases, and the establishment at Athens, as early as Solon's time, of a customary order in which sections of the epic *corpus* were to be recited, perpetuated the plan and content of the poems as they then were. For clearly there was in some sense a plan, if there was a risk of such deviations as sensibly detracted from the significance of the distinct sections. On the other hand a very large part of the criticism of the earlier Alexandrians was concerned with the expurgation of spurious lines, which had therefore slipped into the poems between the date of their composition and that of the copies, official and otherwise, collected from all over the Greek world for the Alexandrian Library. How much was lost by the same processes we have no means of judging. The number and quality of the lines rejected by the critics illustrate the looseness of Homeric syntax and the extent to which almost inevitably clauses were coextensive with lines. At most it is only a reasonable interpretation of the critics' allusions to their own and each other's procedure to suppose that they compiled a text which included all extant lines known to them, while obelizing in it those lines which they themselves respectively rejected. But we know enough of their materials and of their practice to be aware that they regarded the poems as having been more seriously affected by deliberate interpolation than by mere careless omission; and this, so far as it goes, is reassuring in respect to the structure and contents of the poems which have been preserved at all.

Of the poet's personality, it has been observed by J. A. Scott, a champion of the unity and uniqueness of Homer, that "different traditions in regard to Homer, his life and his work, become fuller and more definite as they get further away from any possible sources of knowledge".[1] Of himself the poet says nothing, and of his own country, even of his topographical surroundings, almost as little; and he never names either of his poems, any more than Hesiod mentions *Iliad*, *Odyssey* or Homer when he quotes or corrects them. All the more important, then, are the few personal clues which rest on something else than the guesses of late and lazy commentators. First, the name Ὅμηρος is known to occur in Greek inscriptions from districts which were historically Aeolic, and hitherto has occurred only there.[2] As to its meaning there was controversy already in antiquity; but it is a real personal name, not merely an epithet or description meaning "blind", "hostage" and so forth. Secondly, while in a sense all who owed their inspiration or their livelihood to Homer's work were his offspring and of one kindred after the spirit, they had not necessarily more to do with their namesake than the Rechabites have with theirs. There was, indeed, in early classical times a guild of singers who called themselves Homeridae and seem to have had some footing or connexion with the island of Chios. Whether they were Founder's Kin or graduated professionally is not known, but their existence is in either case proof of the respect in which the Homeric tradition was held and the care taken to maintain it by those interested.

The numerous *Lives* of Homer, mostly composed as editorial

[1] *The Unity of Homer* (1921), p. 3.
[2] Paul Mazon, *Introduction à l'Iliade* (1942), p. 263.

introductions to late editions of the poems, seem to be careless versions of a single body of tradition, collected not much earlier than the time of Augustus. A few of the statements contained in these *Lives* can be traced back in other writers also as far as the fifth century. The half humorous notion of an "imaginary conversation" and competition between Homer and Hesiod, which as we have it is later than the accession of Hadrian, was probably taken from the *Mouseion* of Alcidamas, a sophist of the fourth century, and it preserves a number of epic verses which seem to be ancient. Now, Plato had heard somewhere, or pretended to have heard somewhere, that the Guild of the Sons of Homer had a store of "private verses",[1] and these may have included a traditional biography of their namesake and been the source of the verses. To such conjectures and Jacob's ladders are we reduced when we try to discover from the learned of Greece, *who Homer was*.

Yet the Greeks from first to last accepted on traditional evidence a personal Homer, the single author of the *Iliad* and (as all but one short-lived group of sceptics believed) of the *Odyssey* also. Herodotus writing about the religious beliefs of his countrymen, distinguishes three main sources of tradition.[2] The first of them is Egypt, with which for Poseidon and Athena he associates other parts of North Africa; and here his argument shows that what he is summarizing is Ionian speculation based on comparisons of certain Greek cults with Egyptian cults, with which Greek travellers and residents in Lower Egypt had been able to make superficial acquaintance since the end of the seventh century. Egypt, however, had no worship of heroes at all, and the cult of Hermes and certain venerable aspects of the worship of Zeus had no parallel there. For these, and for the essentials rather than such superficial details as divine names (where it is obvious how his Egyptian information had led him unawares to argue in a circle) he looks to the relatively barbarous north-western frontier between Greek lands and the rest of the sub-continent of which they are the shallow frontage towards the Aegean. But archaic observances at Dodona and in Samothrace—his two principal examples—do not carry him far; and he dates the revelation of Greek personal gods with their names and of the rational order of the world, not from ancient times, but, as he says, "from yesterday and the day before". "Hesiod and Homer I believe to have been in date four hundred

[1] *Phaedr.* 252 b.　　　　　　　　[2] II, 49–53.

18

years before my time and not more, and these are they who composed a 'birth of the gods' for Greece, and gave the gods their titles and ranks and functions and described their appearance. The poets who are said to have preceded these men came later, in my belief." This he gives as his own opinion, and distinguishes it from what he had heard at Dodona.

The Hesiodic poem on the *Birth of the Gods* has survived. It is a close-knit metrical catalogue of genealogies, divine and heroic, declining at times into a mere list of names, conventional and often prosaic in style. What is preserved runs to 1022 lines, or as much as two books of the *Iliad*. It ends with a list of the goddesses—Aphrodite, Thetis, Circe, Calypso—who bore hero children to mortal husbands, and the prelude to a similar list of human women, γυναικῶν φῦλον, which is lost. It contains a few simple explanations of ritual and folklore: the origin of the sacred stone at Delphi (497–500); the reason for the reservation of the bones and fat of sacrifices to the God, while the worshippers ate the meat (535–60); the origin of fire and the creation of woman, of whom the poet has only a poor opinion (562–612). The most important revelation of this kind, however, the Five Ages of Humanity, is not included in the *Theogonia* but appears in an early section (90–201) of that earlier and perhaps only original Hesiodic poem, the *Works and Days*, where it follows an alternative version of the creation of fire and womankind. So far as it goes, that is, the Hesiodic *Theogonia* is planned to fulfil the function ascribed to it by Herodotus, to "give the gods their titles and ranks and functions"; only rarely does it describe their appearance, or enter into ceremonial details.

On the other hand, if the "Homer" in this passage of Herodotus means the *Iliad* and the *Odyssey*, it is not at first sight clear how these poems do what is described at all. They are narrative poems, of war, and of adventure and intrigue respectively. They contain hardly any didactic matter, and what there is, appears as illustrative digression to explain some point in the action. The Gods, and especially a few Gods of the first rank, take part in the story and profoundly affect its course; by studying their doings, we get a partial and none too favourable impression of high life in Olympus, and of a world-order in which the Gods have really little more authority or responsibility than the heroes. Behind the fretful, voluptuous, henpecked figure of Zeus we have glimpses of a fatality, Μοῖρα, which none can resist

19

and man challenges at his peril; of the Angels of Death—κῆρες θανάτοιο; of Ἄτη, an impersonal devil, almost in the Christian sense of that word, a power not ourselves which makes for un-righteousness. The Gods are neither the makers of the world, nor even (as has been said) its landlords. Of Poseidon it cannot be said that "the sea is his, and he made it"; it became his share of the loot, when the Olympians conquered, by force and fraud, an older dynasty of gods like themselves. Zeus can cloud the sky and send abroad his thunderbolts; but it is not he who sends the seasons in their order, any more than he piled up Olympus or Mount Ida. The problem is not solved by the suggestion that by Homer a fifth-century writer meant not only the *Iliad* and *Odyssey* but the rest of the poems eventually canonized as Cyclic; for the contents of these, so far as we know them, are of the same narrative construction and content as the *Iliad* and *Odyssey*; like them, if they were included in the "Bible of the Greeks" at all, they taught by illustration not by precept, as the books of Samuel and Kings may be described as "written for our learning". Clearly, whatever Herodotus meant when he assigned to Homer, side by side with Hesiod, this high function as interpreter of the ways of Gods to men, it is of no assistance to us in distinguishing between what Herodotus regarded as Homeric, and what he did not.

Xenophanes and Heracleitus, two generations earlier, took the same general view of the literary function of Homer. It was the things that Homer let the Gods do, not his system of theology, which roused the wrath of educational reformers. And the inference seems to be unavoidable that in the sixth century the Homeric poems had to be endured, by all but such extremists, because they could not be cured; that they had already a traditional form and content, and were not susceptible of expurgation or amendment; that they were already in the same sense "canonical books" as the Hebrew scriptures had come to be at the same stage in their history; that they were attributed to a personal Homer, in popular belief, in the same way as the *Works and Days* and the *Theogonia* were attributed to a personal Hesiod; and that the sole difference in respect of origin between these "great originals" and the schoolpieces which supplemented and imitated them, was that they were indeed original, in the sense in which the others were not; older, superior in beauty and finish as literature, authoritative in moral and theological significance, a voice from beyond the local and personal, self-justifying and therefore precarious varieties of what we may justly describe as "apocryphal" epic. It is worth noting here that the Hesiodic *Works and Days* differs from the *Theogonia* in this very point. The *Works and Days*, though addressed to the individual, Perses, are silent about their author. The *Theogonia* in a very pretentious prelude leads up to the introduction of the man Hesiod into the poet's calling by the Muses whom he serves.[1] It is in the manner of the *Hymn to Apollo* and the *Margites*, not of the *Iliad* or *Odyssey*.

It has been thought that from the middle of the fifth century onward the volume of literature which was accepted as in the strict sense Homeric became steadily less. A principal argument is that Herodotus regarded the *Cypria* as the work of another poet, not of Homer, on the ground of discrepancy with the accounts given in the *Iliad* and *Odyssey* of the route taken by Paris and Helen; Herodotus doubted also whether the *Epigonoi* was Homer's work, though he gave no reason for this opinion.[2] In spite of Wilamowitz's ingenious advocacy and Allen's acceptance of this view, there is no good reason for supposing either that Herodotus was the first to challenge the Homeric authorship of the *Cypria* and *Epigonoi*, or that the rest of the poems later described as "cyclic" were ascribed to Homeric authorship either originally or even at all. When this opinion is given in the *Certamen*, it is only as "some people's theory", $\phi a\sigma i$ $\gamma \acute{a}\rho$ $\tau\iota\nu\epsilon s$.[3] The circumstance that in the narrative the decision takes the form of a preference for the Hesiodic type of epic, dealing in advisory fashion with events of daily life, over the narrative epic of wars and adventures, proves indeed that Homer's works were regarded as typical of a class, but it is very far from confirming the view that all narrative epic was originally believed to be in one and the same sense Homeric, any more than it would prove the complementary view that all didactic poems were regarded as alike Hesiodic. And if the tradition may be trusted that at Athenian festivals in the sixth century precautions were taken to ensure that what was then accepted as "Homeric" should be recited in proper order, not in selections offered by the performers, it follows that the

[1] 22–34.
[2] II, 117, IV, 32. Wilamowitz, *Die Ilias und Homer*, p. 399; Allen, *Origins and Transmission*, p. 130, n. 2.
[3] 260.

21

total length of the poems then accounted "Homeric" did not exceed what could be recited on such an occasion; and consequently did not include in any sense "all epic", nor even the poems other than the *Iliad* and *Odyssey* which were eventually grouped into an Epic Cycle. Indeed, all that we know of ancient opinion about the Cycle, except the two passages of Herodotus already mentioned, goes to show that a clear distinction was maintained between the *Iliad* and *Odyssey* on one side, and all other epic poems on the other. If there was an early poem on the War with Thebes, as is not improbable, and if it was at one time attributed to Homer, which is doubtful, it seems in any case to have been superseded early by the *Thebais* of Antimachus (which was regarded in Roman times as a fine piece of work), much as the *Argonautica* of Apollonius of Rhodes probably caused the neglect and loss of any early poems on that subject which may have existed in his time. But even the Homeric mention of the Argo as a popular subject ('Ἀργὼ πᾶσι μελοῦσα[1]) does not prove that there was a Homeric poem about it; still less do the Homeric allusions to the Theban War prove a Homeric *Thebais*.

The belief in a personal Homer could not, and did not, blind Greek critics of Homer to "anomalies" as they called them—discrepancies and inconsistencies within poems which were admittedly Homeric in the fullest sense, improbabilities as to the conduct of the War, such as attracted the notice of Thucydides,[2] differences of usage between events as described in the poems and the customs of everyday Greece. Had the poems been regarded as anonymous folk poetry, like the popular epic of the Serbs, short work could have been made of such anomalies, by rewriting or by explanatory additions. But Alexandrian editors of Homer thought that little more had been done in this direction than by mere carelessness in transmission. They treated therefore both kinds of contamination alike, signalled all attempted amendments as un-Homeric, and concentrated their critical activity, not on bringing Homer up to date, but on reconstituting the original words of a personal author, already ancient and therefore in some respects antiquated. Now this is quite different from the procedure of Greeks of all known periods in their treatment of the rest of their epic repertoire. For example, the *Little Iliad* and the *Sack of Troy* cover in part the same ground, drawing from a common store of popular tales and handling them freely. Again, granted

[1] μ 70.   [2] I, 10.

22

that there was an old *Thebais*, or old poems about the *Labours of Hercules* or the *Voyage of the Argonauts*, nothing prevented Peisander in the seventh or sixth century from composing a *Heraclea* of his own, nor did this prevent Panyassis in the fifth century from repeating the venture. Antimachus of Colophon wrote his new *Thebais* in the fifth century, Apollonius his *Argonautica* in the third, and so forth. Similarly the later literary forms, lyric and tragic, borrowed and remodelled freely the contents of the Cycle and *Thebais*; from the *Thebais* alone we have the *Seven against Thebes*, the two Oedipus plays, the *Antigone*, and the *Phoenissae*. Yet they almost completely avoided the main episodes of the *Iliad* and *Odyssey*, and only rarely used even subsidiary incidents, as the story of Dolon was used for the *Rhesus*, and episodes from the *Odyssey* for the *Cyclops* of Euripides, or, to take the nearest approach to a serious loan, for the *Agamemnon* of Aeschylus. But we should note that the story of the fate of Agamemnon, so far from being canonically registered in Homer, is told more than once and in different ways. Clearly, where Homer himself had taken a second helping from the "great banquet" of legend spread before him, Aeschylus felt himself free to eat from the same dish. This general abstention from the ground covered by the *Iliad* and *Odyssey* is only partly explained by the fact that in some Greek states, perhaps in many, and notably in Athens since Solon's time at least, the two poems had been canonized by habitual, public and officially-conducted recitations. What is much more striking is the very small use made by the great linguistic critics of the grammar and vocabulary of the cyclic poems in illustration of the Homeric text. Clearly the two poems attributed to the personal Homer were felt to stand in a class by themselves, just as they were assigned by common consent to a period considerably earlier than any other poems of the same narrative class, and even a little earlier apparently than the earliest Hesiodic poems of daily life.

Now, in this ancient history of Homer we must make the same distinction as we did in general at the outset. There was customary, unthinking enjoyment of Homer, as part of the necessary furniture of civilization in Greece; there was conscious, intentional utilization of Homer, as a school text in education, elementary and other, and as a guide to correct literary style; and there was the critical approach to both—reasoned analysis and evaluation of the sources of the enjoyment, in literary and historical interpretation, and reasoned defence of the use of the poems in education. As we have seen, the systematic conservation of the traditional text, including as far as possible recovery of its damaged passages, was a necessary preliminary to any such analysis and estimate of its value.

For the first (Homer as a classic) we have the fact that by the time the Greeks began seriously to think about Homer and examine his works, as the works of Plato and Hippocrates were examined by students of morals and medicine, the poems were already a popular possession all over the Greek world. The Alexandrian critics had the use of manuscripts from places as remote as Massilia by the mouth of the Rhone and Sinope on the Black Sea and Cyrene in North Africa. For the second, we have the typical schoolboy in Aristophanes,[1] the stories about Alcibiades and the schoolmasters of the age of Pericles,[2] and the testimony of Xenophon's friend for about 420 B.C.: "My father, eager to have me become a good man, compelled me to commit to memory all the poetry of Homer, and thus it happens that even now I can repeat from memory all the *Iliad* and *Odyssey*";[3] not because there were no written texts, but because what was desired was not the skill to find a given passage by chapter and verse in a book, but that intimate familiarity and inseparable companionship which a good many people even now retain in some measure from their school days, if not of Homer, at all events of the Bible and of the *Pilgrim's Progress*, the Christian *Odyssey*. It is when we come to the third aspect of the Greek view of Homer as an object of criticism that we are conscious, as the Greeks were themselves, of disillusionment.

In the first place, Greek political institutions, and indeed the structure of Greek societies generally, were already very different from those described in the poems. At the period when we have the first glimpse of Homeric literature, the Achaean dynasties, with a few remote exceptions, had long ceased to exist; the very word πόλις in Homer means always a fortress, not a state; the πολῖται are its garrison, not the governing body of a free city. There are clans, Λαοί, who hold together in war and in rough and ready reprisals for murder and other serious offences; and there are elder statesmen, γέροντες, who hear pleadings and in some fashion assist in settling disputes; but there is neither council of elders nor mass-meeting of citizens,

[1] *Daitaleis* fr. 222. [2] Plutarch, *Alcibiades* 7.
[3] Xen., *Symposium* 3, 5.

24

regularly convened, and there is a political as well as a social gulf between the "divine-born" Kings and their subjects. Even the brief description given by Thucydides of the earliest phase of constitutional history known to him in Greece, "hereditary monarchies on terms of stated privileges",[1] sits very ill on the great Achaean chieftains. Consequently the political knowledge and most of the political wisdom of Homer were obsolete and inapplicable in most city-states. We see this disillusionment looming up already in Aristophanes' contrasts between the classical and the modern side in education; and Isocrates was flogging a dead horse when he quoted the Trojan War as an incentive to a pan-Hellenic invasion of Persia.[2] Greek morality, too, under the severe constraint of that period of migrations and collapse of old *régimes* (from which those city-states emerged, fully organized, when we first have knowledge of them), had matured rapidly, and, what was more significant, had begun to turn upon itself and ask introspective questions about the *grounds*, as well as the *rules*, of conduct. Here the great conceptions of *Aidos* and *Nemesis*, as Gilbert Murray has shown,[3] which are fully presented in Homeric discussions of behaviour, are aspects of a conception of *conscience* and of a social morality far in advance of the political structure of the societies which sheltered them; and it is to these conceptions mainly, and to the graphic illustrations of the application of them to the conduct of individuals, that the poems owed whatever authority they retained in the classical age. Murray himself is so conscious of this "anomaly"—to revert to an Alexandrian term—that he regards the higher morality of the poems not as original but as superimposed, the result of a long half-unconscious process of expurgation and moralization. But (however this may be) the conceptions themselves remain unanalysed, and even undefined. $N\acute{\epsilon}\mu\epsilon\sigma\iota s$ is, briefly, my feeling about this man's behaviour, or that man's feeling about my behaviour, that "this sort of thing is not done", and that, if done, it incurs not only disapproval but material consequences. $Ai\delta\acute{\omega}s$, its correlative, similarly, is my feeling about myself, and that man's feeling about himself, that such behaviour "does not do" for me or for him. But why this or that "is not done" by decent people, or obviously "would not do" for me or any one of them, is nowhere explained. Only in the wrath of the

---

[1] I, 13, 1.　　　　　　　　　　[2] *Panegyricus* 158–9.
[3] *Rise of the Greek Epic*[4] (1934), pp. 82–92, 120–45.

25

Gods, or of a God, does νέμεσις reach an intensity which is deterrent, because it is coercive and not moral at all. Similarly the Homeric conception of μοῖρα, μόρος, the share or portion which falls irrevocably to a God or a man, has not been reconciled in the poems either with the purpose of Zeus, Διὸς βουλή, which plays so perplexing a part in the *Iliad,* nor with the notion that a man may even act or suffer ὑπὲρ μόρον, beyond his fate. Most disquieting of all, the Homeric presentation of the Olympian theocracy, which was still the official expression of Greek religious beliefs, with its ruthless anthropomorphism, and its reckless insistence on the bad temper, bad faith and bad habits of certain Gods, seemed to destroy any disciplinary value which the notion of a Divine Wrath might have for ill-doers who did not respect the wrath of their fellowcitizens. Gods who interfered in wartime to protect their worshippers were intelligible; if they disguised themselves and gave treacherous advice to the enemy at a critical moment in a duel, it was only what a human patriot might do in wartime without disgrace; but Gods who could not be kept off the course during a race and interfered with two of the competitors, came out badly beside the human sportsman who had to clear himself on oath of the suspicion of even trying to cause a foul.[1]

These were inconsistencies between Homeric and Hellenic beliefs and behaviour, which shocked educational reformers from Xenophanes and Heracleitus at the close of the sixth century, to Plato in the fourth; and there were others which became apparent in the Alexandrian age, when the dynasties of the Succession Kingdoms had made Greeks more familiar with the behaviour proper to Kings' courts than they had been since the time of Croesus. That Athena should herself carry a lamp to light Telemachus along a corridor,[2] was a lapse of manners unthinkable in a Berenice or a Cleopatra. But the worst disillusionment came from the change of outlook in the Greeks themselves; or rather among those Greeks of whose Homeric studies we happen to know most, namely the scholars of Alexandria. Here, though in Greek communities throughout Egypt we trace a pathetic attempt to retain the traditional attitude of mind to Homer, the teacher and guide of life, in the numerous copies of the poems

[1] Γ 373ff.; X 226ff.; Ψ 382ff., 566ff., 768ff.

[2] τ 33–34. It was, however, saved from athetesis by the explanation λείπει τὸ ὡς.

26

which were dog-eared and scrapped in the process, the Alexandrian College of All Muses appears to have lost touch with life just as it seemed about to gain real touch with Homer. The study of vocabulary, which had begun in the fifth century as a necessary aid to interpretation, served now mainly to provide curiosities of diction for the court poets; the study of metre served only the same people, now that public recitations were out of fashion; history, even of the free Greek states of the classical age, still more, that of the Homeric age, had almost ceased to have any bearing on politics or diplomacy, now that the masters were no longer city-states like Athens, Sparta or Thebes, but upstart Macedonian adventurers and their descendants in the Succession Kingdoms. Consequently the study of the Greek *classics* —for such they had already become—and not least the study of Homer, became an indoor pursuit, a library subject; and it was because the Homeric poems accorded less with this new outlook than the rest that we have Eratosthenes saying that Odysseus' account of his adventures was suited rather for entertainment than for education.[1] What indeed was there for the great geographer to say about the *Odyssey*? Cyclops island, Calypso island, even Phaeacia, were not on the map at all; the Cimmerian country was in the wrong place; Scylla and Charybdis, located in the Straits of Messina, had lost their terrors; the Planctae, the Wandering Islands, once charted at the entrance to the Bosphorus, were no longer a danger to navigators. In a civilization where even Aristotle complained that "everything would soon have been found out",[2] and the specialists of the Museum had multiplied Aristotle's knowledge tenfold, there was less scope for insisting on the numberless trivial points on which Homer's observation was true and vivid, than for discussing alternative theories as to why he was wrong when his imagination led him into Outland. And meanwhile the rise of a proficient school of literary epics, such as the new Argonaut poem of Apollonius of Rhodes, threw the older epic out of fashion even for recreation, in a city where Homer was in any case as much out of his element as he was in the dull, gaudy, modern, cosmopolitan Alexandria. We have seen something of the same kind in our own time, when the

[1] Strabo 7. οὐδὲ γὰρ ἀληθές ἐστιν ὅ φησιν Ἐρατοσθένης ὅτι ποιητὴς πᾶς στοχάζεται ψυχαγωγίας οὐ διδασκαλίας. Strabo's defence of Homer occupies most of his first book. See especially 22–25.

[2] Cic. *Tusc.* III, 28, 69.

disillusionment of the nineteenth century with the authority of early Hebrew literature in matters of geology, natural history and to some extent even of morals and religion, has been followed by the picture-house pageantry of the *Ten Commandments*,[1] and the latter-day creation myth of Bernard Shaw; to go *Back to Methuselah* [2] is only halfway back to Genesis.

One result of that lack of local *mise-en-scène* in this Greek Chicago, squatting on a flat foreshore of the Wild South, was to increase the impression, which as I have suggested was already beginning to be felt by the earlier Greeks, that Homer was not quite of this world. Even the later epics, collected now into some kind of orderly cycle according to their subject matter, stood further and further aloof from the *Iliad* and *Odyssey*, as the differences of vocabulary and diction, still more of plot and contents, were revealed by the new methods of verbal criticism. For so long as there could even be a doubt whether the *Cypria* or the *Epigonoi* were in the strict sense Homeric or not, their contents at all events might count, as indeed they counted for Aeschylus, as "dainty dishes from the great banquet". For the Alexandrians they were demonstrably not *that*, and if even they were not admissible as evidence—well, there was nothing for it; Homer, like the Almighty, must be his own inter-preter, a doctrine of despair which we shall see looming up again later,[3] in circumstances which in certain respects recall those of Ptolemaic Alexandria. Consequently Alexandrian criticism found its horizon fatally contracted, just at a moment when in every direction the range of observation and the principles of classification as a basis for inference to fresh results, were amazingly and very rapidly extended. While Aristotle's *Poetics*, and especially his epoch-making comparison between Homer and the Tragedians,[4] became obsolete, his discoveries in logic and his application of them in physics and natural history opened a new period in ancient sciences. In the absence of material for comparative treatment, Homeric study lost touch with other kinds of humanity and was divested of historical background and perspective. Standards of taste and truth to fact became subjective and personal; the spontaneous music and free naturalism of Homer were judged by composers of verses according

[1] Directed by Cecil B. de Mille for Paramount, 1923.
[2] London, 1921. [3] See p. 93 below.
[4] 23. 1459^a 23—1460^a 21.

28

to rule, and by dependants of a court which inherited or revived the ceremonial of an Egyptian dynasty.

Let us, however, see the positive results of Alexandrian criticism, as well as its dreary failure. It developed the methods of philological criticism initiated by the sophists of the fifth century, when the search for ὀρθοέπεια led Protagoras to classification and Prodicus to definition.[1] The boys who used Homer as a school-text must be helped to understand the actual phrases of the narrative by etymological explanations, and the subject matter could be elaborated in the manner of a sermon or lecture, as Gorgias does in his surviving *Praise of Helen*.[2] This exegesis or interpretation of the subject matter drew attention to "anomalies" in the poems, and raised the same controversy between "anomaly" and "analogy" in literary criticism as in grammar. For those who adopted the one hypothesis about Homeric criticism, analogy pointed to the need for a scientific text. They possessed a criterion for recognizing genuine material, and anything in the poems which did not satisfy it could be regarded as "un-Homeric" and properly obelized. The "real Homer" was held to be the single, personal author of the *Iliad* and *Odyssey*; the other epics were more or less successful imitations of the "real Homer", foisted on him more or less clumsily by their real authors; οἱ περὶ Κύναιθον, οὕς φασι πολλὰ τῶν ἐπῶν ποιήσαντες ἐμβαλεῖν εἰς τὴν Ὁμήρου ποίησιν, or Stasinus, who more ingeniously claimed to have received the *Cypria* as dowry with Homer's daughter.[3] For their opponents, anomaly pointed to the need for literary and historical criticism of the poems as they existed, in their contexts and against a historical or even evolutionary background. The first step to the separatist conception of an Epic Phase with plural authorship was the separation of *Odyssey* from *Iliad*. This should logically have proceeded to a rehabilitation of the Cycle and the older *Thebais* and *Argonautica*, but unfortunately the previous Hellenic age had degraded these poems irretrievably. In any case, the *Iliad* and *Odyssey* were themselves so vast a problem that neither school of criticism had energy to look beyond them. Literary and historic exegesis passed in Stoic hands into allegorizing, or at best mythological commentary, or indulged in an uncritical form of Euhemerism; while heroes

[1] Plato, *Phaedr.* 267 c, *Protag.* 337 a–c.
[2] Diels, *Vorsokr.*[6], II, pp. 288–94.
[3] Sch. Pind., *N.* II, *init.* For *Cypria*, Homer V (*O.C.T.*), pp. 116–18.

became modern virtues, the Gods became prehistoric men. The difference between the methods of "analogy" and "anomaly" was really one of degree not of quality. Aristarchus, for example, went back to bed-rock, in the shape of the text re-established by Zenodotus and Aristophanes. He made a fresh collection of "Homeric usages", both in language, including even the commonest words, and in custom and belief. Only on the strength of his own independent generalizations from Homeric "anomalies" thus inductively established did he venture to revise further the "reformed" text which had come down to him from his immediate predecessors. Even in this, a large part of his own work was conservative. Especially he restored many lines which had been prematurely condemned by Zenodotus. At the same time, he discovered new "anomalies" within the Homeric usages so formulated, and therefore raised afresh the question whether this or that deviation from Homeric usage was due, in a particular passage, to a mistake in transmission.

Two points need to be emphasized here, if the work of these great pioneers in scholarship is to be rightly estimated. Firstly, our information about their procedure and results has been transmitted in a controversial form. Where they agreed, there was in the existing state of knowledge nothing further to be said about the passage. Consequently we are left in ignorance of a very large part of their activity, especially their application of the principle of "analogy" when it established the traditional text instead of throwing doubt on it, and their deliberate allowance for "anomaly" where, for example, metre precluded uniformity of grammar. This defect is common to our knowledge of all ancient research work. Secondly, the critics accepted all the material within the poems as homogeneous. It was the fundamental contention of the separatist heresy that the differences of style and treatment between the *Iliad* and the *Odyssey* were too great to be compatible with single authorship. But the separatists were put on a false track by their contemplation of the two poems as wholes. One of the greatest advances in modern criticism, made essentially by Grote about 1840,[1] is that the resemblances with the *Odyssey* (and the contrasts too) are more marked in some parts of the *Iliad* than in others. This led to the conception of the *Iliad* as consisting of a shorter poem on the *Wrath of Achilles*, expanded by the insertion of episodes unconnected with Achilles and handled less with reference

[1] pp. 91–2 below.

to the wrath *motif* than to the course of the Trojan War as a whole. The Alexandrian critics accepted the one personal poet, at very least of each poem; consequently their concessions to "anomaly" were far less than become at once obvious on the alternative hypothesis of multiple authorship. Preoccupied with the previous question of re-establishing the text and starting from a mass of very various details, they were separatist without scruple as to single lines, but omitted in general to apply their minute knowledge of grammar and content to the larger literary structure of the poems. They did, however, apparently, admit the *Doloneia* as interpolated.

Aristarchus in particular accepted (for some reason or other) the belief that the personal Homer was Athenian. Consequently the occasional use of Attic forms of speech and the presence of passages showing special knowledge of Attica or interest in Attic history, though occurring in essentially Ionian poems, did not disturb him, any more than Ionic forms had disturbed Zenodotus; indeed he re-admitted one of those which Zenodotus had ejected.[1] The principal passage of this kind is one of the occasions on which the presumption that Zenodotus had already ejected it has deprived us of the reasonings of either critic.[2] The effect of these same passages on the Megarian historian Dieuchidas was that his Megarian patriotism and acceptance of the common belief that the personal Homer, like his general language, was Ionian, led him to accuse the Athenians of having inserted passages, about Salamis, in particular, and the Salaminian hero Ajax, in their own political interest.[3] Long afterwards we hear of an alternative Megarian version, but it never appears in our texts.[4] That this was a real political issue, at least as early as the fifth century and apparently also in the sixth, is clear from the special explanation given by Herodotus of the fact that Ajax, though not an Attic hero, was selected to be the patron saint of one of the new tribal divisions of Athens in the constitutional reforms of Cleisthenes before the end of the sixth century.[5] A further consequence of Aristarchus' belief in an Athenian Homer is that he took no interest in the theory, which was already current before the end of the fourth century, that it was Hipparchus the son of Peisistratus who introduced the Homeric poems into Attica as a deliberate measure of educational policy. Yet it was in fact the argument of

[1] *B* 553–55, cf. *H* 475.   [2] *B* 558.   [3] *F. Gr. Hist.*, 485. 6.
[4] Strabo 394.   [5] V, 66.

31

Dieuchidas that the poems were already in use in Attica and that Solon had provided for their proper conservation; anything that could be ascribed to the Peisistratids had been in the way of corruption, not improvement.

The Alexandrian Age of scholarship, and of Homeric criticism in particular, lasted about as long as the modern critical period of scholarship; from Zenodotus to Aristophanes is about as long as from Wolf to Lachmann (1785–1884), and from Zenodotus to Aristarchus about as long as from Wolf to the present day. During this century and a half they collected and collated a mass of manuscript material from all parts of the Greek world, large enough to be representative of the Homeric tradition as it stood at about 250 B.C. They confirmed that the tradition was in essentials well founded, with the exception of a small proportion of "anomalous" lines scattered all through the poems. The earlier excesses of the theory of "analogy" were for the most part corrected by the more cautious judgment of Aristarchus, and it was recognized that "the usage of the poet", τὸ ἔθιμον τοῦ ποιητοῦ, discovered from study of the texts themselves, demanded greater concessions to "anomaly". The only recorded attempt, that of the *Chorizontes*, to explain "anomalies" by plural authorship, was defeated,[1] largely because of the narrowness of its approach, but even the school of "analogy" conceded the *Doloneia* and the *Continuation* of the *Odyssey*. In general, however, the Unitarian belief was (fortunately) so strong that even Aristarchus' rejections were only signalled, not omitted, and were perpetuated in the standard tradition; and some "expanded" copies, resembling the pre-Alexandrian versions, remained in popular use for a while, at all events in Egypt.

Alexandria was not the only school of Homeric criticism in Hellenistic times, but the accident which has given us our knowledge of its services to the text has no parallel. Demetrius of Scepsis, a typical local antiquarian, wrote a vast commentary on the Homeric *Catalogue of Priam's Allies*; and from the copious use which Strabo made of it in the thirteenth book of his *Geography*, supplemented by some anecdotes and allusions, we form some idea of the school of Pergamum. It was as romantic in its outlook and, like later romantics, as inclined to jump to conclusions as the Alexandrian was austerely philological. But the political history of the Kingdom of Pergamum

---

[1] Aristarchus wrote a monograph πρὸς τὸ Ξένωνος παράδοξον.

was short and its end unworthy; its school of scholarship established no living tradition, and a good deal even of what has been preserved about its contentions is triumphant rejoinder from Alexandria. It has its counterpart in mediaeval learning, in the craze for identifying "sacred places" on slender evidence; Attalus I thought he had discovered on Mount Ida the very pine tree under which Homer in one of his extant *Lives* is said to have slept.[1]

Independent criticism faded out before the Augustan Age. Even the possibility of research into Homeric origins was precluded by the underlying assumptions. The prevalent Unitarianism reduced this question to a matter of biographical detail and left us *Lives* of Homer instead of an account of the "Homeric Age". Moreover, the growing acceptance of the belief in a Peisistratid Recension carried with it the conviction that Homer's own work had been disarranged and that even the Alexandrian collections could not carry the traditional text back beyond the late sixth century. Especially the rarity of actual quotations from the other epics and the demonstrable slovenliness of the later commentators and encyclopaedists, who copy from one another, raises the suspicion that only the *Iliad* and *Odyssey*, and perhaps the *Thebais*, remained in general circulation. Pausanias, quoting Callinus and "many other reputable authorities" for the Homeric authorship of the *Thebais*, adds that he himself appraises the poem next after the *Iliad* and *Odyssey*, whereas Hadrian thought it superior to them[2]; but we may wonder if Hadrian was referring to Antimachus' poem. There is the same doubt about the *Thebais*, which must be assumed to have survived long enough to be used by Statius. Pausanias quotes the *Cypria* as if he knew the text,[3] and Atilius Fortunatianus, if we may believe him, had a copy of the *Margites* perhaps as late as the end of the third century A.D.[4] We hear a good deal more of the Stoic interpretation of Homer, and it concerns us a good deal less.

There had been allegorical explanations, on a generous theory of hidden meanings, far back in the sixth century, the rejoinder probably to the criticisms of reformers like Xenophanes. As the Homeric text could not be altered—and to the allegorists we may at least be grateful for having shown us *that*—and as it could not be decently taught as meaning what it said, it must be supposed to mean some-

---

[1] *Vita Herodotea* 275–85. [2] IX, 9, 5.
[3] X, 31. 2. [4] Homer V (*O.C.T.*), p. 156.

thing else; in which event the field was open to the most ingenious or the most devout, to discover what that hidden meaning was. This doctrine crops up in different places and at different periods. Theagenes of Rhegium, who explained the Homeric gods as symbols of the forces of nature, may have been a Pythagorean, and we know that Pythagoras was one of the most outspoken of the early critics of Homer and Hesiod on the ground of their sayings about the gods. Anaxagoras of Clazomenae in Ionia, and Metrodorus of Lampsacus in the Hellespont, extended this kind of explanation from what Pope calls the "machinery of gods" to the heroes and even to material objects like Penelope's web, which was to illustrate the rules of argument.[1] We are reminded of Aristotle's condemnation of those "ancient critics of Homer, who see small resemblances but overlook large ones",[2] a tribe by no means extinguished by that exposure of their methods. That there was a good deal of nonsense talked about Homer in the fifth and fourth centuries, we know from Xenophon's description of professional reciters "who are perfect in their lines but quite silly themselves",[3] and from the remarks of Isocrates about the absurd theories that were propounded at the Lyceum.[4] Of such people Plato makes good-humoured fun in the dialogue between Socrates and Ion. This kind of criticism, if it deserves the name, appears among the Stoic philosophers from the foundation of the School. Zeno himself taught that the Homeric gods were natural forces, and Cleanthes supplemented allegory by etymology adding verisimilitude (I suppose) to a bald and unconvincing story.[5] Similarly Crates of Mallus, a Levantine like Zeno and in general a prominent defender of "anomalies" in Homer, as they were understood at Pergamum, found hidden meanings in the geography of the

[1] Diels, *Vorsokr.*[6], 8. 2 (Theagenes); 59.A.1.11 (Anaxagoras); 61 (Metrodorus); 82.B.29 (Gorgias and the Web).

[2] *Metaph.* 1093 α 26.

[3] *Mem.* IV, 2, 10.

[4] 12, 33–4.

[5] Plutarch, *de Iside et Osiride* 66. δεύτερον, ὃ μεῖζόν ἐστιν, ὅπως σφόδρα προσέξουσι καὶ φοβήσονται, μὴ λάθωσιν εἰς πνεύματα καὶ ῥεύματα καὶ σπόρους καὶ ἀρότους καὶ πάθη γῆς καὶ μεταβολὰς ὡρῶν διαγράφοντες τὰ θεῖα καὶ διαλύοντες. ὥσπερ οἱ Διόνυσον τὸν οἶνον, Ἥφαιστον δὲ τὴν φλόγα. Φερσεφόνην δέ φησί που Κλεάνθης τὸ διὰ τῶν καρπῶν φερόμενον καὶ φονευόμενον πνεῦμα. Cf. A. C. Pearson, *Fragments of Zeno and Cleanthes*, pp. 13, 155, 287, 295.

Odyssey.[1] And so we come down into Christian allegory, in which Achilles, for example, is "in a figure" Adam.[2] It is this kind of nonsense which trickles through later antiquity into the voluminous "Allegories" of Tzetzes in the twelfth century. It was only a trifle better if the characters of the heroes were treated as texts for sermons on the departmental virtues, as we have known to be the fate of good and bad men alike in the Old Testament; or if the Gods, instead of being evaporated into sunlight and storm clouds, were crystallized by Euhemerus into kings of prehistoric Crete or Arcadia.[3] In any case, anything seemed to be better than to take Homer literally and let him tell his own story in his own way. After standing, as he had stood for Pindar and Herodotus and Thucydides, at the dawn of authentic history, his very naturalism had pushed him back beyond the frontier of reality, and relegated him to the Twilight of the Gods.

[1] W. Kroll, *RE* XI, p. 1635; cf. Porphyrius, *Cave of the Nymphs*, 4, in *opuscula selecta* (*Teubner*, ed. 2, A. Nauck, 1886) τοιούτων ἀσαφειῶν πλήρους ὄντος τοῦ διηγήματος πλάσμα μέν ὡς ἔτυχεν εἰς ψυχαγωγίαν πεποιημένον μὴ εἶναι ἀλλ' οὐδ' ἱστορίας τοπικῆς περιήγησιν ἔχειν ἀλληγορεῖν δέ τι δι' αὐτοῦ τὸν ποιητήν, προσθέντα μυστικῶς καὶ ἐλαίας φυτὸν πλησίον.

[2] Pierre Bersuire, a Franciscan monk, d. 1362, wrote: "Vel dic quod Peleus et Tetis est Adam et Eva qui s. filium se maiorem Achillem i. Christum de sua progenie produxerunt. Et Christus Adam. Vel dic moraliter quod Iupiter est iustus qui revera cum Tetide i. cum aqua deliciarum seu cum voluptate non debet contrahere ..." (P. Ghisalberti, 'L' *Ovidius Moralizatus*', *Studj Romanzi* XXI (1931) p. 101).

[3] *F. Gr. Hist.*, 63, especially pp. 302–3.

Chapter Three

FROM THE GESTE DE TROIE
TO BENTLEY

In what follows I propose still to adopt a generally chronological order. Beginning, as we were bound to do, with the Greek view of Homer, we have seen that the assumption of a personal Homer, while it greatly simplified the whole problem, nevertheless left it an open question how this personal Homer stood in relation to the composers of other epic poems and how his subjects were related to theirs; also that it did not touch the questions how the poems had been transmitted and how nearly the current text of them should be regarded as corresponding with what came from the poet. Since the belief in a personal author involved belief in a design running through the poems, it facilitated the comparison of this type of design with that presumed in other kinds of literary composition, and so led directly to conclusions on literary art in general, as it had developed within the Greek city-state. It also went far to determine the course of discussion on the purpose and meaning of the poems, and consequently on the limits of their legitimate uses, as works of art and as sources of information. Coming next to the reception of Homer into the new world of the Classical Renaissance, we shall see how the circumstances of transmission to the west determined the course of discovery, and in particular gave a common inheritance to each of the principal nationalities which came into being during the dissolution of the mediaeval world order which that Renaissance made possible; but that in spite of the recovery, in due course, of the main outlines of the Greek view of Homer, the literary pioneers of crit-

36

icism in each of those national states took their own line, and reached views about Homer which are as instructive as they are, precisely because they are characteristic of the people who formed them. We shall see, in the modern world as in the Hellenistic, new methods of enquiry applied to the text, the language, the design and the substantial contents of the poems, and from these disconnected and often divergent lines of investigation, a new body of conclusions in process of formation, of which the full meaning and implications are not even yet clear; though some avenues, once tempting, are found to lead nowhere, and some questions are discovered to have been so framed that they do not admit of any answer at all.

Though almost wholly replaced in the mediaeval West by prose narratives of the Trojan War, of doubtful age and authority, by Latin versions, old and new, not very widely distributed, and by the French *Geste de Troie*, composed in the twelfth century and based of course directly on these, the multiplication of manuscript copies in the thirteenth century stands to the short-lived Latin Empire of Constantinople much as the crowd of late fifteenth-century manuscripts stands to the Turkish conquest in 1453. The Homeric references of writers as different as Dante, Roger Bacon and Chaucer agree, however, in showing that it was still through the Latin versions or through earlier books *about* Homer that they had their acquaintance with Greek epic. More than once in this period we have the complaint that Homer is so hard to translate; and a little later it is one of the ironies of literary history that Petrarch, who was at pains to acquire a manuscript of the *Iliad*, could not read it because he did not know Greek. But others did read Homer, and manuscripts were multiplied rapidly, all however derived from a quite small number of Byzantine originals—not more than a score—of not very different value. A printed edition was produced in Florence, by a Greek, Demetrius Chalcondyles, in 1488, and was followed by the Aldine editions of 1504 and 1517. The twelfth-century commentary of Eustathius, bishop of Salonica, printed in 1542–50, was not quite the first introduction of the traditional interpretation to Western readers; for the tenth-century manuscript known as Venetus A, acquired at an uncertain date by the great library of St. Mark's, contains a very copious ancient abridgment of a commentary, or commentaries, based in their turn mainly on the annotated editions of Aristarchus himself and other Alexandrian critics. This all-important link between ancient and modern scholarship was not however appreciated at its true value till the latter part of the eighteenth century; and the significance of other ancient annotations, such as those of the Burney and Townley manuscripts, was only realized when that of the Venetian collection was discovered.

Partly for this reason, partly because Homeric poetry stands in such vital respects apart from the Greek literature of the classical age, and consequently from those aspects of ancient culture which had the most direct appeal to the scholars of a Latinized Italy, Homer exercised a far less profound influence on the Renaissance of the fifteenth and sixteenth centuries, than we should perhaps have been prepared to expect. As a source for the inspiration of Virgil and other writers of the conventional Latin epic, he stood on the shelves of the learned side by side with the *Argonautica* of Apollonius, and the *Works and Days* of Hesiod; but he had no such popular vogue as Euripides, for example, gained by the side of his imitator Seneca. We have the same experience when we turn to the classical sources of Renaissance painting and sculpture; it is the Graeco-Roman sarcophagi and the productions of the Pergamene and other Hellenistic schools that filled the palaces and public buildings of Italian patrons of learning; the temple-sculptures of the Parthenon, Aegina, and Phigaleia remained unmolested by antiquaries till it was too late to rescue more than the wreckage of them.

In France, the Counter-reformation purged the classical Renaissance of its revolutionary force, that essential protestantism which had made it a revival of free learning and free thinking. The great scholars drifted away to the Low Countries, to German courts and free cities, to Elizabethan England. There was, it is true, controversy enough about Homer, with La Motte, Perrault, Fénelon and Fontenelle leading vigorous attacks on his manners, his colloquialisms, his theology; those being "loudest in their abuse of Homer . . . who did not understand the language in which he wrote", as our own best interpreter frankly says of them later.[1] For the defence, there were Boileau, with some glimpses of historical perspective, Boivin, with more liberal taste in literature, and above all Madame Dacier, who was not only a respectable scholar, but a fair poet and a woman of the world; a judge of character, a humanist with a real sense for natural beauty very rare in that circle and much more akin to what

[1] Robert Wood, *On the Original Genius of Homer* (1775), p. 144, note a.

we are to find in English criticism of that time. For she made a translation which in more favourable circumstances might have acclimatized Homer in French literature as Pope kept him familiar among ourselves, after Chapman's and Ogilby's versions had ceased to please.

In England alone, during this period, did the Wandering Poet really find a home. What Keats experienced *On First Looking into Chapman's Homer*, we know; what that discovery meant to many thousands of young Englishmen of the generation after 1598, we can only guess from the popularity of the book. They were ripe to share the importunity of the three scholars in Marlowe's *Faustus* that he should show them "Helen of Greece, . . . the admirablest lady that ever liv'd, . . . whom all the world admires for majesty".[1] And Chapman was himself a poet of "full and heightened style",[2] with a reputation which we know from the repeated allusions of his greatest contemporary to the "proud full sail of his great verse", to "his spirit, by spirits taught to write Above a mortal pitch".[3] Born about 1559, he was a scholar, a dramatist, "a person of most reverend aspect, religious and temperate, qualities rarely meeting in a poet",[4] with a "wealth and vigour of humorous invention, a tender and earnest grace of romantic poetry", a man "who held of no man and acknowledged no master, but . . . held on his own hard and haughty way of austere and sublime ambition"; "romantic, laborious Elizabethan",[5] to quote the judgment of a great Victorian. If he was not the ideal

---

[1] *Dr. Faustus* V. i., *Arden edition*, ed. F. S. Boas, p. 159 and footnote.

[2] John Webster, *The White Devil*, printed 1612, *To the Reader*.

[3] If the Rival Poet of *Sonnet LXXXVI* is Chapman.

[4] Anthony à Wood, *Athenae Oxonienses* (ed. Philip Bliss, 1815), II. 576.

[5] Swinburne in *Encycl. Brit.*[11] (The other quotations have not been traced.) He thought all the words denoted faults in the translator. Some critics did not like Chapman. He says in his *Preface*, "And much less I wey the frontlesse detractions of some stupide ignorants; that no more knowing me, then their own beastly ends; and I, ever (to my knowledge) blest from their sight; whisper behind me vilifyings of my translation: out of the French affirming them; when both in French, and all other languages but his owne, our with all-skill enriched Poet, is so poore and unpleasing, that no man can discerne whence flowed his so generally given eminence and admiration." But Ben Jonson wrote verses to head his *Hesiod*:

> . . . If all the vulgar tongues that speak this day
> Were ask'd of thy discoveries, they must say,
> To the Greek coast thine only knew the way.

translator of Homer, at least, to draw again on the same critic, he reared "the superstructure of a romantic poet on the submerged foundations of Greek verse", of which "the power, the freshness, the indefatigable strength and inextinguishable fire" have secured its high place in our literature.

It was an age of great translations, of the naturalizing of desirable aliens among a nation that was just finding itself, to which there is, I think, no parallel. Read the great prefaces of the sponsors for those aliens, the prefaces to North's *Plutarch* and to Philemon Holland's *Livy*, or to the *Authorized Version* of the Hebrew Scriptures "appointed to be read in Churches"; for the chained copies of all three stood side by side in the room over the Church Porch. Listen to Philemon Holland, presenting his candidate for graduation into this *universitas nostrorum*: "And thus I recommend unto my countrymen, *Livie* in English habit; *Livie* (I say) who whether he were more honoured whiles he lived, than beloved at this day of forrein nations, I cannot easily determine. For like as then . . . there repaired many great and noble personages from the farthest parts of Spaine and Fraunce, only to see his face, for the admiration they conceived of him by the fame of his incomparable eloquence: even so of late time, his spirit (which yet liveth in his writings) hath made a voyage by Florence into the same Fraunce and Spaine: and hath passed as far as into Arabia one way, & Almaine another. In which dissite and remote parts he hath found such kind entertainment, not only in courts of emperours and kings, in pallaces of princes and great potentates; but also with the people in generall; that they seeme to

(p. 39, n. 5 contd.)

> Such passage hast thou found, such returns made,
> As, now of all men, it is called thy trade;
> And who make thither else rob, or invade.

Daniel in *A Defence of Ryme* called him (perhaps too truly) "our Homer-Lucan". In 1802 Lamb wrote of his *Odyssey* to Coleridge, "It has the most continuous power of interesting you all along, like a rapid original, of any", and Coleridge also thought that "Except his quaint epithets . . . it has no look, no air of a translation . . . For Chapman writes and feels as a poet,—as Homer might have written had he lived in England in the reign of Queen Elizabeth" (*Coleridge's Miscellaneous Criticism*, ed. T. M. Raysor, 1936). But when Lamb writes to Elton in 1821, "I shall die in the belief that he has improved upon Homer, in the Odyssey in particular", it suggests that those are loudest in their praises who least understand the language of the original.

strive no lesse (who may endow him with most ample franchises and free burgeoisie) than those seven citties in old time who every one chalenged to themselves, the birth of the poet *Homer*. Since then, he hath thus long been desirous to crosse the seas into this noble Iland, not as a travailer to soiourne for a time, in the Court onely or the Vniversities; but to remaine here still both in citie and countrey, and thereto hath learned our language indifferently; let it now appeare that this nation of ours (like to reap as great fruit and benefit by his acquaintance as any other) is readie also to receive and embrace him as friendly as the rest."[1]

Thus, what Roger Bacon had pronounced impossible, though there is no evidence that he himself attempted it, was achieved for Elizabethan England; and Homer too, "having arrived long since and conversed as a meere stranger in this . . . famous Iland, and now for love therof learned in some sort the language" in Chapman's sonorous periods, came to be "ranged with other free-denizens of that kind: so long to live under [the Queene's] princely protection as hee shall duly keepe his owne allegeance, and acquaint [her] liege subjects with religious devotion after his manner, with wisdome, pollicie, vertue, valour, loyaltie; and not otherwise".[2] The *Whole Works of Homer, Prince of Poets, his Iliads and Odysseys* began to appear in 1598. When the complete edition came out in 1614, Milton was six years old; his father is described as a man of "ingeniose" tastes, and took ungrudging pains with his early training.[3] We can hardly doubt that the *Whole Works of Homer, Prince of Poets* were familiar in such a household. Not that Milton did not become, in early course, one of the most accomplished classical scholars of his age; but I think we may attribute something of that rugged and full-mouthed utterance which distinguishes even his early verse from that of other young Spenserians, and something of that almost Homeric breadth of design and genius for sustaining a breathless interest by mere suspending of the action, to the naturalized Homer of George Chapman no less than to the great original.

It might have been expected that in the next generation, so

[1] Philemon Holland, *The Romane Historie written by T. Livius of Padua*, 1600. *To the Reader*.

[2] Holland, *ibid., Dedication to Queen Elizabeth*.

[3] *"Brief Lives", chiefly of Contemporaries, set down by John Aubrey between the years* 1669 *and* 1696, ed. A. Clark (1898), II, p. 62.

susceptible in its manners and in its art to the *baroque* superficialities
of French classicalism, there should have been some slackening in
English appreciation of Homer. But what did happen—which was
itself paradoxical enough—is undesigned testimony to the hold which
the poems, and especially the *Iliad*, had upon educated Englishmen.
If the poet had but "in some sort learned the language" in the
brusque roaring of Chapman, there could be no doubt of his
naturalized eloquence, when he spoke through the lips of Alexander
Pope.[1] From *Her Royal Highness the* PRINCESS, the *Duke of* Argyle,
and Joseph Addison, *Esq*, who head the list of subscribers, past the
Duke of Buckingham *and* Normanby and *Lord Viscount* Bolingbroke,
who ordered "ten setts" each, and *The Reverend Dr*. Swift, *Dean of
St*. Patrick'*s*, to *Captain* Young and *Mr*. Edward Young, *Fellow of*
All-Souls *College*, Oxon, who close it, we are in the heart of English
society. Cambridge, indeed, took no stock in the venture, but the
University of Oxford and no less than ten College Libraries subscribed; evidently a new version of the *Iliad* was not beneath the
notice of Oxford Commonrooms in 1715. But it is not the public,
but the translator that deserves our attention; and most of all his
motive for the work.

> Non ita certandi cupidus, quàm propter Amorem,
> Quòd Te imitari aveo,

he quotes from Lucretius on the title-page; and what he sees beyond
all comparison in Homer, is what he calls his *Invention*. "Homer" he
says "is universally allow'd to have had the greatest Invention of any
Writer whatever. . . . Nor is it a Wonder if he has ever been acknow-
ledg'd the greatest of Poets, who most excell'd in That which is the
very Foundation of Poetry. It is the Invention that in different
degrees distinguishes all great Genius's. . . . It furnishes Art with all
her Materials, and without it Judgment itself can at best but *steal
wisely*: For Art is only like a prudent Steward that lives on managing
the Riches of Nature. Whatever Praises may be given to Works of
Judgment, there is not even a single Beauty in them but is owing to

---

[1] *The Iliad of Homer*, 1715–20. Quotations are from the folio edition.
Pope said that he would not have made the attempt if Dryden had completed his version. Dryden translated *Iliad I* and in his old age wished to
translate the rest (*Preface to the Fables*, 1700; Ker, *Dryden's Essays*, II,
pp. 246ff.).

the Invention: As in the most regular Gardens, however Art may carry the greatest Appearance, there is not a Plant or Flower but is the Gift of Nature. . . . And perhaps the reason why most Criticks are inclined to prefer a judicious and methodical Genius to a great and fruitful one, is, because they find it easier for themselves to pursue their Observations through an uniform and bounded Walk of Art, than to comprehend the vast and various Extent of Nature." (In the name of Queen Anne and the Muse of Alexandria, what has happened to the man?)

"Our Author's Work is a wild Paradise, where if we cannot see all the Beauties so distinctly as in an order'd Garden, it is only because the Number of them is infinitely greater. . . . It is to the Strength of this amazing Invention we are to attribute that unequal'd Fire and Rapture, which is so forcible in *Homer*, that no Man of a true Poetical Spirit is Master of himself while he reads him. . . . It seem'd not enough to have taken in the whole Circle of Arts, and the whole Compass of Nature; . . . but wanting yet an ampler Sphere to expatiate in, he open'd a new and boundless Walk for his Imagination, and created a World for himself in the Invention of *Fable*. That which *Aristotle* calls the *Soul of Poetry* was first breath'd into it by *Homer*."[1]

Then, classifying Fables as either *Probable*, *Allegorical*, or *Marvelous*, he notes how the Homeric plots fall into the first class. "That of the *Iliad* is *the Anger of* Achilles, the most short and single Subject that ever was chosen by any Poet. Yet this he has supplied with a vaster Variety of Incidents and Events . . . than are to be found even in those Poems whose Schemes are of the utmost Latitude and Irregularity." Similarly, the characters are natural and real, the speeches are in accord with them and vividly direct. "*Homer* makes us Hearers, and *Virgil* leaves us Readers". "What were alone sufficient to prove the Grandeur and Excellence of his Sentiments in general, is that they have so remarkable a Parity with those of the Scriptures: *Duport*, in his *Gnomologia Homerica*, has collected innumerable Instances of this sort." This is an aspect of Homeric commentary which later greatly exercised the pious ingenuity of Gladstone.

After dealing with the Expression, and especially with Homeric

---

[1] It is curious that Lamb in his letter to Elton should speak of "the pert modern Frenchify'd notes, etc., in Pope's translation".

Epithets (for "as a Metaphor is a short Simile, one of these Epithets is a short Description"), Pope goes on to summarize contemporary scholarship, mostly Dutch, and to anticipate some modern German work, in a brief examination of Homeric dialect. "He was not satisfy'd with his Language as he found it settled in any one Part of *Greece*, but search'd thro' its differing *Dialects* with this particular View, to beautify and perfect his Numbers. ... What he most affected was the *Ionic*, which has a peculiar Sweetness from its never using Contraction, and from its Custom of resolving the Diphthongs into two Syllables; so as to make the Words open themselves with a more spreading and sonorous Fluency. With this he mingled the *Attic* Contractions, the broader *Doric*, and the feebler *Aeolic*, which often rejects its Aspirate, or takes off its Accent; and compleated this Variety by altering some Letters with the License of Poetry." (Pope wrote this, of course, just too soon to profit by Bentley's rediscovery of the Homeric digamma.) "Out of all these he has deriv'd that Harmony, which makes us confess he had not only the richest Head, but the finest Ear in the World."

Against critics of the morals and manners described in the poems, he makes a defence which anticipates quite another aspect of Homeric criticism. "When we read *Homer*, we ought to reflect that we are reading the most ancient Author in the Heathen World; and those who consider him in this Light, will double their Pleasure in the Perusal of him. Let them think they are growing acquainted with Nations and People that are now no more; that they are stepping almost three thousand Years backward into the remotest Antiquity, and entertaining themselves with a clear and surprising Vision of Things no where else to be found, and the only authentick Picture of that ancient World." He protests against contemporary and "injudicious Endeavour to exalt *Virgil*; which is much the same as if one should think to praise the Superstructure by undermining the Foundation: One would imagine by the whole Course of their Parallels, that these Criticks never so much as heard of *Homer*'s having written first. ... Others select those particular Passages of *Homer* which are not so labour'd as some that *Virgil* drew out of them: This is the whole Management of *Scaliger* in his *Poetices*. Others quarrel with what they take for low and mean Expressions, sometimes thro' a false Delicacy and Refinement, oftner from an Ignorance of the Graces of the Original; and then triumph in the

Aukwardness of their own Translations. This is the Conduct of *Perrault* in his *Parallels*." Others again perversely excuse the ancient popularity of Homer as founded "upon the Ignorance of his Times and the Prejudice of those that followed". "This is the Method of Mons. *de la Motte*." Again anticipating the Homeric criticism of another great people, he concludes, "They who find the justest Faults, have only said, that a few Branches (which run luxuriant thro' a Richness of Nature) might be lopp'd into Form to give it a more regular Appearance."

An essential supplement and commentary to the *Preface* is the *Poetical Index*. Here you may see the subject-matter of the poem classified as in a commonplace book, under such headings as: FABLE, *Allegorical Fables*, *Allegorical or Fictitious Persons*, and *Marvelous or Supernatural Fictions*: CHARACTERS or MANNERS: SPEECHES, *deliberative, vituperative, in the Pathetick* and *in the Irony or Sarcasm*, not forgetting *Speeches to Horses*: DESCRIPTIONS or IMAGES, *of places, persons and things, of the weather, of the operations of War, of the internal passions or their visible effects*. The similes are classified under their subjects, from lions to low life, and from the arts to rural affairs. It is a *thesaurus* or *vade-mecum*, a manual of applied Homerology, to which the only close parallel is the Homeric Concordance projected by Gladstone. The object of both is the same, to make Homer useful; useful to the poet as a classical dictionary and literary rag-bag, very necessary in an Augustan Age; useful to the schoolmaster, if not to his boys; useful to the politician in the House of Commons, for the whole contrivance begins (under the general heading Fable, I must admit), with "The great *Moral* of the *Iliad*, that *Concord, among Governours, is the preservation of States, and Discord the ruin of them*; pursued thro' the whole *Fable*". It is a very suitable "moral" for the early days of George I. Pope himself did not mean to be didactic or to moralize Homer; witness his protest against Eustathius' allegorical treatment of Hermes' escort of Priam in Ω (verse 447): "sure it requires great Pains and Thought to be so learnedly absurd." His own alternative "by having recourse to the Pagan Theology" is, however, that "*Homer* might intend to give his Readers a Lecture of Morality, by telling us that this unhappy King was under the Protection of the Gods. Madame *Dacier* carries it further", in a comparison between Priam and Tobit, to which Pope devotes some twenty lines.

I have quoted Pope's estimate at some length, not because I can suppose it to be specially unfamiliar, but because it is so typical of English views about Homer throughout. Anything that Pope could write about the *Iliad* and *Odyssey* today, educated Englishmen were thinking, not tomorrow but yesterday and the day before. The Duke of Buckingham, who subscribed for ten copies, had himself given Homer "(in his excellent *Essay*) the finest Praise he ever yet receiv'd.

> 'Read *Homer* once, and you can read no more;
> For all things else appear so mean and poor,
> Verse will seem Prose; yet *often* on him look,
> And you will hardly need another Book.'"

And like Lord Bolingbroke, Sir Samuel Garth, and William Congreve, he was one of those who made the translator free "not only of their Advice for the Conduct in general, but their Correction of several Particulars of this Translation. . . . In short I have found more Patrons than ever *Homer* wanted. . . . If my Author had the *Wits* of After-Ages for his Defenders, his Translator has had the *Beauties* of the present for his Advocates".

What it was that acclimatized Homer so wholesomely in our own Augustan age, I leave to the modern representatives of his various kinds of patrons to judge for themselves.

The first note of scepticism about the transmitted text came from Isaac Casaubon, who was not born till 1559: "we can hardly hope for a sound text of Homer, no matter how old our Manuscripts may be."[1] He found reason for this scepticism in the statement of Josephus that the reason why the poems present such difficulties and discrepancies was that between their composition and their first committal to writing there had been a long period of oral transmission. Though he does not expressly mention it, Casaubon can hardly have failed to notice even more disastrous allusions by Pausanias to the services of Peisistratus in collecting poems which had been dispersed and were treasured by memory in divers places; and to the still more desperate situation as it appeared to Cicero, when he speaks of the same Peisistratus as the first editor of many poems originally distinct—*qui primus Homeri libros confusos antea sic disposuisse dicitur ut nunc habemus.*[2] Nearly a century later, the

[1] *Notae ad Diogenis Laertii libros* (1583), IX, 12.

[2] Cic., *de or.* III, 34, 137; Jos., *contra Apionem* I, 12; Paus., VII, 26, 13; cf. T. W. Allen, *Homer: the origins and the transmission* (1924), pp. 226–38.

Dutch scholar Perizonius, who held the chair of Eloquence and History at Utrecht from 1682 to 1693, and is at the same time one of the founders of the scientific study of grammar and a pioneer in historical criticism, more especially in the history of the Roman republic, amplified Casaubon's commentary on the statement of Josephus and collected those other fragments of ancient tradition which bore on the early history of the poems, especially on the part played by Peisistratus and Hipparchus in their conservation.[1] Obviously if these stories were trustworthy, the belief of Aristarchus in an Athenian Homer of very ancient date rested on a foundation of sand.

Meanwhile, in a very different quarter, similar doubts were being expressed about the traditional history of the poems. François Hédelin, Abbé d'Aubignac, who had been in turn lawyer, scholar, dramatist, and literary critic, is best known by his *Pratique du Théâtre*, an attempt, suggested to him by that great organizer of learning and the arts, Cardinal Richelieu, and completed in 1656, to acclimatize to the modern French stage the principles of Greek dramatic construction. With this varied and not inappropriate equipment, he turned his attention to Homer,[2] whose admitted excellences, as we have seen from Pope's *Preface*, were being variously depreciated and misinterpreted by the stricter French classicists, mainly on the ground of their anomalies and the difficulty of reconciling Homer's treatment of his subject with modern conceptions of what classical literature ought to be. D'Aubignac's scholarship and real sense of literary art appreciated the vigour and beauty of Homeric diction and the realism of Homeric narrative and description; but as a lawyer he was sensible of the discrepancies and anomalies of the action, and as a dramatist, practical as well as theoretical, he deplored the looseness and wayward construction of the poems as they stood. The prelude to the *Iliad*, for example, announces Achilles and his Wrath as the central theme; but, after the first scene of *Quarrel*, Achilles disappears from the action until the sixteenth book out of twenty-four. Something clearly had gone very wrong here. That such productions could have been transmitted orally in the way described by Josephus seemed to him in any event impossible; but the proceedings ascribed to Peisistratus, and still

[1] *Animadversiones historicae* (1685), c. 6.
[2] *Conjectures académiques ou dissertation sur l'Iliade.*

more the similar but earlier proceedings of Lycurgus at Sparta, provided an alternative. Within the comparatively narrow limits of the
principal episodes, flaws of construction did not seem to occur; it was
in the connexions of one episode with another that the weak spots lay.

D'Aubignac's solution of the problem was simple and ingenious.
What had there been for Lycurgus and Peisistratus in succession to
put together as described? Clearly not the complete sections of an
originally continuous composition, but a number of shorter poems,
each dealing with a single episode and observing the unities as required by the classical theory, but composed independently and not
necessarily, or even probably, by the same poet. Differences of
handling, style, and diction favoured the probability of such multiple
authorship; but all were Homeric in a general way. What was *not*
Homeric, was that inferior workmanship and clumsy contrivance by
which these forty or more separate poems had been combined into a
single composition, in the eighth century by Lycurgus at Sparta, and
in the sixth by Peisistratus for use in Athens. The fame of the poet or
poets was saved at the expense of his editors and publishers—of what
Pope loosely describes as "the Ignorance of his Times and the Prejudice of those that followed". Had Pope known of the work of
d'Aubignac, I fear he would have classed him with those "Criticks"
who "are inclined to prefer a judicious and methodical Genius to a
great and fruitful one, . . . because they find it easier for themselves to
pursue their Observations through an uniform and bounded Walk of
Art, than to comprehend the vast and various Extent of Nature".
D'Aubignac in fact had followed the Ptolemaic and mediaeval
astronomers who accumulated epicycles to account for the perplexing movements of the planets, instead of joining Kepler and
Newton in exploring the peculiarities of an ellipse. By a curious
accident, d'Aubignac's essay was not published until 1715, nearly
forty years after his death. It was known, however, before this to
Charles Perrault, one of the depreciatory critics of Homer whom
Pope chastises, saying that "there were learned men who did not
believe in the existence of Homer at all, and said that the *Iliad* and
Odyssey were nothing but a pile of many little poems by different
authors which had been pieced together"; and Perrault mentions
d'Aubignac expressly as having written on the subject. The next
step forward in Homeric criticism was taken the year before
d'Aubignac's essay appeared.

Richard Bentley, born two years after the Restoration, had even before he was thirty won a place in the first rank of English, and indeed of European scholarship, by his famous *Letter to Dr. Mill* which reconstituted the text of the late Greek Chronicle of John of Antioch with a mastery of materials and a critical insight which marks a real turning point in classical learning. At the age of thirty-three he was a Fellow of the Royal Society, and in the previous year no less a scholar than Graevius had paid him the compliment of a dedication. With his other contributions to scholarship we are not here concerned; and of his projected edition of Homer there are only the manuscript materials in the library of Trinity College, Cambridge. But in two important directions he turned a new page in Homeric criticism.

The first emerges only in a casual reference in his *Remarks upon a late Discourse of Free-thinking*, published under a disguised name in 1713.[1] Collins, the author of that *Discourse*, had described the *Iliad*, in the style with which Pope has made us familiar, as "the epitome of all arts and sciences"; Homer "designed his poem for eternity, to please and instruct Mankind". This is once more the Pergamene allegorizing conception, which had made of Homer a romance and a schoolbook, as the Protestant Reformation had made an oracle and an encyclopaedia of the Bible. Bentley thought otherwise. "Take my word for it", he wrote, "poor Homer in those circumstances and early time had never such aspiring thoughts. He wrote a sequel of Songs and Rhapsodies, to be sung by himself for small earnings and good cheer, at Festivals and other days of Merriment; the *Ilias* he made for the men, the *Odysseis* for the other Sex. These loose songs were not connected together in the form of an epic poem, till Pisistratus' time about 500 years after." Here we have evidently a very concise summary of a whole philosophy of Homeric study; every clause in it is significant; and it comes from a man who by this time had the world's learning about Homer at his fingers' ends. We note first that he does not dispute the single authorship of the poems, nor the coherence of them in a great design or pattern in the poet's mind. Though he dates the poet about five hundred years before Peisistratus (that is to say in the generation of 1060–1030, and therefore contemporary with the traditional founding

[1] Cf. H. L. Lorimer, "Homer and the Art of Writing", *AJA* 52 (1948), pp. 11–23.

of the cities of Ionia) he assumes that he could write. This "sequel of Songs and Rhapsodies" was intended to be sung, canto by canto, on public occasions; he conceives the poet as a compeer of Phemius, Demodocus and Thamyris in the poems themselves. He accepts the late classical tradition that between the poet's time and that of Peisistratus the Homeric sequel of poems had been dishevelled and dispersed, and that it was only through the Peisistratid recension that these poems were conflated, rather than reconstituted, in the two coherent wholes in which we have them now. The programmes, however, of the two sequels were original and distinct, and the *morale* and *motif* of each had its own literary quality, the greater abundance of sentiment and romance in the *Odyssey* distinguishing it from the chivalry and political rhetoric of the *Iliad*. How every one of these points has challenged the judgment and ingenuity of the next two centuries of critics, it will be our business to discover later on.

Bentley's other contribution to Homeric study concerned the language of the poems, not their literary form, and is one of the corner-stones of modern scientific philology. The Alexandrian critics inherited a living tradition of the way in which the poems should be read, or rather performed as a work of art before an audience. Consequently they were not troubled by the fact that the verses as written did not conform to the usages of metrical quantity and the elision of open vowels which prevailed in lyrics and dramatic verse, though they did something to simplify Homeric scansion within the limits of their respect for manuscript tradition and Homeric usage as they collected it from the tradition. But from the Renaissance onwards this living tradition was lost. In Italy and France some attempt seems to have been made to pronounce Homeric and other kinds of Greek at least as the refugee Greeks from Constantinople now pronounced it, but this ignored two thousand years of phonetic change.[1] In England Greek, like Latin, rapidly came to be pronounced as it was

---

[1] Robert Wood drew the moral. "Could Homer have heard his Poems sung or recited, even at the Panathenaean Festival, I dare say, he would have been offended at the elegance, perhaps the affectation, of the Attic accent and articulation; not to mention the various changes to which Greek pronunciation has been and is daily exposed.—I remember, when I was at Athens, that I sent for a Greek schoolmaster, and when we read the Iliad together, we could not bear each other's manner of pronunciation." (*Essay on the Original Genius of Homer*, 1775, p. 240.)

written, with the English values for vowels and consonants alike. This made for wholesome acclimatization, as our amazing vocabulary shows—we speak, for example, of *neuralgia* while a Frenchman says *nevralgie*, as a modern Greek says *nevralyīa*—but it paralysed the study of the language as a form of speech, and it made much Homeric verse as unmetrical as an English schoolboy's reading of Molière. Hence the repeated allusions in Pope's preface to contemporary criticisms of Homeric verse as barbarous, or at least primitive; look for example at his metrical note on the first line of the *Iliad*.[1]

What Bentley discovered—and it was a very great achievement of scientific imagination, worthy of a Cambridge man of the age of Newton, and a Wadham man of the age of Wren—was that the largest and most important class of these metrical difficulties disappears if it be supposed that the words as originally pronounced included a consonant with a value between F and V. The Greek alphabet of the manuscript tradition had no symbol for it, though the Roman alphabet, itself borrowed from the Greek colonies in South Italy, did both contain the letter F which we still use, and also employ the letter V both as a vowel, representing the Greek *upsilon*, and as a consonant. Early Greek inscriptions from districts of Greece other than Ionia demonstrate the source of the Latin symbol F, in the *digamma* symbol of identical form; further study of Greek dialects other than Ionic and Attic has shown how gradual was the disappearance of the V sound which it represented; and comparative study of Greek and Latin vocabulary has proved the common origin of such pairs as *vicus* and οἶκος, *vinum* and οἶνον, *virus* and ἰός, *ovis* and ὄϊς, *viola* and ἰόν. It was a curious paradox that the oldest surviving examples of the Greek language should be composed in one of the dialects which seem to have lost both the symbol and the sound itself soonest; for the V sound disappeared from Ionic at least before the earliest surviving inscription, and in Attic makes only an occasional appearance to mark the glide before *v*. Revolutionary as Bentley's discovery was from the point of view of Homeric

---

[1] Πηληϊάδεω Ἀχιλῆος. "Make but a Diphthong of the second *Eta* and the *Iota*, instead of their being two Syllables (perhaps by the fault of Transcribers) and the Objection is gone. Or perhaps it might be design'd that the Verse in which he professes to sing of violent Anger should run off in the Rapidity of Dactyles. This Art he is allow'd to have us'd in other Places, and *Virgil* has been particularly celebrated for it."

dialect and metre, it was still more significant in the general interpretation of language and early literature. For it was the first direct proof that within the limits of literary tradition the Greek language had been undergoing change, and had in fact a historical perspective; and it emphasized by material evidence the width of the gulf which separated the period at which the Homeric poems were composed from the classical civilization which inherited them. No wonder that Bentley felt himself justified in estimating the interval between Homer and Peisistratus at as much as five hundred years; very considerably greater than was believed, for example, by Herodotus. Bentley is thus the founder of historical philology, and once again, as in Alexandrian days, it is the problem of the Homeric poems which furnished scholarship with a new instrument of research. But Bentley, self taught, had to create his own method; and his knowledge of literary history, and of any language except Latin which was sufficiently akin to Greek to be comparable with it in a scientific way, was necessarily too limited to permit him to make extensive use of his discovery. Nor had any English or Dutch scholar the training, still less the insight, to carry the matter further. Heyne, sixty years later, had some idea of the significance of Bentley's work, Wolf, on the other hand, very little. It was only after the revelation of Sanskrit by Sir William Jones, at the very close of the eighteenth century, that what we know as comparative philology became possible; and then it was again from the problems of the Homeric dialect that Hermann and Buttmann went on to reconstruct the whole study of Greek Grammar, and Hermann in particular to systematize and extend Bentley's observations on Homeric and other Greek metres.

What was momentous in Bentley's discovery was that Homeric language was found to exhibit facts of a kind which the Alexandrian critics had quite failed to see. Once these were realized, the spell of the Alexandrian tradition was broken. It had long stiffened into a meaningless collection of so-called "rules of grammar" and irrational "exceptions" to them, and the study of their "analogies" had become a substitute for independent analysis of the traditional text, and even an obstacle to it. Like some other English discoveries, Bentley's restitution of the digamma in the Homeric text bore more fruit abroad than at home. Pope's hostility to Bentley had other roots than that the scholar had "talked against his Homer", though no doubt he was personally affronted by it; "It is a very pretty poem, but you must not call it Homer". Bentley was a professional scholar, and when he crossed swords with his amateur opponents, he committed the unforgivable sin of being right. And so he was satirized as a second Aristarchus, apostrophizing his mistress, the goddess of Dulness:

> Thy mighty Scholiast whose unweary'd pains
> Made Horace dull, and humbled Milton's strains.
> Turn what they will to Verse, their toil is vain,
> Critics like me shall make it Prose again.
> Roman and Greek Grammarians! know your Better:
> Author of something yet more great than Letter;
> While tow'ring o'er your Alphabet, like Saul,
> Stands our Digamma, and o'er-tops them all.[1]

Bentley's own marked copy of Homer fell later into the hands of the German scholar, Heyne, who acknowledged his obligation handsomely in the great commentary on the *Iliad* which he published in 1802, at a time when comparative philology was (it is true) still in its infancy, but the significance of Bentley's observations could be appreciated; and it was one of Heyne's greatest pupils, Immanuel Bekker, who first printed, in 1843, a text with the digamma.

Yet a further consequence may be noted. Bentley supposed, as we have already seen, that Homer could *write*, and that the period of oral tradition described by Josephus rested on a misapprehension. As the poems preserved so faithfully, in their metrical form as in their orthography, evidence for the lost consonant, it was not unreasonable to suppose that they had originally been committed to writing in an alphabet which included the digamma sign, and that it was only when they came to be disseminated among Ionians who had no use for a digamma sign in their ordinary writings, because they had lost the sound which it represented, that the poems came to be copied without the insertion of that obsolete letter. At all events, Bentley's words stand, that Homer, in his opinion, *wrote*.

[1] *Dunciad* IV, 211 ff.

Chapter Four

POET AND PAINTER

———————————————

THE general interest in Homer, whether as a Prince of Poets or as an *enfant terrible* without respect for the dramatic unities, received during Bentley's life-time a fresh stimulus from quite a different quarter. The custom of illustrating historical books can be traced far back in the Middle Ages, and Strzygowski's work,[1] in our own time, has wellnigh completed the proof that this is also an inheritance from the early days of the use of parchment. On papyrus, obviously, nothing more elaborate than a geometrical or astronomical diagram was practicable. The practice is illustrated for Homeric subjects by the joyous vignettes of French fourteenth-century manuscripts of the *Geste de Troie*, to which we must return in another connexion later.[2] With the invention of block-printing, book illustration took a new lease of life. One of the earliest printed editions of Terence, for example, has a full series of wood-cuts showing episodes in the plays as they should be staged, sometimes on a classical stage with architectural façade and the traditional three doorways, sometimes on an in-and-out stage with central tabernacle, such as is familiar to us in Elizabethan revivals.[3] From the originals the custom passed to

[1] *Eine Alexandrinische Weltchronik*, 1906. In 1932, the year after this lecture was given, Josef Strzygowski's 70th birthday was honoured. For Greek and Egyptian illustrated papyri and codices, see Kurt Weitzmann, *Illustrations in Roll and Codex* (*Studies in Manuscript Illumination* 2), 1947.

[2] p. 127 below and Pl. 2. *α*.

[3] Grüninger, 1503. For the *Adelphi*, the central tabernacle has been provided with wings to make three doors. This may not be the edition to which Myres refers, but it is the nearest that could be traced.

the translations. Ogilby's *Virgil*, printed in 1653, and his *Odyssey* of 1669, of which Pope speaks so severely, have copper-plates, some Dutch, some engraved in London, which render selected scenes in the manner of Rubens, or *longo intervallo* of Mantegna. The Plantin-Moretus Museum of early printing at Antwerp has great store of such original plates. There was, however, no pretence that these were more than works of a lively imagination in the prevalent classical mode.

In 1683, however, the distinguished Italian antiquary, Raphael Fabretti, one of the most active field archaeologists of the seventeenth century, published a monument in the Capitoline Museum of Rome, which goes by the name of the *Tabula Iliaca*, the *Picture of Troy*.[1] This was only the first of what is now a considerable series of ancient relief-sculptures,[2] not only representing scenes from the Tale of Troy, but identifying them and the personages in them by short explanatory titles. The discovery had a double importance, first as supplying a clue to the meaning of a very large number of other ancient reliefs and other monuments of various dates and styles, and opening a new and fertile storehouse of Homeric commentary; and secondly because the *Tabula Iliaca* included scenes from other epic poems besides the *Iliad*, and gave the names of these, and also of their respective authors. This threw quite a new light on the scanty references of ancient grammarians to the other poems of the so-called Epic Cycle; and this was the more important, seeing that it was already known that these poems had been among the sources of Virgil for the second book and other parts of the *Aeneid*, where the *Iliad* and *Odyssey* were not applicable, and that this whole class of reliefs turned out to be more or less careful copies of an original which could be referred to so early a date as the first century B.C. The effect of Fabretti's publication was immediate. In 1699 Lorenz Beger supplemented it by printing, at Berlin, a rich *corpus* of other such illustrations of Homer, under the title, *The War and Destruction*

---

[1] *De columna Traiani syntagma: accesserunt explicatio veteris tabellae anaglyphae Homeri Iliadem atque ex Stesichoro Arctino et Lesche Ilii Excidium continentis, et Emissarii Lacus Fucini descriptio*, pp. 315–84. It is a noble work, with a fine, full-size drawing and a good description.

[2] For a list of the tablets, see Kurt Weitzmann, "A *Tabula Odysseaca*", *AJA* 45 (1941), pp. 166–81.

of Troy, from the Ancient Monuments;[1] and the study of Homeric Archaeology came into being. Subsequent landmarks in this aspect of Homeric study were the discovery of famous Homeric scenes among the fresco-paintings of Pompeii, in the generation after 1763; the printed reproduction of the *Codex Ambrosianus Pictus*, a magnificent early manuscript of Homer in the library at Milan, by Angelo Mai in 1819;[2] and the publication of Inghirami's *Galleria Omerica*.[3] For English students of Homer all earlier attempts at pictorial inter-

---

[1] *Bellum et Excidium Trojanum, ex antiquitatum reliquiis, Tabula praesertim, quam Raphael Fabrettus edidit, Iliaca delineatum, et adjecto in calce Commentario illustratum.* Beger (with reason) hesitated because Fabretti's publication was such "ut post Homerum Iliada conscripturus videri posset, qui denuò id studium decurrere, aut doctius quid in medium proferre conaretur." He also doubted if his commentary were necessary, because "non tantum sublimi eruditione fulgentes, sed et mediocriter docti would recognize the familiar scenes. sed vicit publicae utilitatis studium, *tum* quòd Fabretti liber in Germania rarior fit, *tum* quòd etiam Doctioribus quibusdam, et praesertim in deliciis nostris minus exercitatis, interdum haerere soleat aqua, ubi minus id cogitares. ... illud etiam vel maxime movit, quòd Antiquitatis studium hodiè etiam ad juvenes descenderit, quorum commodis vel praecipue erat studendum." His own interest is wholly in the identifications. The drawings are poor; it is instructive to compare, e.g., his No. 5 with its original on p. 357 of Fabretti.

[2] *Iliadis fragmenta et picturae. Accedunt scholia vetera ad Odysseam, item Didymi Alexandrini marmorum et lignorum mesurae*, Milan. The drawings are excellent, and were produced in the same year in a more popular book, *Picturae antiquissimae Bellum Iliacum repraesentantes, nunc primum ex Homeri codice non sine descriptionibus editae*. For the codex (F. 205. P. inf.) see *Pal. Soc.* I (1873–83), pp. 39, 40, 50 and 51, or *Ilias Ambrosiana*, ed. A. Calderini, with reproductions in colour and Mai's historical commentary. Greeks are distinguished by helmets, Trojans by Phrygian caps, and gods usually by coloured nimbi which in Mai appear as neat halos.

[3] *Galleria Omerica, o Raccolta di Monumenti Antichi esibita dal Cáv. Francesco Inghirami, per servire allo studio dell' Iliade e dell' Odissea*, Florence, 1831–36. Sculptures, gems, and the *codex Ambrosianus* predominate, but there are some black-figure and red-figure vases. Pl. XLVII is a water-colour of the gallery at Tiryns—"il più antico monumento tra gli Omerici che vantar possa questa collezione. ... Ecco pertanto i pregevoli avanzi di quelle mura militari di Tirinto che da Omero fecero dare alla città l'epiteto di ben murata." The shift of interest from illustrations (from any period) of the poems to illustrations (of any subject) from what is taken to be the poet's own period, is well shown by a comparison of Inghirami with Franz Winter, *Kunstgeschichte in Bildern* I, iv, *Die Kunst der Homerischen Zeit*, n.d., Leipzig.

pretation were superseded, and further attempts in this direction prevented, by Flaxman's drawings, produced before 1794,[1] and by his
exuberant reconstruction of the Shield of Achilles, executed about 1818
and now preserved at Oxford in the Ashmolean Museum (Pl. 2.b.).

To see Homer in pictures was to think of him, in some sense, in
time and place. In the *Scienza Nuova* of Giambattista Vico, a pioneer
in what is sometimes called the philosophy of history, Homer stands
by the side of Orpheus, Lycurgus, and other symbolic types, to
illustrate different phases of social and national development. In
Vico's earlier essay on Universal Law, published in 1722, he had
already insisted that "Homeric poetry is not a conscious effort of
profound philosophy", as was contended by the didactic school of
criticism, "but the mirror of a simple age"; an interesting advance
towards a profounder historical perspective of early Greece. More
notable is what he proclaims in 1730 as the "discovery of the true
Homer"; that Homer is a collective name for many men's work; that
the poems were produced gradually, and stereotyped only when they
were collected by the Peisistratids. More notable still, he returns,
though probably unawares, to the Separatist Paradox of Xenon, and
anticipates the views of Grote and Geddes more than a century later,
when he distinguishes, within this Homeric school of epic, two pre-
eminent poets, the Homer of the *Iliad*, who belonged to North
Eastern Greece, and the Homer of the *Odyssey*, who came from the
Peloponnese and the islands in the South West.[2] Vico gave no proofs
of his theories, and had apparently no direct influence on the views
of Wolf half a century later; but his views run closely parallel with
the thesis of Zoëga in the same generation (1788), that "those Greek
peoples *were* that Homer of ours",[3] and Wolf wrote a review of
Vico's work twelve years after the publication of his *Prolegomena*,
which is of some personal interest.[4]

[1] Published Rome, 1793, London, 1793–5. See W. G. Constable, *John
Flaxman 1735–1826*, 1927.

[2] Works of Giambattista Vico, ed. F. Nicolini, 1931–42, *Il Diritto
Universale* (1722), pp. 375–78, 675–700; *La Scienza Nuova Prima* (1725),
§§79–89; *La Scienza Nuova Seconda* (1730), §§ 780–904.

[3] Adolph Michaelis, "Georg Zoëgas Betrachtungen über Homer", in
*Strassburger Festschrift zur XLVI Versammlung deutscher Philologen und
Schulmänner* (1901), pp. 1–12.

[4] "Giambattista Vico über den Homer", in *Museum d. Alterthums-
Wissenschaft*, I (1807), pp. 555–70.

Bentley, as we have seen, used phrases which show that while he pictured Homer to himself as living in humble circumstances, he supposed without hesitation that he could write, and that his verses had been preserved in writing. The same conception reappears in the title of Thomas Blackwell's *Enquiry into the Life and Writings of Homer* which appeared in 1735. "It was when *Greece* was ill-settled, when Violence prevailed in many Places, amidst the Shock and Confusion of the wandering Tribes, that *Homer* produced his immortal poem." "And yet, with all these Chances, the Period I have mentioned, when the *Manners*, the *Religion* and *Language* of *Greece* were at their *proper Pitch* for *Poetry*; to that Period, I say, the World stands indebted for *Linus*, and *Orpheus*, for *Olympus*, *Musaeus*, and *Amphion*; Men who are handed down to us as the Masters of Verse, by the greatest of their successors." While insisting on the originality of the poet, he leaves open the possibility that both Homer and Hesiod may have acquired some of their knowledge from books, rare though such written sources probably were; and though he mentions the theory that Homer did not write out the poems himself, he clearly thought that what he describes as his "posterity in Chios" had written copies, from which the professional reciters "came at last to have them by heart". He mentions the notion that one of them, Cynaethus, "did intermix a good deal of his own inventions", but only to reject it as resting on insufficient authority.[1] In these phrases of Blackwell, we encounter for the first time in English scholarship two fresh notions, probably derived from the captious criticism of the preceding century. The one is that Homer and Hesiod had access to sources of some kind; that is to say, that they did not stand at the beginning of this kind of literature but had predecessors. The ancient commentators and biographers, it is true, had no hesitation about this; Orpheus, Musaeus, Linus, were all of earlier date than Homer, though opinions had differed as to their relations, if any, with the poet of the *Iliad* and *Odyssey*. And it had been discussed, even in Alexandria, whether the tenth book of the *Iliad*, about Dolon the spy and the capture of the horses of Rhesus by Diomedes and Odysseus, was not really a separate poem which had somehow been incorporated. But it is doubtful whether the evidence for these ancient beliefs was generally known in Blackwell's time. The other novelty was the revival of those ancient but

[1] 2nd ed. (1736), pp. 66, 73, 110–11, 129.

late and for the most part fanciful statements about the contamination of the Homeric poems with later materials. It goes as far beyond d'Aubignac's suggestion that inconsistencies and lapses from the truly Homeric manner were due to incompetent editors of a later age, as it does beyond the Alexandrian belief that single lines or short groups of lines had been inaccurately transmitted, and that this was a remediable accident which might occur at any point in the text. For what was now contemplated was that later reciters deliberately tampered with Homer's original work, to improve it or bring it up to date. Thus both before and after the "real Homer" there lay unexplored phases of poetical composition, and newly-realized risks that what we possess in the transmitted text might not be wholly due to Homeric "invention". Homer, an editor or a compiler himself, might have been himself edited.

It was a great step forward, as we have seen already in regard to Bentley's discovery of the lost consonant, to conceive the poems as standing in any sort of context and historical perspective at all; and once again, it is in Homeric study that this new conception of historical development takes shape, which was to revolutionize both history and scholarship in the next two generations. But it is necessary to insist that all these scruples about the workmanship of the poems had their origin in a school of austerely and pedantically classical criticism which regarded as anomalies and therefore as blemishes whatever did not accord with the critic's own standard of style. The significance of this will become clearer as we proceed.

While Vico was insisting, in his theoretical way, on interpreting Homer as the representative of a definite period of history and phase of human advancement, Robert Wood was raising the same question in a typically English way.[1] He was by no means the first of those English travellers who did so much to lay the foundations of a classical geography and to widen the basis of classical archaeology beyond the limits of Italian collections. During the great days of the Ottoman Empire, and even in the first century of its decline, travel in the Near East was probably easier than at any later period;

[1] *An Essay on the Original Genius of Homer*, privately printed, 1767. Published, London, 1769. Posthumous edition, with additions and corrections, London, 1775, *An Essay on the Original Genius and Writings of Homer, with a Comparative View of the Ancient and Present State of the Troade*. All quotations are from the 1775 edition.

certainly far easier than it became when the conquered peoples, Greeks, Armenians, Arabs, were awakened to the idea of modern nationalism, and became the objects of suspicion and reprisals of a conqueror who was forgetting how to govern. Wood had travelled widely overland; he had explored and described the ruins of Palmyra and Baalbec; and he had done what was much more unusual—he had cruised about in the Mediterranean with the conscious object of familiarizing himself with Greek waters as well as Greek lands; "particularly", as he says in the preface to his Homeric essay, "we proposed to read the *Iliad* and *Odyssey* in the countries, where Achilles fought, where Ulysses travelled, and where Homer sung."

"Our expectations", he goes on, "from this object of our curiosity were by no means disappointed, yet I almost despaired of a satisfactory method of conveying to others a tolerable idea of the entertainment we received from it on the spot." His difficulties "do not arise so much from a scarcity, as from an exuberance of matter, which crowds upon my choice too abundantly. . . . A review of Homer's scene of action leads naturally to the consideration of the times, when he lived; and the nearer we approach his country and age, the more we find him accurate in his pictures of nature, and that every species of his extensive Imitation furnishes the greatest treasure of original truth to be found in any Poet, ancient or modern". His embarrassment was overcome by the encouragement of travel companions (for as he says, "the beauties of the first of Poets were enjoyed in the company of the best of friends", Dawkins and Bouverie), and not least of his patron, Earl Granville, "who while he presided at his Majesty's councils, reserved some moments for literary amusement. . . . I seldom had the honour of receiving his commands on business, that he did not lead the conversation to Greece and Homer". Wood goes on to record an affecting instance, only a few days before Lord Granville's death.

Wood's discovery was as simple as it was fundamental to Homeric criticism. Where the poet's words could be tested, Homer meant what he said; there could be an end of allegory and pedagogy. "We shall admit his ancient title of Philosopher only as he is a Painter. Nor does it come within our plan to examine his pictures, except so far, as their truth and originality are concerned." In criticism of this kind, as Wood justly says, "he enters most into the spirit of the Copy, who is best acquainted with the Original." He contests, on this ground, the prevalent opinion that the *Iliad* is finer than the *Odyssey*: "a superiority, which, if I am not mistaken, must still gain ground, in proportion to our distance from, and ignorance of, the times, which the Poet describes". For the "paintings" of the *Odyssey* are "often of that finished kind, which produces resemblance and character out of very trivial incidents; and these delicate touches, though essentially concerned in making out the likeness, are so minute, as to escape observation, if the copy and original be not confronted". Wood insists on the gulf which separates the Homeric Age from the Hellenic Age of his first great critic, Aristotle, in outlook and manners; "I will venture to say, that they differed as much, with regard to their reigning virtues and vices, their state of police and degree of civilization, their modes and tastes, in short, the great business and leading pleasures of life, as we do in these respects, from our Gothic ancestors in the days of Chivalry and Romance".

Chivalry and Romance—these then are the keynotes respectively of Homer's *Iliad* and *Odyssey*; and that, not in antiquarian retrospect, but a direct transcript from the pre-Hellenic original. "His great merit, as an instructor of mankind, seems to be that of having transmitted to us a faithful transcript, or (which is, perhaps, more useful) a correct abstract of human nature, impartially exhibited under the circumstances, which belonged to his period of society, as far as his experience and observation went. ... Elegant imitation has strange powers of interesting us in certain views of nature" (the vocabulary of romantic criticism was still rather scanty and frigid in 1769). "These we consider but transiently, till the Poet, or Painter, awake our attention, and send us back to life with a new curiosity," and the copies "have this advantage over real life, that they are susceptible of a more deliberate examination and close comparison, than the fleeting and dispersed originals will admit".[1] Out of the wealth of Robert Wood's illustrations of Homeric naturalism, it is not possible here to give more than illustrations. Beginning with a study of Homer's winds and weather-lore, he identifies his homeland somewhere on the west coast of Asia Minor. He had verified from the peak of Mount Ida the prospect which lay before Zeus and Hera and the journey of Poseidon among the islands of the North Aegean. His discussion of the topography of Menelaus' visit to Egypt is masterly;[2] and his explanation of the "turning-places of the sun", in

[1] From the *Preface*.   [2] pp. 93–115.

the account of Syria the home of Eumaeus, is in accord with the experience of every later traveller—now that we have learned from Wood what to look for! "Let us suppose the Ionians looking south-west from the heights of Chios at the winter solstice, they would see the sun set behind Tenos, and towards Syros, the next island in the same south-west direction: and having observed, that when he advanced thus far, he turned back, they would fix the turnings ($\tau\rho\sigma\pi\alpha\iota$) of the sun to this point".[1] He knew Greek waters, loving them as those only can love them who know them as he did; and he knows his Poet too, because he has been himself under the spell. "I have often admired the spirited theatrical action of Italian and Eastern poets, when they recite in the open air, pointing out each object of description in an imaginary scenery of their own extemporaneous creation, but availing themselves at the same time of every real appearance of Nature within view of their Audience, that is applicable to their subject, and connects it, in some degree, with the spot, where the recital is made." And in this connexion he makes happy use of the daily rise in the Gulf of Smyrna of the *Inbat* wind from the west, which, "from the first dark curl on the surface of the water, to its greatest agitation, which was sometimes violent", he recognized in the similes[2] which Homer drew from it.

Then, he had the good luck in 1742 to be present at just such an altercation between pilot and ship's officers, as to the course to be steered from Mytilene southward—inside or outside Chios—as occurred between Nestor, Menelaus and Diomedes, on the way home from Troy,[3] and was enabled to deal summarily both with Eustathius and with Madame Dacier; "the first was led into an error by mistaking the meaning of one word"—this was the bishop of Salonica—"and the last" (the lady from Paris) "by mistaking the distance from Lesbos to Euboea; but both by attending more to grammatical criticism than to the genius and character of the Poet, and of the age when he wrote".[4] With Pope's edition, Wood deals no less candidly, while acknowledging that "though Madam Dacier comes nearest to the Poet's meaning, I believe it will be acknowledged, that of all the languages we know, in which Homer has hitherto appeared, it is in English alone that he continues to be a Poet". His principal grievance against Pope, as in less degree against

[1] p. 17. [2] Δ 275–80, 422–7, H 63–5, I 4–8, Λ 305–9.
[3] γ 168 ff. [4] pp. 40–46.

Virgil, is that they cannot let well alone. Virgil, it is true, usually confines himself to omitting phrases inapplicable to an Italian occasion; Pope must needs replace them by a "florid profusion of unmeaning ornament", "loaded with English ambiguity, and even contradiction, for which there is no foundation in the Greek"; as when Achilles lies "stretch'd along the shore", which is "rocky", "sandy" and "grassy" within a few lines: "a sort of prevarication (if I may use that expression) impracticable upon canvass";[1] and for Wood, Homer is before all things a Painter; as incapable of fudging his landscapes as of mystifying his religion or his morals. For his religion "looks much less like the religion of mystery, than of common sense". If he borrowed from the older world of Egypt and the East, "his figures, I may say portraits, were his own; and the scenery of his Mythology is Grecian."[2]

Wood goes on to discuss Homer's "manners" in the light of his own camping experiences at Palmyra among bedouin Arabs, and concludes here too that what Homer describes, he had seen and known in a state of society, different from that of classical Greece but no less worth studying; for societies are formed in accordance with external circumstances; and where circumstances remain constant, there is no reason to suppose that institutions change. Hence we may confidently use our experience of modern Arabs and Greek seamanship, as commentary on Homeric narrative and the Homeric manner in poetry. This is as far in advance of the political philosophy of Montesquieu, as Montesquieu is in advance of Thucydides; Wood anticipates indeed all that is essential in the work of Herder in the next generation. He stands on the very threshold of modern anthropology, as Tylor and Lubbock understood it. In the same way, he says that "it is impossible to do this subject justice, without taking likewise into consideration the manners of the sacred writers, which come so much nearer those of Arabia than Homer's, as they lived nearer that country, and as most of the scenes, which they describe, lie either in it, or contiguous to it"; so that it is not necessary to explain the resemblances by "Homer's supposed knowledge of the Jewish learning through the Egyptian priests, as some ingenious men have too loosely conjectured".[3]

Most of all, Wood appreciated the necessary accord between the Poet's surroundings and his own manner of delivery. A test case is

[1] pp. 77–86. [2] pp. 127–30. [3] pp. 155–6.

humour "whose genuine spirit is so subtle and volatile in its nature, that it evaporates upon the least change in the circumstances, which produced it, leaving nothing behind but the insipid dregs of low buffoonery"; and in this respect he claims, with some justice, that we English have a better chance of enjoying Homer than others, for "if we have excelled other countries in this walk of humour, it may be ascribed to our rich diversity of original character, open to every artist, without those restrictions, which seldom check licentiousness without suppressing genius";[1] another sly hit at "our polite neighbours the French", who "seem to be most offended at certain pictures of primitive simplicity, so unlike those refined modes of modern life, in which they have taken the lead".[2] He appeals especially to Swift, Addison and Hogarth; like each of these, Homer "was a faithful Historian, because he was a correct Painter". "From the greatest uniformity of simple manners that ever fell to the share of any Poet, he drew the greatest variety of distinct character that has ever been produced by the same hand." But whence did Homer get his incidents? Here again Wood's own experience gives him a clue. "Having followed him through most of the countries which he visited, I would say, that he is a writer of veracity in his descriptions of what he saw, but of credulity in his relations of what he heard." As he took his scenery from "ocular examination" and his characters from life, so for his history he drew on the "prevailing traditions of the times ... perhaps from those who were eye-witnesses of the siege, and had signalized themselves upon the Scamandrian plain; or at least from their children".[3] That is to say, Wood follows Bentley, as Bentley had apparently followed Eratosthenes, in assigning to the poems a date of origin within a century or so of the historical events which they describe; a Trojan War and an Age of Wanderings in the early years of the twelfth century B.C. Only if this intimacy of the poet with his subject, and the early date which follows from that, are realized, can critical justice be done to his language or his style.

But how were the poems composed, and preserved? Here we reach the only part of Wood's criticism which has been popularized in Homeric commentaries. He was a good enough observer, though no specialist, to be aware how late and rare were the examples of archaic stages in the Greek alphabet; he knew that habitual intercourse between the Greeks and Egypt did not go back beyond the days of

[1] pp. 175–7.   [2] p. 144.   [3] pp. 180–4.

the XXVIth Dynasty, that is to say the seventh century B.C.; consequently, before that date, the materials as well as the skill for book production were, at best, very rare. Provisionally he offers his "opinion, as matter of conjecture, ... that the art of Writing, though probably known to Greece when the Poet lived"—a point usually overlooked by those who have quoted—"was very little practised there; that all knowledge at that time was preserved by memory, and with that view committed to verse, till an alphabet introduced the use of prose in composition". He quotes ancient authority in support of this opinion, and suggests (in the same sense as d'Aubignac and Bentley, but with a very different estimate of the origin of the poems) that the first written versions of the poems may have been due to later men, Lycurgus, Solon, Peisistratus or his son Hipparchus; "just as some curious fragments of ancient poetry have been lately collected in the northern parts of this island, their reduction to order in Greece was a work of taste and judgment: and those great names which we have mentioned might claim the same merit in regard to Homer, that the ingenious Editor of Fingal is entitled to from Ossian". We remember at this point that Macpherson's Fingal was published in 1761 and Wood's Essay in 1769.[1]

Consequently, to do justice to Homer's diction and styles, we must go back behind the written text, and recover by that scientific use of the imagination, which John Tyndall[2] was to expound so eloquently just a century later, the poems as Homer delivered them. For "the language which we bring into the world with us is not confined to the organs of speech; but it is made up of voice, countenance, and gesture". But for the devices of an elaborated grammar "the simple tones of Nature, with the varieties of modulation, which are now assigned to the province of music, might have been applied to the purposes of common life, as we are told they are in some degree among the Chinese"—I do not know whether Wood had ever travelled in Wales—"Speaking and singing would differ little, as the original Greek words, which signify both, seem to imply; the human countenance would have not only retained but improved its natural powers of expression, which it is now the great business of education

[1] The edition privately printed in 1767 did not contain the Chapter on *Homer's Language and Learning*.

[2] *On the Scientific Use of the Imagination*: *A Discourse Delivered Before the British Association at Liverpool*, 1870.

to suppress, and the dumb language of gesticulation would have made a very significant part of conversation". I do not know whether Wood would have agreed that the English were the best educated, as well as the most humorous nation; but I have encountered the opinion that English is the only language that you can really talk with your hands in your pockets. From the very circumstances of his age, then, it results, "that Homer, though the oldest, is the clearest and most intelligible of all ancient writers. The Greek Vocabulary, though copious in his time, was not yet equivocal; ambiguity of expression was little known before the birth of Science"—and I had better not go on to quote what he says of the achievements of Philosophy! He notes especially, in this connexion, the profuse employment of particles in Homeric Greek: "they contribute very much to the clearness of his meaning, as well as to the length of his verses"; they are, indeed, "to hexameter verse, what small stones are to a piece of masonry, ready at hand to fill up the breaks and interstices and connect those of a larger size, so exactly as to give a smooth compactness to the whole". The compounding of epithets and the free treatment of metrical quantity were "not only advantages, which the Greek language possesses above all others; but which, in all probability, Homer enjoyed above all Greek Poets", thanks to his early date and freedom from the trammels of writing. Here indeed is Aristarchus' insistence on the usage of the poet (τὸ ἔθιμον τοῦ ποιητοῦ), but applied in commendation of a liberal theory of *anomaly*, not of Alexandrian *analogy*. "For when Criticism took its rise as an Art, and Aristotle found in the *Iliad* and *Odyssey* those rules of composition, which the Poet drew from Nature, those bounds of Poetical licence were prescribed for others, which his unlimited fancy had freely suggested to himself; and the liberties he chose to take, became the laws which they were obliged to follow."[1]

Wood was very modest about his contributions to Homeric criticism; "the humble duty" (as he says) "of bearing testimony, as an eye-witness, to the Poet's veracity. If I endeavour to rescue him from errors, not his own, by bringing within the observation of a cursory perusal of his works their truth and consistence, as to time, place, persons and things; it is as a Traveller only, that I can hope to do him that justice."[2] But the traveller and explorer was also a citizen of the world; and it is Wood's unique service to scholarship

[1] pp. 276–90.   [2] p. 302.

66

that he could go behind the commentaries and the texts, to the scenes, the events and the men of a Homeric Age, and indicate the veracity of a Homeric Homer.

Before we go on to the period which was dominated by Teutonic methods of criticism, let us summarize those advances towards a fuller knowledge and appreciation of Homer which were achieved in more or less Latinized Europe up to the middle of the eighteenth century.

In Italy, which had the first and fullest opportunity for Homeric scholarship, the more intimate appeal of Virgil and other Roman writers of conventional epic diverted scholars into studies more immediately serviceable in the renewal of that contact with antiquity which was indeed their first business, as well as their people's need. Italy furnished indeed the materials for objective, archaeological illustration of Homeric incidents; but it was an exclusively Hellenic, and in great part Hellenistic and Graeco-Roman commentary; and we have already seen how very imperfectly Greek critics had appreciated the nature and extent of that aloofness of Homeric descriptions from their own experience, even while they recognized that it was there. Only in Vico's rediscovery of "the true Homer" as the "mirror of a simple age" and the key to one stage in what was at bottom an evolutionary presentation of culture and history generally, is there any advance beyond the traditional commentary inherited through Strabo from Pergamene criticism and through Eustathius from Alexandrian.

In France, political and religious reaction from the revolutionary protestantism which in part resulted from the Revival of Learning, though indeed it had partly made it possible, confronted Homer with a more than Alexandrian classicalism, which found in the poems a stone of stumbling—a *scandal* in the strict sense of that disastrous word—and a challenge on matters of fundamental principle which only d'Aubignac had the courage to surmount, and Madame Dacier to excuse; because Madame Dacier alone had the good heart and good taste to know good work when she found it; and because d'Aubignac alone by lucky accident had the leisure, as well as the technical experience, to study the poems for their merits of construction and presentation, not for their anomalies and nonconformity with classical usage and baroque convention. And even d'Aubignac had only contrived to save the soul of the poems by annihilating their creator, as he was prepared to annihilate Fénelon's Deity in the cause of a more liberal creed.

In England Chapman, translating for a generation of explorers, had set his readers upon a Peak in Darien, as King James' translators set them upon Mount Pisgah overlooking the Land of Promise and Performance; as North and Holland set them on Mars' Hill and the Roman Capitol. Ogilby, seizing those very colloquialisms which had shocked Perrault and La Motte, had sketched a vernacular Homer "sung for small earnings and good cheer" which had at least the concurrence of Bentley.[1] Pope, in the same way, concentrated on the poet's limitless invention, and at least commented upon the poems as if he supposed they were being read for enjoyment as well as for instruction. Bentley, though he never achieved either the edition or the commentary that he planned, laid the foundations for scientific study of the language and the metre, and shot out one realist searchlight into the problem of their origin. Finally, with Blackwell and Wood we reach a stage where it became at last possible to study the poems in their geographical context, and in some sort of historical perspective, as masterpieces still, but as masterpieces within a school, with "primitives" and "old masters" earlier, imitators later, and a great phase of fixation, when they came to be written down for a reading public, "as well as floating living through the ears of men, from the mouth of the living poet". For in that historical perspective, as Wood clearly saw, questions of language and metre, as well as of manners and historical events, are transfigured and clarified. We break away from the tradition of the elders—even if it be the monumental work of Alexandrian scholarship; at the touch of Homeric wind from North and West, blowing out of Thrace upon Greek lands and Greek seas, the sleeping beauty has awakened from her Egyptian sarcophagus; from dogmatic slumber to the renaissance of romance.

[1] John Ogilby, *Odyssey*, 1665.

Chapter Five

FRIEDERICH AUGUST WOLF

W E have already seen how the Catholic Counter-reformation in France paralysed the classical scholarship of that country, at whatever countervailing advantage in the creation of a national literature, classical in pretensions and outward form, but singularly remote from all that we now regard as Hellenic essentially. Some few scholars went east across the Rhine, others to Basle and Geneva; but the majority went to the Low Countries, and it is to the long succession of Dutchmen from Vossius to Ruhnken that classical learning owes most during the seventeenth century and the first half of the eighteenth. The only one of these, however, who paid any particular attention to Homer was Lodewyk Kaspar Valckenaer, a man of extraordinary breadth of learning who became professor at Franeker in 1741.[1] His critical text of *Iliad* XXII with commentary, published in 1747, marked a considerable advance in method. Graevius, rather earlier, had illustrated in his edition of Hesiod (1667) his conception of the way in which ancient literature may be interpreted as a revelation of ancient life, and had laid the foundations of the scientific study of the material remains of antiquity, and we have seen how promptly and graciously he saluted the rising star of Bentley; but he did not contribute specifically to the text or to the interpretation of Homer. It was only with the foundation of the Universities of Halle in 1649, still more of Göttingen in 1737, that the contribution

---

[1] In his *Antrittsrede, de causis neglectae literarum Graecarum culturae*, he blamed the use of translations. "Versionibus in lucem prolatis, Graeci sermonis studia negligi coeperunt et obsolescere. . . . Quid Homero Latino, Gallico, obscurum magis et jejunum? Quid insulsius? Quid putidius?"

of the German people to scholarship became more than the struggle of isolated students; and it was Johann Matthias Gesner, one of the original staff at Göttingen, whom we must regard as the founder of that organized system of literary and linguistic research which the German universities have made in a very special sense their gift to mankind. Gesner in particular deserves recognition, not only as the man who reintroduced Greek into the normal university course, but as the pioneer in that characteristic instrument of German higher education, the informal conference between the teacher and his maturer pupils, which we know by its German name as the *seminar*, the seed-bed of the academic garden. Then in 1763, Gesner was succeeded, on the recommendation of the great Dutchman, David Ruhnken, who refused to migrate thither himself, by an almost unknown man of thirty-four, Christian Gottlob Heyne, for the next forty years the most encyclopaedic researcher, the most amazingly productive writer, and by far the most influential teacher, of his generation. He was not himself a scholar to compare with the greater Dutchmen, but in the Germany of the eighteenth century he was eminent; and he was fortunate in his pupils.

What Gesner and Heyne stood for was what eighteenth-century Germany needed most, namely a new Renaissance. Its classical traditions were inherited indeed from the great days of Rudolf Agricola (d. 1485), John Reuchlin (d. 1522), and the *praeceptor Germaniae*, Philipp Melanchthon (d. 1560), but they had been starved and frozen to sterility in the following century. The mountainous unmeaning erudition and the pathetic attempt to clothe Teutonic thoughts in the trimmings of classicalism which was, in fact, rather Gallic than Latin or Greek—these had to be shed, if German humanism was to live and to revive a "living cultural intercourse with the classical authors themselves as the highest patterns of art and taste".[1] In this new humanism, the study of antiquity

[1] Friederich Paulsen, *The German Universities* (1906), p. 47; cf. his *Geschichte d. Gelehrten Unterrichts* (1885), pp. 427–40. Even at Franeker Valckenaer said that Greek scholarship was despised as "literarum venatrix; syllabarum fugientium auceps; speculatrix rerum futilium superstitiosa; foeta difficilium nugarum proseminatrix", and the scholar as "homo, si non stolidus, . . . a rerum quotidianarum usu semotus; ridiculus veterum admirator; in musaei squalore deses; in Homero, Sophocle, Menandri versiculo dimetiendo, restituendo, seu in ritu obsoleto eruendo, totos dies occupatus; qui, dum studiosus est antiquatae vocis indagator,

once more acquired a reasonable and humane purpose—the culti-
vation of a sense and taste for the beautiful and sublime in literature
and also in other arts, not in opposition to contemporary German
poetry, but in "living, reciprocal relation with it". Of German
poetry, the centre at this time was, for the best of reasons, at Göttingen itself. The *German Society* founded there by Gesner was the
complement of his classical *seminar*. We have seen how Robert
Wood's *Essay on the Original Genius of Homer* opened a new period
of Homeric criticism in England. Published in 1769, it fell into the
hands of Heyne at Göttingen in 1770 and delighted him;[1] for it
supplied a whole aspect of appreciation which his own conception of
the humanities required. No doubt it was he who induced the son
of a Göttingen colleague, Michaelis, to translate Wood's *Essay*
into German in 1773; and the translation must have sold well,
for a second edition was published in 1778. The arguments were
elaborated and reinforced in a substantial essay by J. B. Merian.[2]
It was not, however, from the "good boys" of Heyne's seminar
that the greatest literary achievements were to come, but from
two whom he quite failed to attract, or even to tolerate on his own
part.

Johann Heinrich Voss came to Göttingen when he was already
twenty-one, self educated, a strong liberal, something of a free-
thinker, a fluent versifier if not a poet, and above all a fervid member
of the *Hainbund* of literary revolutionaries. After reading philology,
he became a schoolmaster, and long afterwards (1805) a Professor at
Heidelberg. He was vigorous in the polemics of his day. Heyne,
with whom he had not got on at Göttingen, was attacked for his
mythological theories, and Georg Friederich Creuzer even more
violently for the symbolical interpretation of ancient history which
he was popularizing at Heidelberg.[3] But Voss devoted most of his
leisure to translations. Of these, more famous even than the *Shakespeare* which occupied his later years, was his translation of Homer,

dum rerum nihil profuturarum thesauros colligit, sensu communi vacat;
Philosophiae, quam vocant, expers penitus et imperitus. O audaciam! O
impudentiam! . . . Quis enim, nisi cui indoles sit et natura divinior, facile a
se impetraverit, ea ut persequatur, quae abjecta iacent?"

[1] He reviewed it in *Göttingische Gelehrte Anzeigen* I (1770), pp. 257–70.
[2] In *Nouveaux Mémoires de l'Académie Royale des Sciences et des
Belles-Lettres*, 1774.
[3] *Mythologische Briefe*, 1794; *Anti-Symbolik*, 1824–6.

of which the *Odyssey* volume appeared in 1781 when he was just thirty.[1] Regardless of the grammatical contrasts between Greek and German, he retained the sonorous and unwieldy hexameter lines. His rendering is sometimes faulty, often as uncouth as Chapman's, but his heart was in the work, and he achieved for Germany very much the same result as the great Elizabethan translators in England two centuries earlier; he naturalized Homer and made him a national classic only second to Luther's rendering of the Bible. Historians might continue to write history as though it had never happened, scholars who held the key of knowledge might use it to double-lock the door of ancient life on "this people that knoweth not the declensions"; but for readers of Voss's translations there was no manner of doubt as to "what actually happened", *was eigentlich geschehen ist*, to borrow Ranke's famous definition of the historian's goal. A whole generation of young perfervid Germans, in the days of the French Revolution, "wandered through the realms of gold" as young Englishmen had wandered in the realms of Chapman and Pope. We may take some consolation, in a generation which has invented *Greek Without Tears* as a substitute for *Greek Under the Rod*, from the thought that the modern school of scientific criticism itself arose very largely out of the inspiration of a vernacular Homer. I give only one example of what was going on in modest households all over Germany. Boie, Voss's personal patron, used to pay visits to a travelled countryman then living in Denmark, and, having with him the new translation, read it aloud in the evenings. For months after that visit the six-year-old boy of the family would "talk of nothing but Odysseus and Penelope", playing *Odyssey* games with his little sister. That is our first glimpse of Barthold Niebuhr, at fifteen "a small miracle of knowledge and of intellectual maturity", at nineteen writing, "if my name is to live it will be as an historian and publicist, as a classic and philologist"; at thirty, the confidant of Stein, Hardenberg and the King of Prussia in the "evil time of Prussia's humiliation"; the reorganizer, not only of Prussian finance, but also with Heyne's pupil von Humboldt of the Berlin University, "to regenerate", as he said, "the young men, to render them capable of great things, to put before them the noble example of antiquity"; and then, the great critical historian of early Rome, the founder of modern antiquarian and documentary research, the teacher who

[1] A new edition was published in 1950.

"felt and explained antiquity as if its figures had been his own contemporaries". If Voss had done nothing else but find Niebuhr, the labour of his translation of Homer would have been well spent.[1]

Eight years younger than Voss, another *bête noire* of Heyne was preparing himself to attack this eternal problem, *what are we to make of Homer*, on very different lines. Friederich August Wolf was ten years old when Robert Wood published his *Essay*. At eighteen, with a competent knowledge of six languages already, he caused some flutter in the University of Göttingen by insisting on registration as a student in philology, "one of those prophecies which spring from the conscious power to bring about their fulfilment". Even to reformers like Heyne, it was as if Mr. Verdant Green had told the Principal of Brazenface that he proposed to take his degree in Natural Science.[2] For the old "Arts Faculty" in a German university had long ceased to fulfil its proper purpose as a preliminary course for Theology, Law or Medicine; and the new purpose was being only dimly conceived, of a school of Humanities which should rank not below but abreast of the old professional studies. It chanced that young Wolf had read Robert Wood's *Essay* and showed up work of his own suggested by it, which Heyne disapproved. Probably he knew quite well where Wolf had got his ideas. On another occasion we hear that Heyne turned him out of his class-room. Lessing however was kind to him, for he realized that Philology, as Wolf conceived it—the knowledge of human nature as exhibited in antiquity—should include the study of other Arts besides Speech. Disillusioned with the humanities as professed at Göttingen, but obviously one of the coming men, Wolf was called at the age of twenty-four to a Classical Chair at Halle, Göttingen's older rival. This was in 1783; beyond the Rhine "all the foundations of the earth were out of course", as they are beyond the Dniester today, and in Germany too "there were great searchings of heart"; and not only about the relations between the *ancien régime* of education and the new subjects, modern languages and national literatures. It was no accident that one of Wolf's first productions at Halle, an edition of

---

[1] *Lebensnachrichten über Barthold Georg Niebuhr* (1838), especially I, pp. 5ff., 104. "Wenn mein Name genannt werden sollte, wird man mich als Geschichtschreiber und politischen Schriftsteller, als Alterthumsforscher und Philologen kennen" (1794).

[2] Cuthbert Bede, *The Adventures of Mr. Verdant Green*, n.d.

Demosthenes' *Speech against Leptines* on a matter of finance, suggested to his greatest pupil, August Boeckh, that masterly essay on the *Public Economy of Athens*[1] which made the fortune of the new chair of Ancient History established by Niebuhr at Berlin. For this kind of scholarship and interpretation of the old world to the new world that was now in the making, the times were indeed ready. Nor was it quite an accident, but an almost inevitable consequence of the naturalization of Homer by Voss, that about 1795 the study of Homer in the original had already such a vogue in German schools that a new school edition was needed; and who so obvious an editor as the brilliant young professor at Halle? For Wolf was even now only thirty-seven, though in the full noon of his academic fame.

It *was*, however, an accident, and a momentous one, that in 1788, a French scholar, Villoison, had published the marginal notes in an unusually early manuscript of the *Iliad* at Venice, and indicated their importance as a revelation of the objects and methods of Alexandrian scholarship. For not only did they supply a vast amount of material, far older than the readings of any extant copy of the poem and of primary value as evidence for the state of the text in Hellenistic times; they disclosed also the procedure of the great Alexandrian scholars, their principles of textual criticism, the variety, sources and something about the quality, of the manuscripts at their disposal; and gave, on first acquaintance at all events, a most disquieting impression of the state of the traditional text before the Alexandrians took it in hand. With longer time for examining this great windfall of new evidence, and for comparing conclusions in leisurely controversy with contemporaries over the large preliminary questions raised by these Venetian Notes—questions of which the most fundamental were hardly formulated until the work of Lehrs in 1833, La Roche in 1866, and Ludwich in 1884 and 1898[2]—Wolf might have found himself very differently equipped and prepossessed from his actual state of mind when the publishers' demand for a school-text of Homer reached him. The little book was literally

---

[1] *Die Staatshaushaltung der Athener*, 1817; *Trans.* G. C. Lewis[2], 1842.

[2] Karl Lehrs, *De Aristarchi studiis Homericis*, 1833; *Quaestiones Epicae*, 1837; Jacob La Roche, *Zeichen und Scholien des berühmten codex Venetus der Ilias*, 1862; *Die homerische Textkritik im Alterthum*, 1866: Arthur Ludwich, *Aristarchs homerische Textkritik nach den Fragmenten des Didymos*, 1884–5; *Die Homervulgata als voralexandrinisch erwiesen*, 1898.

written against time[1]; only the first part of the editor's introduction, the famous *Prolegomena ad Homerum*, ever appeared in print at all; and although Wolf published eventually, in 1804, a serious edition in four volumes, its contents are very far from supplying the scientific proofs of the brilliant, revolutionary theories of the school book of 1795.

Nor was it apparently Wolf's Homeric theories, profound as their influence immediately was, that mainly determined Von Humboldt's offer to him of a chair in the new Berlin University in 1807, but partly his success as the founder of a general school of the humanities at Halle, partly the fact that during the French invasions of 1806 Wolf's own university had been summarily closed, and consequently one of the best scholars in Germany was at the moment actually out of work. Wolf, at all events, was deeply disappointed with his reception at Berlin; he became involved in bitter controversy with his old professor Heyne, who after excluding him from his lectures, accused him now of stealing his ideas, and he had already a similar feud with Johann Gottfried Herder, who had instituted a very suggestive comparison between the literary form and historical significance of Homer, the early Hebrew poets, and the folk-songs of the Germans themselves.[2] Wolf hardly lived to see the first phase of the counter-attacks of more conservative or less courageous scholars, still less to take a side in the controversies between men like Hermann and Lachmann, who in the main were working out his ideas.

Briefly stated, Wolf's theory amounted to this. In the absence of alphabetical writing, the composition of a poem as long as the *Iliad* or the *Odyssey* was unthinkable and therefore impossible. Therefore the unity of design which had hitherto been thought to exist in each of the poems resulted, not from premeditation or single authorship, but from the ingenuity of compilers and editors, interpreting the vague folk-memory out of which the "sequel of songs and rhapsodies", in Bentley's phrase, had sprung. Even if there had been

[1] But after long thought and with full knowledge of its implications. "Iacta est alea, ad quam certe non inparatus accessi. Superstites adhuc sunt (et utinam diu sint) et meminerunt fortasse duo litteratissimi viri, quid ego annis 1780 et 1781 de hac re secum et sermonibus et litteris egerim" (*Prolegomena* xxvi, note 84).

[2] p. 81 below. In 1796 Wolf violently attacked Herder for plagiarizing his ballad theory in *Homer, ein Günstling der Zeit*.

any primary coherence, in general relation to such folk-memory, it had been for centuries at the mercy of piecemeal recitation by more or less careless professionals. Not all the primitive songs which must be thus presumed are the work of the same composer, or even of the same age; this is inferred from, and accounts for, the minor inconsistencies within the poems as we have them, but it is not possible now to distinguish between original and supplementary work. We can trace the poems to the recension of them by Peisistratus at Athens in the sixth century B.C., but no further back with any certainty.

What was it, which made Wolf's *Prolegomena to Homer* the spark to a whole barrel of explosive matter, and set the Homeric Question, as he formulated it, in the forefront of the battle in which the new classical scholarship of Heyne's pupils was to be engaged all along the line? To understand this we must go back a little into other lines of work, and link up the *Prolegomena* themselves with other aspects of contemporary German thought. In England, as we have seen, the seventeenth century had fallen less disastrously into the *baroque* than in France. Freedom of thought before and after the Civil War, and even during it and on both sides in it—such is the paradoxical outcome of so much of our queer history—had given us in succession Hobbes, Locke, Berkeley and Hume; freedom of investigation had given us Newton, Wren and Bentley; freedom of taste—not a little assisted by the sojourn of royalist *émigrés* in Italy and the Netherlands—had given us the Arundel, Pomfret and other collections of "ancient marbles", and a succession of travellers and antiquaries, in the three generations before Robert Wood. This more wholesome outlook, and especially this reaction towards naturalism, had in due course its effect in France; we need only look at Montesquieu in relation to Locke or Voltaire in relation to Hume, to see how things were moving in larger aspects of the philosophy of history. But, for French taste, poetry in imitation of nature was still reconcilable with a good deal of flimsy finery which was tolerated mainly because it was classical and *de bon ton*. History in particular remained a branch of rhetoric; and the historical significance of an early source like the Homeric poems was unappreciated, for example, by so good a classic as Diderot. In Germany things went differently. The counterpart of those earlier English naturalists we begin to see in Lessing, whose real appreciation of mature Hellenism, together with his personal preference for Roman poetry, set him closely in the same plane as Bentley. But Lessing failed to discover Homer, as he failed to discover either the Tragedians or Plato. Only in chance phrases, such as his brilliant inference from the opening words of the *Odyssey* that there had been *Epics of Return* before Homer, and his description of the *Odyssey* itself as "one of the *Return* poems", do we realize how narrowly he missed that discovery.[1] Lessing, however, contributed indirectly. He broke the spell of the Latinist models for epic, Tasso and Virgil, and set Goethe on the way to a real epic style, though in the first instance rather through English models than through Greek; one sometimes wonders whether alongside of Shakespeare he is not thinking after all of George Chapman. But why should the young Goethe or anyone else in Germany be looking about for a real epic style, or have any use for new non-Latin models?

We have seen how Robert Wood, though no philologist in any special sense, appreciated the importance of the Homeric poems as a document in the early history of language; and also just alludes to the recent discovery of similar relics of early oral composition "in the northern part of this island" and to the contemporary editor of Ossian, in illustration of the part ascribed by d'Aubignac and Bentley to Peisistratus in the collection and interconnexion of a "sequel of songs and rhapsodies", the rambling poems of a rambling poet. Now, it cannot be too forcibly insisted that the strength both of the psychology and of the morals of English thinkers in the seventeenth century had rested on what I think we may fairly describe as their anthropology. Hobbes, Locke, and in a less degree also Hume, had been close students of the newly discovered types of mankind and of human societies which the great age of exploration had revealed. That amazing mirror of the background of all this school of thought, Daniel Defoe, had characterized, with just that touch of caricature which reveals men to themselves, the procedure of Locke with his "Indian in the backwoods of America", his "Hottentot from Soldantia Bay", in that delicious (but little read) passage of *Robinson Crusoe* where Man Friday is interrogated about the state and contents of his immortal soul, his possession of innate ideas about the eternal verities. The shipwrecked Englishman "goes back to nature" in enjoyment of this new specimen, as he had

---

[1] *Hamb. Dramat. Stück*, 36; *Philologischer Nachlass Hempel* XIII, i, p. 284. *Laokoon* is ignored, presumably because, as Herder objected, it failed to see Homer in time and place.

meditated on the habits of his goats and the products of the island, like any Fellow of the Royal Society, or like Elias Ashmole, in his private diary, interrogating his gouty legs or his still more disastrous liver.[1]

Not least among these problems of research, attacked from different sides by men so different as Locke and Bentley and the Jesuit Lafitau who is one of the sources of Montesquieu,[2] a problem which hovers on the margins of Wood's *Essay*, was that of the origin of language; and next to that, the problem of the origin of that first use of language on a more than utilitarian plane, those glimpses of primitive narrative and description, which Leopold Stolberg later described as "Nature describing herself". Pioneers in this kind of discovery are two of our own countrymen. Thomas Percy, born in 1729, became the Hesiod of the Baltic and the North Sea by the virtual discovery of the creation-epic of Scandinavian explorers in his *Northern Antiquities*, published in 1763 and 1770, and produced his *Reliques of Ancient English Poetry* in 1765. James Macpherson, a little younger and more precocious, began his eccentric career in 1758 with a volume of verse about the Highlands, which might have passed as original if he had not been over-persuaded to reveal the sources of his inspiration in those *Fragments of Ancient Poetry collected in the Highlands of Scotland, and translated from the Galic or Erse Language*, with which he astonished the literary world in 1760.[3] Percy and Macpherson had gone "back to Nature" with a

[1] *Memoirs of his life, drawn up by himself*, ed. C. Burman, 1717. I could not find the liver, and offer instead, "I took, early in the morning, a good dose of Elixir, and hung three spiders about my neck, and they drove my ague away—Deo gratias" (p. 359).

[2] Joseph François Lafitau, *Mœurs des sauvages americains comparées aux mœurs des premiers temps*, 1724.

[3] Otto L. Jiriczek published a full critical edition, *James Macpherson's Ossian*, in Heidelberg in 1940, because of the great influence of the poems. Voss was not alone in preferring Ossian to Homer; see L. M. Price, *English Literature in Germany* (1953), pp. 125-6. Macpherson appeals seductively to admirers of the primitive. In the preface to the first collection, he writes: "They are not set to music, nor sung. The versification in the original is simple; and to such as understand the language, very smooth and beautiful. Rhyme is seldom used: but the cadence, and the length of the line varied, so as to suit the sense. The translation is extremely literal. Even the arrangement of the words in the original has been imitated; to which must be imputed some inversions in the style, that otherwise

vengeance, and found her not dumb but eloquent. For this new kind of research, encouragement and funds were only too promptly at hand. *Fingal, an ancient Epic in Six Books, together with several other poems composed by Ossian, son of Fingal, translated from the Gaelic language,* appeared in 1761, *Temora* in 1763, and the complete Works of Ossian in 1765. With the respective responsibilities of Ossian son of Fingal and of James Macpherson for these productions, we are no more concerned at this point than with those of Homer and Peisistratus for the *Iliad* and *Odyssey.* It is sufficient to note that the Homeric Question had already been asked by Perizonius and answered by Bentley and Vico, and that the impossibility of any scientific answer had been anticipated a century before by Casaubon. But that did not prevent both questions from being discussed. Dr. Johnson in 1773 satisfied himself that Macpherson had "found names and stories, and phrases, nay passages in old songs, and so made what he gives to the world as the translation of an ancient poem".[1]

would not have been chosen". And he has a note, "In these early times, suicide was utterly unknown among the people, and no traces of it are found in the old poetry. Whence the translator suspects the account that follows of the daughter of Dargo killing herself, to be the interpolation of some later Bard", which might have been written on Σ 34.

[1] Boswell's *Journal of a Tour to the Hebrides* is naturally full of the controversy: 23 August 1773, "We spoke of Fingal. Dr. Johnson said calmly, 'If the poems were really translated, they were certainly first written down. Let Mr. Macpherson deposit the manuscript in one of the colleges at Aberdeen, where there are people who can judge; and, if the professors certify the authenticity, then there will be an end of the controversy. If he does not take this obvious and easy method, he gives the best reason to doubt; considering too, how much is against it *a priori.*' " 23 September, "Dr. Johnson proceeded, 'I look upon M'Pherson's *Fingal* to be as gross an imposition as ever the world was troubled with. Had it been really an ancient work, a true specimen how men thought at that time, it would have been a curiosity of the first rate. As a modern production, it is nothing.'—He said, he could never get the meaning of an Erse song explained to him. They told him, the chorus was generally unmeaning. 'I take it (said he) Erse songs are like a song which I remember: it was composed in Queen Elizabeth's time, on the Earl of Essex; and the burthen was

"Radaratoo, radarate, radara tadara tandore" ' . . .

When Mr. M'Queen began again to expatiate on the beauty of Ossian's poetry, Dr. Johnson entered into no further controversy, but, with a pleasant smile, only cried, 'Ay, ay; Radaratoo radarate.' " Next day, confronted with some passages in the original, he made the reply quoted in

Macpherson lay low, pleading the prohibitive expense of a Gaelic *Corpus Poetarum*; Malcolm Laing waited till Macpherson was dead, before denying the existence of those authorities in his *History of Scotland*.[1]

But Macpherson's *Ossian* was read everywhere; it was translated early into German, and in Germany it came under the notice of Herder, whose attention had been directed early to the Homeric poems by Lessing and Klotz,[2] and who had been brought up in the

the text. "If this was the case, I observed, it was wrong to publish it as a poem in six books. JOHNSON: 'Yes, sir; and to ascribe it to a time too when the Highlanders knew nothing of *books*, and nothing of *six*;—or perhaps were got the length of counting six.' " 10 November, Johnson made a gentleman of "talents and integrity", who claimed to have heard a great part in the original, admit that he did not understand the language. " 'He would undertake (he said) to write an epick poem on the story of Robin Hood, and half England, to whom the names and places he should mention in it are familiar, would believe and declare they had heard it from their earliest years.' " Boswell gives his own view, "That *Fingal* is not from beginning to end a translation from the Gallick, but that *some* passages have been supplied by the editor to connect the whole, I have heard admitted by very warm advocates for its authenticity. If this be the case, why are not these distinctly ascertained? Antiquaries, and admirers of the work, may complain, that they are in a situation similar to that of the unhappy gentleman whose wife informed him, on her death-bed, that one of their reputed children was not his; and, when he eagerly begged her to declare which of them it was, she answered, '*That* you shall never know'; and expired, leaving him in irremediable doubt as to them all." Worth noting, too, is the argument on 21 August, "whether the Savage or the London Shopkeeper had the best existence", Lord Monboddo, "as usual, preferring the Savage". Cf. T. L. Peacock, *Melincourt*, 1818.

[1] *Essay on the supposed Authenticity of Ossian's Poems*, in *The History of Scotland from the Union of the Crowns to the Union of the Kingdoms*, 1800, 2nd ed. 1804, IV, pp. 409–502. He also published *The Poems of Ossian*, 1805, with a commentary to show where they imitated the Bible or classical writers. Patrick Graham, *Essay on the Authenticity of the Poems of Ossian*, 1807, is a solemn defence. Macpherson died in 1796.

[2] *Epistolae Homericae*, 1764. It contained criticisms of Homer which provoked replies from Lessing (*Briefe antiquarischen Inhalts*) and Herder (*Kritische Wälder* II-III) in 1769. R. T. Clark in *Herder, his Life and Thought* (1955) speaks of "Halle, capital of pseudo-classicism, where Christian Adolf Klotz (1738–1771) held sway with a coterie which can be described by no more fitting appellation than that of a gang of literary thugs" (pp. 68–9).

new nationalist romantic notions which were to revolutionize German literature and create a new method for the investigation of history. He had learned philosophy from Kant, at a time when Kant was still working on those anthropological, observational, naturalist lines which had been so fruitful for Locke and Montesquieu. He had learned from that wandering star, Hamann,[1] also at Königsberg, to look to the study of words and grammar for a clue to the mysteries of ideas and the processes of the working mind. One of his own earliest essays had been *On the Origin of Language*[2] as the central problem in any scientific examination of human nature. He was profoundly concerned in the new movement towards a nationalist literature, which should interpret the German soul as language in general interpreted the innate ideas of mankind. He seems to have become acquainted somewhere about 1771 with the collections of Percy and Macpherson, and soon after he published two books which focused these earlier experiences on what was for him the central problem of all. His *Plastic Art*,[3] an examination of the principles of all material art, was at the same time a challenge to the dominant classicalism of Lessing and Winckelmann, and the first formal rediscovery of mediaeval art as a manifestation of a stage in human advancement worthy of serious study. It is, indeed, one of the fountain-heads of the Gothic Revival, though anticipated in point of time by the work of Browne Willis in England,[4] and those others who refounded the Society of Antiquaries in 1743, a year before Herder was born. His *Voices of the Peoples in their Songs*[5] started in his own country the same studies of folk-lore and folk-poetry which were already well under way in England. Though his main interest turned from his early studies on Homer, his essay *On the Spirit of*

---

[1] His *Aesthetica in nuce* began "Poetry is the mother tongue of the human race" (*Sturm und Drang: Kritische Schriften*, Heidelberg (1949), p. 121— a useful selection of essays).

[2] *Über den Ursprung der Sprache*, 1772.

[3] *Plastik*, 1778. In 1769 Herder reviewed Denis' *Die Gedichte Ossians* I, and in 1771 he wrote *Über Ossian und die Lieder alter Völker*, before he first read Ossian in English and just after he had read the *Reliques*, which confirmed his belief that Ossian was lyric, not epic. "Ossians Gedichte *Lieder, Lieder des Volks, Lieder* eines ungebildeten sinnlichen Volks."

[4] Joan Evans, *A History of the Society of Antiquaries* (1956), pp. 55f.

[5] *Stimmen der Völker in Liedern*, 1778-9. Herder himself called it *Volkslieder*.

Hebrew Poetry[1] picks up another of the fertile germs which we have found already in Robert Wood's *Essay*, and heads the long roll of German contributions to the scientific study of Jewish literature, no less than to the literary appreciation if it.

With Herder's masterpiece, the *Ideas for a Philosophy of the History of Mankind*,[2] which only began to appear in 1784, we are only concerned to note how its successive instalments prepared the ground for the reception of the new art and science of interpreting ancient history and ancient literature, for which Heyne's seminar had been laboriously preparing the craftsmen. For while Herder was feeling his way, under the guidance of Kant, Hamann and Lessing, to the conception of Homer as a *Favourite of Time*,[3] the inspired interpreter of a period and a civilization, much as the significance of the period of French influence in Germany might be summed up in the one word *Voltaire*, yet another of Heyne's pupils, the Danish antiquary Zoëga, was advancing on the lines both of the archaeological commentary initiated by the publication of the pictorial *Tabula Iliaca*, and of those evolutionary notions about history and literary forms which had been popularized in Italy by Vico. Zoëga was a man of many friends and few books; of wide artistic training, strict historical method, and vivid imagination. Like Wood, he could see through the texts to the people who composed them. A short *Essay on Homer*, written in 1788 and long unpublished, though it lived in the work of his great pupil, Welcker, is significant for two reasons. Firstly, he doubted, like Vico, the personal existence of Homer, whom

---

[1] *Vom Geiste der ebräischen Poesie*, 1782–3.

[2] *Ideen zu einer Philosophie der Geschichte der Menschheit*, 1784–91; *Trans.* T. Churchill, *Outlines of a Philosophy of the History of Man*, 1800.

[3] *Homer, ein Günstling der Zeit*, 1795. Herder has the same idea in verse (*Suphan*, Vol. 26, p. 38), for which the editor offers:

> Years come, and are gone;
> Still Homer is there.
> His song is alone.
> It rings through the air.
> All the victor's laurels
> Garland his head.
> Long brooded Nature
> And toiled. Her work done,
> She looked on her creature,
> And rested, and said—
> "Earth has her jointure!
> A Homer is made."

he put in the same category as Orpheus and Lycurgus, regarding them as types of successive phases in the cultural development of the Greek people: *essi popoli Greci erano quell' Omero*—those peoples of Greece *were* that Homer of theirs. Secondly, he restated the question raised by the *Tabula Iliaca*, whether the Alexandrians had been right in setting such a gulf between the *Iliad* and *Odyssey* on the one hand and the rest of the epic literature on the other. Might not the other poems have been "Homeric" in the same general sense as these two; representative of the same general phase of civilization; trustworthy commentary on the two extant poems; illustrations, even, of stages on the way by which those poems had come to be what they are? Though Zoëga wrote so little, we have probably a good deal of his thought in Welcker's great book on the same subject. The first volume appeared in 1835, under the title, *The Epic Cycle or the Homeric Poets*,[1] which sufficiently illustrates its scope and conclusions, and the second volume in 1849, just too late to be used by Grote in his first edition of his History, though Grote evidently owed much to Volume I. For it went far to bridge the gap between Homeric and Hellenic which was now seen to be, not necessarily a gulf between contrasted principles, but rather a lacuna in our knowledge, corresponding with a plane in the picture, a phase in a historical development.

Thus, side by side with Wolf's realization, through his study of the Venetian Scholia, of the processes by which our actual text of Homer had been established by the scholars of Alexandria, and his belief in an Athenian edition or recension of the poems in the sixth century, stood his acceptance, even more literally than in the very tentative and guarded phrases of Robert Wood, of the assumption that before the seventh century at earliest (and for Wolf it seemed far more likely to have been the sixth) those poems had not been systematically written down at all. This was strengthened by the profound impression which had been made on him, as on all his contemporaries, by the discovery that such oral tradition did in fact take place, in Gaelic Scotland, in England and in his own country. For he found that this traditional ballad-literature was being interpreted as one of the phases through which the literary history of any people must necessarily pass, between its first hardly articulate aspirations and the moment when a Macpherson or a Herder or a

[1] *Der epische Zyklus oder die homerischen Dichter.*

Peisistratus arrested the process of spontaneous generation and fixed its products in an *Anthology* or an *Ossian*. For a generation which had been forced by its own spiritual growing pains to set up anew the old sophistical distinction between φύσις and νόμος, between Nature and Art, as the only way to get out of a school of art which had in fact merely gone stiff and stale, hardly any other explanation of the "freshness and simplicity" of the Homeric poems was conceivable than that the composer or composers of those naturalistic verses had lived literally "in the state of Nature", like "the Carib on the Banks of the Orinoco" in the writings of Rousseau, or the Polynesian children of nature who were being popularized by Chamisso and George Forster, the naturalist who sailed with Captain Cook.[1] Overlooking the complete anonymity in which the poet of the *Iliad* and *Odyssey* has so successfully involved himself, Wolf seems to have thought, like d'Aubignac and Vico before him, that in dissipating those impressions of personality which led the later Greeks to compile *Lives* of him, to set up statues to him, and to rank him with other personal heroes for reverent commemoration, he was restoring the poems to their proper niche in the library rather than the temple of Fame, among the folk-poetries which had now become the accepted type of the literature of the "state of Nature".

Wolf's services to his contemporaries were of two distinct kinds, in classical studies and in German literature. We are here, of course, primarily concerned with the former, but if criticism stands, as I have suggested at the outset, in any real relation to life, we cannot overlook at this point the contribution of Wolf to the many-sided maturity of Goethe. Herder had introduced Goethe at Strassburg, when he was a young law student,[2] to the Homer whom Leopold Stolberg

---

[1] George Forster, *A Voyage round the World in his Britannic Majesty's sloop Resolution, commanded by Captain James Cook, during the years 1772-5* (2 vols. 1777). Actually it was his father, Reinhold, that sailed with Cook, but when the Admiralty forbade him to write an account, he got his son to do it. According to *D.N.B.*, this Forster (Johann Georg Adam, d. 1794) is often confused with George Forster (d. 1792) who wrote *Sketches of the Mythology and Customs of the Hindoos* (1785). Adelbert von Chamisso was appointed botanist in 1815 to the Russian ship *Rurik* which Otto von Kotzebue commanded on a scientific voyage round the world; he published a diary of the voyage, *Tagebuch*, 1821.

[2] A bitter and unhappy Herder, as Goethe tells us in *Dichtung und Wahrheit* X.

called, in the mode of the time, the "mirrored truth of a primaeval present", the inspired child of nature, whom he described in Romantic verse which I can only paraphrase here.[1]

> Said the Spirit of God, Let a Poet be.
> Earth gave him her nurture all motherly;
> And on the blue breast of her ocean flood
> His fancy was cradled to poethood.
>
> Blind stood the bard by the sounding sea.
> The waves surged round him unendingly,
> And the giant deeds of the Golden Days
> Surged round him with all their pageantry.
>
> Songlike, swift as a swooping swan,
> Fell inspiration his soul upon.
> As songlike sprang from the singing sea
> An *Iliad* and an *Odyssey*.
>
> Had sight been his, he had seen that day
> Heaven, Earth and Sea dissolve away;
> But 'twas they revealed to his sightless eyes
> Heaven, Earth and Sea for a Paradise.

From Winckelmann[2] Goethe had that conception of beauty as no less a creation of organic and living development than truth. His own nature-study and his acquaintance with Italian art, where the fact of such development from primitive to mature was already demonstrated, were deepening and widening that conception, when he set out on his Italian journey. Experiments in elegy, where his models were necessarily Hellenistic, as Winckelmann's artistic models had been necessarily almost wholly Graeco-Roman, took him a certain distance and then failed to satisfy him. Tragedy, on an Homeric model already, the story of *Nausicaa*, took him a further stage; it was the first morsel snatched from the great banquet since the death of Euripides. But as he moved still southward, and found himself at last, like Wood, on the frontiers of Homer's own countries, tragedy too gave way to epic, and the fragmentary *Achilles*, a twenty-fifth

[1] *An das Meer*, lines 25–40 (*Der Göttinger Dichterbund*, ed. Sauer, III, pp. 109–10).
[2] *Gedanken über die Nachahmung der griechischen Werke in der Malerei und Bildhauerkunst*, 1755; *Geschichte der Kunst des Altertums*, 1764.

book of the *Iliad*, to take up the story of the hero where Homer had left it, was already on his pen, when Wolf's *Prolegomena* appeared, and he hailed—strangest of all welcomes from a great poet to a great critic—"the man whose courage has at last delivered us from the name of Homer, and called us to a wider career. Who dares fight against Gods, and who against the only God? Yet to be of Homer's lineage, even if only the last born, is great".[1] While there was a personal Homer ahead of him, the way was blocked, even for a Goethe; without him, with only the other disciples far ahead and ever climbing Homerwards, there was an apostolic succession and a mansion prepared even for the least of the apostles. In such romantic fashion did the scales fall from the eyes of this least of the apostles; and he wanted to begin his apostolic career with a German translation of the *Prolegomena*.

Among the learned, Wolf's *Prolegomena* had a mixed reception. Heyne, as we have seen, thought that Wolf had stolen his ideas. But it was some while before the real weakness of his interpretation was detected. In the first place, he underestimated the evidence for the antiquity of alphabetic writing in Greece, even as known in his time; and it was not long before his Berlin colleague, August Boeckh, set the Prussian Academy of Sciences to work to investigate this very question by the collection of whatever evidence there was in that *Corpus* of Greek Inscriptions which bears his name; a work as essential for the sound criticism of Homer, in this respect, as for Boeckh's own special studies in ancient economics and administration. In 1884 Wilamowitz could say that alphabetic writing is not only not so late as Wolf thought, but is in fact as early as Homer.

[1] *Hermann und Dorothea* (1796), 27–30; cf. his letter to Wolf, 26 December 1796 (*Weimar*, iv *Abtheilung*, xi Bd., p. 3455). But the poet in Goethe soon won.

> You have with ingenuity
> From any reverence set us free,
> And we confessed too liberally
> That *Iliad* but a patchwork be.
>
> May this defection raise no ire;
> For Youth can urge us with its fire
> Rather to think of it as One
> And so delight in One alone.

(J. Boyd, *Notes to Goethe's Poems* II (1786–1832), p. 72; translation by M. Jacobs of St. Hugh's College.)

And by a curious irony, it was almost exactly a hundred years later that the announcement was made by Arthur Evans, at the Oxford meeting of the British Association in 1894, that quite independently of any kind of alphabetic writing such as was in use later in Greece, in Phoenicia, and in other coastlands of the Near East, there had been a far earlier and quite different system in Crete and other parts of the Greek archipelago, consisting not of linear characters (γράμματα—scratchings, as Wood had rightly interpreted the Greek word for such signs) but of σήματα—symbols, more or less pictorial, for objects, acts and conceptions related to them; strictly in accordance with the one Homeric reference to a material and portable message, the folded tablet with its baleful symbols which is described as carried by Bellerophon from the Peloponnese to Lycia, and containing the instructions for his own murder.[1]

In the second place, Wolf's own assumption that in the absence of written record, the transmission of a long poem is not possible, was really refuted in advance by Robert Wood's experiences among the Arabs and among Greek ballad-mongers; and has been disproved again and again by other travellers in many parts of the world. The memory of people unspoiled by reliance on notebooks and works of reference is indeed amazing, even without the aid of metre; and quite apart from that, and in the midst of a literate society, the practice of the older English public schools in Wolf's own time included the memorizing of the whole of the Homeric poems, and the works of Virgil as well, within two or three years at most. I can vouch for the permanence of such early impressions in old Eton and Winchester men within my own experience.

Further, Wolf relied on the late and scanty statements about the activity of Peisistratus, which he describes quite inaccurately as supported by the unanimous agreement of antiquity. But even if it were better attested, it would yet prove little as to the previous state of the poems. One of those very passages asserts that Solon did more for Homer than Peisistratus; and what Solon did, which is equally well attested, was to insist that at public recitations in Athens the competitors should take their turns each where his predecessor left off, so that the poems (whatever they were) should be recited, not in capricious selections, but in the customary order; it follows that a generation before the administration of Peisistratus

[1] Z 168–9.

there *was* a customary order, and all that was necessary was to provide against the preferences of individual performers for particular episodes.

Wolf's conception, too, of schools of professional reciters with their own repertoire of traditional verse, neither rested on ancient authority (for even of the so called "sons of Homer" in Chios we know little more than their name) nor did it help his other contentions much. If there were such schools, how did it come about that the traditional poetry was in such fragmentary disorder as the theory of a Peisistratid Recension presupposed? And whence did they derive their traditional materials? For Wolf seems to have conceived them rather as clumsy transmitters than as original composers of epic. It was also, among his German colleagues at all events, no small defect in Wolf's presentation of his ideas, that he had evidently not worked them out in detail, with chapter and verse; and further, as time went on, that he had little intention of doing so. His eventual edition of Homer, published in 1804, did not seriously advance the particular aspect of the subject which he was supposed to have made his own. This did not, however, prevent his ideas from having very wide popularity and enduring influence. As the preface to a school textbook, which became popular as a result of the general movement in literature which had led to its production in the first instance, his essay fell into the hands of everyone who aspired to be a scholar at all, and his ideas accorded sufficiently well with the trend of literary criticism to be accepted, in view of his really great repute as a scholar, with less question than they might otherwise have incurred. There was, indeed, little controversy over them till after his death. Then Nitzsch raised the objection that the art of writing is proved by extant inscriptions to have been known before the time of Peisistratus[1] and K. O. Müller, while accepting his views on writing, disputed his inferences.[2] Further study of the Cycle also showed that the *Iliad* and *Odyssey* had influenced other epic literature and should therefore be appreciably older.[3] In essentials, however, his theories were widely accepted, and comment on them gradually took two principal forms.

[1] *Meletemata* I (1830).

[2] *History of the Literature of Ancient Greece*, 1840.

[3] Nitzsch, *Meletemata* II (1837); Welcker, *Der epische Zyklus oder die homerischen Dichter*.

Gottfried Hermann, yet another pupil of old Heyne and in closer touch with his master than almost anyone, devoted himself to some of the numerous preliminary studies which were required before conclusions as brilliant and, if the truth must be spoken, as premature as those of Wolf could be accepted as more than conjectural hypotheses. He laid the foundation for the scientific study, not of the Homeric hexameter merely, but of Greek metre in general. He faced the perplexing problem of the Homeric dialect, with its curious intermixture of Aeolic and Ionic forms and its archaic syntax, in the light of the rapidly growing selection of Greek dialect inscriptions of which at any rate the relative age could be established. He did pioneer work, on the lines suggested by Zoëga and more fully explored by his own contemporary Welcker, on the poems attributed to Hesiod, on the so-called Homeric Hymns, and on the fragments and ancient summaries of the other epic literature. In particular, he made the first systematic and critical analysis of the structure and contents of the two poems (which Wolf does not seem to have attempted), and devoted special attention to one of the most obvious and characteristic and at the same time most unusual marks of Homeric style, namely the frequent repetition of whole passages, in identical words, even where the context would seem to demand at all events a change of standpoint and interpretation of the facts to be related. This peculiarity gained especial interest when it was realized that it recurred in other bodies of traditional poetry and might be regarded, for some reason yet to be discovered, as an habitual procedure in such compositions. But was it simply a reciter's device for spinning out material of his own composing? Or did it mean that such stock-passages were drawn by different composers from some common stock, in which case it was reasonable to regard them as presumably traditional already and representing an earlier stage in the development of epic diction? Or again were they to be regarded as the tedious and tasteless insertions of mere transmitters of a tale originally more concisely and crisply told?[1]

On the whole, Hermann's view of the whole question was conservative. We may compare him with the cautious and minutely-learned Aristarchus, revising and often reversing the judgment of that

---

[1] *De metris poetarum Graecorum et Romanorum*, 1796, and *Elementa doctrinae metricae*, 1816. Papers on Homer (1831–2) in *Opusc.* V, pp. 52ff., VI, i, pp. 70ff., and VIII, pp. 11ff.

enthusiastic pioneer Zenodotus; more careful to establish, by systematic collection of instances, the usage of the poet and to accept, as facts to be examined and explained, what had at first sight seemed irregular and corrupt. Hermann, like Aristarchus, admitted as certain a large class of such blemishes, and saw his way to *explain* how they had come to stand in the text; but he regarded the poems, in their present shape, as preserving in essentials the plan and contents of the original composition, a rendering of the central motive, in the one the *Wrath of Achilles* and in the other the *Wanderings* and *Return of Odysseus*; and he saw no reason, in their conception or style, to assign them to different authors. Hermann's principal publications appeared between 1832 and 1840, and his standpoint was shared in essentials by scholars of the learning and distinction of Kayser and Immanuel Bekker.

A more drastic line was taken by Karl Lachmann, briefly a pupil of Hermann but more indebted to Bentley in general, and to Wolf directly, in his treatment of Heroic Poetry. As a young scholar, he took Homer with him on the campaign which was ended before it began by Napoleon's defeat at Waterloo, but at that time he was applying Wolf's conclusions to the *Niebelunge-not*. It was more than twenty years later, and he was a professor at Berlin, when he turned from German epic to the *Iliad* and dissected it into eighteen *Kleinlieder*.[1] It was his contention that contradictions in the subject matter between these lays preclude unity of original conception or authorship of the poems as we have them, but he also found divergencies of spirit between some of them. His tendency, therefore, is to give less prominence to "one first poet" than Wolf did; *Die Einheit der Ilias ist eine gefallene Burg.* He had no difficulty in demonstrating that there were anomalies. They had, indeed, been recognized in antiquity, and excused on the ground that the personal Homer sometimes fell short of perfection; *quandoque bonus dormitat Homerus*.[2] He contended further that the only argument accepted as valid by *all* Unitarians was the evidence of the tradition. His conclusion that all theories of single authorship, sources or evolution are alike hypothetical is unshaken, and we may wonder if in this we have gone any further since 1874. He failed, however, to note that his own lay theory was equally hypothetical. His "objectivity" is only

[1] *Betrachtungen über Homers Ilias* (1837–41; definitive edition, 1874).
[2] Hor., *A.P.* 359.

apparent. It is not that he believed the evidence for a Peisistratid recension to be stronger than the evidence for a single Homer, but that he required the Peisistratid recension to support his lay theory; and the lay theory itself finds no support in Greek literature, but is based on the analogy of the lays he thought he had detected in the *Niebelunge-not* and *Edda*. Yet he himself warned his pupil Lehrs of the danger of arguing from analogy with other literatures. We may note, too, that later criticism has not confirmed his analysis of the *Niebelunge-not*.[1] His own arguments against the *Iliad* are valid against his lays; they have no Aristotelian "unity" of composition, neither the epic unity which Aristotle at least thought the *Iliad* had, nor unity as conceived in a tragedy or a Pindaric Ode. It was left to Wilamowitz to ask how the lays could exist except as fragments of a pre-existing Cycle. Lachmann used historical premisses as hypotheses for a literary conclusion about what must have been the condition of poetry in early times, instead of working inductively from the poems. In fact, he rushed to conclusions in the spirit of the creative romanticism in which he had grown up. He became a great leader; but leaders only achieve their tasks when they are outrun.

Of these two interpretations of Wolf, George Grote followed Hermann's rather than Lachmann's.[2] In extant literature, he distinguished two classes of Greek epic poetry, represented by the poems ascribed respectively to Homer and Hesiod. The Hesiodic, didactic, type is more closely related to the culture of the historic Greeks than the Homeric and is therefore probably nearer to it in date. The Homeric poems are the survivors of a much larger class of such literature and seem to be early examples of it. The classical traditions about the personality of Homer are worthless, and the personality of Homer may itself be a myth, invented to explain that which the historical guild of the Homeridae was constituted to conserve and transmit. The poems were popular in the sense that they were meant to be performed publicly, and suffered innovations, especially as to the use or disuse of musical accompaniment. The question of writing raised by Wolf has no necessary connexion with the problem of single authorship; it is easier to suppose long memories than long manuscripts, and the existence of the *Catalogue of Contingents* in *B*,

[1] See Mary Fleet, "The Recent Study of the Niebelungenlied" (*Journal of English and Germanic Philology* LII (1953), pp. 32ff).

[2] *History of Greece*, I-II, 1846.

a kind of gazetteer of the Trojan war, proves the existence of a comprehensive narrative of that event. The absence of allusions to events and customs of the Peisistratid age is negative evidence in favour of an early date for the poems as a whole. Wolf had laid most stress on the problems offered by the *Iliad*, but this attacks the problem at its more difficult end. The *Odyssey* has a structure so closely compacted that, whatever the materials available when it was composed, it appears to be one man's work and design as it stands. The *Iliad* is more complex. Grote saw in it an original poem of single design about the *Wrath of Achilles*, which has been expanded by additions which have no necessary or original connexion with the incident of the *Quarrel* between Achilles and Agamemnon. The parts of the poem in which Achilles is in the picture are coherent and consecutive in themselves, but the interval between the first and the eighth books, nearly a third of the whole poem, is inexplicable except on the supposition that another hand has been at work. Similarly the ninth book, in which a further attempt is made to propitiate Achilles, is inconsistent with points in the main narrative, and the episode of the fortification of the Greek camp makes the tactics in other parts of the action unintelligible. The character of Zeus in the non-*Achilleid* sections is inconsistent with that assigned to him in the *Achilleid*. Finally, the last two books, after the death of Hector, are in a style and contain matter perceptibly different from all that precedes and should be regarded as a supplement of later date. The history of the poem may be summarized. Early in the eighth century, "Homer", using earlier lays, composed an *Achilleid* or *Menis* ($A\Theta\Lambda$-X; later critics expelled Θ). It was expanded into the *Iliad* by the addition of B-HIK (later critics make K later still). $\Psi\Omega$ make a further supplement.

This is the first example of a plausible theory of expansion. What Grote saw was that the Wolfian theory of a piecemeal Homer, patched together by Peisistratus, and still more Lachmann's theory that the minor poems which he detected had once had a separate existence and consequently a literary form and method of composition of their own, failed to explain the strong traces of design in the larger sections even of the *Iliad*. He conceded, therefore, the gradual accretion of episodes, while insisting that there must have been some nucleus around which they might cohere.

Grote's challenge on the *Odyssey* was accepted by a pupil of

Lachmann, Adolf Kirchhoff.[1] He distinguished three stages in the poem's creation, independent poems on the *Wanderings* and on the *Revenge*, brought together by a later poet who added the *Telemachy*. He dated the final stage to about 600 B.C. Kirchhoff performed the inductive work which Lachmann had indicated as necessary but did not do. His concentration on the *Odyssey* marks a change of emphasis; from now on, it becomes more prominent in controversy. He raised the question whether analysis of the poems is the only way to reach a solution, the alternative being to treat the whole question historically, with the use of external evidence. Aristarchus had denied Homeric epic a past and a sequel, a view which is not yet obsolete. "Homer is only interpreted by himself" is a valuable principle, but not of universal application. From another point of view, "Homer" is the whole Epos, which has a lifetime coming down into historic times and traceable back thence. Wolf's ill-founded corollary to Wood's ill-founded thesis became in turn the foundation of sand for nearly a century of "higher" and "higher" criticism, chiefly in Germany but increasingly copious in England as German notions of scholarship came into vogue from about 1850 onwards; but the generation after Lachmann put the Homeric Question on to an entirely different footing, even from that in which Lachmann left it.

[1] *Die Homerische Odyssee*, 1859, 2nd ed., 1879; *Die Composition der Odyssee*, 1869.

Chapter Six

GLADSTONE'S VIEW OF HOMER

T HE earlier chapters of this book traced the principal achievements
of Homeric criticism in antiquity, in the classical renaissance, and in
the eighteenth century. In the first of these we saw the birth of textual
criticism, in the formulation of grammatical rules as a test for errors
of transmission and as a guide for amending them, and in the appeal
to the usage of the poet as a criterion of authenticity, applied to his
subject matter as well as to his verses. We saw the first separatists
overwhelmed by the authority of Aristarchus, and the first attempts
at historical criticism smothered between austere philology and
exuberant allegory until the brilliant early climax of Alexandrian
scholarship declined into pedantic traditionalism. In the Revival of
Learning, Italy was diverted from Homeric to Virgilian studies by
pardonable pride of birthplace; France was precluded by the baroque excesses of an official cult of a false and frigid classicalism from
appreciating the spontaneous realism of Homer; and Holland erected
laboriously an unwieldy superstructure of true scholarship on the
basis of traditional learning. England, happier in its translators than
in its critics, enjoyed Homer and naturalized him, but it was here
that Bentley made the first serious discovery in Homeric scholarship
since Alexandrian days, and that Robert Wood initiated a realist,
even materialist, interpretation based upon eyewitness and acquaintance with Mediterranean and oriental life. The contribution of
German scholarship after the middle of the eighteenth century we
found to consist of applying to poems, which antiquity had accepted
almost without question as the work of a personal Homer, the

94

microscope of a meticulous analysis of phrase and plot. It assumed, in the light of contemporary discoveries about the popular poetry of northern Europe, an initial fragmentariness and incoherence, and a subsequent insecurity of transmission, which appeared to involve the rejection of the traditional unity of composition and the acceptance in its place of the very ill-attested episode of the Peisistratid recension of the *disiecta membra poetae*. We saw this purely literary criticism inherited from Wolf by Lachmann and Hermann, from Hermann by Grote, from Grote and Lachmann by Kirchhoff. The assumption of a sixth-century reconstitution of the poems was supplemented by the theory of an original poem or poems of relatively high literary merit, expanded and interpolated by clumsy and spiritless patchwork. The question how the collective result had acquired its admitted vigour and charm remained, not only quite unanswered, but almost unasked.

In the nineteenth century new influences were at work. Systematic archaeology began but, for reasons which will be discussed in the next chapter, its results were small until the end of the century. But the generation which was adding chemistry, physiology and geology to the list of the "natural sciences" had other new weapons with which the old problems of early history were being attacked afresh. The revelation of Sanskrit language and literature, about 1800, led to the establishment of a new science of comparative philology, and unfortunately also to a long period when philological conclusions were applied with pardonable enthusiasm to historical and ethnological research; as though it could be assumed that, because two groups of people spoke the same language or languages of kindred structure, they had wandered by the same or similar routes from the same "home" of origin, and retained their physique and manners with only such amount of modification as was exhibited in their speech. The result was an orgy of speculative dogmatism about Aryan migrations, Aryan civilization, and even Aryan blood, which was only prevented from being more misleading than it was, by the difficulties which its exponents found in making their own conclusions tally with one another.[1] A by-product of comparative philology

[1] In an article, "The Olympian System versus the Solar Theory", in *The Nineteenth Century* for October 1879, Gladstone discussed: Ernest Renan, *On the part falling to the Semitic Races in the History of Civilization*, 1870, Max Müller, *Introduction to the Science of Religion*, 1870, and George Cox, *Mythology of the Aryan Nations*.

was the discovery that among Aryan-speaking peoples there was a large common stock of stories, in part explanatory of natural occurrences such as the courses of heavenly bodies and changes of seasons and weather, in part, like the tales of early wars in the *Iliad* and the *Mahābhārata*, neither so clearly aetiological nor so closely parallel. Scholars brought up in the contemporary schools of romantic literature found little difficulty in detecting myth and symbolism in such stories and fitting them, as the Romanticists of the Hellenistic Age had done, into cosmologies and theogonies based on the common stock of more obvious nature-myths. Thus Achilles, Jason and Penelope, with Lycurgus and Codrus, on the one hand, and Minos, Cadmus and Helen on the other, passed over from history to philosophy and ceased to need archaeological commentary at all. Old-fashioned amateurs might "believe in the Trojan War", as old-fashioned parsons might "believe in the Exodus", but the seats of the mighty were occupied by critics and sceptics, masters of the comparative method.

Into this period of nascent philology, nascent mythology, and nascent archaeology, still dominated by German higher criticism as interpreted by the cold commonsense and great historical authority of Grote, comes the meteoric Homerology of William Ewart Gladstone, which had an immediate and widespread influence from the appearance of his *Studies on Homer* in 1858, and remained a principal factor in English scholarship till the no less meteoric intervention of Schliemann in 1871.

Gladstone plunged early into public life, and we can best appreciate his work on the Homeric Question if we consider the way that it connected itself in his mind with his public career and especially with his work as an Oxford reformer. The training with which he came to the study of Homer was one which professional scholars might envy. At Eton, where, to use his own words, "We knew very little indeed, but we knew it accurately", he could already exchange Homeric banter with Arthur Hallam.[1] He passed with high honours through the Oxford Classical School, and acquired from that discipline a habit of mind which many of his contemporaries shared but which three generations of reform have abolished rather than improved. Fortunately, the Terminal Examinations of the Christ Church of that day have left, in a volume called the Senior Censor's

[1] John Morley, *The Life of William Ewart Gladstone* (1903), I, p. 28.

JOHN LINTON MYRES, 1931

PLATE 1

(b) Flaxman's "Shield of Achilles"

(a) Jason, from a Flemish MS. of *Le Roman de la Rose*, c. 1500 A.D.

PLATE 2

(a) Wm. Dörpfeld lecturing in the open air at Mycenae

(b) East fortification wall of Troy VI: a, lower wall; b and c, tower; d, parapet; f, house of Troy VIIa; g, debris of Troy VIII

PLATE 3

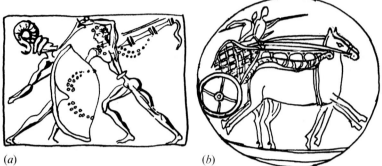

(a)   (b)

(c)

(d)

BRONZE AGE FIGHTING

(a) Mycenae, saec. XVI   (c) Mycenae, c. 1200
(b) Vaphio, saec. XV   (d) Battle of Kadesh, c. 1288

PLATE 4

(a)

(b)

(c)

BATTLE SCENES

(a) Nestor and the Molione (?), Attic, end of eighth century
(b) The death of Achilles, Corinthian, c. 690–80 B.C.
(c) The death of Achilles, West Greek (?), sixth century

PLATE 5

(*a*)

(*c*)

(*b*) (i)   (ii)

(*d*)

SOLDIERS IN FORMATION

(*a*) Mycenaeans, *c.* 1200   (*c*) Athenians, saec. VIII
(*b*) Battle under Rameses III   (*d*) Assyrians, *c.* 700

PLATE 6

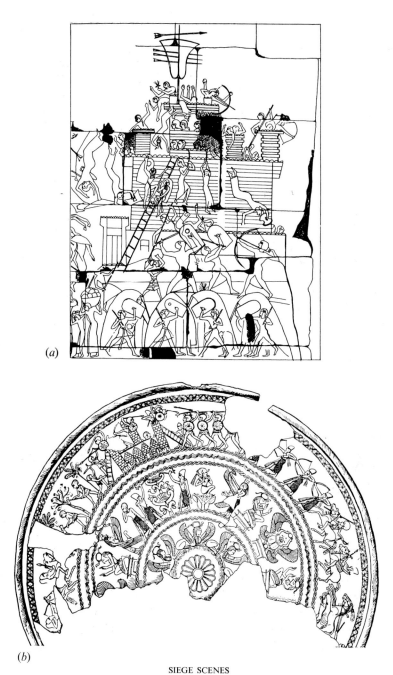

(a)

(b)

SIEGE SCENES

(a) c. 1290   (b) Saec. VII

PLATE 7

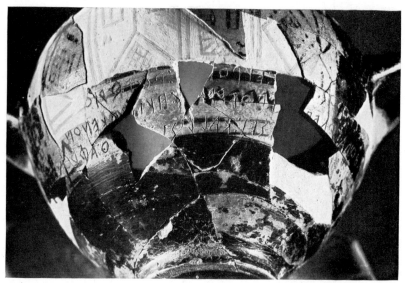

(a)

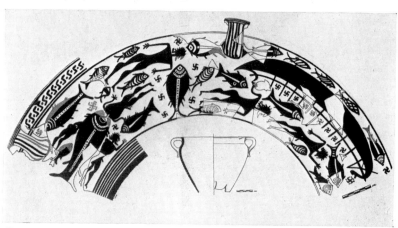

(b)

VASES FROM EIGHTH-CENTURY GRAVES ON ISCHIA
(a) The "Cup of Nestor" inscription
(b) Shipwreck (of Odysseus?)

PLATE 8

Book, what must be an almost unique survey of the practical work-ing of the old Classical School. Until it became clear to a man's tutor that he was proficient in exact science as it was then understood, he was tied rigidly to Trigonometry, Optics and Hydrostatics as a real element of the term's work. Gladstone's reports in these subjects, though not on a level with his classical performances, are creditable enough, and his name appeared in the First Class of the non-Classical School. Philosophy, History and Theology had their separate courses; Theology was of course compulsory and the other two indispensable. History, indeed, somewhat outweighed Scholar-ship, and Philosophy, under Scottish rather than German auspices, was beginning to outweigh History. In the departments of Logic, of Morals, and above all of Political Philosophy, it included all that modern thought had based on the foundations of Socrates and Aristotle. So much for the broad basis of general culture on which an Oxford First Class man was built. On the side of Classics, too, it was no question of special periods and set books, or of limited aspects for the evidence of ancient life. It was the Graeco-Roman world in all its fulness, with the whole of its literature and all its antiquities which the Renaissance or recent endeavour had recovered, "the study", as Gladstone wrote to Hallam, "of the great master-pieces of antiquity in their substance and spirit".[1] The only limits to the quest were the will and endurance of the student, the wisdom of his advisers, and the contents of the Bodleian Library. For the "read-ing man", Oxford was a place where, as Cyril Jackson said, "You must work like a tiger, and not be afraid of killing yourself by work."[2] Obviously a course of only three years made some selection necessary, and the College provided formal teaching on a few authors only. The selection was determined partly by good sense, partly by unwritten custom, at Christ Church greatly also by the inclination of individual tutors. But what a width of reading is disclosed! A mere gentleman-commoner like Ruskin—and it was of course nobody's business to see that a gentleman-commoner did anything but pay his footing and exist gracefully—was examined in a single term in five plays of Aeschylus, and two books of Aristotle's *Rhetoric*, together with a revision of the whole of Herodotus and Statics, Trigonometry and Differential Equations. A Gladstone or a Liddell was expected to

[1] John Morley, *The Life of William Ewart Gladstone* (1903), I, p. 50.
[2] *Ibid.*, p. 49; Cyril Jackson was Dean of Christ Church 1783–1809.

master, on a high standard of scholarship, practically all the first-rate literature of classical antiquity and the whole of its social and political background. Nor was there then any latter-day separation between style and substance, between the form and the matter of the books. The state of the text, the grammar and idiom, the aesthetic and historical value of the work, were alike fair field for the examiners. The questions in the written papers were framed on a broad humanist plan, and the *viva voce* was frankly a duel of wits between candidate and examiner, in which the former not infrequently scored.

Like many men of his time, Gladstone "kept up his classics" when he went out into the world. Whatever the value of his view of Homer may be shown hereafter to have been, he was at least fortunate in his generation. He grew up at a time when the world was ready for a real rereading of the poems and when the materials for a new judgment were beginning to accumulate rapidly; and the particular work which most needed to be done was the one most easily compassable by a busy man, provided only that he "would but read him four or five times over every year" and "let no day pass without having Homer in his hand."[1] He contributed a scholarly review of Lachmann's *Iliad* to the *Quarterly Review* of 1847, but it was not till 1857 that he had the inclination, perhaps even the opportunity, to print, also in the *Quarterly*, two short articles which show very clearly which way Homeric studies had led him. One is an essay on *Homer and his Successors in Epic Poetry*, which brings out well the existence of a great gulf between the Homeric and all later forms of epic; the other is a careful study of an important group of the data, *Homeric Characters, In and Out of Homer*, in which the same distinction is traced and insisted on in detail. But it was not as a young graduate but as a statesman that he came before the world in 1858 with the three thick volumes of his *Studies on Homer and the Homeric Age*.

As he went through his classical course at Oxford, he was already aware of its defects, as of its merits. "The classical knowledge acquired here", he wrote home in 1830, "though sound, accurate and useful, yet is not such as to *complete* an education."[2] But looking back upon it afterwards, he could give noble testimony to its effect. In spite of obvious deficiencies, he thought that it tended strongly "to

---

[1] Jackson's advice to Peel, John Morley, *The Life of William Ewart Gladstone* (1903), I, p. 49, note 2.

[2] *Ibid.*, p. 50.

make the love of truth paramount over all other motives in the mind, and thus that it supplied an antidote for whatever it had of bane".[1] Scattered utterances and his letters to personal friends show clearly that he never relaxed this attitude of friendly criticism. He represented his university in Parliament from 1847, and in the years which followed he was brought into relations with it of a peculiarly delicate kind. In 1850, when University Reform first became a burning question, he opposed it staunchly; but he was far from satisfied and the Commissioners' Report convinced him wholly. It was "one of the ablest productions", he thought, "submitted in his recollection to Parliament."[2] He saw that once public attention had been aroused, public action was certain to follow, unless the cause for action ceased to exist in the necessary lull between enquiry and legislation. He was unwearied in urging his friends at Oxford to make use of this golden opportunity for reforming the university from within, and in warning them that delay would be dearly purchased. "As one of your burgesses", he wrote, "I stand upon the line that divides Oxford from the outer world, and as a sentinel I cry out to tell what I see from that position."[3] He was already Chancellor of the Exchequer; but he could "work like a tiger", and his energy and insight were the admiration even of his opponents. He was indeed the inevitable man to frame a workable bill. "My whole heart", he wrote, "is in the Oxford Bill; it is my consolation under the pain with which I view the character my office [the exchequer] is assuming under the circumstances of [the Crimean] war."[4] The Bill was drafted for reform, not for revolution. "What I therefore anticipate," he could write of the university to Burgon of Oriel, "is not the weakening of her distinctive principles, not the diminution of her labour, already great, that she discharges for the church and for the land, but a great expansion, a great invigoration, a great increase of her numbers, a still greater increase of her moral force, and of her hold upon the heart and mind of the country."[5] Under this sign was inaugurated the measure which Jowett, for example, could describe as the greatest boon that Oxford ever received;[6] a boon moreover which would

[1] John Morley, *The Life of William Ewart Gladstone* (1903), I, p. 70 (1865).

[2] *Ibid.*, p. 499. [3] *Ibid.*, pp. 500–1.
[4] *Ibid.*, p. 500. [5] *Ibid.*, p. 504.
[6] *Ibid.*, p. 503.

have been ten times greater, had the bill passed into law in at all the clear working shape in which it was drafted.

But Gladstone knew very well that in academic as in political life, it is the spirit, not the letter, which is vital; that the best of constitutions may be barren, if the men and their practice are not a living, propagating force. On another aspect of University Reform, a letter to Pusey makes this clear enough. "If the church of England has not strength enough to keep upright, this will soon appear in the troubles of emancipated Oxford: if she has, it will come out to the joy of us all in the immensely augmented energy and power of the university for good. If Germanism and Arnoldism are now to carry the day at Oxford (I mean supposing the bill is carried into law), they will carry it fairly; let them win and wear her (God forbid, however); but if she has a heart true to the faith her hand will be stronger ten times over than it has been heretofore, in doing battle."[1]

Now in scholarship, as in theology, there was Armageddon in Oxford; "Germanism and Arnoldism" were fighting with an older, and wholesomer because more acclimatized tradition of what education meant when the classics were employed to effect it. The Oxford tradition, in Gladstone's own day, had meant a harmonious and proportionate study of the Graeco-Roman world as a whole. But in the generation which followed, the attempt of the more active tutors to keep their own heads above the rising tide of foreign scholarship, led to needless rivalry in impressing that learning on their pupils. The Classical School, in spite of Gaisford's discouragement, had become unwieldy, over-weighted, unmanageable; and in 1850 it had broken in two. That Germanism, in Gladstonian phrase, might work its will upon the form, and Arnoldism upon the matter of the texts, Scholarship and Literature parted company from History and Philosophy: the result was Honour Moderations, created like Eve from a rib of sleeping Greats. Yet all the while the leaving age of the candidates stayed fast at twenty-two; and the public schools were sending out fewer men each year who could read even a Latin author at sight.

This, broadly speaking, was the situation when what was left of Gladstone's Bill became law. The old vintage, crusted though it had

[1] John Morley, *The Life of William Ewart Gladstone* (1903), I, pp. 504–5. For *Germanism* and *Arnoldism*, see Duncan Forbes, *The Liberal Anglican Idea of History* (1952).

become, had been sound and strong; but new wine had burst the bottles; new bottles of his handiwork lay ready now for the coming vintage; it was but human that he should desire that in spirit and aroma the new wine should be worthy of the old vineyard. He was conscious that he knew and appreciated the humanist training of the place. He had certainly laid his finger early on a weak spot, and that weak spot was in danger, as he believed, of breaking out into a sore. Was there anything further that he could do to give the new mechanism a fair start on the right lines?

The reply to this question I believe to be given in his return to Homeric studies. *Studies on Homer* was confessedly a book with a purpose, and the objects of its publication are stated on its opening page. "These objects are twofold: firstly, to promote and extend the fruitful study of the immortal poems of Homer; and secondly, to vindicate for them, in an age of discussion, their just degree both of absolute and, more especially, of relative critical value. My desire is to vindicate at least, if I cannot hope to establish, their proper place, both in the discipline of classical education, and among the materials of historical enquiry." Striking passages in the *Prolegomena*, repeated from his *Essay on the Place of Homer in Classical education and in Historical enquiry* of 1857,[1] make it quite clear that he intended his book to be a direct contribution to the teaching apparatus of Oxford and a further step of educational reform. He reasoned that the existing state of knowledge of Homer was enough to show that the ancients were right in the high value they put upon the poems; they were indeed a mirror of human life, a compendium of discipline, moral as well as intellectual. The Classics as a means of education were then on their trial, and nothing less than a complete humanistic curriculum would justify their retention under the new conditions. The best and widest must be prescribed, and the widest and best of all is Homer. He had fallen into neglect compared with the masterpieces of Classical Greece and, though the recent admission of a part in Moderations was better than nothing, the value of Homer is not in his dialect or his diction but in his picture of unsophisticated man. "There is an inner Homeric world, of which his verse is the tabernacle and his poetic genius the exponent, but which offers in itself a spectacle of the most profound interest, quite apart from him who introduces us to it, and from the means by which we are so

[1] In *Oxford Essays*.

introduced. This world of religion and ethics, of civil policy, of history and ethnology, of manners and arts, so widely severed from all following experience, that we may properly call them palaeozoic, can hardly be examined and understood by those who are taught to approach Homer as a poet only. . . . If we take into view his date, the unpreparedness of the world for works so extraordinary as his, the comparative paucity of the traditional resources and training he could have inherited, he then becomes the most extraordinary, as he is also the most ancient, phenomenon in the whole history of purely human culture. . . . Life, to be rightly understood, should be studied in its beginnings. There we may see in simple forms what afterwards grew complex, and in clear light what afterwards became obscure."[1]

Homer for Gladstone came to stand on something more than the pedestal of a great literary monument. The poems seem to have occupied in his mind a place wholly apart, and second only in dignity to the archives of Christianity. He distinguished rigidly, as by training and inclination he was bound to do, between civilization and religion, as co-efficient factors in the progress of mankind, "destined" as he held, "to combine and coalesce" in the end. In the Homeric poems he recognized "a vast depository of knowledge upon subjects of deep interest, and of boundless variety", and he contended, not without justice, that "this is a knowledge, too, which can be had from them alone. It was the Greek mind . . . in which was shaped and tempered the original mould of the modern European civilization", and it was Homer, as he believed, who had shaped and tempered the Greek mind. "The power derived from this source was to stand in subordinate conjunction with the Gospel, and to contribute its own share towards the training of mankind. From hence were to be derived the forms and materials of thought, of imaginative culture, of the whole education of the intellectual soul." Of this Hellenism, copartner with Christianity in the shaping and tempering of us, Homer was for Gladstone the fountain-head. For emphatic as he always was on the great gulf which lay between this and all other Greek literature, he was equally convinced of the essential Hellenism of Homer. "As regards the Greeks," he writes, "it is Homer that furnishes the point of origin from which all distances are to be measured." The Greek mind "cannot be fully comprehended without the study of Homer, and is nowhere so vividly or

[1] *Studies on Homer*, I, pp. 12–14.

so sincerely exhibited as in his works. He has a world of his own, into which, upon his strong wing, he carries us. There we find ourselves amidst a system of ideas, feelings and actions, different from what are to be found anywhere else; and forming a new and distinct standard of humanity." The poems of Homer, in fact, show us man "in the free unsuspecting play of his actual nature".[1]

At this point, let us for a moment recall the dates. The *Origin of Species* did not appear till the year after the *Studies on Homer*. Lyell's *Antiquity of Man* was published in 1863 and Lubbock's *Prehistoric Times* not till 1865. The probability of a sequence of the cultures of Stone, Bronze and Iron had indeed been promulgated by Thomsen in 1832, but the stratigraphical proofs of Gabriel de Mortillet did not come till 1860 and were not reviewed in the *Quarterly* till 1862. Even the palaeolithic discoveries of Boucher de Perthes were not confirmed by Prestwich and Evans till the autumn of this same year, 1858. It was still justifiable, therefore, to set Homer by the side of Genesis among the archives of Man. Gladstone's conception of Homeric literature as a kind of secular Bible was, of course, wholly consistent with minute and accurate study of the text and its literal meaning. It was only when it came to commentary and constructive work that it led to perilous junctures between what was in the Homeric text and what was not. In 1858, for example, it was no untenable position for an educated Englishman that reminiscences of a happier past might have been treasured in popular memory during long migrations from a primaeval home. Such migrations were in fact quite in the fashion then among the historians of mankind. But it was a different matter, even in 1858, when the hypothesis of a Dispersal was used to derive Homer's Achaeans from Media or to trace Trinitarian groupings among the Homeric Olympians.[2] It was, moreover, an argument in a circle to contend that the single authorship of the Homeric poems made a single author probable for the Pentateuch, while using the Mosaic origin of the Pentateuch as a proof of a personal Homer. The two works have indeed their points of resemblance; but it does not follow that they stand or fall together, and even if this were established, it would not follow that both ought to stand.

There was, of course, another point of view on Oxford Reform and

[1] *Studies on Homer*, I, pp. 5–7.
[2] *Ibid.*, I, pp. 545 ff.; II, pp. 138 ff.

Oxford's relation with the Country. In a speech on the Oxford Bill, Disraeli put this point very neatly. The talk (he said) about the erudite professors of Germany as so superior to Oxford was non-sense. The great men of Germany became professors only because they could not become members of Parliament. (The disastrous collapse of German liberalism was then hardly two years old.) "We, on the contrary, are a nation of action, and you may depend upon it, that though you may give an Oxford professor two thousand a year instead of two hundred, still ambition in England will look to public life and to the House of Commons, and not to professors' chairs."[1] Gladstone's reply was to dot the i's in Disraeli's speech, with a demonstration that one Cabinet Minister at least was capable of quite professorial work in the intervals of Parliament and office. But his amazing work over the Budget of 1853, over the Oxford Bill, and over the Italian Nationalists, was having its effect even upon him; and difficulties, personal and partisan, made him contemplate retirement from politics. "The House of Commons", he wrote in 1857, "would sooner and more healthily return to a sense of its own dignity and of its proper functions, if let alone by a person who had so thoroughly worried both it and the Country as myself."[2] But with the slackening of political interests, "literature", he writes again, "has of late acquired a new and powerful hold upon me";[3] and opponents, clutching at the chance, made merry over the "Simeon Stylites", the "man of speculation misplaced and lost in the labyrinth of practical politics".[4] As in every time of trouble, it was to Homer that he turned; and thus the *Studies* were produced. In a very real sense therefore they mark a crisis in his career. They were published in March and were reviewed copiously and with care; the public, here and abroad, seems to have read them attentively. Ill-wishers hoped that the ex-Minister would turn Professor after all; the political prospect for him became more perplexing than ever. Then came the turning-point. Gladstone evidently needed rest and change of scene; his Homeric book had reached and delighted the Greeks who were getting rather tired of their own Bavarian rulers. In November the Government needed a strong and sympathetic man to enquire into the misgovernment in the Ionian Islands, then a British dependency; and though some of his friends were uneasy, Gladstone was not

[1] Morley, *op. cit.*, p. 507. [2] *Ibid.*, p. 567.
[3] *Ibid.*, p. 557 (1856). [4] *Ibid.*, pp. 581–3.

sorry to accept and be out of England. Politically the mission was a failure, for reasons which could not have been foreseen, and the islands were ceded to the Greek Kingdom; but it gave Gladstone a grand holiday, reciting Arabian Nights like another Thamyris to the Pasha of Janina, and playing leap-frog with his staff along the shore; it completely restored his confidence and spirits; above all it gave him an interval for reflection and opened a new chapter of his life. Almost his first public act on his return to England severed him from his political past and marked him for Liberal leadership. "Gladstone is now the real leader of the House of Commons", wrote the Prince Consort in 1859, "and works with an energy and vigour altogether incredible".[1]

We come now to the substance of Gladstone's view of Homer as trustworthy material for history. The position which he took up in the *Studies* of 1858, does not differ appreciably from his matured pronouncement in his *Homeric Synchronism* of 1876. "I am among those", he says, "who have, in previous works, contended or admitted:

"(1) that the poems of Homer are in the highest sense historical, as a record of 'manners and characters, feelings and tastes, races and countries, principles and institutions'.

"(2) that there was a solid nucleus of fact in his account of the Trojan War.

"(3) that there did not yet exist adequate *data* for assigning to him, or to the *Troïca*, a place in the established Chronology.

"(4) that his own Chronology was to be found in his Genealogies, which were usually careful and consistent, and which therefore served to establish a relative series of persons and events, within his proper sphere, but did not supply links of definite connexion with the general course of human affairs outside of that sphere in time or place.

"(5) that there was no extravagance in supposing he might have lived within a half-century after the War, though he was certainly not an eye-witness of it.

"(6) that there was very strong reason to believe that he flourished before the Dorian Conquest of the Peloponnese."[2]

[1] Morley, *op. cit.*, II, p. 28.
[2] *Homeric Synchronism*, pp. 9–10.

This, in broad outline, is the hypothesis upon which he sets out to examine the subject matter of Homer, and his work is best viewed as a series of tests of the validity of this hypothesis.

It will be seen that he assumes throughout the existence of a personal Homer, a single poet of transcendent genius, the author of two poems which (with whatever vicissitudes in detail) are essentially the *Iliad* and the *Odyssey* as we have them. It is at first sight remarkable that a scholar, with so exact and minute a knowledge of the Homeric text, should have held so tenaciously to the belief in a personal Homer. But we must remember, first, that the school of classical study in which Gladstone was trained was one which set greater store by the matter of an author than by his form, whereas a large part of the best work of the German separatists had been done on little points of language and style. We must remember, too, that it is a common experience that in face of a mass of quite unfamiliar matter, observation dwells on the large generic unfamiliarities, and neglects specific points of difference and resemblance. But when familiarity with the essentials of the subject sets attention free to dwell upon details and accidentals, a wonderful diversity is disclosed. It is all a question, on the one hand of unfamiliarity among the objects themselves, on the other of the observer's absorption in his own particular quest. It is no wonder, therefore, if English scholarship, which has looked at Homer almost wholly as literature, found the contrast of the Epic with Hellenic literature so striking and the naturalist savour of the Epic itself so overpowering, that the poems presented themselves as the single ordered outcome of one stupendous mind. Still less should it surprise us that a scholar so saturated with English scholarship, so masterfully intent to realize his conviction that in the Homeric literature there lies enshrined a history, should cling with proud confidence at all times, and at last with almost passionate conviction, to the belief in a personal Homer, one and indivisible.

We must remember, too, that much of Gladstone's life had been spent in regions where rigid conformity of detail was neither practicable nor expected; and that he himself was one of those men whose early maturity is but the screen of a slower and deeper adolescence, of a second nature behind the first, almost of a new man into whom the former personality is at last transformed and vanishes. As he himself wrote in another connexion "there have been two great deaths, or transmigrations of spirit, in my political existence. One, very slow, the breaking of ties with my political party." To such an intellect, the verbal slips and inconsistencies which distressed the separatist school, would be but straws on the surface to show which way the deep currents of the poet's life were setting. In a long life, in a wandering existence from town to town, each with its own local idiom, and in an age of transition, such as Gladstone conceived the Homeric Age to have been, it was no cause for wonder if the poet's diction changed, or if his studies of heroic character mellowed and matured in literary power. To a great personality like Gladstone's, too, with its immense range of sympathies and gifts of action, there was less improbability that the active talents of a great poet could be many-sided too. A man like Gladstone stood for a personal Homer because, as far as ability went, he could have written an *Iliad* himself. Consequently, on the question of Homeric personality he almost never argued, and never stated a case for the defence. It was for the prosecution to prove single authorship impossible; for himself, he knew—because he *felt*—the possibility of single authorship; and the objections of the critics seemed to him capricious and invalid.

For us, three generations later, the crucial struggle of Homeric controversy still rages about the same question of single or multiple authorship. Both sides have found themselves fresh weapons; each has shifted its ground again and again; and leaders in either camp have set their names to pages in Homeric ἀριστεῖαι. On both sides extreme views have gone to the wall. Few believe now that the *Doloneia*, or the last book of the *Odyssey*, came in the form in which we have them from the mind which created the *Death of Hector*, or the meeting of Odysseus and Nausicaa. Fewer still believe that the great structure of the poems was in the making in the days of Peisistratus. On all hands it is agreed that there is a great gulf fixed, not merely between Homer and the literature of Olympiad Hellas, but even between Homer and Hesiod and between Homer and the Homeric Hymns, and that, whatever the date or the home of the Epic, its place is in a world of its own, of which the Greek world knew little and understood less. Of this Homeric world even we in these latter days are in a position to know more than Thucydides knew, more perhaps than even Hesiod knew, when he interposed his Age of Heroes between the Ages of Bronze and of Iron.

[1] Morley, *op. cit.*, II, p. 149.

But the other question still remains; was there, or was there not, a great gulf fixed between Homer himself and the Trojan War? Does he belong to the Achaean Age, to the Age of the Pelopid Confederacy and the Sea Raids on the Egyptian Delta, or was all this a vain shadow already in his time, a thing of legend and regrets, "an Eden guarded by the flaming sword of time long past"? For this question, textual criticism and the detailed analysis of phrase and idiom stand almost out of account. If the poems as we have them fail to exhibit a definite picture of a real, habitable world and a livable mode of life, then indeed the study of style is indispensable to explain how the poet's image has come to be distorted and blurred, to tell us, as an art critic might of an ancient altarpiece, "This and that has happened to the picture. Here it has been repainted over the old lines; there the old paint has faded away. This is all modern; I cannot tell what the artist meant to have put." But so long as the main outlines of the picture are clear, so long as the details which conflict are details and accessories merely, it is not to the textual critic but to the historian and the archaeologist that we look for its interpretation. And standing as Gladstone did on the margins of the world of scholarship, drilled in its methods, saturated with its better spirit but untroubled by its smaller heart-searchings, he was in a position to do an inestimable service to Homeric study in England. No one could be more conscious than he of the limitations which his public life imposed on assiduous study, of the necessarily patchwork character of anything he might hope to achieve, or of the impossibility of keeping a steady eye on the kaleidoscope of "exact scholarship". But no one knew better that the English instinct, like that of the Greeks, looks for all-round excellence in its leading men. Athens could send Sophocles to maintain the blockade of Samos, because his *Antigone* succeeded in the theatre; England would read its Homer again, and read it aright, if Gladstone, orator and financier, would come forward and show the way. Critics and detractors might say in later years that if this and that essay were not by Gladstone, no one would look at it; but Gladstone might retort, in the manner of Themistocles, that many great books were little read because they were not by Gladstone.

Side by side, moreover, with his conviction that there had been a personal Homer, Gladstone seems to have seen from the beginning that there was no such necessary connexion as many scholars had held between this question of authorship and the question whether Homeric literature depicts a real period of history. "Even the dissolution of his individuality," he said in the *Prolegomena* of 1858, "does not get rid of his authority. For if the works reputed to be his had proceeded from many minds, yet still, according to their unity of colour, and their correspondence in ethical and intellectual tone with the events of the age they purport to describe, there would arise an argument, founded on internal evidence, for the admissibility of the whole band into the class of trustworthy historical witnesses. But, first of all, may we not ask, from whence comes the presumption against Homer as an historical authority? Not from the fact that he mixes marvels with common events; for this, to quote no other instance, would destroy along with him Herodotus. Does it not arise from this, that his compositions are poetical—that history has long ceased to adopt the poetical form—that an old association has thus been dissolved—that a new and adverse association has taken its place, which connects poetry with fiction—and that we illogically reflect this modern association upon early times, to which it is utterly inapplicable? If so, there is no burden of proof incumbent upon those who regard Homer as an historical authority. . . . The immense mass of matter contained in the *Iliad*, which is beyond what the action of the poems requires, and yet is in its nature properly historical, of itself supplies the strongest proof of the historic aims of the poet. Whether in the introduction of all this matter, he followed a set and conscious purpose of his own mind, or whether he only fed the appetite of his hearers with what he found to be agreeable to them, is little material to the question. The great fact stands, that there was either a design to fulfil, or, at least, an appetite to feed—an intense desire to create bonds and relations with the past—to grasp its events, and fasten them in forms which might become, and might make them become, the property of the present and the future. Without this great sign of nobleness in their nature, Greeks never could have been Greeks."[1] There is here of course all the difference between the two solutions proposed—between a "design to fulfil" and "an appetite to feed". But the contention is a sound one, that either mode of production is compatible with the creation of genuine history.

But here again Gladstone held no extreme position as to the unity

[1] *Studies* I, pp. 22–3.

of the poems. "It is of course admitted," he says, "that these lays, even though ideally one as they came from their framer, were in many cases actually separated", and if actually separated, some one must have put them together. Moreover, for Gladstone, as for the best Greek critics, the poems were "not only the special charge and pride of particular poetical schools, but distinct objects of the care of legislators and statesmen. ... They had thus to depend for their transmission, not only on the fire of national and poetic feeling, but upon a jealous custody much resembling that which even a comparatively rude people gives to its laws."[1] This comparison of traditional poetry with traditional legislation is indeed particularly apposite; and it lends itself further to the same choice of regarding the tradition as the outcome either of a "design to fulfil", where there was an encyclopaedic personal legislator, or of an "appetite to feed", where a code has grown up piecemeal by accumulation of case-law during a long period of time. In either case, the sole limiting condition is that within the lifetime, whether of the individual or of the period, there shall have befallen no such catastrophe as to snap the fine chain of personal or cultural identity. This prudent view which Gladstone held of the nature of Homeric authorship leads naturally to his view of the proper mode of studying our present text. Granted that there may be earlier and later sections in the poems as we have them, that earlier sections, as we have them, may have been reworked at a later phase, and that later sections may include genuine fragments of older verse, yet, if the poems are to be treated as materials for history at all, they must be treated as a whole and not as a collection of fragments of which some may be taken into calculations and others left out. It is essential, he says, "that we should adopt the text itself as the basis of all Homeric inquiry, and not any preconceived theory, nor any arbitrary standard of criticism, referable to particular periods, schools or persons"; and that "as we proceed in any work of construction by evidence drawn from the text, we should avoid the temptation to solve difficulties found to lie in our way, by denouncing particular portions of it as corrupt or interpolated; should never set it aside except upon the closest examination of the particular passage questioned; should use sparingly the liberty even of arraying presumptions against it; and should always let the reader understand both when and why it is questioned".[2] The reference is, of course,

[1] *Studies* I, pp. 47–9. [2] *Ibid.*, pp. 43–4.

partly to the brilliant but erratic work of Payne Knight,[1] but mainly to Lachmann, on whose dissection of the *Iliad* into sixteen independent lays Gladstone had commented vigorously in the *Quarterly Review* of 1847, and to his followers who, with greater zeal and inferior scholarship, had carried the dismemberment of the text far beyond the bounds of proof—or even of reason.

Let us now trace out some consequences of Gladstone's thesis and see whither they lead us. From his first position "that the poems of Homer are in the highest sense historical", follows at once a conclusion which necessitated a complete re-working of Greek history, as the Greeks themselves and most modern writers had constructed it. If Homer's poetry is early poetry, then its authority on matters relating to the Homeric Age lies in a wholly different plane from that of any other Greek writer whatsoever. "It is an error," he writes, "to regard and accept all ancient traditions, relating to the periods that precede regular historic annals, as of equal value, or not to discriminate their several values with adequate care. Above all, I strongly contend that we should assign to the Homeric evidence a primary rank upon all the subjects which it touches, and that we should make it a rule to reduce all other literary testimony, because of later origin, to a subordinate and subsidiary position." Frequently for instance the same story is told both in Homer and in a Hellenic writer; and often the stories differ, even in the essentials. "A story of this kind, say in Apollodorus, may indeed by bare possibility be older than anything in Homer; but if it comes to us without the proper and visible criteria of age, it has no claim upon our assent as a truthful record of the time to which it purports to refer. Traditions of this class only grow to be such, as a general rule, for us, at the time when they take a positive form in the work of some author, who thus becomes, as far as his time and circumstances permit, a witness to them. It is only from thenceforward, that their faithful derivation and transmission can be relied on as in any degree probable. Again, I cast aside statements with respect to which the poet, being carried beyond the sphere of his ordinary experience,

---

[1] Richard Payne Knight, *Carmina Homerica, Ilias et Odyssea, a rhapsodorum interpolationibus repurgata, et in pristinam formam, quatenus recuperanda esset, ... redacta; cum notis ac prolegomenis, in quibus de eorum origine, auctore, et aetate, itemque de priscae linguae progressu et praecoci maturitate diligenter inquiritur*, 1820.

must, on that account, not be presumed to speak historically; yet even here, if he is speaking of matters which were in general belief, he is a witness of the first class with respect to that belief, which is itself in another sense a matter of history; and here also those, who have followed him at a remote date, are witnesses of a lower order." He instances particularly such test cases as are supplied by what he well describes as "the stubborn facts of geography". "Or again," he goes on, "it is conceivable, though I do not know whether it has happened, that Homeric testimony might come into conflict, not with mere counter-assertion, but with those forms of circumstantial evidence which are sometimes conclusively elicited by reasoning from positive *data* of architecture, language, and ethnology. *I claim for Homer no exemption from the more cogent authority which may attach to reasoning of this kind.*"[1] It follows clearly from all this that, in regard to the religion, history, ethnology, polity and life at large of the Greeks of the heroic times, the authority of the Homeric poems, standing far above that of the whole mass of the later literary traditions in any of their forms, ought never to be treated as homogeneous with them, but should usually, in the first instance, be handled by itself—and the testimony of later writers should, in general, be handled in subordination to it, and should be tried by it, as by a touchstone, on all the subjects which it embraces.

Gladstone himself, of course, had neither the time, nor possibly the desire, to undertake the task of re-writing Greek history on these lines; and for a variety of reasons, that task still waits to be performed. For one thing, it was fully another generation before that external evidence came, which Gladstone was convinced would come, and without which the Homeric picture, construct it how you will, stood suspended in the void, almost without point of contact with the rest of history. For another, specialized linguistic criticism, divorced from study of the context and too often even from the feeling for literature, led powerful minds to interpret Homeric Greek, and by consequence Homeric culture, in a totally different direction. For another thing again, the great contemporary discovery that the mythologies of the Aryan-speaking peoples, no less than their languages, form dialects (so to speak) of a single anthropomorphic reading of the facts of Nature, set speculation to work to

[1] *Studies*, I, pp. 72–3 (Myres's italics).

interpret Achilles, like Apollo himself, as the Sun, the quarrel with Agamemnon as a solar eclipse, Hector and the Trojans as the scattering clouds and the whole Trojan War, in fact—Gods, men and the Scamander river—as astronomy tinged with emotion.

For these and other causes, Gladstone's view of Homer suffered long discredit among the majority of scholars. From this discredit only two things could rescue it. The first was such a reconstruction of the Early Age of Greece, upon Homeric evidence essentially, as would stand consistent and take its place in Mediterranean History as a whole; which would present Homeric places and people as a Homeric poet saw them, not as Pausanias or Apollodorus guessed centuries after that perhaps they might have been, or as the soaring imagination of Ephorus convinced Greece that they must have been. And, as I said, such a history as this has not been written yet. The other would be an account based solely on the facts of archaeology, on the sequence of events over the whole of those long vicissitudes of cities and tribes which lie between the downfall of the Cretan Empire of Knossos and the Renaissance—for a Renaissance in great part it was—of the Hellas of Olympiad reckoning. Only if Aegean Greece, as archaeology recovers it, answers to Homeric Greece as Homer knew it, is Gladstone's hypothesis to be accepted as a demonstrated thing; but in proportion as the two pictures do answer one another, as one figure after another becomes traceable in each, so does this hypothesis become by degrees more probable, and the alternative of an Ionian Homer sink westward to join the Sun-God Achilles.

The *Studies on Homer and the Homeric Age* were published as we have seen in 1858. In the ten years which followed, Gladstone himself was immersed again in affairs and the Homeric Question went its own different way. Among the learned world, Gladstone seemed on the whole to have been fighting a losing case. Comparative mythology came to the aid of comparative scholarship to emphasize the unhistorical, almost the allegorical, character of the Trojan legend. Linguistic study seemed to be forcing a belief that the poems, in their present shape and almost in their origins, were the work, not of Achaeans, but of Ionians of Asia Minor, the citizens of towns which in the Heroic Age for the most part had not even been founded. But beyond the inner circles, the vigour and simplicity of his exposition, as well as his personal prestige, gave his views wide currency; and in time he was persuaded to restate them in an abridged and maturer form. The title of the little book was *Juventus Mundi: The Gods and Men of the Homeric Age*. It was mainly the produce of the two Recesses of 1867 and 1868, and appeared in the spring of 1869. To compensate for the excision of much detail from this popular outline of his views, he foreshadowed at this time a great Homeric Concordance, of which specimens, dealing with Athene, Aeolus, and a few other topics, were printed experimentally; but increasing occupations, and perhaps also the appearance of *Die Homerische Realien* of Eduard Buchholz,[1] of which he had a high opinion, prevented him from publishing the whole.

Meantime, what had been the progress of enquiry in the directions which he had foreshadowed and which he most desired? His mode of study, as we have seen, was the Book, the whole Book, and nothing but the Book: and when he wrote his *Studies* even the last clause was applicable in its literal sense, as a sound canon of Homeric criticism. There was hardly an error of Homeric scholarship which was not traceable either to neglect of some part of the Homeric evidence, or to the inclusion of non-Homeric evidence in the premises to a Homeric conclusion. And the reason why this was so was precisely the circumstance which Gladstone himself so often emphasized, namely that the Homeric poems "float, like Delos, on the sea of time"; that they stand so wholly in a world by themselves that no security exists, except total abstention, to prevent the misapplication of evidence from later authors, and particularly from authorities of the rationalist ages of Greece. But the very hypothesis on which Gladstone's whole work rested was this, that the direct, forcible naturalism of Homer presupposed the real existence of an Homeric Age and an Homeric World; and it follows from this that if once evidence should be presented—from whatever non-Homeric source— which should correspond with the *data* of the poems as a whole, and yet should be demonstrably of earlier than Hellenic date, then such evidence would be admissible as commentary upon Homer, in precisely the same way as is the physique of the Aegean sea and sky. Nay more, if once the greater antiquity of the new evidence were made out—most of all, if it could be proved to be approximately contemporary with the Homeric age—such evidence would clearly rank at least as high, and conceivably higher, than the evidence of the poems

[1] 1871–85.

themselves; for the poems after all are poems, and include, by common consent, episodes which are imaginary—like the fight between Diomedes and Ares—however historical may be the setting and the accessories of them.

Now, this is precisely what occurred. Even before the publication of the *Studies*, the Egyptian heroic rhapsody which is known as the *Poem of Pentaur* had been published by the Vicomte de Rougé and had given rise to transitory speculations as to the nationality of certain peoples whom the poem describes as fighting for the Hittites against Rameses II. Similar allusions in documents of the reign of Merneptah and Rameses III, a generation later, supported the statements of Pentaur, and made it clear that the later part of the Nineteenth Dynasty and the opening years of the Twentieth fell in a period when the Eastern Mediterranean swarmed with piratical adventurers very like those whom Odysseus describes more than once when he is trying to make a really plausible tale[1]—a tale, that is, which shall be convincing not only to Penelope and Eumaeus, but to the original audiences of that part of the *Odyssey*. De Rougé returned to the subject of these peoples in a formal memoir in the late sixties, and pointed out that a number of their names closely resembled the names of peoples familiar to Homer, such as Danaans, Achaeans and Dardanians,[2] and in 1867 Lauth of Munich reformulated the whole position in an essay called *Homer und Aegypten*.[3] Gladstone himself did not apparently become acquainted with Lauth's work till 1873, but when he did, he saw its importance at once.

Meanwhile, events had moved rapidly in another quarter also. We shall come in the next chapter to Heinrich Schliemann, whose life-long quest of Homeric reality, whose simple faith in his author, whose vivid imagination and invincible optimism in his cause, gave him much the same place in German Homerology as Gladstone had attained in this country. To find on the hill of Graeco-Roman Ilium, beneath some forty feet of the debris of as many centuries, a prehistoric town which had perished in a great burning, and whose

[1] ξ 245ff., ρ 424ff.

[2] *Rev. Arch.* XVI (1867), pp. 35ff. and 81ff.; for the texts see J. B. Pritchard, *Ancient Near Eastern Texts*[2], pp. 255ff. and 262ff.

[3] Franz Joseph Lauth, *Homer und Aegypten* (*Programm des königl. Maximilians-Gymnasiums in München*), 1867.

inhabitants had vainly attempted to save a great treasure of gold jewellery of strikingly Homeric forms, seemed to many a "nucleus of fact" beyond their most daring dreams. Even the sceptics admitted that a new chapter was open in the prehistory of Greek lands, and that judgment must be reserved on a number of questions which the philologists had held for settled. Gladstone had long been prepared for some such revelations as these. In *Juventus Mundi* he had expressed his belief that it was close at hand. In Schliemann's work he saw the beginning of the new era, and the almost simultaneous arrival of an author's copy of Lauth's book set him on the warpath at once. No sooner was he out of office in 1874 than he printed in the *Contemporary Review* two papers on the *Place of Homer in History*, in which he summarized the new discoveries in Egypt and at Troy, and showed their bearing on the Homeric problem. With some expansion, these papers were reprinted in 1876, under the title of *Homeric Synchronism: an Enquiry into the Time and Place of Homer*; and on the flyleaf appears the triumphant extract from the Delian Hymn: "Therefore no longer didst thou float indefinite, in the waves of the Aegean hast thou planted the roots of thy feet."[1] Homer's feet, too, he felt, were rooted fast now in the waters and on the shores of the Aegean; yet of an Aegean which was not yet the Greek lake of historic times, but the sea frontier still between the powers of Agamemnon and of Priam.

Homeric Synchronism consists of two parts. The first contains his comments on Schliemann's work at Troy; Mycenae, Agamemnon's capital, was not excavated, of course, until the autumn of 1876, and the results were not published till 1878. The second part gives the conclusions to be drawn from the Egyptian evidence, as to the historical identity of the Homeric Age with the period of the Sea Raids in the thirteenth century B.C. "By these contentions", he says, "I seek to lead up to a general conclusion as follows. There are probable grounds, of an historical character, for believing that the main action of the *Iliad* took place, and that Homer lived, between certain chronological limits, which may now be approximately pointed out to the satisfaction of reasonable minds."[2] He is particularly explicit as to the place of Schliemann's work as a crucial test of Homer's nearness to his subject. "My warrant," he says, "for introducing the topics treated in Part 1 is to be found in this; that, if

[1] Callimachus, *Hymn. in Delum* 53.　　　　　　[2] p. 15.

Homer were an Asiatic Greek, of the period most commonly supposed, at some time after the Dorian Conquest, it is idle to talk of placing him in any particular relation to the Egyptian Chronology, and a waste of labour to trace out in detail his possession of Egyptian knowledge and traditions; for, to Asiatic Greece, Egypt was but the name of one among foreign lands, and its wide-reaching Empire was neither any longer felt in action, nor witnessed of by patent and accessible records, nor retained in the living memory of man."[1] If, however, Homer could be shown, as Gladstone believed that Schliemann had shown, to be acquainted personally with the pre-Greek phase of Aegean society and manners, then all this was reversed; Homer's allusions to Egypt and the East acquired the value of contemporary evidence; and it became justifiable to look for more allusions of the same kind, now that our knowledge enabled us to verify them.

Yet that it was "idle talk" and "waste of labour" to correlate Homer with Egypt, was of course just what those scholars were thinking who stood committed to an Asiatic and post-Dorian Homer, and did not see their way to change their minds. It was unfortunate too, that, in admitted ignorance of hieroglyphics and of the Egyptian language, Gladstone had encumbered his case with a good deal of minor matter borrowed from Lauth, which would have added little to the argument, even if it had been accepted fact, and which has not for the most part passed into currency at all. We still need to know much more than we do about Egyptian intercourse with Aegean visitors, before we can accept Egyptian derivations for names like Phoenix, Elysium and Briareus. But among the few who had the new learning, *Homeric Synchronism* came as a landmark of acceptance. Like all Gladstone's work it was brightly and breezily if somewhat loosely written; the case was stated with spirit and skill; and though it was a pamphlet rather than a book, it formed a very proper pendant to *Juventus Mundi*.

Schliemann, in particular, was delighted, and insisted that Gladstone should write him a preface to his book on Mycenae which had been on the point of being excavated when *Homeric Synchronism* appeared.[2] Gladstone consented; but the new evidence was too

[1] pp. 14–15.

[2] *Mycenae; a narrative of researches and discoveries at Mycenae and Tiryns*, 1878.

new, its complexity and unfamiliarity too great, and perhaps the enthusiasms of Schliemann himself too contagious, to allow him to do justice to his case. Almost the only points of criticism which emerge in this *Introduction* are these. First, that unless Schliemann's Troy was to be regarded as exceptionally impoverished by long war, the gulf between the meanness of Trojan equipment and the splendid luxury revealed in the tombs at Mycenae was incompatible with a contemporary dating. This was the first step forward towards a larger perspective than Schliemann had ventured to allow himself, and it anticipates at one step a decade of tangled controversy, till Ferdinand Dümmler in the islands and Schliemann himself at Troy could show by excavation that the wider vision was the true one. Secondly, Gladstone's vivid appreciation of Homeric realism enabled him to catch at once the real identity of Homeric and Mycenaean imagery. "Possibly," he says, "a knowledge of the Mycenean treasures may have prompted or aided a vigorous imagination, in that wonderful anticipation of excellences which had not been realized in practice." We must remember of course that the inlaid work on the "Lion Dagger" which so exactly reproduces the workmanship of the Shield of Achilles, was not visible at that time, and was only revealed by careful cleaning nearly fifteen years later on. "The most remarkable feature, I think," he goes on, "of all Homer's delineations of art, is the force and reality with which he confers animation on things inanimate. And perhaps the eye may be struck, on examining Schliemann's illustrations, with the vigour of life and motion which asserts itself in many of the Mycenean works, where the delineation is technically most imperfect."[1]

But he does not seem to have gone further. Tiryns and the problem of its relation with the House of Odysseus in the *Odyssey*, which came up in 1885, found him in the very crisis of the Irish question and the first Home Rule Bill, and so far as I know he never put pen to paper on that matter. Moreover, in those later years, it was a totally different side of ancient history which most attracted him. Gladstone had always kept Homer and the Bible in adjacent chambers of his mind; and when, with Schliemann's work, the fight for Homer seemed strategically won, he turned from Egypt and the Mediterranean to Babylonia, and its influence on the ancient Land-World. First fruits of this, incorporated in a third restatement of the whole argument,

[1] p. XV.

appeared in 1890 in his *Landmarks of Homeric Study*. On the occasion of a visit to Oxford in 1891 he was prevailed upon to speak at the Union on some Homeric subject; and the topic which he chose was the influence of Babylonian Mythology on certain fundamental conceptions of Homeric Religion. The analogies were certainly there, and many of them had not been pointed out before. I was fortunate enough to find squatting room, as an undergraduate, on the crowded floor close to the speaker's feet. As we listened, the grand figure, the superb voice, the obvious earnestness and enthusiasm of the lecturer carried conviction; but afterwards as we talked it over, it was still not clear how the contact had been effected between the East and Greece, and consequently whether the analogies themselves were coincidences or something more.

Considering how hard the Phoenician Myth is dying even now, it is interesting to find Gladstone, at the end of a long life, hesitating as to the precise significance of the name. "Now is the time," he says, in a paper contributed to the Oriental Congress of 1892, "to make an observation of vital importance with regard to the comprehensive meaning which attaches in Homer to the Phoenician name. Whether the Achaian Greeks themselves devised that name to describe a set of strangers who frequented their coasts, we have no means of knowing. It derives, however, no support from the Pentateuch, or (as I believe) from the monuments." He gives up, that is to say, all claim that the name represents any identifiable people of any identifiable shore of the Mediterranean. "But for Homer it seems to cover everything found in the Achaian Peninsula that was of foreign origin. ... Whether the question be of persons settling in the Peninsula, or of things brought by or learned through maritime visitors who came from the south-eastern corner of the Mediterranean" (the Φοινίκη of the *Odyssey*), "all these apparently had but one vehicle, and that vehicle was the Phoenician ship. Consequently all came to carry the Phoenician name, or to run up into Phoenician association, for the contemporary Achaian. Much as to the Turk of later days every European was a Frank, so to the Achaians of Homer all persons and things reaching them from over sea were bound up with this Phoenician name. ... What it indicates is a channel; and all that came through that channel is embraced by it. ... Egyptians or Egyptian subjects were reckoned as Phoenicians (Φοίνικες), because, all reaching the Achaians in Phoenician ships and Phoenician company, they presented in this particular a real unity of aspect."[1]

It was in this spirit, we must remember, that writing soon after, in 1893, to the German excavator, Max Ohnefalsch-Richter, to acknowledge his new work entitled *Kypros, the Bible and Homer* and to send him a copy of the paper last mentioned, he anticipates by only three years one of the largest accessions to our knowledge of Aegean craftsmanship within the centuries of which Homer sang. "Cyprus", he says, "was I apprehend a great advanced post of Phoenician navigation, commerce and civilization, and it may prove to have become the richest storehouse of illustrative remains supplied by that race, which played so momentous a part in human development." The Turner Bequest to the British Museum permitted this also to be tested by the spade, with disastrous results to Phoenician claims in the narrower Syrian coast sense. Instead, it provided new proofs of the extent, the date, and the remarkable vitality of Aegean enterprise; for in Cyprus alone did Homeric institutions like monarchy and chariot fighting persist into Hellenic times. And later on in the same letter, he speaks in very similar phrase of the Νέκυια as "altogether *exotic*, that is to say Phoenician, in its character".[2] The first clear British pronouncement on the new aspect of the Phoenician problem was made at the meeting of the British

---

[1] *Trans. of the Ninth International Congress of Orientalists* (1893), II, pp. 429–30. W. M. Ramsay has a good note on Gladstone's address in *The Bookman*, October 1892. "In the first place, he has always felt that works which were able to influence so profoundly the religion and thought of the Greeks must have a foundation in reality; only because they represented a real Greece could they succeed in creating a Hellenic unity. The remark needs only to be stated to carry conviction, provided that we do not define too narrowly what is meant by reality; but Mr. Gladstone stood alone in making it the fundamental principle of his work. In the second place, he has learnt in the career of politics to judge of men and the way in which they show their character in practical life; and he has found in the *Iliad* and the *Odyssey* the characteristics of real human beings engaged in real life, not creatures of poetic fancy. . . . Agreement between Mr. Gladstone and Professor Sayce on Homer is a sign almost as portentous and prophetic of a new era, and almost as fitted to pass into a proverb, as the lion and the lamb reclining in amity side by side (we make the comparison without specifying too precisely which part best suits each hero)." And he goes on to joke about Sayce's Home Rule principles of the autonomy of different parts of the poems.

[2] Reproduced at the beginning of *Kypros, the Bible and Homer.*

Association which was held in Liverpool in 1896. In an address entitled *The Eastern Question in Anthropology* Arthur Evans laid the cornerstone of an interpretation of the early Aegean as an independent focus of advancement, with Crete (as he showed so fully later) as its principal leader in the arts; and he followed up his presidential address with a communication on *Tree and Pillar Cults in the Aegean*, which cut away the whole ground from beneath one of the mainstays of the *Mirage Oriental*. Gladstone, who was at Hawarden at the time, was delighted, and expressed his keen interest in this new line of work, which, as he saw at once, fulfilled so completely his own persistent conviction that, if only we could reach it, there existed in the Aegean a highly organized culture of pre-Hellenic date and non-Hellenic quality, of which Homer was the poet and the historian.

Here let us leave him. In nearly forty years since the publication of his *Studies on Homer*, he had seen the whole school of mythological interpretation rise, bloom and vanish away. He had seen the Asiatic, Ionic Homer revived, elaborated and in a fair way to be discarded again, for those very reasons—his late date, his alien culture, the impossibility of saying what old Ionic Greeks were really like—which had prevented Gladstone from accepting his existence at all. He had seen one dissection of the poems after another attempted, discredited and abandoned, because it did violence to the text or failed to conform with the larger conditions of the question. He had seen, in fact, two generations of scholars reduced, after all their labour, pretty much to his own simple canon of Homeric criticism—*the Book, the Whole Book, and nothing but the Book*; and an impression revived that in essentials poems like the *Iliad* and the *Odyssey* might be the life work of a single man, planned as organic wholes. But he had also seen a small but efficient school of Homerology (as he called it) spring up in English universities. More than one of these Homerists was engaged, like himself, in active public or professional life, yet snatching evenings and odd moments for Homeric work of high quality. Above all, he had seen an Homerologist after his own heart set spade to Hissarlik and the acropolis of Mycenae; he had seen a real historical background reconstituted by many workers in all its amplitude of space and millennial time. The Homeric Question, when he first touched it, was: "How little earlier can Homer be than Herodotus?" It had been transmuted before his death into the problem: "How little later must he be than Agamemnon and Achilles

who fought in the Great War, than Pelops and Laomedon, the intrusive founders of the conflicting powers, and than Menelaus,
Odysseus and Paris who toured or raided Egypt and landed in Sidon
and Cyprus before the decline of hundred-gated Thebes?"

And the means by which this transformation had been effected
were essentially his own: the persistent, painful study of the Homeric
text; the acceptance of Homeric statements as to kinship and descent
as the sole credible witness to lapse of time within the Homeric Age;
the steady refusal to take the word of Pausanias or Ephorus or
Herodotus or even Hesiod, in preference to that of Homer, as to
persons or peoples or countries of the Homeric world; above all, the
confidence that the Homer whose observation is so unerring and
whose workmanship is so subtle in simile and landscape and the
spear-play of his warriors, would be found to be credible up to the
very limits of his knowledge in the art and manners, the politics and
the beliefs of the heroic age and the range of the world in which it
moved. Parts of his work, it is true, fell short of his own canon and
have passed away; other parts have been superseded in academic
leisure by finer workmanship than his. But Gladstone stands as a
large, generous figure in Homeric scholarship, not perhaps so much
for actual discoveries, as for his instinct for great literature and
great history, and for the labour of love to which he put his powers
of heart and pen; "to provoke," as he said, "the close textual study
of the Poet, as the condition of real progress . . .; to encourage and
facilitate the access of educated persons to the actual contents of the
text; to commend conclusions from the Homeric Poems which
appear to me to be of great interest with reference to the general
history of human culture." In his own fine words therefore let us
inscribe this epitaph to Gladstone the Homerologist:[1] "No exertion
spent upon any of the great classics of the world, and attended with
any amount of real result, is really thrown away. It is better to write
one word upon the rock, than a thousand on the water or the sand."

[1] *Studies*, I, p. 91.

Chapter Seven

THE EPIC OF THE SPADE:
1. HEINRICH SCHLIEMANN

T HE word "archaeology" is commonly used in several senses. To some, it is the general study of antiquity as a whole, the study of life as it was within selected limits of time in a selected region. In this sense we speak of Greek or Roman or Mediaeval archaeology. Others limit archaeology more strictly to the study of the material remains of antiquity. I have even heard it described as "technology in the past tense"; for as technology is concerned with the ways in which man satisfies material needs by material means, so archaeology is the comparative study of such craftsmanship in bygone times. Others again, realizing as we all do that the strictly technological view does not accord with modern practice, would extend the definition to include the study of the ways in which man has satisfied his aesthetic needs also by some material means. Archaeology in this context becomes, or at least includes, the past tense of art-criticism. The material for such criticism necessarily includes all those examples of craftsmanship, however utilitarian, which have an artistic or aesthetic quality as well as mere utility. Buildings, for example, or metalwork, or vessels of clay or glass, may be themselves beautiful and characteristic achievements of artists brought up in a particular set of social and geographical conditions. But it includes also "works of art" in the special sense that their aesthetic aim dominates or even obliterates all considerations of usefulness.

Here for our present purpose we must make a further distinction; for the ways in which material means are employed to achieve

123

aesthetic ends are different according to whether the artist's use of them is in action only or in production. By "use in action only" is meant the class of activities ($\pi\rho\acute{a}\xi\epsilon\iota\varsigma$ or in artistic phraseology *performances*), whereof nothing materially perceptible survives the occasion. The event, the act, is itself an artistic achievement, as when a man sings or dances or makes poses or gestures.

> "I breathed a song into the air,
> It fell to earth, I knew not where."[1]

By "use in production", on the other hand, some result is achieved which outlasts the creative act. It may be a building or a painting or an object of daily utility—anything which perpetuates something of the designer's imagination and recreates the craftsman's emotion when he looks upon the work that he has made, and "behold, it is very good". Now, it is instructive that in Greek the words which describe artistic production ($\pi o\acute{\iota}\eta\sigma\iota\varsigma$, $\pi o\acute{\iota}\eta\mu a$, as distinct from $\pi\rho\hat{a}\xi\iota\varsigma$ and $\pi\rho\hat{a}\gamma\mu a$) came to be applied also specifically to that art which most nearly bridges the gap between these two kinds of activity. To complete the lines quoted just now:

> ". . . The song, from beginning to end,
> I found again in the heart of a friend."

And this may be true, not only in emotional content but in exact linguistic form—in a poem which the friend in turn may sing or publish in a book for the delight of a nation. Unless the study of such a work of art in relation to its subject and occasion, as an element in the creative product of a people in a particular period of advancement, is to be ruled out of the scope of archaeology altogether, such a term as "Homeric Archaeology" would seem rightly applicable to a proper subject for enquiry. What did the composer of any part of the Homeric poems himself know or believe that he knew, or assume his own audiences to know, about the persons and events with which his production, his $\pi o\acute{\iota}\eta\mu a$, dealt? How did he and they come by that knowledge or those beliefs? How far and by what methods is it possible to verify that knowledge, supplement those beliefs, and in general reconstruct in historical perspective the background of an Homeric Age?

But again, what exactly do we mean by an "Homeric Age"? Do we

[1] Longfellow, *The Arrow and the Song.*

mean the period of civilization in which the poet (or poets) lived and
the Homeric poems were composed? Or the earlier period in which the
events in the poems took place in material circumstances which
the poets describe to the best of their ability? Or is it premature to
describe this period as "earlier" than that in which the poems were
produced? Should we rather conceive the events as so recent and the
equipment as so familiar that the poet is to be accepted as standing
in the same contemporary relation to the Trojan War as Phemius
and Demodocus themselves? These are questions to which ancient
critics, so far as they were confronted with them at all, gave an answer
which is sufficient evidence how impossible it was in antiquity to deal
with such matters coherently. Our only fifth-century witness dated
the poet's lifetime to the ninth century B.C. The latest of the dates
given for the Trojan War was the early part of the eleventh century.
There should, therefore, have been an effective chronological gap of
at least two centuries between the poet and his subject. The interval is
comparable with that which separated Thucydides from the colonization of the west which he describes at the beginning of his sixth book,
or Livy from the Punic Wars. Yet the poet was accepted as historical
authority for the duration of the siege, the numbers, equipment and
tactics of the forces, the genealogical background of history before
the Trojan War, and the character and even the complexion of the
heroes. No less notable is the confident unanimity of Hellenic
illustrators of Homeric episodes that the Heroic Age, as described
by the poet, was in essentials Hellenic and homogeneous in material
culture with their own. Homeric scenes carved on fourth century
sarcophagi are not idealized more than is Alexander's hunting scene
on the sarcophagus from Sidon.[1] The weeping Briseis in a copy of a
fourth-century painting would not be out of place on the grave
monument of Sostrate or Lysistrate.[2] On a red figure vase, Helen at
her abduction and recovery wears normal fifth-century dress.[3]
Thetis and her Nereids, coming to Achilles on a black figure vase, are
the familiar "penguin women" of the sixth century.[4] Patroclus on a
cup by Sosias and Heracles in the pedimental sculptures from
Aegina are armed like the "Marathon warrior" on his tombstone at

[1] G. Rodenwaldt, *Die Kunst der Antike* IV, Pl. 442–3.
[2] *MuZ.* 655: Rodenwaldt, *op. cit.*, Pl. 446–7.
[3] *MuZ.* 435–6.
[4] *Ibid.*, 175.

Athens.[1] On black figure vases heroes wear the rigid breastplate of the sixth century.[2] The Euphorbus plate and Protoattic and Proto-corinthian vases carry the practice back into the seventh century.[3] Before this there are no recognizable pictures of Homeric scenes at all. There was, therefore, every excuse for Flaxman when he assumed that the right way to "illustrate Homer" was to conform with the strictest current idealization of "classical" style, as the eighteenth century conceived it; and Wolf himself, the founder of Homeric criticism, accepted Flaxman's drawings as appropriate to his own edition of the Homeric text.

It follows from all this that, though critics in the Hellenic age accepted traditional dates, both for the poems and for the Heroic Age, which set them apart from each other and still further apart from the great age of Greece, they not only regarded the poet as a trustworthy authority for the Trojan War and as intimately ac-quainted with its details, but also assumed that in detail his experience was that of a writer of their own day. In certain respects, it is true, Hellenic, or rather Hellenistic criticism recognized that the manners of the Homeric and Heroic Ages differed from those of the critics and their contemporaries. There was the Homeric contempt for a diet of fish, as highly appreciated in the Athens of Aristophanes as among the Greeks of our own day.[4] There was the paradox, the dis-covery of which Herodotus attributes to his Persian informant,[5] that the epic represents the Trojan War as originating from the mis-behaviour of Helen—and on this principle of *cherchez la femme* Aristophanes, too, has something to say in the *Acharnians*.[6] There was the supersession of the leather sling ($\tau\epsilon\lambda\alpha\mu\grave{\omega}\nu$ $\sigma\kappa\acute{\upsilon}\tau\iota\nu\sigma$) by a handbar ($\mathring{\delta}\chi\alpha\nu\sigma\nu$) for carrying a shield, also noted by Herodotus and assigned by him to those Carian invaders who flooded back into the island world in post-Minoan and *ex hypothesi* post-Achaean times.[7]

[1] Rodenwaldt, *op. cit.*, Pl. 236–7, 245: *C.A.H. Plates* II, 24c. *MuZ.* 418.

[2] *MuZ.* 236, 241, etc.; cf. Pl. 5. c.

[3] *MuZ.* 117: *BSA* XXXV, Pl. 52: Johansen, *Vases sicyoniens*, Pl. XXVII, 1b; cf. Pl. 5. b.

[4] μ 330–3.   [5] I, 4.   [6] 528–9.

[7] I, 171. Vase painters from the seventh century always showed the shield worn with arm-band and hand-grip, though they sometimes depict it unconvincingly as an Hourglass shield, and later set an uneasy Gorgo-neion on its waist. *BSA* XLII (1947), p. 93, fig. 7 (here Pl. 5. b), with the article by H. L. Lorimer: *MuZ.* 163, 234, 237 and 274.

But these were differences of detail, ranking with the replacement of some Homeric words by modern synonyms and, as Aristarchus at any rate knew, with differences between the Homeric and modern sense of certain words. They were justifiably explained by the lapse of time which was admitted between the generation of Homer and that of the critics. They were not felt to infringe the continuity which was accepted in principle as existing between Homeric and Hellenic culture.

This Hellenic conception of an Homeric Age essentially Hellenic in its material civilization might, in default of other evidence, be admitted as possible, and was in fact so accepted until about 1870. But there were already well-known facts which pointed to a different conclusion. It was not only Hellenic illustrations of various dates that rendered each detail of equipment in close accord with the fashions respectively prevalent at the date when each monument was designed. The fourteenth-century illuminator of the *Geste de Troie* shows Jason, in contemporary plate armour, against a diaper background and killing a dragon which might have come off Nôtre Dame, while the golden fleece beyond is supported by a Gothic foliage-capital.[1] The Elizabethan stage, for all its acquaintance with classical literature and the classicizing art of the Renaissance, deals with an epic subject in the same spirit. Look for instance at *Troilus and Cressida*. The stage direction is "Lists set out; enter Ajax, armed." Hector swears "by Mars his gauntlet", as Helen "swears still by Venus' glove", and heroes wear riveted armour and fight with scimitars.[2] Such phrases are for the theatre where Brutus in doublet and slashed hose stabs Caesar with a rapier. But they put in a fresh light the Hellenic assumption, as we now see it to have been, that Homer conceived of the Heroic Age as an anticipation of the Hellenic centuries. The notion of staging a subject with accessories archaeologically correct for the presumed date of its episodes is a late product of the romantic reaction against the convention of pedantic classicalism which draped the statues of Hanoverian Kings and Whig Ministers in Roman toga and sandals. Indeed the fantastic notion of enhancing the poet's appeal by a parade of the results of historical research is as foreign to Hellenic art and literature as to any work of imaginative genius. And further, if this is so with

[1] This illumination could not be traced, but cf. Pl. 2. a.

[2] IV. v. *init.* and ll. 176–8; I. iii. 174–5; V. vi. 29; V. i. 2.

Hellenic attempts to render pictorially the spirit of Homeric epic, for a public for whom the poems were a national inheritance and an inspired exemplar of national ideals, what are we to infer as to the beliefs and the practices of the poets themselves? Firstly, we must regard the descriptive enhancements of epic narrative as an attempt on the part of the poet to visualize the story, as he tells it, in the imagery most vividly familiar both to himself and to his audience, namely, the material civilization of their own age and country. Secondly, if in any particular the descriptions are demonstrated to be out of accord with ascertained peculiarities of the civilization of the age to which the poems demonstrably belong, then we must infer that both audience and poet, early as they are shown to stand in the history of Greek literature, were themselves acquainted not merely with the topics and personalities of epic as traditional history, but with formal works of literary art (ποιήματα) which had been transmitted to them from a phase of creative achievement earlier still. In that earlier period the anomalous descriptions must have been a normal, realistic account of the fighting, the dwellings, and the daily life of their original audience and of the poets who composed for its entertainment and for the satisfaction of their own creative souls.

There was, of course, no lack of attempts at any period of scholarship to illustrate the recorded customs of prehistoric, and particularly of Homeric Greece by the monuments of Hellenic civilization. But until about 1870 these attempts rested uniformly on the assumption that the representations of Homeric subjects by Hellenic artists were good evidence for the dress, armour and architecture of Homeric times. There were several reasons why this state of things continued. In the latter part of the nineteenth century students of classical antiquities began to be infected with those evolutionary notions which had been current for a generation in all other departments of ethnology. Their attention was, therefore, confined to the mature and decadent phases of Greek art. Everything which could not be assigned to a century subsequent to the sixth was either dismissed as barbaric or discounted as a "Phoenician importation". We shall have occasion to deplore more than once the part which "Phoenician" fables, ancient and modern, have played in the historical study of Mediterranean peoples. Another serious obstacle to archaeological work was the scarcity of new material. This resulted directly from changes in the political situation in Greek lands. In the seventeenth and eighteenth centuries there seems to have been no greater difficulty in bringing back to Europe objects of ancient art, if anyone cared to do so, than in making the journeys that led to their discovery. But with the political decline of the Turk, suspicions arose as to the motives of any kind of traveller in the Ottoman Empire. The fear of being plundered by the detested "Franks" spread from provinces to potsherds and made exportation hazardous. Occasionally a powerful state like Great Britain might extort a concession to excavate an ancient site, or put a gunboat at the disposal of a consular enthusiast or a wealthy connoisseur; but long after scientific excavation had been employed in Italy and on Roman or pre-Roman sites in Western Europe, it was only on rare occasions that anything of the kind was practicable east of the Adriatic. Moreover, the "great powers" of the middle of the century became industrialized and the former patrons of the arts lost political influence at home. It is noteworthy that the two great enterprises which open a new period in the classical and prehistoric archaeology of the Greek world were both promoted by the newly-unified *Reich* of the Germans, and were a prompt and symbolic warning of that Empire's interest in the affairs of the Nearer East.

There had, indeed, been a few isolated discoveries, which might have provoked more systematic work if the conditions had been more favourable. About 1810 the Marquess of Sligo visited Mycenae and carried off fragments of the carved façade of the "Treasury of Atreus";[1] but for nearly a century they lay unregarded in his Irish country house and were transferred to the British Museum by his descendants only in 1905. In 1841 K. G. Fiedler, a German geologist, published the contents of some early graves in Naxos and other islands, including marble figures of the Early Cycladic style.[2] About the same time Ludwig Ross collected in Melos and other islands a peculiar class of engraved seal-stones, some of which resembled the earliest Greek coin-dies, while others were clearly more crudely barbaric and others again, though of admirable workmanship, were not in Hellenic style at all, but showed a vigorous naturalism which

[1] P. E. Laurent, *Recollections of a Classical Tour through various parts of Greece, Turkey and Italy in* 1818–19 (1821), p. 145.
[2] *Reise durch alle Theile des Konigsreiches griechischen Regierung in den Jahren* 1834 *bis* 1837, II (1841), pp. 314–5.

we now recognize as Minoan.[1] From Melos, too, come vases which are described in Brongniart's *Catalogue* of the Sèvres Museum[2] and which evidently belong to an early phase of the Cycladic culture revealed in 1895 by excavation on the town site at Phylakopi; and some Mycenaean vases from Cephallenia from an excavation by the Governor, de Bosset, in 1836, found their way into the Museum at Neuchâtel.[3] A Greek antiquary, Pappadopoulos, opened Cycladic tombs in Syros in 1861, but thought that they contained Roman convicts.[4] In the course of a geological investigation in the island of Thera in 1866, the relics of an early settlement of non-Hellenic appearance were found by Fouqué, buried beneath a thick bed of volcanic *debris* from some eruption of pre-Hellenic times.[5] They were accepted almost without question as confirming the Greek legend of a Phoenician colonization of the island, and much ingenuity was expended in extracting from the geological evidence a chronology which would agree with the traditional date for the voyage of Cadmus. Similarly when between 1858 and 1871 Biliotti excavated graves

[1] *Reisen auf den griechischen Inseln des ägäischen Meeres*, III (1845), pp. xii, 21.

[2] Alexandre Brongniart, *Description méthodique du Musée céramique de la manufacture de Porcelaine de Sèvres* (1845), no. 388, pp. 52–3, Pl. xiii, I, 3, 5, 6.

[3] *Rev. Arch.* XXXVII (1900), pp. 128–47.

[4] *Rev. Arch.* VI (1862), pp. 224–34.

[5] F. Fouqué, *Santorin et ses éruptions* (1879), pp. 94–131 and Pl. XXXIX–XLIV. He deserves to be quoted on the Phoenicians. After discussing the geological evidence, he continues: "Enfin, les faits historiques confirment encore cette manière de voir, car on sait, d'après des données positives, que l'invasion des Phéniciens dans les îles du sud de l'Archipel date du quinzième siècle avant notre ère. Or les constructions, les instruments et les vases de ces peuples et de ceux qui les ont remplacés plus tard sur le même sol sont entièrement différents de tout ce qui a été découvert à Thérasia et à Acrotiri. Les populations contemporaines de l'effondrement de la baie de Santorin ont donc occupé l'île avant les Phéniciens, et par conséquent antérieurement au quinzième siècle avant Jésus-Christ; et comme la grandeur des ruines de leur habitations, l'abondance et la variété des poteries, dont nous retrouvons les débris en les points éloignés l'un de l'autre, montrent qu'elles y ont eu des établissements stables, on est en droit de penser qu'elles y ont vécu pendant plusieurs siècles, et, par suite, qu'elles pouvaient y habiter deux mille ans avant notre ère" (pp. 130–31). Moreover, the pottery is well illustrated, in colour, with provenience given.

at Ialysus and Salzmann others at Camirus in Rhodes,[1] although they recognized the difference of style between their contents, the finds were described indiscriminately in the inventories of the British Museum as "Graeco-Phoenician"; and the assumption that the vases and other objects from Ialysus are immediate predecessors of those from Camirus is only recently extinct. With rather more reason, the same "Graeco-Phoenician" compromise was thought sufficient explanation of the peculiar styles of decorative art which were being revealed by General di Cesnola's excavations in Cyprus from 1865 to 1879.[2]

Except for the spurious Phoenician connexions, these sporadic discoveries lacked any context within which they could be related. The first attempt to apply to Greek lands and sites the methods of systematic archaeology which had been yielding remarkable results in the lake dwellings of Switzerland, in the terremare villages in the Po valley, and among the peat bogs of Denmark, was an essay by George Finlay, the historian of Greek independence, published in Greek in 1869 under the title of *Prehistoric Archaeology in Switzerland and Greece*.[3] It described the recent Swiss finds and illustrated, by a small collection of stone implements made by himself in Greece, the probability that similar settlements existed around the lakes and fens of Boeotia and Thessaly, and above all in Macedonia where Herodotus had described lake dwellings still in use in the fifth century.[4] Finlay did not himself excavate, but his contribution shows how widespread was the interest excited by the Swiss lake dwellings, and especially by the stratigraphical evidence which was for the first time applied to determine the sequence of periods and styles, which had hitherto been classified solely on grounds of morphological resemblance. The Swiss excavations were indeed the beginning of scientific archaeology, and Finlay in Greece was among the first to see the value of the new method of research.

---

[1] *Annuario della R. Scuola Archaeologica di Atene e delle Missioni Italiane in Oriente* VI–VII, pp. 251 ff.; Charles Newton, *Edinburgh Review*, 1878 = *Essays on Art and Archaeology*, pp. 246–302.

[2] Louis Palma di Cesnola, *Cyprus: its ancient cities, tombs and temples*, 1877; *Cyprus Antiquities*, 1880; *Salaminia*, 1882.

[3] Παρατηρήσεις ἐπὶ τῆς ἐν Ἑλβετίᾳ καὶ Ἑλλάδι προιστορικῆς ἀρχαιολογίας, 1869.

[4] V, 16.

In 1868 a successful merchant, Heinrich Schliemann, was at last enabled to execute his life-long ambition of testing with the spade the Hellenic tradition that the site of the Graeco-Roman town of Ilium at Hissarlik in the Troad, was also the site of Homer's Troy. The tradition had indeed been roughly handled more than once already, by Demetrius of Scepsis, a local antiquary of the second century B.C., on the geological ground that the Plain of Troy was of recent alluvial formation,[1] and by other critics on the score of inconsistency with the Homeric narrative. But Bunarbashi, the site suggested by Demetrius, which is moreover the only alternative, is as a matter of fact still more inconsistent; it never supported an inhabited site of any importance at all; and it was put out of question finally by Schliemann's discoveries at Hissarlik. Here, in eight seasons between 1870 and 1890 he laid bare, not one, but six cities, built one after another on the same site and forming an accumulation of walls and debris some thirty feet deep; and in addition to these six, two sub-sidiary layers were distinguished after his death by Dörpfeld's con-firmatory excavations in 1893–4.[2] The second city of this series, reckoning from the lowest upwards, was found to have perished in a general conflagration, and the discovery among its ashes of a great hoard of primitive jewellery and vessels of gold and silver convinced Schliemann that he had indeed found the Great Treasure of Priam himself, in the ruins of the Troy which Agamemnon burned with fire. Although, as we shall see, the identification of the "Burnt City" with the Homeric Troy was mistaken, and even the close connexion which Schliemann hastily assumed to exist between the Great Treasure and the burnt city may be disputed with good reason,[3] it was almost universally admitted from the first moment of the discovery that the whole question of the credibility of early Greek traditions had entered upon a new phase, and that it challenged investigation by totally new

[1] Strabo 598.

[2] H. Schliemann, *Trojanische Alterthümer*, 1874. *Eng. trans. Troy and its Remains*, by Philip Smith, 1875; *Ilios*, 1880; *Troja*, 1884; *Bericht über die Ausgrabungen in Troja*, 1890. Wilhelm Dörpfeld, *Troja und Ilion* (1902).

[3] The conclusion from the excavations conducted by the University of Cincinnati, 1932–8, is that "it seems likely that most of the 'treasures' which Schliemann attributed to the 'Burnt City' actually did belong to the final phase of the Second Settlement, II g, as revealed in our excavations; but in almost every instance the evidence is insufficient to preclude a later date" (C. W. Blegen, *Troy* I (1950), pp. 207–10).

methods and new canons of evidence. We shall have to return to these "Trojan" discoveries later on in more detail and in relation to later discoveries elsewhere.

With the same indomitable purpose of testing Homeric tradition by the spade, Schliemann went on in 1874–6 to excavate the citadel of Mycenae, the traditional centre of Agamemnon's Confederacy.[1] Here too the results were totally unexpected in detail, but (as it seemed at the time) no less confirmatory in outline of the Homeric story. The so-called Treasury of Atreus and the other "beehive" tombs in the lower town, were found to have been plundered and damaged in antiquity, and it was nearly fifty years before more expert handling recovered fragments of their original furniture and ascertained their dates.[2] Within the sculptured "Lion Gate" of the citadel, Schliemann had better luck. Under only a few feet of *debris* washed down the hillside, a stone-fenced burial place was brought to light, within which deeper excavation revealed at rock level no less than six "Shaft Graves" of royal magnificence. The amazing wealth of gold vessels and ornaments which they contained, though all utterly un-Hellenic and executed in a new and sumptuous style of art, seemed ample confirmation of the legendary wealth of "Golden Mycenae" and of the description, based on local Hellenic legend, which is given of this part of the site in a well-known passage of Pausanias.[3] In the first ecstasy of discovery Schliemann telegraphed to Athens, "To George, King of the Hellenes; I have found Agamemnon, King of all the Hellenes", and for a while it seemed as if the sober truth were but little short of his claim.

The civilization which was brought to light at Mycenae, though quite un-Hellenic, was at the same time very far from barbarous. It was also greatly in advance of all but the very latest layers at Hissarlik and incomparably richer and more elaborate even than these; and it exhibited so clearly, despite all its unfamiliarity and splendour, the decadent conventionalism which follows every period of mature

[1] *Mycenae*, 1878.

[2] A. J. B. Wace in *BSA* XXV (1921–3), pp. 293–397; cf. his *Mycenae*, 1949.

[3] II, xvi, 4. See A. J. B. Wace, "Pausanias and Mycenae" in *Neue Beiträge aus antike Kunst: Festschrift B. Schweitzer* (1950), pp. 19–26, and G. E. Mylonas, *Ancient Mycenae* (1957), pp. 171 ff. The contents of Schliemann's Shaft Graves were fully published by G. Karo, *Die Schachtgräber von Mykenai*, 1930.

artistic advancement and marks its decline, that more than one archaeologist of distinction regarded the relics from Schliemann's "Shaft Graves" as the handiwork of Gothic adventurers in the Byzantine Age. But it was recognized, widely and at once, that the art and civilization of Mycenae were not merely identical with those of Ialysus already mentioned and closely akin to those of Thera, but also explained a large number of casual finds already made at various times and in many parts of the Mediterranean basin, from Marseilles, Etruria and South Italy in the west, to Lycia, Egypt and particularly Cyprus eastwards. It was also realized, though more slowly, that a number of the painted potsherds which had been observed in the upper and later layers at Hissarlik were of the same general style as the commoner pottery of Mycenae; and this gave at once a rough relative perspective, for it showed that a considerable lapse of time must be presumed between the destruction of Schliemann's "City of Priam", and the closing of his "Tomb of Agamemnon". It was, however, nearly ten years later that the first attempt was made, by workers less enthusiastic but better equipped, to discover how this intervening period was filled.

Other excavations followed—by Schliemann himself at Orchomenos (1880–1)[1] and Tiryns (1884–5);[2] by the Greek Archaeological Society on the Acropolis of Athens[3] and at Vaphio in Laconia;[4] by the German Archaeological Institute at Dimini in south Thessaly,[5] and at Menidi[6] and Spata[7] in Attica; and by the other foreign Institutes in Athens on a number of other sites in Greece and the Aegean Islands. They demonstrated that this civilization, to which the name "Mycenaean" had been given provisionally, was widely represented in the Aegean, especially in the southern part. Trial diggings and surface exploration in Crete[8] made it clear that this island was a stronghold of "Mycenaean" culture, and even that on the Kephala hill, within the site of the Greek city of Knossos, a great

[1] *Orchomenos*, 1881.

[2] *Tiryns*, 1886.

[3] Δελτ. 1888, pp. 30ff. Kavvadias-Kawerau, *Die Ausgrabungen der Akropolis* (1907), pp. 71ff.

[4] *EA* 1888, pp. 197ff.; 1889, pp. 129ff.

[5] *Ath. Mitt.* 1886, pp. 435ff.; 1887, pp. 146ff.

[6] Lolling, *Das Kuppelgrab von Menidi*, 1881.

[7] *Ath. Mitt.* 1877, pp. 261ff.

[8] *Ath. Mitt.* 1886, pp. 135ff.

complex of "Mycenaean" buildings stood in the same relation to the legend of Minos as the Shaft Graves and Lion Gate of Mycenae to that of Agamemnon. Schliemann paid it a short visit in 1887, but it was not followed by any systematic digging. Further researches made at Mycenae itself from 1886 onwards by Chrestos Tsountas,[1] for the Greek Archaeological Society, confirmed in all essential points the first general impression of "Mycenaean" civilization which was conveyed by Schliemann's discoveries; but the excavation of numerous tombs in the lower town, of rather more decadent style than the Shaft Graves on the citadel, made it possible to trace stages of development among the products of Mycenaean art, and to extend the limits of the "Mycenaean period" very much lower down the chronological scale than the point represented by the Shaft Graves. But even the latest varieties of Mycenaean style showed not the slightest sign of anything which could be ascribed to Hellenic influence. Subsequent excavations in every part of the Mediterranean from Sicily to Syria and from Chalcidice to Egypt, have contributed much to fill in the picture and to enhance the perspective of a prolonged period of civilization.[2]

Another important piece of pioneer work in interpretation belongs to the year 1883. Since Ross's exploration of the Cyclades for King Otto about 1840, a class of engraved gems, the so-called "island-stones", had been established and enlarged by many casual finds. These "island-stones" are small, lens-shaped or almond-shaped objects, perforated for suspension from edge to edge or from end to end like beads. They bear decorative designs engraved on one of their convex surfaces, and very occasionally on both, in styles some of which resemble those on the earliest Hellenic coin-dies, and the subjects too of some of these were derived from Greek legends. Others recalled the linear, angular work of the "geometrical school" which was found to dominate all important sites in Greece and the Aegean during the phase immediately preceding the Hellenic, and had been shown by the tomb-groups at Camirus to pass over into its Orientalizing and archaic Greek phases. Others again were in a

---

[1] Tsountas, Μυκῆναι καὶ ὁ Μυκηναῖος Πολιτισμός, 1893. Conclusions somewhat modified in Tsountas and Manatt, *The Mycenaean Age*, 1897.

[2] See C. W. Blegen, "Preclassical Greece—a Survey", *BSA* XLVI (1951), pp. 16–24, and for detail, Friederich Matz, *Die Agäis*, in *Handbuch der Archäologie* II, i. (1950).

style as vigorously naturalistic as the Greek, but quite distinct from it. These alone were frequently, though not always, in hard stones such as porphyry, jasper, agate, cornelian and amethyst, requiring really high technical skill; the linear and the quasi-Hellenic designs were all on softer materials—marble, serpentine, steatite, or occasionally ivory or bone. The occurrence of several fine examples engraved in the naturalistic style, in agate and other hard stones, in the Shaft Graves of Mycenae, where they were associated with gold rings in the same fine style, made it certain that this class belonged to the earlier end of the series and fixed their approximate age; and it became clear that in the island-stones there was a practically complete series of objects linking Mycenaean art with Hellenic. The comparative abundance of these "island-stones" in Melos and Crete suggested to Adolph Milchhöfer that the origin and chief centre of production of such works of art must be sought rather in the South Aegean than on the Greek mainland; and his essay *Die Anfänge der Kunst in Griechenland*, published at Leipzig in 1883, was one of the main inducements to Schliemann's visit to the traditional site of Knossos in 1887. Milchhöfer, however, damaged his case a good deal by insisting that workmanship so excellent must be in the purest and earliest sense Indo-European, and by the attempt to bring Hissarlik into the story, though in fact such engraved stones do not occur there, through an elaborate comparison of the mythology of Crete and Phrygia.

Meanwhile, what was the relation of the "Mycenaean" civilization of the Argolis and the Islands, with its wheel-made painted pottery, bronze implements, rich gold-work, engraved gems, and evidence of intercourse with Egypt and other foreign lands, to the civilization of Troy, with hand-made, self-coloured pottery, mainly copper implements, and very much simpler gold-work, mainly of twisted wire and flat plates? The casual finds from Thera and Melos, as far back as 1840, suggested a solution. Following these clues, F. Dümmler of the German Archaeological Institute in Athens visited Amorgos and other of the remoter Cyclades in 1885, and then went on to Cyprus.[1] In the Cyclades he found tombs like those discovered in Syros in 1862, with pottery like that of Thera and bronze implements which resembled Troad types but were more varied and specialized. Marble idols of the type described and illustrated by Fiedler in 1841 were

[1] *Ath. Mitt.* XI (1886), pp. 15 ff.

fairly common in these tombs, and also obsidian flakes, such as had been recorded by Ross in Melos. Dümmler, however, probably misled by Ross, missed the town-site at Phylakopi in Melos, from which the vases in the Sèvres Museum probably came, and also a smaller town-site in Amorgos which was certainly familiar to his guide. His collection went astray after his return to Athens, but the more important objects were re-identified in 1893 and secured for the Ashmolean Museum.

We may now summarize the position as it appeared to Schliemann and his contemporaries. The long stratified series at Hissarlik had already its fragmentary counterparts—in the Cycladic tombs, with their unpainted pottery and leaf-shaped daggers of copper or its "natural alloys"; in the earliest series of tombs in Cyprus; and on the Greek mainland, in the stone implements and unpainted pottery from the Athenian Acropolis and from trial pits at Tiryns, where it was known that only the upper stratum had been laid bare as yet. Analogies between Hissarlik and Neolithic and Early Bronze Age sites in central Europe (where Schliemann's work gave a great impetus to prehistoric studies) were felt to be closest in the First City; those between Hissarlik and Cyprus in the Second City and its successors. The significance of the painted pottery from the denuded remnants of the Sixth City was already appreciated as indicating closer contacts with the "Mycenaean" world, and the exploration of this stratum was being planned. The region over which "Mycenaean" objects were found to be distributed already included South Thessaly, Cephalonia, Laconia, Crete, Rhodes and Cyprus. From the mainland of Asia Minor there was as yet very little. From Hissarlik VI there were as yet only some very late fragments, and there were other even later and more barbarous imitations from Tsangli (Mycale) opposite Samos,[1] and from Assarlik near Halicarnassus in Caria.[2] There were also a very few casual finds—a vase from Pitane in Aeolis,[3] and another from Mylasa in Caria.[4] It looked as if even the

---

[1] *Ath. Mitt.* XII (1887), pp. 229–30; cf. V. R. d'A. Desborough, *Protogeometric Pottery* (1952), p. 323.

[2] *JHS* VIII (1887), pp. 64 ff.; cf. XVI (1895), pp. 203–4, *Ath. Mitt.* XIII (1888), pp. 275–80, and Desborough, *loc. cit.* These graves are Protogeometric.

[3] Perrot et Chipiez, *Histoire de l'Art dans l'Antiquité* VI (1894), p. 923, cf. Bossert, *Altanatolien* 7.

[4] *Ath. Mitt.* XII (1887), p. 230, fig. 10.

west coast of Asia Minor had somehow escaped Mycenaean influence though the islands off the coast were occupied, from Rhodes northwards to Patmos. Certain Germans, however, clung to a "Carian theory", based on a misinterpretation of a well-known passage of Thucydides;[1] and this "Carian theory", in spite of disproof by persons who had been in Caria, devastated German work on this subject for another whole generation.

Mycenae itself was already recognized as representing only the decadence, and perhaps (in the Shaft Graves) the late maturity of "Mycenaean" culture. But the Cyclades illustrated a rather earlier phase of the same or a similar culture, reminiscent of a barbaric past like that of Hissarlik; Crete, to judge from its gems and the trial-excavation at Knossos, promised earlier and richer material; and the lower levels at Tiryns might be expected to provide the missing links. Indications of intercourse with Egypt, such as the scarab of Queen Tii found at Ialysos,[2] the tomb-ceiling at Orchomenos, and other loans from Egyptian to Mycenaean art, pointed to intercourse during the Eighteenth Egyptian Dynasty, rather than the Twenty-sixth, already known for its Philhellenic policy; and the discovery of a Mycenaean vase in the Maket tomb at Thebes, dated to the reign of Thothmes IV (about 1500),[3] had already supplied the necessary counterpart of the proof: for Mycenaean tombs and manufactures, being thus both "not earlier" and "not later" than the Eighteenth Dynasty, must therefore be regarded as contemporary with it.[4] As to the racial or national identity of the originators of "Mycenaean" cultures, nothing could be concluded yet. But the contrast between the earlier finds in the Cyclades and in Cyprus on the whole supported the inference drawn from the late and sparse occurrence of Mycenaean objects in Cyprus, that the fountain head of "Mycenaean" culture was to be sought not in the Levant, but rather within the Aegean.

Though Schliemann's discoveries, and still more his method and outlook, mark a turning point in the history of archaeology—since

[1] See note by A. W. Gomme on Thuc. I, 8 in *A Historical Commentary on Thucydides* I (1945).

[2] Furtwängler-Loeschcke, *Mykenische Vasen* (1886), *Textb.*, pp. 4, 9, 75, Pl. E.1.

[3] W. M. Flinders Petrie, *Illahun, Kahun and Gurob* (1891), p. 21, Pl. 26, no. 44.

[4] Tsountas and Manatt, *The Mycenaean Age*, pp. 317–21.

Hissarlik was actually the first wholly dry-land site to be explored with the stratigraphical experience hitherto mainly won among northern lake-dwellings—it was some while before his challenge to the dominant school of Homeric criticism provoked any serious response. Geddes in 1878[1] amplified Grote's theory that the *Iliad* consisted of an early Thessalian *Achilleid* expanded later by a poet or poets better acquainted with the Troad and Ionian civilization. He added in a footnote that "it might be premature to venture an opinion how far Dr. Schliemann's discoveries will modify opinion as to the mythical character of the war of Troy, but they will tend decidedly in that direction". For his own part, he was prepared to "assume, without reference to prior questions, the early Grecian standpoint, and accept the *Iliad* and *Odyssey* as poems historically, and not merely poetically conceived, that is, that they embodied or were conceived to embody a certain substratum of traditional incident believed in as once veritable fact and not 'a past which never was in any sense a present' ", as in ancient times Megacleides had regarded "all these things as fictions".[2] "The evidence supporting this thesis", he thought, "is weightier than is usually believed", and he detected "glimpses of something like an historic consciousness on the part of the poet, so that he restricts himself as to the features and inventions of his own age (e.g. κέλης and σάλπιγξ), and, while he may and does use them as similes, refrains from introducing them into the *action* of an age prior to his own". But "a certain allegiance in him to external fact and a subordination to historic conditions" was compatible, in Geddes's view, with the admission "that much of the adornment, and many of the incidents, may have been in origin purely mythical and imaginative, and that ideas and situations, taken, we shall say, from Solar or Storm mythes, may have been adopted as poetic imagery to body forth the struggles and victories of actual flesh and blood heroes". This was no advance on Welcker's view of the Trojan War as *Wahrheit und Dichtung*, a mixture of Poetry and Fact.[3]

Indirectly, however, new notions consequent on Schliemann's work profoundly influenced the trend of literary criticism. In the

[1] *The Problem of the Homeric Poems*, especially pp. 242–3.

[2] Schol. X 36, Μεγακλείδης φησὶ ταῦτα πάντα πλάσματα εἶναι quoted by W. D. Geddes.

[3] Geddes quotes the phrase with approval from *Der epische Zyklus* II, p. 21.

first place, the long vista of prehistoric civilization—or barbarism, if you will—revealed by the superimposed layers in the mound of Hissarlik, revolutionized the perspective in which the early history of the Greek world must thenceforward be studied. Whether Homer's Achilles was a sun-god or a Thessalian prince, *somebody* had burned Schliemann's "Second City" many generations before the Aeolic colonization, and earlier still somebody had built the wall and gates of that city; some chieftain had lived in the "great house" which crowned the settlement, and had accumulated treasure, some of it from afar—amber, jade, ivory, lapis lazuli, faience and obsidian, as well as gold vessels and jewellery and silver "talents". If the Second City were indeed Priam's Troy, the Trojan War must be antedated by centuries; if even the Shaft Graves had anything to do with the "Golden Mycenae" of Agamemnon, the House of Atreus must belong, not to the twelfth century, as Greek tradition said, but at latest to the fourteenth, like the graves at Ialysus. To the historian this was a revolution in chronology. To the philologist it was a revelation; for it gave him far ampler time both for the stages which were now generally recognized to have existed in the composition of the poems, and (more important still) for the growth of the Greek language and the phonetic and structural changes which had been detected already. And these changes were now recognized as more far-reaching and complex than Bentley had dreamed of when he demonstrated the disuse of the *digamma*.

Secondly, the quite un-Hellenic character of the civilizations (for they were obviously distinct from each other) disinterred at Hissarlik and at Mycenae, posed a new set of problems of interpretation of Homeric descriptions of the craftsmanship and art of the heroic age. Quite apart from the question, what was the date and character of the Trojan War, of the confederacies led by Agamemnon and Priam, and of the civilization which they enjoyed, it must now be asked further, what was the material culture enjoyed by the poet, and by his audience for whom those amazing descriptions flowed so spontaneously—descriptions of golden armour, golden cups, decorations of inlaid metals, of blue glaze, of amber, of ivory stained scarlet, of richly-figured textiles. What sort of a world was it, in which Achaean freebooters harried the lands of the King of Egypt, lived in honourable detention at his court, raided Sidon or traded in partnership with a Phoenician merchant, and knew at all events something of a Wild

West with perilous straits and delectable islands, and of a grim north, with midnight sunrise and sunset, or sunless gloom along the scouring ocean?

Thirdly, general attention was recalled to the correspondences between the Homeric and the actual topography of the Troad, on which travellers, from Wood to Leaf, have insisted in the face of sceptics who had not seen the country; for as the poets have been usually convinced of a personal Homer, so explorers have stood for a real Troy, if not always for an historical War. Such familiarity with the region favoured the view that the poems, or at all events the most ancient portions of them, belonged rather to the north Aegean than to the Ionian area. An *Achilleid* of Thessalian origin, such as Grote and Geddes supposed, was more likely to have been the inheritance of Aeolic Greeks, whose colonial settlements ranged from Smyrna and Cyme northwards to Lesbos, Tenedos and Achilleum, and eventually to the mouth of the Hebrus river, than to Ionians whose mother countries lay along the Euboean and Saronic Gulfs; and consequently it was more likely to have been expanded and embellished by poets of that Aeolic-speaking area. Yet the poems, as we have them, are in a dialect which in the main is that of the Ionian cities of Asia Minor, which according to the traditional dates were founded about the middle of the eleventh century. Since the personal Homer did not live before the end of the ninth century, a fourth question had to be asked. How could these dates be reconciled with the impression of personal acquaintance with the material culture of Mycenae? One possible answer was that the culture had lasted until the traditional date for the personal Homer—as was insisted by Alexander Murray of the British Museum.[1] Alternatively, the Ionic dialect might have been differentiated before the foundation of the Ionian colonies, in some region of peninsular Greece where the Mycenaean civilization prevailed. A third possibility was that the poems as we have them represent the result of some kind of translation or paraphrase. The Ionicized version would be the work of an Ionian at a relatively late date. The original composition would have been made in Mycenaean surroundings, not necessarily in Ionic Greek, or in Greek at all,[2] or

[1] A. S. Murray, "A new view of the Homeric Question", in *The Contemporary Review* 23 (1874).

[2] The work of Michael Ventris has saved us from the difficulty of the translation of an epic *Kunstsprache*.

in poetic form, and transmitted somehow across the gulf which separated the "Golden Mycenae" of Schliemann from the Ionia of the traditional Homer.

The effect of this group of considerations was to formulate new antitheses and alternatives, between which Homeric criticism was now asked to make its choice. Were the actual poems essentially Ionian in origin as well as Ionic in dialect, or were they relics of a pre-Ionian world, shattered, as Greek tradition told, by the *Coming of the Dorians* and other immigrants into peninsular Greece, about the end of the twelfth century? If the poems were Ionian, still more if they were Ionian of the ninth or eighth century, was it possible— and if so, how—to distinguish within them between original compositions of that age, and versions, paraphrases or excerpts from materials ancient enough to have served as the vehicle for Mycenaean experiences into that Ionian world? If the poems were not Ionian, but pre-Ionian, what had been their history between the date of their composition and their acceptance as an heirloom of the Ionian Greeks? How far back could they be traced, on internal evidence interpreted by the new archaeological materials? And in what relation did descriptions of works of art in a style of the fourteenth or fifteenth century stand to the narrative of a Trojan War between dynasties which tradition assigned to the twelfth or thirteenth? To these questions, answers were attempted on two general lines.

In 1883 August Fick published an edition of the *Odyssey*, followed by an *Iliad* in 1886,[1] in which he claimed to penetrate behind the present Ionic form of the poems, and to restore them to an earlier state in the Aeolic dialect. It had been recognized in antiquity that the Homeric dialect presented a mixture of forms, some of which survived in Aeolic, some in Ionic Greek. Fick observed that many of the Ionic forms might be replaced by the corresponding Aeolic forms without damage to the metre; but that many of the Aeolic forms could *not* be replaced by the corresponding Ionic forms, because the latter would not scan. He also satisfied himself that in the parts of the poems which for other reasons were regarded as older, these unreplaceable Aeolisms were more numerous; and further that in other parts, which for similar reasons he thought later, Ionic forms occurred

---

[1] *Die homerische Odyssee in der ursprünglichen Sprachform wiederhergestellt* and *Die homerische Ilias nach ihrer Entstehung betrachtet und in der ursprünglichen Sprachform wiederhergestellt.* D. B. Monro devoted Appendix F of his *Homeric Grammar*[2] (1891) to criticism of Fick's theory.

which, unlike those first mentioned, were not replaceable by Aeolisms. He inferred from all this, first, that the parts characterized by ineradicable Aeolisms had been originally composed in Aeolic and subsequently translated into Ionic so far as the metre allowed, and secondly, that the parts wherein ineradicable Ionisms occurred had never been in Aeolic shape, and consequently were supplements composed by the Ionian poet or poets who had translated the original Aeolic poems. Fick thought that this translation into Ionic from Aeolic occurred in the latter half of the sixth century, and he attributed it to Cynaethus of Chios, who is said to have been the first to recite Homer's poems at Syracuse, about 504 B.C. In this extreme form his theory is refuted by the fact that before that date Simonides quoted from one of the *older* passages of the *Iliad* in Ionic, and attributed it to a "man of Chios" who can hardly have been his own contemporary Cynaethus.[1] Far more valuable, indeed, was the suggestion made by Friederich Ritschl as long before as 1838,[2] that the personal Homer had been one of the Aeolian emigrants from Old Greece, and had composed at Smyrna short Aeolic poems which Ionian poets had supplemented and Ionicized until the eighth century. It was Fick's particular merit that his analysis of the Homeric dialect, in so far as it was valid at all, was applicable to such an earlier adaptation of the poems as Ritschl had contemplated. It is, indeed, in this alternative guise that the "Aeolic theory" has generally been discussed. If it were established, it would obviously be of the greatest value as an objective criterion of the relative dates of the constituent parts of the poems.

But in the first place, Hinrichs showed that a good many of the so-called Aeolisms were to be explained otherwise, and Sittl was able to go very much further than Hinrichs in reducing the number of indisputable forms;[3] whole classes of Fick's examples have not been shown to occur in Aeolic; others are not confined to Aeolic; others, especially in proper names, may go back to a phase of Greek anterior

[1] *Z* 146. Diehl accepts the attribution to Semonides, fr. 29. But see J. A. Davison, "Quotations and allusions in early Greek literature" (*Eranos* LIII (1956), pp. 125–40).

[2] *Die Alexandrinischen Bibliotheken unter den ersten Ptolemaeern und die Sammlung der Homerischen Gedichte durch Pisistratus* (*Opuscula Philologica* I (1866) esp. pp. 59–60).

[3] Gustav Hinrichs, *De Homericae elocutionis vestigiis Aeolicis*, 1875, and *Herr Dr. Karl Sittl und die homerischen Äolismen*, 1884.

to the establishment of any surviving dialect. In the second place, Fick's metrical argument would be inconclusive if there were any reason to suppose that the poet was familiar with alternative forms of words, and used them as they best pleased his ear; and the large residue of "exceptions" which Fick had to admit, made it probable that this had at some time or other been so. Smyrna, one of the most famous of the traditional birthplaces of Homer, had been an Aeolic city before it became a colony of Ionian Colophon, and Chios in the fifth century still spoke a variety of Ionic peculiar to itself. Thirdly, the probability was growing that in some form or other considerable parts of the poems reflected a phase of culture earlier than had been supposed and radically different from that of historic Ionia. Consequently it was becoming more probable that the dialect of the poems also belonged to a phase of the Greek language in which it could not be proved that either Aeolic or Ionic had as yet been differentiated as organic dialects at all, and that the traditional spelling of archaic forms, whenever the poems were first written, followed approximately that of similar forms then in ordinary use.

Subsequent revision of Fick's data in the light of more copious and earlier examples of Aeolic and Ionic speech, by more trustworthy methods of philology and with a more scientific text of the poems, shows that the problems of Aeolism are very much more complicated than he supposed. His own later work did little to clear the main issues and much to confuse them. But his work had two immediate results of considerable importance. He gave new significance to the questions already outlined. Were the poems essentially Ionian or pre-Ionian? And if pre-Ionian, had they originated among the Aeolic Greeks whose cities lay wholly north of Ionia and adjacent to the home-district of the Trojan confederacy, or had they been transmitted even to these colonial Greeks from an earlier home in Thessaly or some other Aeolian-speaking district of peninsular Greece? In the latter event, what was the bearing of this purely philological consideration on the literary distinction formulated by Grote and elaborated by Geddes, between a primitive Thessalian *Achilleid* and the enlarged *Iliad* of which that poem now formed the kernel?

Fick's Aeolian Theory began to influence the interpretation of the poems almost at once. This is evident already in Adolf Holm's *History of Greece*, the first volume of which appeared in 1886 and explained the Trojan War as a probably historical incident of the

Aeolian colonization. Another aspect of the same idea appears also quite early, in Dümmler's essay on Hector printed in Studniczka's *Cyrene*,[1] and in Bethe's *Theban Epic Poetry*.[2] Dümmler's contribution was to explain the "tomb of Hector" which was shown in antiquity at Boeotian Thebes,[3] not, as had been customary, as a quite independent affair with accidental similarity of a name which is in any case a normal Greek word meaning "hold-fast", but as indicating the place of origin of any possible tradition about any possible hero of that name. The plausible catchword that "myths originate where the monument is, and are derivative where it is not", set people searching for analogies; and as the chemist Berzelius said, "It is the easiest thing in the world to discover what you are looking for".

If there had been an original *Achilleid* of Thessalian composition, it was argued that there must have been not only a Hector somewhere thereabouts, but a Troy to be besieged, an Agamemnon to quarrel with, and so forth. There was, moreover, Homeric allusion to a great war between Thebes and Argos, in the days of Eteocles and Polynices, the sons of Oedipus, and to another war, a generation later, in which the children of the famous "Seven against Thebes" were involved.[4] There was also a lost poem, sometimes attributed to Homer, about the *Taking of Oechalia* by Heracles.[5] Accordingly it was argued that the original *Taking of Troy* had been a similar episode of local Aeolian history before the Aeolian colonization of the Troad coastlands. This

[1] Ferdinand Dümmler, *Hektor* (Franz Studniczka, *Kyrene, eine altgriechische Göttin* (1890), pp. 194–205). "Es ist wohl allseitig anerkannt, dass die dem troischen Kriege zu Grunde liegenden Sagen älter sind, als ihre Fixierung auf troischem Boden infolge der äolischen Besiedelung jener Küsten. ... so ist doch eine nothwendige Consequenz dieser richtigen Grundansicht praktisch noch nicht zur Genüge gezogen, nämlich die, dass auch die Gegner der Panachaier zum grössten Theil jenen älteren Kriegsschauplätzen angehören."

[2] *Thebanische Heldenlieder*, 1891.

[3] Pausanias IX, xviii, 5.

[4] Δ 376–410, E 126, 800–8, Z 222–3, Ξ 113–25, Ψ 678–80, ο 244–7. There is no mention of the War in the story of Oedipus, and Eriphyle is just a name in λ 271–80, 326.

[5] First attributed to Creophylus by Callimachus (ed. Pfeiffer) Epigram VI. Name Οἰχαλίας ἅλωσις first in Strabo 638. Creophylus was known to Plato as ὁ τοῦ Ὁμήρου ἑταῖρος (*Respubl.* 600 B). The story was used by Bacchylides (ed. Snell) 16 and *fr.* 22. For other references see Homer V (*O.C.T.*), pp. 144–7.

hypothesis was a good deal helped by ancient uncertainties about the meaning and usage of the word *Argos*; and it was suggested that the original Argos, with its Argive population, had been situated in South Thessaly, and that its name and fame had somehow been transferred to the Peloponnesian district and city. These ideas were popularized by Paul Cauer's *Fundamental Questions of Homeric Criticism*,[1] by far the most comprehensive summary of recent and current opinions on these matters, and in its third edition still an invaluable handbook to the whole subject. In the next decade there appeared a series of works treating Homer as part of an epic tradition. Richard Wagner's *Process of Development of Heroic Legend* elaborated the displacement theory still further.[2] Bethe followed up his earlier book in due course with his *Homer and the Heroic Legend* and his *Trojan Excavations and Homeric Criticism*.[3] Even a serious piece of geographical work like Otto Kern's *The Country of Thessaly* gave considerable attention to the supposed localities of this pre-Trojan War.[4] Friederich Stählin's essay on the *Thebes under Plakie*, the home of the Boeotian Andromache, is another piece of special pleading.[5]

But meanwhile a very awkward thing had been happening. Ancient tradition and modern travellers had located the Trojan War on the Trojan Plain; Schliemann had dug in the Trojan Plain, and found a prehistoric city which had certainly been captured and destroyed more than once. If scholars better skilled in interpretation now located the Trojan War in pre-Trojan Thessaly, here was the chance for a new Schliemann to discover, if not Hypoplakian Thebes, at all events some archaeological counterpart of the pre-Trojan Achilles and Hector. It happened also that political consideration for the feelings of the Turks had held Teutonic explorers aloof from the "promised land" of Crete, which the successful insurrection of 1896–8 had now thrown open to British and Italian excavators. But

[1] *Grundfragen der Homerkritik*, 1895, 3rd ed., 1923.

[2] *Entwicklungsgang der Heldensage*, 1905.

[3] "Homer und die Heldensage" and "Die trojanischen Ausgrabungen und die Homerkritik", in *Neue Jahrb. für Klass. Alt.*, 1901, pp. 657 ff. and 1904, pp. 1 ff.

[4] "Die Landschaft Thessaliens und die Geschichte Griechenlands", in *Neue Jahrb. für Klass. Alt.*, 1904. Reprinted in *Nordgriechische Skizzen*, 1912.

[5] *Das hypoplakische Theben*, 1907.

if the insular Minoans had been appropriated by the sea powers, there were still the Minyans of continental Greece to be won by a continental power. Moreover Orchomenos, the traditional centre of the legendary power of the Minyans whose famous Argo had been the first ship to force the Dardanelles, had been earmarked in 1880 by Schliemann, but only superficially examined. Here was the chance to find a second Knossos; for Achilles at all events looked on Orchomenos as the wealthiest centre of exchange in the Achaean world; it ranked for him, we remember, with Egyptian Thebes.[1] So with some flourish of trumpets, no less a personage than Adolf Furtwängler of the Berlin Museum, set out to excavate Orchomenos. But it is also the easiest thing in the world "to find what you are *not* looking for". The German excavators found no Knossos at Orchomenos; no palace, no frescos, no painted pottery, even, worth speaking of; instead, a strange, monotonous, drearily barbaric settlement, of great antiquity but slow advancement. Only at a quite late stage and as an outpost in alien territory, had some chieftain of the Mycenaean *régime* planted himself here in a blockhouse which could not be found, and built for posterity rather than for his contemporaries one gigantic beehive-tomb of the same type as those at Mycenae. The German excavation was rather hurriedly shut down, and for many years only one instalment of the results was published.[2] It was left for others to follow up what in fact was the most important discovery in continental Greece since Schliemann's at Mycenae and Tiryns, the extent and the history of a non-Aegean, non-contagious culture, which had, however, the characteristically negative function of interposing an impenetrable obstacle to the northward spread of the Mycenaean culture, except in a few precarious footholds along the seaboard of northern Greece. The first intelligible account of this whole affair is a paper on Minyan pottery by Sir John Forsdyke in 1914.[3] And only gradually were other consequences realized. The contrast of quality between the Mycenaean civilization of the Mainland south of the Isthmus and the Minoan civilization of Crete was eventually seen as the result of the impact of Minoan influence on the Minyan sphere. This was first interpreted as a colonization of the

[1] *I* 381.

[2] *Orchomenos* I (Bulle), 1907; II (Kunze), 1931; III, 1934.

[3] *JHS* XXXIV (1914), pp. 126ff. See A. J. B. Wace, "Middle and Late Helladic pottery", in Ἐπιτύμβιον Χρ. Τσούντα (1941), pp. 354ff.

Argolid from Minoan Crete; the Minoan colonists had to fight their way even into the southern margin of this Minyan sphere of influence, and to fortify themselves against its hostility in the great castles of Tiryns, Mycenae and the "Pelasgic Walls" of Athens; they had made good their conquests only at the cost of considerable modification of the culture which they brought with them, and eventually of a disastrous breach between the continentalized descendants and the Cretan motherland, which brought the seapower of Knossos to its downfall at the close of the fifteenth century; but this disaster made possible that liberation of the pent-up energies of the mainland populations of which the Achaean Confederacy of the twelfth century was the now almost historical creation. Later the idea that Minoan civilization was propagated not colonially but culturally gained ground, but that did not alter the fact that its character was determined and its sphere limited by the Minyan culture of its pupils. None of this, however, was immediately apparent. For the moment, there was disillusionment; if the origin of the legends was to be sought where the monuments were to be found, what was the predicament of the enquirer if the wrong sort of monuments were turned up? Schliemann's "Burnt City" had totally failed to answer expectations of the civilized and powerful Troy of King Priam—and this was one reason why people were prepared to look elsewhere for a satisfactory tomb of Hector. What was to be done with the Minyan Argo, and with the pre-Trojan warfare of central Greece, in face of dug-outs and middens like those of archaeological Orchomenos?

But this was not all. Equally surprising and even more destructive discoveries were being made during the same years in Thessaly, and indeed all over north-eastern Greece, this time mainly by Greek and British excavators with less anxiety about finding the right things. As early as 1884 painted pottery had been reported from the surface of some of the flat-topped mounds which are numerous in the Thessalian plain.[1] In 1886 one of these mounds, near Volo, had been found to have a rather late "beehive tomb" intruded into its steep side;[2] and this put everyone on the wrong track. For it seemed as if it was only a question of time before the Pelasgian Argos of the north would yield the same kind of results as the Peloponnesian

[1] H. Lolling, *Ath. Mitt.* IX (1884), pp. 99 ff.
[2] *Ath. Mitt.* XI (1886), pp. 435 ff.; XII (1887), pp. 136 ff.

Argolis. Once again international politics took a hand in the archaeological game; it was not until after the comic-opera war of 1897 and the closer watch kept over the relations between Greeks and Turks, that excavation was practicable even for Greeks in Thessaly. But the Thessalian corollaries of the Aeolic theory about the *Iliad* made temptation irresistible. From 1901 to 1910 every year saw fresh mounds opened, and always with the same results, which were summarized in the stout volume of Tsountas in 1908[1] and more fully explained in 1912 in the *Prehistoric Thessaly* of Wace and Thompson, who were greatly aided by the contemporary work on Serbian, Bulgarian and especially Roumanian sites. Later still, the entrenchments of Salonica in the first world war more than made amends for the interruption of these studies which the war had caused.[2] For, so far from yielding the archaeological counterparts of the displaced legends of Achilles and Agamemnon, the upshot was that until the very close of the Bronze Age and the latest days of Mycenaean decline, Thessaly and indeed all northern Greece had nothing to do with the Aegean.[3] Before the Minyan barbarism spread over central Greece, these regions had been occupied by southward extensions of modes of life which were at home in the middle Danube and on the South Russian steppe. When that Minyan obstacle grew—and at its greatest extent its south front was in north-eastern Peloponnese, and its northern wall within the limits of Thessaly itself—these inland continental cultures persisted in the rear of it; and eventual exploration of the Pagasaean seaboard by seafaring pioneers from the South Aegean had barely begun, when the Mycenaean *débâcle* occurred in the twelfth century.

Consequently what the archaeological exploration of Thessaly seemed to demonstrate was that there was not only no material counterpart to the proto-Aeolic *Achilleid* or those inter-tribal struggles which it was supposed to commemorate, but in fact a state of things which precluded there any such long folk-memory as that theory required. What on the other hand was most unexpectedly explained was a state of things in which any early *catalogue of allies* of a King of Mycenae could not be expected to have accurate information about places or peoples north of the Spercheius valley; but in which any later revision attempted not earlier than the thirteenth

---

[1] Αἱ προιστορικαὶ ἀκροπόλεις Διμηνίου καὶ Σέσκλου.

[2] *BSA* XXIII (1918–19), pp. 1–103.   [3] See p. 272 below.

century and not later than the twelfth would have in the first place to take account of contemporary extension of the northern frontier of experience; in fact to append to the older document a rather confused (perhaps even inaccurate) sketch of the political divisions of Thessaly, such as is actually appended to the *Catalogue* of Agamemnon's Allies in the second book of the *Iliad*. It is not surprising, then, to find that even in Cauer's second edition, published in 1909, less ardent hopes are entertained of the results of the displacements of legends, or even of the value of the pre-Trojan phase of Aeolic epic in Thessaly; and that since 1910, advocates of the "displacement" theory (as in Carl Rothe's *Die Ilias als Dichtung*, published in that year) begin to play with the notion, originally due to Georg Finsler in 1908,[1] that the plot of the *Wrath of Achilles* has its prototype (for how could anything in the *Iliad* be original for a critic who knew his business?) not in a pre-Trojan Thessaly, but in the story of Meleager as told in illustration of it by Phoenix in the *Embassy*. As Meleager came from Aetolia, his country was at all events safe for a while from the ravages of archaeologists. And yet, and yet ... No soil is sacred to the sapper. By 1911 the *Wrath*, so far from being one of the oldest elements in the poem, was being interpreted in J. van Leeuwen's *Commentationes Homericae* as an original idea of the late composer of our actual *Iliad*, a literary device to give dramatic unity to miscellaneous materials for epic. And in 1916 Wilamowitz was beginning to hark back to the long antiquated notion that the *Iliad* really deserves its name;[2] that it refers to a siege of Ilion in the Troad, after all.

A line of enquiry quite different from Fick's search for an Aeolic Homer was inaugurated almost at the same moment by Wolfgang Helbig, whose *Homeric Epos illustrated from the Monuments* appeared in 1884.[3] It reached a second edition in 1887 and a French translation soon after, and it long remained the best book of general reference in what we may justly call "Homeric Archaeology". Helbig was one of the ablest of the pupils whom Gerhard and the other founders of the German Archaeological Institute in Rome had produced. Concurrently with large contributions to classical archaeology and art criticism, he had followed closely the work of Pigorini

[1] *Homer aus dem Erläuterungswerke.*
[2] *Die Ilias und Homer.*
[3] *Das homerische Epos aus den Denkmälern erläutert.*

and other explorers of the prehistoric antiquities of Italy, and his essay on *Italians in the Po Valley* in 1879 had been a landmark in the application of their discoveries to the ethnology of the peninsula. Between the completion of the first and second volumes of his *Essays on the History of early Italian Civilization and Art*, he paid a visit to Olympia, then newly excavated, and was impressed with the importance of the early bronzes and other portable objects found there as evidence for the stage of civilization which the first Greek colonists in the eighth century had brought with them from the mother country to South Italy and other regions of the West. Accepting provisionally the traditional date for the Homeric poems at the close of the ninth century, he realized the importance of a clear conception of the civilization which they presumed; and he set himself, while writing for the official publication of the bronzes of Olympia, to enquire what archaeological materials existed which might serve to illustrate the "Homeric" civilization, which he regarded as the "indispensable foundation" for his projected examination of that of the western colonies. Realizing that modern scholars were approaching Homeric problems with a traditional predisposition to assume that classical analogies were applicable, he was at some pains to show how different Homeric civilization was, in many ways, from that of historic Greece; and himself assuming, as everyone did assume until the publication of Salomon Reinach's *Le Mirage Oriental* in 1893,[1] that it was mainly by adopting and transforming loans from older and for the most part Oriental cultures, that Greek genius had created the Hellenic civilization of classical times, he set out to take stock of the available indications as to the character of those loans, in the quite reasonable belief that the earlier one could find illustrations of them, the less completely would they be found to have been already Hellenized, and the more clearly would they betray what their chief sources were.

Among such sources, the newly discovered culture represented by Schliemann's finds in the Shaft Graves at Mycenae and similar objects from other sites in the Aegean and the Levant were of course conspicuous. That he should have acquiesced in the common assumption that because they were pre-Hellenic and yet evidently the product of a civilized people, they must owe much to the traditional craftsmanship of the Phoenicians, was very natural; and indeed in a

---

[1] *L'Anthropologie* 4, pp. 539–732.

later essay *La Question Mycénienne*[1] he advocated this explanation of Mycenaean culture, long after the proof was already complete that it was essentially indigenous to the South Aegean region, and that what it owed to Egyptian civilization, it had borrowed actively and independently, not through Phoenician intermediaries. It was an unlucky accident that Milchhöfer's brilliant anticipation[2] that the fountain head of the Mycenaean civilization was to be sought not in the Levant but in Crete, only came into Helbig's hands after the first half of the manuscript of *Das homerische Epos* had been sent to the printer; and he confesses in his *Preface* that he was in two minds whether to recall and revise it in the light of Milchhöfer's suggestions. It was indeed unfortunate that he did not do so; still more unfortunate that a second edition was wanted before he had been able to make adequate study of Schliemann's book on *Tiryns*, which appeared in 1886; and that meanwhile the publication in 1885 of the third volume of Perrot and Chipiez's great *History of Art in Antiquity*, dealing with Phoenicia and Cyprus, supplemented by many striking illustrations the alternative explanation of Homeric works of art to which Helbig himself already inclined. Consequently, though he was at great pains to hold even the balance between the theories of Phoenician and of Aegean sources for the culture of the Homeric Age, the scales were at the moment loaded in favour of the Phoenicians, and also of the later limits of date for Homeric experience generally. And since in the years that followed his essay became the standard textbook of the whole subject, while the progress of Mycenaean exploration was so rapid that he was himself quite unable to keep pace with its results, he must be regarded as one of the chief popularizers of what may be described as the "Mycenae-and-Tiryns" conception of the scope of the new discoveries, and one of the causes for the relative neglect of the wider and (as it turned out) sounder interpretation which had originated with Milchhöfer.

In another direction, also, Helbig's work had an immediate effect which was not wholly undesigned. The good is proverbially the enemy of the best. What was most urgently needed, at the moment, by the advocates of the traditional belief in an Ionian Homer, was an

[1] *Mémoires de l'Académie des Inscriptions et Belles-Lettres* XXXV, 2 (1896), pp. 291–373.
[2] p. 136 above.

authoritative description of the culture of the Ionian cities at the traditional date for that Ionian poet. Only with that pendant picture, to be compared with the splendid glimpse which Schliemann had revealed of a pre-Ionian world, could sound conclusions be formed as to the applicability of Homeric descriptions to the product of either. But the Turk sat tight, as he sat tight for so long, on the great Ionian cities, and as he sat tight on Knossos till the Cretan Revolt of 1896. Even the few early graves from Samos were not opened by Boehlau till 1894[1]. The earlier temple of Artemis at Ephesus was first explored by Hogarth only in 1904.[2] Miletus was not excavated till 1899.[3] Rhodes lay fallow from Biliotti's excavations in 1871 till the Danish expedition in the first years of the twentieth century and the work of the Italians since their military occupation of it in 1912.[4] Smyrna and Chios waited some forty years longer, and other of the traditional birthplaces of the poet are almost untouched today.[5] Next best, as Helbig saw, was to make use of early Hellenic elements in the culture of Southern and Central Italy, and of the votive offerings at Olympia which might be presumed to come from many districts, as provisional indications of what might be expected from Ionian sites when the time came to explore them. For this kind of reconstruction of an hypothetical Ionia, Helbig certainly did much; so much, indeed, that the provisional and inferential quality of his conclusions tended to escape notice, and defenders of the Ionian Homer argued as if the archaeological proof of their theory was complete, and consequently Schliemann's Mycenae and all its works might be set aside as merely "pre-Homeric". Especially in Italian archaeology, these provisional ideas of early Ionian art had a great vogue; even after Boehlau's review of the whole question in the light of his identification, by excavation on one Ionian site, of at least one of the Ionian schools of vase painting, phrases were habitually employed about "Chalcidian", "Milesian", and other Ionian styles,

[1] *Aus ionischen und italischen Nekropolen*, 1898.

[2] *Excavations at Ephesus: the archaic Artemisia*, 1908.

[3] T. Wiegand, *Ergebnisse der Ausgrabungen und Untersuchungen seit dem Jahre* 1899, 1906–36.

[4] Ch. Blinkenberg and K. F. Kinch, *Exploration archéologique de Rhodes* I–VI (1903–12): *Lindiaca* I–IV (1917–26): *Clara Rhodos* (1928–).

[5] Since the war Turkish archaeologists have been active, and an Anglo-Turkish Expedition has excavated at Smyrna. Chios has so far yielded very little between the Bronze Age and the seventh century.

which did not betray the fact that these great centres of craftsmanship had not yet been explored.

A characteristic instance of the current reformulation of the Ionian theory is the *Homeric Enquiries*[1] of Ulrich von Wilamowitz-Moellendorf, which was published in 1884, just too late for Helbig's first edition but in ample time to influence his views in the second. In form this book was an examination of the structure of the *Odyssey*, by the methods of Wilamowitz's own master Kirchhoff. It was dedicated, appropriately and significantly, to Wellhausen, a leading figure in that "higher criticism" of the Hebrew Scriptures which had owed so much in its inception to the Homeric *Prolegomena* of Wolf. But it included also a careful examination of all the major problems of Homeric criticism as they presented themselves in 1884; and it is instructive that about the material civilization of the Age either of the Heroes or of the Poet, it contains hardly a word. The "gigantic ruins of the citadels look down from the hills of the mother country today, as in the days of the Ionians who had fled overseas before the city-wrecking Dorians" and they were as devoid of significance for Wilamowitz as for the Dorians themselves. The culture which they represent is for him "enigmatical", less significant than that of Egypt or Mesopotamia, and as remote from the Homeric order of things. Possibly another generation of scholars might read that riddle; no serious scholar would insult the memory of Achilles or Helen by tactless allusions to lake-dwellings or the borrowed plumage of Phoenician art, any more than a student of Attic drama really figures the Phaedra of Euripides in a tragic mask and stilted shoes. This may be literary criticism, but it was hardly scientific or humanist. "These finds", as he goes on, "have little or nothing to do with the Greece which our epic describes; as little"—and this too is noteworthy, in view of the course of events—"as the Middle High German poems about Dietrich with the monuments of Theodoric at Ravenna." They are simply "pre-Homeric", and therefore irrelevant. On the other hand, the culture of the sixth, perhaps even of the seventh century, as revealed in Italian tomb-contents, has been profitably brought to bear on the epic, above all by Helbig's recent book; *this* kind of archaeology may rank with the evidence of language, metre and mythology as legitimate commentary on Homer. Helbig has avoided dates; but his results tally with those of the other legiti-

[1] *Homerische Untersuchungen.*

mate methods, and confirm a late and Ionian origin. There may be older remnants among the more recent texture of the poems; but what is archaic is conventional, the naturalism of eye-witness is modern. Homer must be studied in the light of Hesiod and the elegiac poets, not of Mycenae and Tiryns. Enough has been said here to show how a scholar of the first rank regarded Helbig's contribution to Homeric studies; and Helbig, on his part, though not professing any competence in literary criticism, expressed in his second edition his complete concurrence in Wilamowitz's presentation of the "Homeric Question" generally. This was very comforting to the literary scholars, who had been a trifle rattled by Schliemann's spade-work and by Gladstone's insistence that when Homer spoke of Golden Mycenae, he meant what he said and described what he knew, not the deserted ruin of which Thucydides and Pausanias wrote. Richard Jebb, for example, in a brilliant little handbook to Homer, which came out in 1887,[1] devoted two whole pages to joyful demonstration that the whole of the Palace of Tiryns was really Byzantine, because a Byzantine church had been built on top of it. These pages[2] were neatly excised in later editions, when the misconception had been cleared up by its author, but a long *Appendix* was retained, partly directed against Schliemann and his architectural adviser, Dörpfeld, partly against J. H. Middleton's identification of the Tirynthian and the Odyssean house.[3] The arrangements of the Tirynthian palace, Jebb insisted, had not and could not have anything to do with those of the house of Odysseus, which he expressly described as "the prototype of the later Greek house of the historical age". As we shall see later,[4] it took another twenty years or so to realize that Jebb's comparison between the Homeric and the Hellenic house rested, not on archaeological evidence, for there was none on either side at the time when he wrote, but on one signal

[1] *Homer: an Introduction to the Iliad and Odyssey.*

[2] pp. 176–7. In the 5th ed. (1894) his concession is still half-hearted. "The advocates of a 'prehistoric' date are fully entitled to all the benefit of such a recantation. If the question of the age of the remains is ever to be settled, it can only be settled by persons specially versed in ancient wallbuilding. But the impression left on most minds by the discussion, so far as it has yet gone, will be that there is ample room for disagreement, even among the most skilful" (p. 177).

[3] *JHS* VII (1886), pp. 161 ff.

[4] pp. 165 ff. below.

group of mistranslations in the *Odyssey*, and another in the text of Vitruvius.

The great authority, however, of Wilamowitz in Germany and of Jebb among ourselves, restored the large majority of literary critics to their dogmatic slumbers; and the excavators had better things to do than to disturb them. Only Leaf, in a notable *Introduction* to the English translation of C. Schuchhardt's book on Schliemann's excavations,[1] outlined an identification of Homer's Achaeans, not indeed with the builders, but with the last occupants of the Mycenaean palaces; a thesis which was worked out independently and with greater elaboration by Tsountas and Manatt in their book on Mycenaean civilization published in Athens in 1893.[2]

Schliemann died, rather unexpectedly, in December of 1890, on the eve of the further excavations at Hissarlik which in fact determined, among other disputed points, that the Sixth City, not the Second or Burnt City, was the Trojan counterpart of the Mycenaean settlements in Southern Greece, though never more than a rather barbarous neighbour of them and only superficially affected by their culture; and also that the Sixth City,[3] like the Second, had perished by violence, had then lain ruinous for a while, then been occupied by a new people of alien culture, and only after a long while had become once again superficially Hellenized from the Aeolic colonies of the coast and inshore islands further south. These new data were announced promptly in outline in 1893 and 1894, but the full details were not published until 1902,[4] by which time the whole question stood in a rather different context.

[1] *Schliemann's Excavations*, trans. Eugénie Sellers, 1891.
[2] p. 135, note 1.
[3] The Sixth City here is Troy VI and VIIa of later reckoning.
[4] Wm. Dörpfeld, *Troja und Ilion*.

Chapter Eight

THE EPIC OF THE SPADE:
2. THE HOMERIC WORLD

I N the ten years which separated Schliemann's death from the winter of 1899–1900, when the political liberation of Crete made it possible for Arthur Evans to begin the long-hoped-for excavation of the Cretan Knossos, research and controversy in Aegean archaeology dealt mainly with four outstanding questions. The first was the question of date. This had been fairly well indicated before Schliemann's time, by the occurrence on an inscribed scarab of Amenhotep III of the Eighteenth Egyptian Dynasty in one of the Mycenaean graves at Ialysus. But though this scarab clearly could not be of later date than the tomb in which it was found, it might have been already ancient when it was placed in it, an "heirloom", to use a phrase of the advocates of a "lowest possible dating" for Mycenaean things. But by 1890 Flinders Petrie had not only multiplied many-fold the evidence for Mycenaean borrowings of Egyptian objects, always of late Eighteenth or Nineteenth Dynasty workmanship, but had discovered the conclusive counterpart to this proof—Mycenaean objects buried in Egyptian tombs of Dynasties XVIII and XIX. As these objects in turn could not be later than the tombs which held them, it followed that, as neither the Mycenaean period was later than the Egyptian nor the Egyptian period than the Mycenaean, they must be accepted as contemporary. This conclusion was abundantly verified by the excavation of the palace of Amenhotep IV at Tell-el-Amarna, effected in 1889 though not published till 1894; and it was supplemented in 1893 by a much earlier synchronism between certain

157

deposits of the date of Dynasty XII found by Petrie in 1890 at Kahun in Egypt and the contents of the Cretan cave at Kamares and Cretan tombs contemporary with it. This extended the outlines of an historical chronology of Aegean civilization back to the nineteenth or twentieth century, as long before the traditional date of the Trojan War as that war was before the days of Alexander the Great.[1] In England, thanks mainly to the advocacy of "latest possible" dates by influential members of the staff of the British Museum, these synchronisms were accepted reluctantly and gradually. Leaf in his introduction to Schuchhardt's *Schliemann's Excavations* and his *Companion to the Iliad* in 1891–2 was, however, more venturesome; and in 1895 Andrew Lang's *Homer and the Epic* frankly accepted the Shaft Graves as dated between 1500 and 1300 B.C., and was prepared to place the personal Homer "conjecturally" between 1200 and 1000 B.C., within easy folk-memory, that is, of the generation which occupied them. In Germany the Greek Histories of Eduard Meyer and Julius Beloch and the second edition of Busolt, all published in 1893, accepted the Eighteenth Dynasty date for the climax of the culture represented by Mycenae and Tiryns, and discussed the whole question of the antecedents of the Homeric poems with corresponding freedom from chronological limitations; they did not, however, seriously question current theories as to the late date and gradual growth of the Homeric poems.

The second question was the origin of the newly discovered culture. Was it, as Helbig for example thought, essentially an early phase of those Phoenician industries whose later masterpieces, metal bowls engraved and embossed in mixed Oriental styles, were distributed over the ancient world from Nineveh and Cyprus[2] to Latium and Etruria? Or was it indigenous, and if so, by what earlier stages had it reached and passed its climax? For the marks of decadence were obvious amid all the wealth and splendour of Mycenae. Here the answer had already been given in principle: positively, by Dümmler's demonstration of its adolescent phases in the Cyclades, connecting the Mycenaean culture backwards with something akin to that of Hissarlik, and by Milchhöfer's inference from the geographical distribution of the engraved "island-stones" to the probability that

[1] See Tsountas and Manatt, *The Mycenaean Age*, pp. 317–21 for evidence available in 1897, and J. D. S. Pendlebury, *The Archaeology of Crete* (1939), pp. 143–6 and 222–5, for summaries with references.   [2] Pl. 7–6.

its principal focus was in Crete; negatively, by the discovery that in Cyprus Mycenaean culture was intrusive and only arrived at a quite late stage during the fourteenth century, whereas, if the cradle of this culture had been in Phoenicia, Cyprus ought to have received it at a much earlier stage than the Aegean.[1] Landmarks in the interpretation of these and similar discoveries are Salomon Reinach's *Le Mirage Oriental*, Beloch's *Greek History* (both in 1893), Evans's *The Eastern Question in Anthropology* in 1896,[2] his *Further Discoveries of Cretan and Aegean Script* in 1897,[3] and his *Mycenaean Tree and Pillar Cult* in 1901. On the archaeological side, the crucial instance was provided by the British excavations at Phylakopi in Melos between 1895 and 1898,[4] where the whole series of phases hitherto known only from different localities was found in regular stratification within the walls of a single settlement.

The third problem, how so civilized and extensive a culture was maintained and administered, was solved in 1894 by Arthur Evans's discovery not only of a highly developed system of hieroglyphic writing on seal stones of the "island-stone" class and other objects, mostly from Crete, but even of a linear script derived from the other. This script was demonstrably itself one of the sources of the Cypriote syllabary, which was afterwards shown to go back to the Mycenaean phase in that island,[5] and it was believed to be a source also of the alphabets of Phoenicia, Lycia and historic Greece. Here was a new and revolutionary fact, with which Homeric criticism had henceforward to reckon. Wolf had in fact been mistaken in supposing that writing was unknown as early as the time when the poems were composed, whatever the date of their composition short of the twentieth century B.C. There remained, fourthly, the question; what had brought this original, widespread, and long sustained culture to such utter

---

[1] pp. 129–37 above.

[2] Delivered to the British Association at Liverpool.

[3] *JHS* XVII (1897), pp. 327–95.

[4] *Excavations at Phylakopi, BSA Suppl. Papers* 4 (1904).

[5] Myres wrote a note on the first inscribed clay tablet from Cyprus, found by P. Dikaios at Enkomi, in *Antiquity* XXVII (1953), p. 105. Dikaios published an important fragment of a second, *ibid.*, pp. 233–7, which suggests that the script was not derived directly from either Linear A or Linear B, but from a different and probably older source (Ernst Sittig, *Zur Entzifferung der minoisch-kyprischen Tafel von Enkomi* in *Minos* IV (1956), pp. 33–42).

disaster, and how was the gulf to be filled which separated its last days from the dawn of classical Hellenism? Greek tradition knew of a *Coming of the Dorians* and assigned it on genealogical grounds to the close of the twelfth century. A generation earlier, on similar evidence, stood the *Coming* of the conquerors of Thessaly and Cadmeian Boeotia. But both of these were subsequent to the Trojan War. Was the Trojan War then fought between the last generation of the Mycenaean Age and an outpost of adjacent barbarism? Or was the process more gradual? For in Homeric tradition, well supported by Greek folk-memory in classical times, the walls of Priam's Troy had been built by Laomedon, only two generations before the war; in Priam's young days the Phrygians had been still extending their occupation into the interior, up the Sangarius river; they had their counterparts in the Brygoi of Macedonia and Epirus; and moreover Pelops himself, the grandfather of Agamemnon, had been the founder of a new dynasty, displacing the ancient Perseids at Mycenae and the Tyndarids in Laconia, and it was from the older royal house that his grandsons married their disastrous heiresses, Helen and Clytemnestra, as Odysseus married their cousin Penelope. Was it accident that the great Aeacid house and the fathers of Diomedes and Nestor were newcomers without known human pedigree, divine-born men "dropped from the clouds", as it were, among alien folk whom they ruled absolutely, as a man owns his sheep and his dog? And how did it come about that Pelops too was in some sense a Phrygian, and his father Tantalus a prince in Thrace? The inference seemed to be that Achaeans and Trojans alike were invaders and conquerors of quite recent arrival, about two generations before their great quarrel and only about four generations before the Achaeans were invaded and conquered in their turn by Thessalians and Dorians out of the North Western highlands.[1]

Both Leaf in 1892 and Andrew Lang in 1893 saw the significance of all this. "Greek tradition and belief", says the latter, "without any variation, assigned Mycenae and Tiryns to the pre-Dorian Achaean age initiated by adventurers from Phrygia".[2] But how had they come? Schuchhardt, working on Schliemann's material, and W. M. Ramsay[3] and others, impressed by the guardian lions carved on tombs in

[1] See also Myres, pp. 297–346.
[2] *Homer and the Epic*, p. 359.
[3] *JHS* IX (1888), pp. 369 ff.

Asiatic Phrygia and on the town gate of Mycenae, followed the suggestion of Thucydides, that "Pelops came from Asia with much wealth, among needy men", and created Golden Mycenae thus.[1] Tsountas, more familiar with the material evidence and with the succession of early and late at Mycenae, equated the Achaeans, as in Homeric tradition, with a recent and not very prolonged phase of Mycenaean culture, supervening on an earlier and aboriginal phase which he assigned provisionally to the Danaoi. Again following Greek tradition about the relationship between Danaos and Aigyptos, he interpreted this legend in the light of the recognized borrowings of Mycenaean art from Egyptian.[2] Attention was recalled to the occurrence, first noticed a generation before by de Rougé, of names resembling those of Achaeans, Danaans and other Aegean peoples in the lists of the Sea Raiders who harried the Egyptian and Syrian coasts between 1230 and 1190, and Eduard Meyer and Andrew Lang independently developed this consideration in its Homeric context.[3] Menelaos, Odysseus and Paris, too, had made piratical journeys around the Levant, according to Greek tradition in the same generation as the Sea Raiders whom Rameses III defeated. A glance at a distribution map of Mycenaean sites will

[1] I, 9. For the Phrygian lions (c. 700 B.C.) see H. Bossert, *Altanatolien*, 1023.

[2] Μυκῆναι, pp. 197–98.

[3] The expert advice of Egyptologists proliferated errors. Flinders Petrie came to Greece in 1891 "to apply the dating which had been found at Gurob to the Mykenaean discoveries". He quotes his report: "The epoch of grand tombs, such as the great treasuries, would be about 1400 to 1200 B.C.; the splendid cups of gold from Vapheio, which show such high art, being about 1200. Then decadence set in, and is markedly shown in the great finds of Schliemann of the graves in the circle of the acropolis; these I date about 1150 by various points, mainly the colour of some green glazed things. Then, about 1000 B.C., came in the impressed glass ornaments, as they are nearly always along with ribbed Egyptian beads of 1000–800 B.C. The tombs of Menidi, Spata, Nauplia and those lately found at Mykenae, all belong to this age. The Doric migration broke up this civilization there, and a date has just turned up for the 'dipylon vases' from two glazed lions in a recent find which cannot be earlier than 650 B.C. As the vases cannot be later, this fixes their date very closely." He comments on this, "It may be worth recording how far matters had advanced in 1891, before the swamping effect of the Cretan discoveries. There seems little to alter in the outline reached then, though forty years have since passed." (*Seventy Years in Archaeology*, p. 130.)

show the significance of these Levantine connexions of Achaean Greece.[1]

We have already seen that pure scholarship and literary criticism had very little use for "external" considerations of this kind. The more insistently archaeologists and historians confronted customary interpretations of Homer with an Heroic Age of wars and wanderings, dated and authenticated by contemporary documents of the thirteenth and twelfth centuries, the more strictly did the literary critics entrench themselves behind their Ionian Homer, and protest that Rameses and the Lords of the North had nothing to do with him or themselves. In two particular directions, however, the new material could not be wholly ignored; and as they happen to concern, the one the main subject matter of the *Iliad*, and the other the setting of three principal episodes of the *Odyssey*, it will be convenient to discuss them here, even at the expense of some anticipation of historical order, as illustrations of how much was possible now that Schliemann and Helbig had shown the way. One of these two questions is that of the plan of the Homeric House (and especially of the House of Odysseus); the other, that of the principal features of Homeric armour. Both controversies were opened by the claim that the newly found Mycenaean culture offered more exact and complete archaeological counterparts to Homeric descriptions than did the Hellenic even in its earliest known stages. In both the defenders of the traditional view have been obliged to modify their case considerably in the process of restating it; in particular they have had to admit that the excavators have forced them to surrender traditional interpretations of the Homeric text which had arisen through the purely literary error of mistranslation. In both, on the other hand, later archaeological discoveries have gone far to provide the terms of an intermediate solution; for though mature Mycenaean and mature Hellenic usages are sharply contrasted, the chronological interval between them has been shown to be sufficient to permit of progressive changes away from the one and toward the other, of a transitional period, and even of a possible period of overlap, with earlier and later usages co-existent.

[1] Such maps go out of date as they are made. See, however, F. H. Stubbings, *Mycenaean Pottery from the Levant* (1951) Map III, which shows the distribution of Myc. IIIB pottery, now supplemented by James Mellaart in *AS* V (1955), pp. 80 ff.

It will be remembered that Schliemann's excavation of a prehistoric Palace at Tiryns in 1884–5 offered early and inevitable challenge to the traditional interpretation of the house of Odysseus. Difficulties in accommodating the episodes as described in the *Odyssey* to the plan of an Hellenic dwelling-house had been perceived in antiquity, and ingenious plans had been drawn by modern scholars to solve them. But until 1885 almost all these plans had been based either on actual Hellenic houses familiar to the commentator, or (since the Revival of Learning) on the description of the Hellenic type of house by Vitruvius, or rather on a conventional but inaccurate rendering of it. Chief among these difficulties were, first, the position of the women's quarters; were they in the rear of the hall or main living room of the house, and entered by a door at its inner end? Or were they independent of the hall and accessible otherwise? Secondly, do the two thresholds mentioned in the poem, of stone and of wood respectively, indicate the existence of two separate doors (as required by one explanation of the women's quarters), or were they both parts of the structure of a single front door opening on the vestibule, portico and courtyard? Thirdly, where were the seats of honour in the hall—at the inner end as in a College Hall or around a central hearth? This question was obviously involved in that of a second door, and led to the belief that the wooden threshold formed part of a raised platform or dais. The main stages of the controversy have been briefly as follows.

Just before Schliemann's discovery, the whole question had been discussed afresh by Percy Gardner, whose conclusions maintained what may be called for short the Hellenic view.[1] This was published in the same volume as Jebb's first attack on the Bronze Age interpretation of Homer.[2] A different view was suggested by E. W. Godwin four years later, when he drew attention to analogies between the Homeric description and the courtyard houses of Egypt under Dynasty XVIII.[3] As soon as Schliemann found the palace at Tiryns, Dörpfeld, the professional architect engaged on the excavation, recognized the resemblance between the plan, with its courtyard, portico and vestibule, its great hall with central hearth and louvre

---

[1] "The Palaces of Homer", *JHS* III (1882), pp. 264 ff.

[2] "The ruins of Hissarlik, and their relation to the Iliad", *ibid.*, pp. 185 ff.

[3] "The Greek Home according to Homer", *The Nineteenth Century*, No. 112, June 1886, pp. 914 ff.

roof, and its bathroom reached from the vestibule, and the building described in the *Odyssey*; and he identified the separate suite of rooms, secluded from the main courtyard, with the women's quarters.[1] The same view was adopted immediately by J. H. Middleton,[2] by a number of other scholars, and with some modifications by Leaf in the second edition of his *Iliad*.[3] But in the same volume as Middleton's article, and again more emphatically in the following year in his *Homer*, Jebb reaffirmed the Hellenic view, and repudiated vigorously the notion that the ruins of Tiryns either did or could throw any light on Homeric architecture.[4] He was followed by Hentze in his edition of the *Odyssey*, by the French architect Chipiez in Perrot's *History of Art in Antiquity*, of which the seventh volume (*La Grèce de l'épopée*) appeared in 1898,[5] and by the American T. D. Seymour in his *Life in the Homeric Age* as late as 1907. Meanwhile the discovery of other palaces, at Mycenae, on the Acropolis at Athens, at Phylakopi, and in a modified form at Gla in the Copais marshes, showed that the Tirynthian type of structure was characteristic of the Mycenaean mainland and islands generally; but also that the arrangement of its main parts was customarily adapted to the peculiarities of the sites. In particular, the secondary suite of rooms might be anywhere, provided that it communicated independently with the courtyard, and not through the hall.

In 1900 I submitted some literary evidence in favour of the Tirynthian theory,[6] especially the discovery that the preposition ἀνά in the *Odyssey*, when used of movements of persons in the

[1] *Tiryns*, Chapter 5.

[2] "A suggested restoration of the Great Hall in the Palace of Tiryns", *JHS* VII (1886), pp. 161 ff.

[3] Appendix C of Vol. I.

[4] "The Homeric House in relation to the remains at Tiryns", *JHS* VII (1886), pp. 170 ff.

[5] pp. 79–104. He had a second door at the back leading to the women's quarter, but he made large concessions to Mycenaean parallels. In Vol. VI (*La Grèce primitive*), pp. 701–6, in 1894 the conclusion had been reached: "L'examen que nous avons fait des grandes lignes du plan a dû laisser l'impression que la concordance est réelle, malgré de légères différences de détail." The main difference noted resulted from a mistaken belief that the "Little Megaron" at Tiryns was the women's suite.

[6] "On the Plan of the Homeric House", *JHS* XX (1900), pp. 128 ff. This was an epoch-making article, both for its expert handling of both kinds of evidence and for its wider implications.

Homeric hall, means *outwards* in relation to the doorway, and κατά *inwards*,[1] and that διέκ was never used of a person first entering and then leaving the hall, but only of movement *across* it. These usages incidentally demonstrated that the wooden threshold formed part of the same main door as the stone threshold. This discovery was accepted at once by Monro in his edition of the *Odyssey* in 1901,[2] and in the main its corollary also, that the Homeric house was Tirynthian, not Hellenic; but Monro was much influenced also by analogies with the houses of the Heroic Age of Scandinavia described in 1889 and 1894 by Gudmundsson and elaborated later by him and Kalund. The discovery of a related but earlier and more elaborate type of hall in the Cretan Palaces at Knossos and Phaistos gave Guy Dickins the occasion for supplementary observations tending towards a reconciliation of the traditional view with the archaeological evidence.[3] Noack simultaneously, in accordance with the prevalent German mode, employed the same archaeological evidence to support a literary dissection of the Homeric narrative into an earlier version, in which the architectural preconceptions were Tirynthian, and a later in which they were Hellenic; and added some ingenious speculations, partly based on the discovery of primitive oval huts at Orchomenos, about the origin and development of the Mycenaean and Cretan types of architecture from a single living room.[4] The Mycenaean character was once more emphasized by S. E. Bassett, in a valuable retrospect of the whole discussion, which added some new suggestions about the main corridor and the position of Penelope's rooms.[5] Meanwhile Ernest Gardner had made some interesting discoveries which took away the foundations from the Hellenic theory.[6] Actual Hellenic houses recently excavated at Delos, at Priene and elsewhere, quite failed to conform to the conventional rendering of the Vitruvian specification for an Hellenic house. The reason for this was that, through mistaken analogies with certain

[1] The editor cannot conceal her doubts about this usage of the prepositions ("Houses in the Odyssey", *CQ* V (1955), pp. 1 ff), but it is not an essential part of the argument.

[2] Appendix V of Vol. II, with references to the Icelandic houses.

[3] "Some points with regard to the Homeric House", *JHS* XXIII (1903), pp. 325 ff.

[4] *Homerische Paläste* (1903); cf. *Ovalhaus und Palast in Kreta* (1908).

[5] "The Palace of Odysseus", *AJA* XXIII (1919), pp. 288 ff.

[6] "The Greek House", *JHS* XXI (1901), pp. 293 ff.

houses at Pompeii which were in fact Italian rather than Greek, the words of Vitruvius had been merely mistranslated; and correctly construed their plain sense accurately described the essential features of the Hellenic houses at Delos and Priene, and the arrangements presupposed by domestic incidents described by Xenophon, Demosthenes and other Greek writers. Moreover it became evident that the Hellenic house, rightly understood, so far from reversing the arrangements of the Mycenaean house, was in fact best interpreted as a direct development from it, made possible, and indeed necessary, by the exigencies of crowded city life and by the circumstance that in a Greek city the menfolk spent most of their time away from home. Consequently the great hall, opening on to the courtyard, was reduced to a mere alcove among the living rooms which surrounded the court; the court and its living rooms became habitually occupied by the women; and so far from Greek women being secluded in a separate suite of rooms, it was only in spacious and well-appointed houses that the men had a room set apart for their special use, like the smoke-room or billiard-room of a Victorian mansion.

Consequently, the upshot of the whole controversy has been to assimilate the Homeric notions of the arrangement of a chief's house in the Heroic Age to those of a transitional phase in a long and evidently complex and variable adaptation of an inherited plan to current usage, and to suggest that the Homeric phase in this development stands early rather than late in this intermediate period between the Mycenaean and the Hellenic type.

[*Additional note.* Since the chronological order has already been broken it is convenient to consider here the last stage of the controversy.

The "Hellenic" plan has found a new advocate. L. R. Palmer rejects Myres's "Tirynthian" explanation as firmly as Jebb did, and proposes a sunk hall with porch and prodomos, and with a door at the back into a two-storey building; the women's quarters he puts in the upper floor, with storerooms underneath; a ladder descended from the upper floor into the λαύρη, which was also accessible from the hall by means of the *orsothyre* and from the courtyard into which it opened directly.[1] He does not, however, base this on Vitruvius, but on a sunken house type which was widely

[1] "The Homeric and the Indo-European House", *Trans. Phil. Soc.*, 1949, pp. 92 ff.

diffused over Asia and Europe from Neolithic times and seems to have made its latest appearance in the Scandinavian Hall. His philological arguments for the origin of the megaron house are valuable, but for the Homeric poems it is more reasonable to look, not to Neolithic Thessaly and Romano-British barns, but to Greece and Anatolia between 1300 and 600 B.C. Buildings of that period recently found have completed the resemblance of the Homeric plan to the Mycenaean and so far suggested no resemblance to post-Mycenaean buildings. A good private house at Mycenae, unusual in plan but made up of the essential parts (single room entered by a columned porch from a courtyard with ancillary rooms round), has given the first and only example of a Mycenaean megaron with a raised second door in one of the long walls.[1] In the *Odyssey* this door is not described as a typical feature, but is introduced as a surprise when the plot needs it; the atypical door at Mycenae is therefore very significant. A second requirement of the plot of the *Odyssey*, two doors in the *prodomos* leading on the one side to Penelope's rooms and on the other to the armoury, happens for various accidental reasons not to be found at Mycenae, Tiryns or Phylakopi. The two doors have now been found in the Palace at Messenian Pylos.[2] This magnificent building has a megaron with central hearth and four pillars, reached only through porch and anteroom. The central block is surrounded on three sides by storerooms, pantries, passages and an archive room and waiting room. The small court has a colonnade on one side, and a columned entrance, in line not with the megaron door but with one of its rows of columns. Stairs led to an upper storey. To judge from the plan in the latest preliminary report, it suggests an explanation of another Odyssean puzzle, the bedroom where Odysseus had built his bed round a growing olive tree. On the far side of the court at Pylos, and reached from the megaron only through the court, there is a small apartment of great magnificence, with its own little court behind (and presumably its own lavatory, though access to both lavatory and bathroom seem from the plan to be inconvenient). This is the position which before the excavation suggested itself for the olive tree bedroom, and a wing reached only by crossing the court is

[1] A. J. B. Wace, *Mycenae* (1949), pp. 91 ff., and "Notes on the Homeric House", *JHS* LXXI (1951), pp. 203 ff.
[2] C. W. Blegen, "The Palace of Nestor: Excavations of 1956", *AJA* 61 (1957), pp. 129 ff.; plan on Pl. 39, fig. 1.

more satisfactory than an isolated building.[1] In the post-Mycenaean period nothing comparable has been found. In the Protogeometric period there are oval cottages at Athens and at Smyrna;[2] the entrance was in the narrow end, but there is only one room and no porch. In the Geometric period rectangular or apsidal houses with porches give the essential megaron plan, and some of the houses, with and without porches, are quite well built.[3] Samos has a temple of some architectural pretensions.[4] In the seventh century, there are typical megara, with central hearth, porch and columns, at Emporio in Chios,[5] and a similar megaron at Smyrna, probably from the end of the century, has a self-contained adjacent room and probably an upper storey.[2] But there is no trace anywhere of the complex of rooms and passages combined with a megaron which is characteristic of Homeric and Mycenaean Palaces.

In the poems there are three groups of houses. Most people live in simple megaron houses, consisting of living room and porch entered from a closed court. The king's palace has the same nucleus, but it has ramifications around and up and down stairs. In the City at Peace and in a simile, housewives can stand at their doors to watch a procession or go into the street to quarrel; the Palace of Alkinoos is something like this from the outside—the finest among other fine houses—but the likeness stops at the outer gate.[6] The simple megara and the houses on a street are not much use for dating. Irregular little buildings are found at all times. Building materials remain the same and building styles do not normally change abruptly. Of the better buildings, it is possible to distinguish two leading types in the Bronze Age. The "open" plan, with free use of stairs and with every room leading into others, is familiar from Crete. A fine example of it from the Middle Bronze Age has been found in the Maeander valley at Beycesultan.[7] Generally similar in type is a remarkable Early Hel-

---

[1] Gray, "Houses in the Odyssey", *CQ* V (1955), pp. 1ff.

[2] *ILN* 28 February 1953, pp. 328–9 (Smyrna); *Hesperia* II (1933), pp. 549ff. (Athens).

[3] To examples in *Monuments*, pp. 406ff., add Siphnos, *BSA* XLIV (1949), pp. 6ff.

[4] *Ath. Mitt.* LV (1930), pp. 10ff.

[5] *ILN* 31 December 1955, pp. 1144–5.

[6] Σ 496, Y 252f., ζ 298f.

[7] Seton Lloyd and James Mellaart, "Beycesultan Excavations", *AS* VI (1956), pp. 101ff. and fig. 3 (Middle Bronze Age) and 2 (Late Bronze Age).

ladic palace, the "House of the Tiles" at Lerna, a singular proof of the sophistication of its inhabitants.[1] The "closed" plan is also found in Early Helladic settlements.[2] Its most characteristic form is the megaron, a term which should be kept for houses wide enough to need some internal support for the roof and entered at the narrow end through a porch or porch and anteroom. It is only doubtfully appropriate, for example, to the thirteenth-century palace at Beycesultan, or to the building which succeeded it after its destruction and which is "perhaps as late as the very end of the twelfth century B.C.";[3] it is a pity that even the later was destroyed too early for Homer, for they look like interesting adaptations of megara to the "open" plan. The main rooms are roughly megaron shaped, but their doors make them thoroughfares rather than traps. The simple megaron house is found in Mycenaean Greece, but it is not peculiar to it. It is found in many countries, and in Greece both in the pre-Mycenaean and in the Geometric period. The Protogeometric oval cottages interrupt the series, but it is likely enough that it continued throughout, and that the great halls of some Mycenaean palaces were turned to religious use.[4] But there is nothing to suggest that any part of the palace except the great hall was so used. The Mycenaean palace had the "closed" megaron as its centre, but it was surrounded by buildings of the "open" plan, connected with the megaron by the common court and by a door or doors in the porch or anteroom. The megaron kept its character much more in Greece than it did in the contemporary palace at Beycesultan, which, it is interesting to note, had no connexions with the Mycenaean world.

The poet's complete familiarity with the plan is a strong argument, as Myres said, for its survival somewhere, and one may yet be found. Since it should in post-Mycenaean times be in the city, there were good hopes of finding a king's house at Smyrna. They were disappointed, and all that can be produced is a poor megaron in the Early Iron Age City of Refuge at Karphi in Crete, which has cupboards rather than rooms at the back and at one side.[5] H. L. Lorimer suggested that it survived to be incorporated in a fourth-century

[1] John L. Caskey, "Excavations at Lerna, 1956", *Hesperia* XXVI (1957), pp. 142ff. and Pl. 44–5.
[2] *RE* XXII. 2. (1954), pp. 1433ff.
[3] See p. 168, n. 7.   [4] Possibly at Tiryns and Athens.
[5] *BSA* XXXVIII (1937–8), Pl. IX, no. 8, 9, 11, 14.

house at Priene but it is poor evidence to bridge so many centuries. There is a better incorporated megaron in the palace of Ilim-ilimma at Alalakh (*c.* 1400 B.C.[1]) and the probability is that in both buildings it is an accidental resemblance. On present evidence the Mycenaean palaces vanished with the kings who lived in them.

The conclusion seems to be that the memory long outlived the buildings; that even the poet of the *Odyssey* expected his hearers to understand immediately what his characters were doing in a house the like of which they had never seen. There are considerations which make this less improbable than it seems. The plan is typical; there is no need to suppose that the poet individualized his palaces or speculated on the floor space needed for each guest.[2] Much of the description is essential to the plot of any palace drama and would be implicit in the story. Many details are preserved in formulae. The farm of Eumaios and the palace of the bow-fight would present no difficulties. And finally there were no Geometric buildings in which a king of heroic status could be decently housed D. H. G.]

The few indications of house plans in the *Iliad* agree with the full evidence of the *Odyssey*, but for the poem of fighting the armour controversy is more important. There was for long no alternative to the Hellenic hoplite armour. Artists depicted the heroes in it, with occasional superficial concessions to the words of the poem, and Aeschylus made fine use of the dramatic possibilities of the hoplite blazon.[3] Yet Herodotus knew that hoplite armour was comparatively recent.[4] He thought it a Carian innovation, and said that it had been preceded by helmets without crests (though they may have had plumes) and shields without blazons or handgrips which the fighters manoeuvred (οἰηκίζοντες) by suspending them from the neck over the left shoulder by a leather τελαμών. Two shields in Homer have κανόνες; both are emphatically metal, as the shield-face of the *Iliad* regularly is when material is specified at all. Hesychius, after explaining Homer's κανόνες as handgrips, struts and so forth, adds, "And also the reeds in the shield to which the telamon was attached". This seems to be a reminiscence of a pre-Hellenic usage, but the

[1] It is shown in Sir Leonard Woolley's *A Forgotten Kingdom* (1953), p. 106, fig. 14, room 24.

[2] Jean Bérard, "Le plan du palais d'Ulysse d'après l'Odyssée", *Rev. d. Études grecques* LXVII (1954), pp. 1 ff.

[3] *Septem* 375 ff.   [4] Hdt. I, 171.

Alexandrian commentators generally have forgotten this earlier type of armour. Schliemann's excavations at Mycenae did not throw much fresh light at first on the defensive armour, but the contrast was obvious between the Mycenaean rapier-like sword, long for its width and flimsily hilted with a marked mid-rib, and the solid-tanged cut-and-thrust sword of Hellenic times. When, however, Athanasios Koumanoudis cleaned the daggers, he revealed the inlaid lion hunt with two quite un-Hellenic types of body-shield in action, and attention was thus called to a number of similar representations of a very peculiar type of defensive equipment (cf. Pl. 4. a.). Unlike any other shield known, the τελαμῶνες were clearly shown passing over the *left* shoulder. Helbig[1] described two main types of shield, which he seemed to regard as a continuous series. (i) The Shaft Grave body-shield, in its Tower, Oval and 8-shape, and the Hourglass, Dipylon shield, which he compared with shields carried by Hittite enemies of Rameses II, and (ii) the small, round shield with a single handgrip seen on a sherd from Tiryns and assumed to be contemporary with the Shaft Grave type, a similar round shield for which very slight evidence then existed before the seventh century, and the hoplite shield with armband and handgrip, which he thought to be in general use (except in Sparta) by the sixth century and which in heroic scenes sometimes had a cut-away waist. The 8-shield and hourglass shield he ejected from the poems; but finding two types in Homer, he identified them with the oval shield (which in fact is the 8-shield) and the round shield. Misled, however, by Rosellini's inaccurate reconstruction of a Shardan mercenary of Rameses II, in which he was shown carrying a hoplite shield, he identified Homer's κανόνες with armband and handgrip, significantly adding that this type of shield must have come to Greece very early, because it is shown on very old vases from Rhodes and Melos—i.e. on seventh-century vases. The result was that a sixteenth-century and a seventh-century shield were in living, contemporary use in the poems, but the supposed Shardan hoplite and the Dipylon hourglass shield did something to bridge the gap. Helbig greatly improved his case in 1909,[2]

[1] *Das Homerische Epos*[2], pp. 311–29. Throughout this section, references which are not given will be found in H. L. Lorimer, *Homer and the Monuments*.

[2] *Ein homerischer Rundschild mit einem Bügel* (*Jahresheft. d. Österr. Arch. Inst.* XII (1909) Heft 1).

bringing in a mass of new material to prove the existence of a pre-hoplite round parry-shield, with telamon and single handgrip; but by that time a quite different view had prevailed.

For, a few years after Helbig's great book, the battle over Homeric armour really began. H. Kluge, in a series of papers between 1891 and 1894,[1] demonstrated the independence of the body-shield and the parry-shield and the poet's acquaintance with both. In the special instance of the Shield of Achilles, he applied the distinction, already noticed by Helbig, between the scenes in monochrome *repoussé* technique and those in the polychrome inlay technique which so closely resembles that of the lion hunt dagger and of rare examples of Egyptian inlay. He accepted Helbig's unguarded assumption that, while this inlay technique was certainly early and disappeared later, the *repoussé* technique was essentially late and belonged to the early Hellenic centuries, and he attempted to distinguish earlier and later strata both in the description of the Shield of Achilles and in the poet's descriptions of Homeric shield-types generally. Kluge thought, however, that in essentials and in general the poet regarded his heroes as using hoplite armour; and he explained the allusions to Mycenaean shields as due to "spectral figures of antiquity" which occasionally confused the poet's vision. They owed their existence, he thought, partly to traditional descriptions in older narrative, and partly to the preservation of old shields, here and there, until the poet's own time, which was that of hoplite warfare.

A more revolutionary interpretation was proposed in 1894 by Wolfgang Reichel and elaborated further in the second edition of his *Homerische Waffen* in 1901. From the rapidly accumulating evidence for the structure and use of the Mycenaean shield, he was able to make out its handling in detail, and with this fresh knowledge, to recognize so many passages in the poems which seemed to refer to this type that the main action seemed now to move in Mycenaean surroundings. Consequently it was the passages in which hoplite fighting was thought to be described which began to require explanation; and in accordance with current practice Reichel made the experiment of excising them as interpolations. Whereupon, in certain

[1] "Vorhomerische Abbildungen homerischer Kampfscenen", *Jahrbücher für classische Philologie* 38 (1892), pp. 369ff.; "Vorhomerische Kampfschilderungen in der Ilias", *ibid.*, 39 (1893), pp. 81ff; "Der Schild des Achilleus und die mykenischen Funde", *ibid.*, 40 (1894), pp. 81ff.

passages where the action had been hitherto very difficult to follow, not only was a practicable feat of arms reconstituted, but a series of grammatical anomalies was explained as well. For example in *H* 251 ff., in the duel between Hector and Ajax, the spear of the latter first perforated Hector's shield, then penetrated his breastplate, and then his chiton right by his flank; yet Hector was able to swerve so as to avoid the point. To do this in close-fitting body armour is impossible; in a breastplate the size of a beer-barrel it would be difficult; only if there were no breastplate would such a movement, if smartly made while the spear was in the air, be a reasonable precaution in case the shield should be pierced, and moreover would leave a loose-fitting vest floating free so that it was caught by the spearpoint and torn, as described. Now, the perforation of the breastplate is given in a single self-contained line.

$$καὶ\ διὰ\ θώρηκος\ πολυδαιδάλου\ ἠρήρειστο,$$

and both the pluperfect ἠρήρειστο and the conjunction καὶ interrupt a grammatical sequence of aorists, ἦλθε—διάμησε—ἐκλίνθη καὶ ἀλεύατο, introduced by μὲν—δὲ—δ'. Similarly in *E* 98 Diomedes is wounded by an arrow in the right shoulder, which perforated the plate of his breastplate, which was forthwith splashed with blood from the wound. This is in itself remarkable, for an arrow fits tightly in such a perforation and in the wound. Moreover in lines 112–13 when the arrow is withdrawn, the blood spurts out afresh but this time through a χιτών, which would not have been visible at all if a breastplate was worn over it. Later in the fight (line 282) Diomedes received a spear right through his shield which "came near his breastplate" (θώρηκι πελάσθη), but did not wound him. His opponent, from his own point of view, thought that Diomedes must be wounded in the flank, but Diomedes was able to disappoint him. Later still (lines 795 ff.) Diomedes, who had sent away his chariot and had been fighting on foot, is found by his chariot and out of action, cooling his wound; and it is noted that as his arm was weary and fretted by the sweat under the τελαμών of his shield, he slipped it off his shoulder. For Reichel who assumed that the shield-strap was worn on his left shoulder, this was his left and unwounded arm, with which he was attending to his wounded right shoulder. But you cannot attend to a wound which is covered by a bronze breastplate, and still less can you perspire through a bronze breastplate on to a shield-strap which cannot have been inside it. Diomedes therefore was still not wearing a breastplate, just as he had none when the arrow was withdrawn from the wound in line 112. Now, it is noteworthy that on the occasion of the wounding, the two lines describing the breastplate are again self-contained and separable from the context; that the context is complete without them; that without them the whole episode makes clear and continuous sense; and that in the intermediate incident in line 282, the very odd phrase "came near his breastplate" fails to explain to the audience how the assailant thought that Diomedes was wounded in the flank. But the phrase θώρηκι πελάσθη is metrically equivalent to διάμησε χιτῶνα, which would have described exactly such a narrow escape as Hector had in H 253. Similarly in other passages the presence of a self-contained θώρηξ-line makes nonsense of the action, whereas the sense is plain without it. It could hardly be an accident, either, that in the description of the armour of Achilles in T and of Agamemnon in Λ, the line describing the breastplate was introduced by the word αὖ, whereas the rest of the armour was introduced by a sequence of μέν and δέ which the αὖ interrupted.[1] Supplementary considerations from other pieces of armour were favourable to Reichel's suggestion. Though the Achaeans are constantly described as "well-greaved", the greaves of Achilles's suit of arms were not of bronze but of tin, and greaves in the arming formulae had ankle-fittings of silver. Reichel noted that, though weapon-proof greaves were superfluous with a great shield which covered "from the neck to the ankles", some kind of shin-pad was required against friction from the lower edge of the shield; and though metal greaves were neither found nor pictorially represented in the Mycenaean culture, he could point to the gold clasps of shin-pads of perishable material which Schliemann had identified in one of the Shaft Graves at Mycenae, associated with a quantity of tubular bronze bindings for some large circular or oval object, also perishable, which was suggestive of the Mycenaean body-shield.[2] Reichel also showed that the Homeric helmet differed in structure and function from the hoplite helmet, and resembled the Mycenaean in having neither cheekpieces nor longitudinal crest. It

[1] T 369–88 and Λ 17–45.

[2] Similar objects have now been found in the new Grave Circle excavated by the Greek Archaeological Service, and it is thought certain that they are not ankle-fittings (G. E. Mylonas, *Ancient Mycenae*, Pl. 72).

was a mere hemispherical cap, with a chin-strap, a metal rim fitting the forehead, and a tassel-like plume attached to a knob at the apex. In particular he recognized the exact Mycenaean originals of the peculiar helmet of Meriones, made of plaited leather protected by a plating of boars' tusks. This point of contact is all the more remarkable because the episode of Dolon, in which it occurs, has been generally supposed to be one of the latest, because one of the least Homeric, parts of the *Iliad*. It should have been a warning against using individual passages as evidence for the date of the longer sections in which they were found.

Though Reichel pressed his interpretation rather hard in some respects and did not attempt an independent analysis even of the *Iliad* in accordance with it, his identifications, coming when they did, called general attention to those features of the poems which were consistent with a date within the age of the Mycenaean civilization. Carl Robert's *Studien zur Ilias*, which appeared in 1901, adopted Reichel's distinction between passages describing early or Mycenaean armour and those describing late or Hellenic armour, and made drastic use of it in his analysis of our *Iliad* into an "original *Iliad*" and later expansions. In particular he argued from the predominance of Hellenic armour in the books from T 19 onwards that the present end of the *Iliad* had been substituted for another version which had been more in accord with the armour described in the earlier books. The reconstructed ending conformed—needless to say—to Robert's own views of the way the story "must have" been told originally. Reichel's opinions have been stated and discussed here with rather full detail, because they were accepted in essentials by Walter Leaf, whose second edition of the *Iliad* came out in 1901–2 and consequently commanded greater attention in this country than usually awaits this kind of work. Andrew Lang discussed them at some length in *Homer and his Age* (1906) and *The World of Homer* (1910), using the Mycenaean coincidences as an argument for a very early date for the personal Homer and consequently, as he held, for the poems essentially as they have come down to us. They are even summarized and discussed in detail in the school edition of Homer by Leaf and Bayfield, and their influence was so great that they came to overshadow (at least in popular esteem) the evidence from the later phases of the Mycenaean Age. They were also one of the considerations which induced the University of Oxford to accept

Homeric Archaeology as a suitable subject for examination. Whether this should be counted to Reichel for righteousness or not, it is perhaps not for me to say.

It was natural that the contrast between Mycenaean and Hellenic armour should be stressed and even exaggerated at the outset. The idea of such a revolution was unfamiliar, and the discovery itself was made at a time when the revelation of the pre-Hellenic culture of the Aegean was in rapid progress. Most important of all, the results of Reichel's own examination of the evidence of the poems seemed to supply the much needed objective test to the large mass of literary criticism which was evoked by Wilamowitz's reformulation of the claims of an Ionian Homer. But the abruptness of this contrast itself challenged closer investigation of the later and rapidly decadent phases of the Mycenaean culture. Fresh excavations by Tsountas in the later tombs in the lower town of Mycenae yielded a painted grave-stone with representations of warriors in exactly the same equipment as those on the "Warrior Vase" (Pl. 6. a.) which had been found in one of the late houses which crowded the space between the Shaft Graves and the later wall of the citadel enclosing them. These two monuments gave an approximate, though still only relative, date for a different type of shield. It too was Mycenaean in age, but it had a handgrip like the Hellenic shield, and it was certainly symmetrical (πάντοσ᾽ ἐίση) in a sense in which the Mycenaean body-shield was not. It was of deeply convex circular form, and it was carried with a close-fitting piece of body armour worn over a short, woven under-garment, quite different from the scanty costume of the fighting men on the gems and the lion hunt dagger from the Shaft Graves. In 1899 the British Museum published, among the contents of rich Mycenaean graves near the Cypriote Salamis, greaves of thin bronze, shaped to the calf like Hellenic greaves but secured by a wire lacing across the calf, which set back the origin of this accessory protection to a date certainly not later than the traditional date of the Trojan War.[1] This discovery threw fresh light on vase fragments from Aegean sites showing men in some kind of leggings as well as a short flowing tunic such as is described where Hector dodges the spear-point. From the same necropolis as the greaves came an ivory relief

[1] For these and other bronze greaves of the same period from Cyprus and Achaea, see now H. W. Catling, "A bronze greave from a 13th century B.C. Tomb at Enkomi", *Opuscula Atheniensia* II (1955), pp. 21 ff.

showing a warrior wearing one of the characteristic helmets armed with boar-tusks (which by this time were known to have been no curiosity but in common use in the Mycenaean phases), and carrying a large round parry-shield ornamented round its broad rim with a row of rivet-like bosses and thus suggestive of the Homeric ἀσπίς ὀμφαλόεσσα. With it he wore a type of body armour already known to be characteristic of the Mediterranean Sea Raiders who were defeated on the Syrian coast in about 1194 by Rameses III.

There was therefore now proof of a much earlier vogue for armour serving the same purpose as the hoplite breastplate than had been supposed, and also greater approximation to continuity of development, at all events so far as concerned the technique of shield construction. The body armour was not, indeed, a breastplate with solid plates behind and in front. At Mycenae it was rather an armoured tunic. On the Cypriote ivory, it consisted of several horizontal belts of rigid material, encircling the wearer's body but sliding over each other like those of the hinder part of a lobster, and affording some freedom of movement. Its importance rather was that, while it confirmed Reichel's argument that the comparative inadequacy of any kind of parry-shield necessitated the provision of some kind of supplementary defence for the trunk and legs, it showed that this characteristic of hoplite armour had been anticipated before the collapse of the Mycenaean *régime*. It also brought very welcome confirmation of the accuracy of Egyptian observation, at a time when (thanks to the British Museum operations in Cyprus) the historical significance of the Sea and Land raids of the years before and after 1200 B.C. was being emphasized (Pl. 6. b.). Some of these Sea Raiders bore names as nearly identical with those of Achaeans, Danaans, Teucrians, Lycians and perhaps even Pelasgians, as an Egyptian transliteration might ever be expected to offer. Consequently the proof that Aegean types of equipment were current among those peoples, and in so central and important a region of the Levant as Cyprus, was a salutary caution to those who during these years were inclined to dispute the historical occurrence of a great expedition like that of the Atreidae to the Troad, or the possibility that, even if such an expedition had occurred, it could have been the subject of a tradition sufficiently trustworthy and copious to be reckoned among the materials available to an Ionian, or even an Aeolian, poet.

In another respect also this horizontal-belted body armour filled a long-perceived gap in our knowledge; for it offered an origin and an explanation of the broad waist-bands of sheet bronze which Helbig had used, fifteen years before, to illustrate that armoured belt of Homeric warriors which is called ζωστήρ in the poems. This supplement to the back and front plates of the Hellenic breastplate could already be traced passing out of use in Crete during the seventh century, though in the West and North-West, in Central Italy and round the Adriatic, it remained in use longer; breastplates were probably still hard to get in those regions. This armoured belt now seemed to point backward, as a survival, to a period when the fully developed breastplate was not yet contrived and the only available armour consisted wholly of such horizontal belts. This would go far to explain both the frequent mentions of the Homeric ζῶμα, ζωστήρ and θώρηξ, all forms of body-armour supported at the hips, and also the obscurity of the poet's descriptions of them. For since they had certainly been superseded in Hellenic times by the fully developed breastplate and are represented, either materially or on early warrior-figures, only by the single broad belt-plate already mentioned, it is intelligible that the poet found mention of them in his sources which he found it proper to preserve, though he did not himself quite understand the use of them.

The upshot therefore of the armour controversy, like that about the Homeric House, has been to show that, although the characteristic armour of the Mycenaean Bronze Age was wholly different in conception and use from the hoplite armour of the classical Greeks, yet there was a period of considerable length during which the old body-shield type and a new type much less remote from the hoplite panoply could have been in use together and perhaps even competitively; and further that, contrary to earlier opinion, the parry-shield, metal greaves and an improved type of sword had already come into use among the seafaring marauders of the Levant—whom there was strong reason to believe to have been in great part of Aegean origin—quite as early as the Greek traditional date for the Trojan War, namely the generation about 1200 B.C. There was therefore no further necessity to associate the round shield and other elements in Homer which did not belong to the Shaft Grave period exclusively with Ionian culture, whatever the Carians of Greek tradition may have had to do with popularizing the round buckler with its handgrip in early Hellenic times or before. It was in any case a novelty in the Aegean, as in the Levant, about the thirteenth century, whatever its actual origin.

[*Additional note*. Again it seems better to complete this discussion, though it means anticipating Ridgeway by half a century. The chief progress has been in the dating of the changes.

Throughout the Bronze Age soldiers used a single thrusting spear. Pairs of light throwing spears are carried by a captain of African irregulars (L.M. I-II), and by huntsmen at Tiryns (Myc. III.B.),[1] but the only evidence for a Mycenaean warrior so armed is a sherd on which two lines might be two spears or might be the rails of the chariot.[2] At first the Mycenaeans had a gentlemanly sword, Minoan in origin, made for use with point and not edge. Pommel, hilt-plates, studs plated with gold or silver, and often inlaid blade made a great show, but the hilt was attached to a fragile tang.[3] Blades tended to become shorter and tangs stronger. One of the earliest, the mighty sword of Mallia, is also the longest, and its pitiably weak hilting, as well as its context, show that it was a ritual weapon.[4] So perhaps was a large sword carried by gift-bearers on the wall of the tomb of Menkheperrasenb, but, like the vessels borne along with it, it may be out of scale.[5] The Shaft Graves at Mycenae contain one more solid weapon, long enough to be a sword but in shape a large dagger, and cleavers or one-edged swords which would make more dangerous weapons and which are perhaps carried by plebeian fighters on some of the stelai.[6] Finally a short stabbing sword with flanged, cruciform tang appears.[7] When this rapier-type sword, as it may be called conveniently if inaccurately,[8] is shown in action, it goes with the body-shields, helmets of various fantastic shapes, and no body armour

---

[1] H. Bossert, *Altkreta*[3], 36-7, 228.

[2] *AA* 1927, p. 250.

[3] Karo, Pl. LXXX–LXXXVII; G. E. Mylonas, *Ancient Mycenae* (1957), Pl. 51; *Antiquity* XXXI (1957), p. 99 and Pl. VIIIb; A. W. Persson, *Royal Tombs at Dendra* (1931), Pl. XX–XXII; *Hesperia* XVII (1948), pp. 156-7 and Pl. XXXIX, 3.

[4] *Palace*, II, pp. 272-3, fig. 162-3.

[5] Bossert, *op. cit.*, 543.

[6] *Ibid.*, 66; Karo, Pl. XCI and XCVII; Mylonas, *op. cit.*, Pl. 45.

[7] *BSA* XLVII (1952), p. 262 (A.J.1).

[8] D. H. Gordon, "Swords, rapiers and horse-riders", *Antiquity* XXVII (1953), pp. 67ff.

(Pl. 4. a.). In the last days of Knossos, however, there is evidence of improved protection. In a warrior grave a fine bronze helmet with cheek-pieces was found, and there are records of the issue of similar helmets and of bronze scale corslets.[1] These were probably the equipment of charioteers who could not carry the huge shield. No soldier in a chariot is ever shown with a body-shield, in spite of the widely held theory that the chariot was intended to relieve men burdened with its weight. Since the King's Grave at Dendra contained only rapier-type swords, the body-shield associated with them presumably continued in use at least until the middle of the fourteenth century. It appears in the poems only in the Periphetes episode (*O* 638 ff.) and in a few epithets and half-understood allusions.

By about 1300 B.C. the mercenaries of Rameses II are shown cutting off the hands of their enemies with the edge of the sword (Pl. 4. d.). Pharaoh's guard sometimes carry single spears and short swords, such as they used for their butchery at the Battle of Kadesh, sometimes longer, more formidable swords;[2] all the swords are sharp-pointed and shaped like elongated triangles, descendants, one would think, of the rapier-type sword and ancestors of a fine tanged blade with the cartouche of Merneptah which was found at Ras Shamra by C. F. A. Schaeffer.[3] They also carry small parry-shields, slung over the right shoulder and held by a single central handgrip, and horned, knobbed helmets high on the forehead. By the end of the century the armour is stronger. The mercenaries of Rameses III have helmets that come lower on their heads and short "lobster" corslets, made of bronze scales sewn on to bands which follow the line of the ribs, the only corslet which, like that of Agamemnon, stops at the waist above a belt (Pl. 6. b.). Another type is a real bronze chiton, with horizontal bands. By this time the same armour is found in Cyprus and Greece; the reinforced jerkins seen on the Warrior Vase (Pl. 6. a.) are less elegant than the Eastern Aegean scale corslets but they were probably

[1] *BSA* XLVII, pp. 256 ff. Similar helmets may be earlier in Central Europe, H. Hencken, "Beitzsch and Knossos", *PPS* XVIII (1952), pp. 36 ff; but it is a normal Aegean type except for the metal facing. Some small copper staples might belong to a body-shield. *Documents*, pp. 379 ff. A clumsy bronze helmet from Dendra is about the same date (Myc. II), Persson, *New Tombs at Dendra*, pp. 51, 119 ff.

[2] *Monuments*, Pl. IV, 1 and V.

[3] *Antiquity* XXIX (1955), pp. 226 ff.

as effective, and the Mycenaeans wore stout gaiters as well.[1] The short stabbing sword is found without a midrib, so that the edge can now be used.[2] Not long before 1200 a straight-edged cut-and-thrust sword with a strong hilt is in use over the whole area; and in Achaea and Cyprus such a sword is found with bronze greaves.[3] It is clear that a more professional equipment had appeared by the end of the fourteenth century and become general in the Eastern Mediterranean in the thirteenth; its uniformity is very marked.

Our next positive evidence is on Attic vases of the eighth century. Here throwing spears have replaced thrusting spears; they are regularly carried in pairs, as is necessary if they are to be launched at the enemy (Pl. 6. c.). A Dinka in South Sudan still takes a handful of hunting spears when he goes for a walk. A fight with throwing spears is faithfully described when at last Odysseus stands at the door "with shield and helmet and two spears". Four men need four shields, eight spears and four helmets. They throw their spears and are able to recover them. They therefore throw them again, but this time they fail to recover them and, not to leave themselves unarmed, use their second spears thereafter at close quarters.[4] How long before the eighth century the change happened is not known. It is worth noting that one grave at Athens, dated to the transition from Protogeometric to Geometric, contained among other tools and weapons two almost identical iron spearheads, 37 cm. long; of the Protogeometric graves, one contained a large and a small bronze spearhead (26 cm and 9 cm. long) and four others single bronze or iron spearheads, from 19 to 23.5 cm. long.[5] As evidence of date, it would be stronger

---

[1] To references in *Monuments* add a lion-slayer from Kouklia, like the griffin-slayer (*ILN* 2 May 1955, p. 710), the chiton and leggings of a man from Pylos and the helmet and arms of another from Mycenae (*ILN* 16 January 1954, p. 89, and 2 February 1957, p. 181), and thirteenth-century ivory heads with boars' tusk helmets from Mycenae (*BSA* XL, Pl. 35, and L, Pl. 25c).

[2] A. W. Persson, *Royal Tombs at Dendra*, Pl. XXXIII.

[3] H. W. Catling, "Bronze cut-and-thrust swords in the Eastern Mediterranean", *PPS* XXII (1956), pp. 102ff., attributes sword and greaves to Mycenaean armourers; the sword has, however, a longer history in Central Europe, J. D. Cowen, "Einführung in die Geschichte der bronzenen Griffzungenschwerter in Süddeutschland", 36 *Bericht der römisch-germanischen Kommission* 1955 (1956), pp. 52ff.

[4] α 256, χ 110ff., 265ff.

[5] *Hesperia* XXI (1952), pp. 286ff.

if the later spearheads were smaller, although in any case one example is not enough. The change from thrusting to throwing spear means a change from hand-to-hand to long-range fighting, and this is much the most significant difference between the Mycenaean and the post-Mycenaean battlefield. Iron for weapons is another, and the horned helmet is no longer found. Both types of sword were made in iron, the cut-and-thrust sword being more common; they were small at first, but there are some substantial weapons from the Geometric period. They now seem to be carried on a belt at the waist, instead of being slung over the shoulder. The parry-shield was identical in action with the Mycenaean shield and carried in the same way. Shapes are hourglass, rectangular or round, all small enough for the knees of the carrier to show beneath. In the eighth century there is for the first time a real counterpart to the metal face which all shields in the *Iliad* have when the material is mentioned. A considerable number of these round faces have been found, some with central boss surrounded by concentric bosses, some with concentric circles cut by a V, some with elaborate figure decoration.[1] Bronze helmets appear at about the same time. Of all these differences, only the spears affect the action, and they affect it fundamentally.

The next change was to hoplite fighting. H. L. Lorimer dated this *at latest* to the early seventh century, when hoplites on vases are unmistakable. Sylvia Benton suggested the late eighth century, when blazons first showed shields which required to be held right side up, and when inferior civilian work could be explained if bronze-smiths were dealing with rush orders for breastplates.[2] The conjecture was confirmed in the same year, when a hoplite breastplate, helmet and greaves, all of bronze, were found in a Late Geometric grave near Argos.[3] Virtually there are no hoplites in Homer. The discovery at Argos does not mean that the hoplite panoply can now be considered Homeric, but that the date of Homeric fighting must be raised to put it earlier than the Argive grave. It also means a raising of the date at which the *Iliad* could have acquired its few, undigested traces of hoplites. To list the half-dozen possible hoplite passages gives them too much importance, but it is worth noting that the

[1] Hugh Hencken, "Herzsprung Shields and Greek trade", *AJA* 54 (1950), pp. 295 ff., with decisive arguments for an eighth-century date.
[2] *BSA* XLVIII (1953), pp. 338 f.
[3] *Archaeology* 9 (1956), p. 172, fig. 10.

blazon, which offers infinite possibilities to a poet, has insinuated itself only in one couplet (Λ 36-7) which is not only superfluous but actually puts two different decorations on the same part of the shield. One or two passages may have been expanded to stiffen Homeric discipline for hearers used to hoplites; Θ 58 ff. is a good example, because three curious "hoplite" lines are isolated by the repetition of "and a great din rose up". But the objection that Homeric armies advance as hoplites and fight as individuals supposes that only hoplites advanced in line. In fact, the soldiers on the Warrior Vase and on Attic Geometric vases are certainly moving in line, though the artist has to show them as in Indian file; Assyrian artists, with great skill and larger scale, could show the formation properly (Pl. 6. d.). What Homer means by "eager at heart to support one another" (Γ 9) is clear from such passages as Δ 422 ff., where a series of linked engagements is both introduced and concluded by descriptions of the battlefield in general.

The Greeks thought Homer master of the art of war, as of everything else,[1] but it is today often assumed as self-evident that his battle-scenes are "garbled to a point of unintelligibility".[2] The chief complaint is that no proper use is made of the chariots. "Homer did not know what battle-chariots were for since his own community did not use them"; why waste shipping space in bringing them, only to drive pompously on to the field and dismount?[3] Édouard Delebecque, noticing that when πεζός meets ἱππεύς, the man on foot always wins, asks, "Si l'homme de char est destiné à la fuite ou voué à la mort, ne ferait-il pas mieux de mettre pied à terre pour se battre?"[4] It is generally admitted that individual duels are varied and exciting, but "c'est magnifique, mais ce n'est pas la guerre".

The mark of Homeric fighting is steadiness combined with mobility. Hector claims to be good at both (H 240-1). Not so old Idomeneus; "His legs were no longer firm enough for a charge, to spring forward after his spear or avoid the spear of his enemy. So he could defend himself in the standing fight but he could not run quickly back out of the fighting" (N 512 ff.). Aias claimed to be as good as

[1] Aristophanes, *Frogs* 1036, Plato, *Ion* 540-1.
[2] M. I. Finley, *Historia* VI (1957), p. 146.
[3] Rhys Carpenter, *Folk Tale, Fiction and Saga in the Homeric Epics* (1946), p. 33.
[4] *Le cheval dans l'Iliade* (1951), p. 94.

Achilles "in the standing fight at least, but with the feet it is not possible to rival him" (*N* 325). Much of this mobility is given by the chariots, which are used as the Numidians used cavalry along with infantry. Normally each chariot had a fighting man and a driver. The fighter fought on foot, but it was the business of the driver to keep the chariot as close to him as his own skill, the fighter's rashness, and the course of events allowed. There is every variation from Asios who had his horses breathing down his neck (*N* 385) to Agastrophos, who was killed because, like a fool, he left his chariot far behind (*Λ* 338 ff.). Idomeneus was old but rash. He came into battle without his chariot. When the Greeks were driven back, he was engaging Hector, and he would have been killed if Meriones and his driver had not driven up to the rescue. Idomeneus sprang up on to the chariot. Hector threw a spear at him, missed him, and killed the driver instead. The driver fell from the chariot, Meriones caught the reins from his hands, and told Idomeneus to whip up the horses; they thus escaped the faster (*P* 605 ff., cf. *Ψ* 638 ff.). In flight and pursuit both sides mount; it is a sign that the battle has ceased to be evenly balanced when we begin to hear that men are falling from their chariots. A fighter might mount in order to fight in another place. It was assumed that a man would mount if he were wounded (*Λ* 191). In fact, the fighters are continually in and out of their chariots, and the poet takes this so for granted that he often does not state it explicitly. If the fighter was killed, the driver could with honour drive away, leaving others to rescue the body; or he could dismount, in which case he was usually killed too, and the chariot often captured, unless someone else took charge of it. Any fighter caught by his opponent in a chariot, or mounting or dismounting, was at a disadvantage and paid for it by defeat. But there is a rare variation. Occasionally two second-rate fighters, usually Trojans and often brothers, fight together in one chariot, trying to throw their spears from a safe distance without dismounting. So the two sons of Dares met Diomedes, they in their chariot, but he attacked them on foot from the ground (*E* 9 ff.). One threw a spear and missed altogether, and his chest was pierced by Diomedes's return throw, so that he fell from the chariot. The other jumped down (presumably to defend him) but he did not dare to bestride him. This second brother was actually rescued by Hephaistos, but Diomedes drove off the chariot. There is a third variation, still more unusual. Athene once

184

condescended to drive Diomedes, and some very unconventional fighting followed (*E* 835 ff.). Very occasionally, two first-class heroes united as fighter and driver.

All three variations are illustrated by the death of Pandaros (*E* 217 ff.). Pandaros complains that his bow is useless against Diomedes, and explains that he did not bring his chariot to Troy because he was afraid there would not be enough fodder. Aineias proposes that they should both go against him in his chariot, offering either to fight and let Pandaros drive or to drive and let Pandaros get down to fight; and Pandaros replies that the horses will go better with a driver they know, especially if they have to get away in a hurry. So Pandaros takes a shield and two spears, and off they go. Sthenelos, the driver of Diomedes, sees them coming and advises Diomedes to get on his chariot and withdraw, because he is wounded and two heroes are coming against him (i.e. not one hero and a driver). Diomedes of course refuses, and tells Sthenelos that, if Diomedes wins, he is to abandon his chariot and capture the horses of Aineias. Aineias drives up. Pandaros, with a boastful speech, throws his spear but fails to pierce Diomedes's armour. Diomedes throws his and kills Pandaros, who falls from the chariot (i.e. Pandaros, a Trojan, a truce-breaker, an archer and a boaster, has not dared to dismount, but has thrown his spear from his chariot, like a second-rate fighter). Aineias leaps down to protect his body, and would have been killed if Apollo and Aphrodite had not rescued him. Sthenelos, who has left his horses at a distance from the fighting with the reins tied to the rail, jumps on Aineias's chariot, drives it to the Greek camp, gives it to a squire, returns to his own chariot and hurriedly rejoins Diomedes (i.e. he has left Diomedes without means of retreat, a thing which the driver could do only on the fighter's specific instructions).

There is a good example of tactics generally when Patroklos has checked the Trojan attack on the ships (*Π* 306 ff.).

"Then each of the leaders killed his man in the scattered fighting." Patroklos kills a man who is turning away in flight (marking the moment when the Trojans waver; after that he takes no part for sixty lines, and he then appears in his chariot in full pursuit of Hector, i.e. the intervening events happen simultaneously). Then come eight encounters, all appropriate to the moment of wavering and ending with a phrase meaning "and so he died".

"Thus each of the leaders of the Danaoi killed his man"—simile of wolves and sheep, and the sheep are terrified, even so the Trojans were terrified and remembered tumultuous flight. "Great Aias was trying all the time to hit bronze-helmeted Hector", but Hector knew how to fight a rear-guard action, swinging his shield to the back as he retreated, and, when he took to his chariot, guiding his horses to the right place.

"And Patroklos pursued, calling eagerly to the Danaoi. . . ." The rout is now complete, and both sides are continually in and out of their chariots as the Trojans flee or make a stand.

The simultaneous engagement of two ranks of men is emphasized by every device the poet knows—the whole pattern, the use of simultaneous imperfects, the position of the similes, the frame of summarizing lines. It is part of the epic technique not to go back in time, and once the scene is set, poet and audience are naturally more interested in the greater heroes; but it is a real general engagement, and neither dull nor unintelligible. In spite of a great wealth of variations, the function of the chariot is consistent and essential. Naturally the man on foot beats the man in the chariot. Either he has caught a first-class fighter at a disadvantage, or he is engaging two second-class fighters, who are bound by poetic justice to be beaten.

War-chariots were used both in the Bronze Age and in the eighth century. The pictorial evidence for tactics is not conclusive, but there is nothing on eighth-century vases inconsistent with Homeric fighting; men and chariots appear together, but no fighter ever attacks from a chariot and no chariot charge is ever shown (Pl. 5. a.). Races and processions of chariots and foot-soldiers at funerals are certainly eighth century, and the vividness and consistency of Homeric narrative are themselves evidence that the fighting described was contemporary. The Mycenaeans, on the other hand, were in touch with peoples who charged in their chariots (Pl. 4. b.), and the Hittites in particular mounted spearmen. They used the chariot itself as a weapon, as the fifth-century Athenians used the trireme. This is how the Hittites and Egyptians fought at the Battle of Kadesh (Pl. 4. d.), and how Sisera fought in his chariot of iron; and Sisera "lighted down" to run away, because his chariot was as deeply involved as he was (Judges 4.15).[1] It is also the way that Nestor

[1] *Y* 401–2 is the *only* place where a man dismounts to flee, and it is made up of *Λ* 423 and *E* 56.

advises his men to fight ($\varDelta$ 297 ff.), keeping in line and thrusting from their chariots with their spears; and this is evidence that the Mycenaeans fought like the Hittites because there is no other source from which it can be derived.[1] Although no one in the *Iliad* ever fights thus before Troy, Nestor's account of one of his early battles sounds like a miniature Battle of Kadesh ($\varDelta$ 670 ff.). His father hid his chariot to keep him at home (Idomeneus could go to battle without one), but he went on foot, killed an enemy, leapt into his chariot, routed the foe, and captured fifty chariots with two men in each. There are other places where we have a glimpse of the knights of Knossos and Pylos. After the death of Patroklos, Automedon was wild with grief (P 458 ff.). "The horses speedily bore the swift chariot to where the Trojans and Achaeans were. Behind them fought Automedon, grieving for his friend, swooping with his horses like a vulture chasing wild geese. For quickly he would dash out from the array of the Trojans, and quickly he would charge down, pursuing them through the great throng." (This sounds like a real chariot charge, and it is a surprise when it goes on:) "But he did not kill any men, when he hastened in pursuit, because being alone in his chariot, he could not both assail them with his spear and hold his swift horses." Then one of his friends laughed at him for being so silly and offered to drive for him; and the battle assumed its normal course. But these few interesting reminiscences do not detract from the clear picture of a quite different use of chariots.

There are three periods of history when the co-existence of different methods of fighting is possible. The first is the late fourteenth and early thirteenth centuries, when there must have been a transition from body-shield to parry-shield fighting. There is no evidence for this overlap, and it is too early for Homeric fighting. The last is the late eighth century; it is probable that all states did not organize hoplite forces simultaneously, but the absence of hoplites from the poems rules it out. There is left the long period from the eleventh to the ninth centuries, between the last evidence for the thrusting spear and the first evidence for the throwing spear. Its craftsmen served archaeologists poorly, and they in turn have virtually nothing to give to historians or critics. But the poems themselves do not show two types of fighting in simultaneous use. They show eighth-century fighting, with a strong but submerged undercurrent of Bronze Age

[1] Not from Assyria, since in Homer bows and chariots are incompatible.

fighting. Men who arm with the formula which gives them one spear, afterwards fight in the same way as men who have two. The only place where the poet seems aware of the difference is where Patroklos leaves the single spear of Achilles and takes a pair of spears instead (Π 140 ff.). And although Achilles has his famous μελίη, he throws it like anyone else; consequently he is once left unarmed, and the poet has to return his spear to him miraculously (X 273 ff.). Elsewhere a second spear is assumed; in H 255 ff., does each use the other's spear? These are strong objections to an historical period of transition[1] D. H. G.]

Both the armour and the house, then, quite independently, seemed at first to suggest intimate Homeric acquaintance with the pre-Hellenic world, and only gradually to commute this intimate acquaintance for the kind of reminiscence which might be expected in an age of transition, when old and new were still to be seen side by side. So matters stood when in 1896 William Ridgeway produced the first draft[2] of a reconstruction of the Homeric Age which is more fully elaborated in his *Early Age of Greece*, of which the first volume was published in 1901 and was then already somewhat antiquated in detail.[3] For him, as for Tsountas and Andrew Lang, and in essentials also for Leaf and for many German writers, the Achaeans were a group of invaders and conquerors. They had nothing to do with the origins of the Mycenaean culture, which indeed they despoiled. They were Phrygian in the sense that they represented the right or western wing of an originally coherent force of immigrant peoples of whom the Phrygians of Asia Minor and the Thracians were on the left or eastern flank. These immigrants were not of Aegean origin at all; they were in a general sense Celtic, in physique tall, blond and grey-eyed; in speech also Celtic; in culture, of that first iron-using culture of the Danubian type most familiar from the great necropolis of Hallstatt in Austrian Tyrol; cattle-keeping, horse-breeding, chariot-fighting swashbucklers, with the superior weapon of an iron sword which could slash as well as thrust, and a handy parry-shield quite distinct from the cumbrous Mycenaean body-shield expounded not

[1] On metals see *JHS* LXXIV (1954), pp. 1 ff.

[2] "What people produced the objects called Mycenaean?", *JHS* XVI (1896), pp. 77 ff.

[3] Vol. II was edited from the proof sheets by D. S. Robertson and A. Gow in 1931. Ridgeway worked on it till his death in 1926, but there was always new material to digest.

long before by Reichel. In the Homeric poems Achaeans burn their dead like the later Hallstatt people but pile a mound over the ashes, whereas Mycenaean folk buried them in chamber tombs, in accordance with a quite different range of ideas about the fate of the departed, to which only faint allusions occur in the poems. In England, Ridgeway's vigorous advocacy of his views and his conservative handling of the literary evidence had considerable influence. Abroad, and especially in Germany, he was somewhat despised for his insistence on a literal interpretation of Homeric tradition, for his omission to distinguish in value between Homer and the late classical evidence with which he lavishly supported his arguments, and for his very defective acquaintance with the details, and even with some of the outlines, of the archaeology of the Danubian culture province; and his more valuable suggestions passed almost unnoticed, until they had been reformulated and re-established by other hands. But his main contention, that the Achaean domination of peninsular Greece was a shortlived reign of violent aggression, and a serious acceleration of the Mycenaean decline, was a solid contribution; his insistence on the historical value of coherent genealogical evidence was a valuable corrective to the current inclination to discredit all folk-memory and therewith the narrative contents of the poems; and his belief that the knowledge of iron as a metal for weapons of war, rather than as a magical rarity, reached the Aegean from the north and overland, not from the east along the seaways, led to much valuable work. With the problems of literary criticism, as practised especially in Germany and by the followers of German methods elsewhere, he had little concern. But his view that, for example, the composer of the poems carried archaism so far as to use the word for bronze habitually when they referred to weapons of the Iron Age, raised the whole question of the limits of such archaism in literary art, and provoked a series of controversies which in the long run cleared this difficult subject of some of its obscurities.

Less permanently valuable, though productive, like all such experiments, of needful and suggestive revisions of current beliefs, were the two principal attempts to do for the historical and geographical background of the *Odyssey* what the excavations of Schliemann and his successors had done for the *Iliad*. Schliemann himself had begun his researches by a flying visit to the little island Thiaki, the Ithaca of classical times and, in spite of grave topographical discrepancies, the traditional home of Odysseus. But in Ithaca there was no obvious site to be dissected, and so long as the Ionian Homer held the field, no one minded very much if his conception of a district so remote from Ionia was less easily recognizable than his account of the plain of Troy. Moreover, the romantic and imaginative quality of the *Odyssey* gave especial point to Eratosthenes's judgment of Homeric poetry generally, that every poet's aim is to entertain, not to instruct. Everyone who has not been to Ithaca knows it, from beach to mountain top, as Homer shows it to him; if it is not the Ithaca of the Admiralty Chart, so much the worse for the surveyors; they have not wandered in the realms of gold.

Was it possible, however, that the poet, though mistaken in his topography, might after all be right in his history and archaeology? Was it in fact conceivable that it was the names, not the places, that had changed? The suggestion was thrown out as early as 1894 by H. Draheim,[1] at the moment when Paolo Orsi's discovery of Mycenaean contacts with Sicily had put the whole significance of Homeric allusions to the far west in a quite new light.[2] Hitherto they had been taken for proof of late composition, on the ground that neither Ionians nor any other Greeks knew anything about Sicily till the generation of 735. But if their predecessors had traded with Sicily, perhaps even settled there, in the days of the twelfth-century Sea Raiders, and if the knowledge of this had been obliterated during the migrations of the eleventh century, Homeric allusions to the west might well join the historical geography of the *Catalogue* and the descriptions of intercourse with Egypt, Cyprus and Sidon, as marks of early composition. The same idea occurred independently to Dörpfeld, who was just completing his interpretation of the long series of excavations on the site of Troy.[3] With characteristic decision he took his annual excursion of German professors and schoolmasters, not to Thiaki, but to the larger island of Leukas north of it, and there, with the sole guide of the British Admiralty Chart, and to the amaze-

[1] *Wochenschrift für Klass. Philologie*, 1894, p. 62f.

[2] He reported a Minoan type of dagger from Plemmyrion, two Mycenaean amphorae from Thapsos, and one amphora from Agrigentum. See T. J. Dunbabin, "Minos and Daidalos in Sicily", *BSR* XVI (1948), pp. 1ff. and *The Western Greeks* (1948), pp. 28 ff; L. Bernabò Brea and M. Cavalier, *Civiltà preistoriche delle isole Eolie e del territorio di Milazzo* (1956), pp. 48 ff.; Brea, *Sicily before the Greeks*, 1957.

[3] *Troja und Ilion* was published in 1901.

ment no less of his Greek skipper than of his learned passengers, lectured on the topography of the *Odyssey* as if he had been Eumaios himself. That was Dörpfeld's way; under the open sky "persuasion sat upon his tongue". It has been truly said that in ancient history "nothing lies like an inscription"; and few things were as convincing as a bit of Greek landscape, or Greek architecture either, when Dörpfeld explained it to you (Pl. 3. a.). His theory was first committed to print in the *Archaeologische Anzeiger* for 1902 and in the *Mélanges Perrot* of 1903; and a lively controversy followed. Wilamowitz naturally led the counter-attack; he was terribly upset that so much was found by Dörpfeld in the *Odyssey* which ought to have been unknown to his Ionian Homer. Dörpfeld's reply was to induce a rich Dutchman, Dr. Goekoop, to provide the funds for excavation in Leukas; and a prehistoric settlement was found in 1905 on the selected site in Nidri Bay. But like Furtwängler at Orchomenos, Dörpfeld found in Leukas something less and more than he wanted. The settlement, though apparently of about the same period as the Late Bronze Age deposits in the Aegean, was of a quite different complexion, comparatively barbarous and inartistic, and almost unconnected with Aegean culture by interchange of products. It was, in fact, the prolongation into Mycenaean times of an older local way of life, standing in much the same relation to the sea-borne culture of the Aegean adventurers as the Minyan *régime* at Orchomenos. Further excavation traced this west coast culture in the neighbouring islands, and on the west coast of the mainland and of the Peloponnese. At Olympia it underlay the foundations of the oldest Hellenic buildings.[1] Only on one site in Triphylia, not far from one suggested locality of the Pylos of the Homeric Nestor, did Dörpfeld strike Mycenaean remains in 1906–8; a rich beehive tomb like those at Mycenae and the similar outlier at Orchomenos, belonging to the Mainland contemporaries of the last rulers of the Palace *régime* of Knossos.[2] As at Orchomenos, too, both public and specialist interest died away in default of artistic or demonstrably "Homeric" finds; and the precise relation of the civilization of pre-Hellenic Leukas, either to the Homeric or the Hellenic world,

---

[1] *Ath. Mitt.* XXXVI (1911), pp. 163 ff., XLVII (1923), pp. 48 ff.; *AA* 1930, pp. 115 ff.; *Alt-Olympia*, 1934.

[2] *Ath. Mitt.* XXXIII (1908), pp. 295 ff., XXIV (1909), pp. 269 ff. and XXXVIII (1913), pp. 97 ff.

remained undetermined for want of persistence. The topographical controversy is best summarized in Peter Goessler's *Leukas Ithaka, die Heimat des Odysseus*, published in 1904, though Dörpfeld himself reopened the question twenty years after.[1] It is, however, probably to Dörpfeld's "troubling of the waters" that we owe the very copious output of literary criticism of the *Odyssey* in the years from 1903 to 1910.

The other excursion into the topography of the *Odyssey* is that of Victor Bérard. *Les Phéniciens et l'Odyssée*, sumptuously published in 1902[2], was just too early to have the use of Dörpfeld's own account of his theory. Among many things romantic, fanciful, and even absurd, and alongside philological speculations about the names of Greek islands and suggestive economic commentary on early Mediterranean seafaring, Bérard applied much the same rather subjective standards of likeness between sites and descriptions as characterized the speculations of Dörpfeld, but without being able to put them to the test of excavation. He too returned to the subject in a six-volume introduction to the *Odyssey*, which did not show much advance in critical skill over his first performance.[3]

The discovery of Knossos in 1900 was of greater importance in Aegean archaeology than in Homeric criticism. It had been foreseen since the Greek trial pits of 1878, predicted by Milchhöfer in 1883, verified in a preliminary way by Fabricius in 1885, and attempted unsuccessfully by Schliemann in 1887. Its urgency had been greatly increased by the Egyptian synchronisms established in 1893 and the announcement of the hieroglyphic script in 1894. But the fact of a long sequence of periods and styles on an Aegean site had already been demonstrated at Phylakopi in Melos. What the great palace sites at Knossos, Phaistos and Ay.Triadha contributed, was a splendid filling to this framework and an unusually precise subdivision of periods and adjustment of the whole perspective. It was now possible to date more accurately the establishment of the mainland sites of Argolis, to show their cultural dependence on Crete, and to offer an explanation of the sudden collapse of the Palace *régime* at Knossos about 1400 B.C., as the result of a schism between Crete and its mainland neighbours, and as itself followed by the wide spread of the Mycenaean type of culture around the Aegean and very widely also

[1] *Alt-Ithaka*, 1927.   [2] 2nd ed., 1927.
[3] 1924, 2nd ed. (Budé) 1933.

in the Mediterranean coastlands beyond.[1] For the Homeric Question, this was the principal novelty in the Cretan evidence; it showed that the decline of the Minoan civilization had been partly abrupt, at the time of that initial disaster at Knossos, and partly gradual, over a period of some three centuries or locally more; and that it was about midway in this long period (from about 1270 to 1180, or in Syria rather later), that the Egyptian records enable us to place the climax of a phase of ubiquitous piracy at sea and migration on land. This obviously threw quite fresh light on the Homeric presentation of the political situation; on the hundred cities of Crete, which nevertheless contributed so little to the forces of Agamemnon; on the traditions of a pre-Achaean Age, with other dynasties and with crises of its own; on the survival into the generation which fought at Troy of descendants of the Minyan seafarers who had explored Pontus and other parts of Outland; and on the piratical familiarity both of Achaean heroes and of Paris with the coasts of the Levant.

Only rarely have any of those who have been most concerned in the literal "making of history" from the archaeological material attempted to apply their special knowledge to Homeric corollaries. This makes the more significant Arthur Evans's presidential address to the Hellenic Society in 1912, on the *Minoan and Mycenaean Element in Hellenic Life*.[2] He swept aside, as based on a series of misconceptions about the details of the finds, the simple bisection of the Minoan civilization into an earlier Carian and a later Achaean period, separated by the coming of the first Indo-European-speaking people from the north. He emphasized the continuity of race and culture, on the Greek mainland as in Crete, far down into the third Late Minoan period. He left it an open question whether the population of the mainland which his Cretan colonists found in possession spoke any kind of Indo-European language, but noted that the fortifications of the colonial centres proved persistent hostility, and that about the thirteenth century the frescos of the later palace at Tiryns distinguished between the normal, dominant occupants, who are painted in red as in Crete, and a "menial type" which is palefaced. On the other hand, he assigned the arrival of that element in the composite population of Cyprus which spoke Arcadian Greek to

[1] It incidentally produced an Encyclopaedia of Aegean Archaeology in *The Palace of Minos*, 1921–36.
[2] *JHS* XXXII (1912), pp. 277ff.

the tenth century at latest, and probably quite a century earlier; but he noted that, while they brought with them at least one cult from their mother-country Laconia, they took over at Paphos the typical aniconic cult of the Lady of the Dove from their Minoan predecessors and that they were probably already familiar with this cult before they left Aegean shores. Similarly, whenever Greek-speaking immigrants may have reached Crete, they adopted here too old local cults under non-Greek names—Dictynna, Britomartis, Velchanos—and the characteristic "mortal Zeus" who was eventually Christianized as *Effendi Christos*. In the other direction, the legendary Cretan element at Delphi was illustrated by the discovery of a Minoan ritual vessel in that sanctuary; the representations of the goddess worshipped as Artemis at Sparta and at Ephesus were modelled on Minoan types; and the Doric architecture of the earliest known Hellenic temples was derived from Minoan constructions and schemes of decoration.

From all this he inferred long juxtaposition of the Minoan and Hellenic elements, and gradual fusion, accelerated by the arrival of "fresh swarms of immigrants from the North-West . . . In the end, though the language was Greek, the physical characteristics of the later Hellenes prove that the old Mediterranean element showed the greater vitality". This gradual fusion and infiltration made it necessary to suppose a long bilingual phase, such as is familiar in "lands where nationalities overlap". In Eastern Crete the two languages are known to have co-existed till the fourth century. Accepting Andrew Lang's inference from the phraseology of the Homeric poems to their composition within a transition period from the use of bronze to that of iron, and implicitly rejecting Ridgeway's contention that χαλκός in Homer is a poetical survival from a Bronze Age that was obsolete, Evans found that transition period at the point dividing the latest Minoan period from the earliest Geometrical, "a period when the great cities, of whose rulers the poet sang, had for some two centuries been heaps of ruins". Consequently "Homer" lay too far up in time for it to be "admissible to seek for illustration among the works of renascent art in Greece, or the more or less contemporary importations", Cypro-Phoenician bowls, and the like. "On the other hand, the masterpieces of Minoan and Mycenaean craftsmen were already things of the past. . . . Only one solution", Evans thought was possible, and it was to be "found in the bilingual condition of the

mixed population. .... We may well ask whether a far earlier heroic
cycle of Minoan origin might not to a certain extent have affected the
lays of the primitive Greek population"; and eventually, "may not
something of the epic traditions of the Mycenaean society have been
taken over?" Many "themes of the Homeric lays", he noted, "postu-
late a state of things which on the mainland of Greece existed only
in the great days of Mycenae. .... The moulding of such inherited
materials into the new language . . . was no doubt a gradual process,
though we may still regard the work in its final form as bearing the
stamp of individual genius". He compared the architecture of the
Arch of Constantine, with its "harmonious incorporation of earlier
sculptures. Not less does Homer personify for us a great literary
achievement, though the materials that have been brought together
belong to more than one age. There is nothing profane in the idea
that actual translation, perhaps of a very literal kind, from an older
Minoan epic to the new Achaean, played a considerable part in this
assimilative process. The seven-stringed lyre itself"(which oblivious
Greek tradition had ascribed to Terpander) "was an heirloom
from the older race—is it then unreasonable to believe that the
lays by which it was accompanied were inspired from the same
quarter?"

Then Evans went on to discuss the familiar problem of the vivid
Homeric descriptions of works of art which were of quite pre-
Homeric date and style; quoting the silver siege-vase from Mycenae,
and the Knossian city-scene in glazed plaques; "executed some five
centuries before the Homeric poems took shape, they may either
have inspired or illustrated contemporary epic". The Shaft Grave
gems with scenes of combat, too, belong to a period (M.M.III–L.M.I)
before body armour was introduced; yet body armour was already
in use before the destruction of the Knossian Palace, and also in late
Mycenaean Cyprus; and it is from Cyprus that Agamemnon received
the breastplate which he wears in *Iliad Λ* 10. On the hypothesis now
proposed, these scenes, so closely resembling Homeric fighting of a
kind which was certainly obsolete when the poems were composed,
may themselves have illustrated "*chansons de geste*" in the days of the
Shaft Graves. Pendants for the *Odyssey* are a seal-impression from
Knossos, and a fragment of a silver vessel from Mycenae, depicting
a dog-headed Scylla attacking a man in a boat at sea.

The naturalistic spirit of Homeric literary art, especially in the similes, has striking affinity with the naturalism of Minoan gem-engraving. Yet this art was obsolete before the close of the Minoan age; and in Homer there is no mention of signets or sealing. Odysseus can only secure his treasure with a cunning knot. Parallels to the hound and fawn on the brooch of Odysseus are sought in vain among Ionian or Geometrical fibulae, "three or four centuries later than the archaeological epoch marked by the Homeric poems", and severely conventionalized in design: for Evans the more probable alternative is that the poet has transferred to a new context, in an age when brooches (unknown in the gem-period) were being worn, a description of a Minoan intaglio—even more conclusive identification of the wearer than any piece of jewellery, because it was at the same time his identification-signet.

The transmission of such descriptions from the period of their material originals to the days of epic-making is fully explained by the "embalming medium of an earlier Epos", co-existence, that is, of late Minoan epic with early Hellenic; and otherwise it is inexplicable; "where indeed would the fly be without the amber?" Such Minoan epic itself, moreover, presumably had its stratification from earlier to later, from body-shield, for example, to buckler and breastplate. In their present shape the Homeric poems "are the result of this prolonged effort to harmonize the old and the new elements": hence patchwork, contradiction, misplacement, for example of similes, of which Gilbert Murray has seen that "their vividness, their directness, their air of freshness and spontaneity are all deceptive": many "were originally written to describe some quite different occasion".

Evans naturally contemplates the existence of written copies of Minoan poems; as well as the recovery (from time to time as in the Italian renaissance) of ancient seal-stones, explaining thus the resemblances of some of the earliest Hellenic coin-types to Minoan engraved gems. And he concludes with a very remarkable example of an ivory copy, by an early Hellenic artist, of such a Minoan intaglio, all the more interesting because the subject is an exact rendering of the peculiar fate of Periphetes of Mycenae in P 645–8, who tripped and fell backwards into his great body-shield. A close Mycenaean prototype, but without the Homeric allusion, is the well-known lentoid sardonyx from the third Shaft Grave.[1]

[1] *Palace*, III, fig. 80.

Chapter Nine

ULRICH VON
WILAMOWITZ-MOELLENDORFF

I T must not, of course, be supposed that, while new methods and materials were being contributed by the archaeologists, historians and geographers, literary criticism was out of action. Wilamowitz's *Homerische Untersuchungen*, with its analysis of the *Odyssey* and its brilliant review of the literary history of the poems, came out in 1884, while Schliemann was at Tiryns, and Paul Cauer's *Grundfragen der Homerkritik* in 1895, while the British School was excavating Phylakopi. The general histories of Greek literature[1] adopted moderate and rather eclectic compromises between radical and conservative views, which fairly represent the general trend of opinion, but do not advance the solution of any of the main problems or make serious contributions to method. The first professed historian since Grote to review the Homeric Question in the light of his own special studies was Louis Erhardt.[2] He deserves mention for an early attempt to ascertain, by comparison with other examples of early epic, the social conditions in which this class of literature usually arises; but, like almost all German scholars since Wolf and Lachmann, he appreciated only very imperfectly the differences between folk-poetry, such as had been by this time collected in a number of regions, and the far more composite and consciously artificial structure of poems like the *Iliad* and *Odyssey*. Indeed, in Germany

[1] A. and M. Croiset, *Histoire de la Littérature grecque*, 1887; Wm. Christ, *Geschichte der griechische Literatur*, 2nd ed., 1890.
[2] *Die Entstehung der homerischen Gedichte*, 1894.

197

especially, the complexity of the whole problem was underestimated, through lack of familiarity with the details. Critics continued to be misled by the earlier bisection of the Aegean Bronze Age into an Achaean and a pre-Achaean period. The latter was variously decorated with names like Carian, Danaan, Pelasgian and was almost always assumed to be non-Aryan—usually on the quaint ground that the Minoan script, which had not been read by the English and could not be read by the Teutons, must be non-Aryan, and therefore pre-Aryan. The script, and the people who used it, could thus be happily sidetracked from any relevance to Homer. The result was more emphatic divergence between the standpoint, methods and objectives of British and German criticism. This was already an old story by 1900. Quite apart from the realist enthusiasm of Gladstone, who did a valuable service by popularizing Schliemann's discoveries, and by showing the application of some of them to the poems, it was the more judicious concurrence of Charles Newton that commended them to serious scholars in this country. Leaf's central criticism in 1891 of Schuchhardt's summary of them was that Schuchhardt was too much obsessed by the Ionian Homer of Wilamowitz to be able to face the Mycenaean evidence squarely.[1] Andrew Lang in 1895 gave the first comprehensive application of archaeological commentary on the new lines now made possible; and he returned to the fray at a later stage with vigorous and original criticism of current theories about armour, dress, funeral customs and the political and social structure of Homeric society, and about the perennial controversy as to the extent to which archaism is to be assumed in such poetry as the Homeric.[2] It was Leaf again, as we have seen, who adopted almost at once and popularized effectively Reichel's interpretation of Homeric armour, though with valuable qualifications prompted by his own maturer scholarship. His combination of literary learning with the traditional English preference for reading ancient texts in classical surroundings, enabled him to apply quite fresh standards of interpretation to the geographical allusions in the poems, and above all to the long-neglected *Catalogue* of the allies of Priam. Similar

[1] In his *Introduction* to the English Translation. Cf. *Companion to the Iliad*, 1892; *Iliad* I–II, 2nd ed., 1900–2; *Troy; a Study in Homeric Geography* 1912; *Homer and History*, 1915; *Strabo on the Troad*, 1923.

[2] In *Homer and the Epic*. Cf. *Homer and his Age*, 1906; *The World of Homer*, 1910.

discoveries in regard to the *Catalogue* of Agamemnon's forces awaited T. W. Allen,[1] as soon as it was possible to plot upon a map the geographical distribution of Mycenaean settlements, as was done in a preliminary way by William Ridgeway in 1901[2] and more fully by Maurice Thompson in 1911.[3] For the result, on both sides of the Aegean, was to show that, whatever the date of composition of the two *Catalogues* as we have them and whatever the stage in the composition of the *Iliad* at which they became incorporated in that poem, they preserve a detailed record of a phase of historical geography as closely in accord with an archaeological reconstruction of Aegean conditions in the thirteenth and twelfth centuries, as it is incompatible with anything in early Greek history later than the beginning of the eleventh.

In a quite different field, Hermann Usener put the Homeric hexameter into a fresh perspective in relation to other early types of metre,[4] and prepared the way for Wilamowitz's eventual treatment of this problem nearly thirty years later. He also formulated more clearly the problem of the relations of a poet to his sources, and especially the part to be assigned, on the one hand to individual imagination, and on the other to those timeless and placeless *motifs* and incidents which form so large a part of the repertory of early story-telling everywhere, in the reshaping of whatever historical traditions are enshrined in works of art of this kind. In a sense, Usener's essay is one of the starting-points for a movement of reaction from the extreme radicalism which was dominant when he wrote. To the same year (1897) belongs Georges Bertrin's *La Question homérique*, one of the earlier and better French restatements of the unitarian view of Homer as a great personality; and it should be noted here that French scholarship, however much it conceded to German claims to have established revolutionary critical results by the method of analysis and more than Alexandrian "analogy", seldom left out of sight the artistic unity of each of the poems as we have them, and the significance of this unity in criticizing inconsistencies

---

[1] A paper in *JHS* XXX (1910) developed in *The Homeric Catalogue of Ships* (1921).

[2] *The Early Age of Greece* (1901), pp. 1–79.

[3] "The distribution of Mycenaean remains and the Homeric Catalogue", (*Liverpool Annals of Archaeology and Anthropology* IV (1912), pp. 128 ff.

[4] *Altgriechischer Versbau*, 1887; *Der Stoff des griechischen Epos*, 1897.

of detail. Andrew Lang also, in addition to his contribution to the appreciation of the contents of the poems, dissected the whole argument of analytical criticism from the point of view of a man of letters, himself a translator of Homer into English prose and also no mean poet. Typical examples of the dominant German criticism by means of what it was the fashion to call "analysis", are two of the principal publications of 1901, E. Bethe's *Homer and Heroic Legend* and C. Robert's *Studies in the Iliad*.[1] It is worth noting that this is the year in which Dörpfeld's *Troja und Ilion* appeared. Bethe, though accounted almost unitarian by those who went further in the way of dissection, allowed himself to be dominated by the notion that everything early and therefore original in the *Iliad* must necessarily have a Thessalian context; and conversely that everything not Thessalian must have been added later to the Thessalian *repertoire*. The girl Briseis is so intimate an element in the story of the Quarrel between Achilles and Agamemnon, and moreover so essentially an Aeolic element, since her home Brisa was in Lesbos, that Fick and Wilamowitz had been content to eliminate her as a topical inter-polation, by a Lesbian for Lesbians, in a poem already traditional. But even she is relegated by Bethe to a still later phase of reworking, because he thinks that the poet who introduced her did not know the simplest fact about her antecedents, but treated the epithet Briseis— the girl from Brisa—as if it were a proper name. Paris, on the other hand, is attributed to the original poem, partly on the strength of a story related only by Plutarch[2] that on some unknown occasion he was defeated in battle on the Spercheios by Achilles and Patroclus, partly on the curious ground that in the *Iliad* all his opponents in battle are Thessalians; to establish which general statement it was necessary for Bethe to discount Menelaus and Diomedes. After the definitive publication of the results of the Trojan excavations, it is true, Bethe made the quite considerable concession that there may have been Trojans in the country which the Greeks called the Troad, instead of *only* in Thessaly; but rather than admit the possibility that a quarrel between men of Thessaly and men of the Troad was the foundation of the legend of a Trojan War, he found reasons for making Ajax, of all people, a local hero of Rhoeteium on the coast of

---

[1] *Homer und die Heldensage* and *Studien zu Ilias*.

[2] *Theseus* 34, on authority of ὁ Ἴστρος ἐν τῇ τρισκαιδεκάτῃ τῶν Ἀττικῶν. See notes on *F. Gr. Hist.*, 334, F 7.

Troad, on the ground that one of the great tumuli in that district was shown as his tomb. Evidently no hero who hoped for immortality could afford to be killed overseas. Robert's method of analysis was even simpler. Reichel had observed (as we have seen) that many of the passages in which the descriptions of armour are applicable to the Hellenic type, with parry-shield and breastplate, occur in parts of the poem which were already regarded as "late" on various other grounds. Robert took this contrast between modes of fighting as his principle of distinction between "Primitive *Iliad*" and later accretions; and he applied it so rigidly that he ejected, sometimes long episodes, sometimes a paragraph, frequently single lines here and there, on the ground of nonconformity in this respect with their contexts. This "Primitive *Iliad*" theory was popularized on much the same grounds by Leaf in the second edition of his *Iliad* XIII–XXIV which came out in 1902, and it had a considerable vogue also in Germany.

It was indeed time that some general account should be given of the logical ground for this kind of criticism, especially as there was growing discrepancy among the results to which it led in different hands; and this was opportunely attempted by Alfred Gercke,[1] with valuable illustrations of similar attempts, as he put it, "to watch the author at his work" in other departments of literature; for example, in the attempts to determine on internal evidence the chronological order of the *Dialogues* of Plato, which had recently given rise to similar controversy. Even unsuccessful analysis is justified, for it leads to revision of received opinions and challenges verification; it is justified no less if the nett result is to show, not that different poets made different use of their sources, but that one and the same poet had different notions at different times, revising his own work piecemeal and incompletely, so that inconsistencies are allowed to stand. Notorious examples, where documentary evidence is available, are provided by Schiller's *Don Carlos* and above all by Goethe's *Faust*. This marks a return to sanity, if not to commonsense, which was long overdue, and which is by no means universal even now. It was at all events something that when an allusion to an episode related in one context was found in another in which the critic did not expect it to occur, it was held to deserve explanation rather than mere

[1] "Die Analyse als Grundlage der höheren Kritik", *Neue Jahrbücher für das Klass. Altertum* VII (1901), pp. 1 ff., 81 ff. and 185 ff.

excision. Gercke's own explanation was but a poor compliment to the poet, whom he supposed to have become conscious of a certain looseness of structure in his own work and used this rather crude device for "clamping it together". A really critical poet, presumably, would have added the footnote, "See line so-and-so". There is, moreover, a certain "poetical" way of thinking, a constitutional weakness to which poets as such are liable; a less considerate critic might have said, more frankly, that poets are as untidy about their verses as about their ties and their hair. But the admission was a valuable one, that a poet might be conceded the same licence as was generally allowed to an interpolator. This concession that the poet himself might make mistakes, and that the most scrupulous interpolator did not manage to detect and rectify all of them, reappears as the upshot of an entertaining controversy between two Italian critics, Giuseppe Fraccaroli and Gaetano de Sanctis, in the years between 1903 and 1905.[1] It was the old controversy between the champions of "anomaly" and of "analogy" which had divided the scholars of the Alexandrian Age. Some of the disconcerting peculiarities of a great poet's work may (it is true) be ascribed, on sufficient grounds, to interference from another hand; but two other causes must be admitted and distinguished. There is the primitive awkwardness of a beginner—and even the greatest poet is most of all a beginner in his art, where he takes the boldest step outwards beyond the guidance of experience. And there are the restrictions imposed by experience itself, by tradition, by convention. Take for example the frequent use of the device of verbal repetition of whole passages, when a command, for instance, is given through a messenger, rehearsed by the messenger, and executed by the recipient of the message; is this an original device for enhancing the appreciation of a fine passage? Or, even if this was its origin, has it become, in a given instance, a conventional respite for the composer or for professional reciters, long afterwards? Or, if it was originally a convention, does the poet ever use it to achieve a special effect? Or again has it become a mere clog on the spontaneous composition of a poet with a style of his own? Once again, unwonted licence is being claimed for the poet; or, to

[1] Fraccaroli, *L'irrazionale nella letteratura*, 1903. De Sanctis, "L'irrazionale nell'Iliade", *Rivista di Filologia* 32 (1904), pp. 41 ff. Fraccaroli, "L'irrazionale e la critica omerica", *ibid.*, 33 (1905), pp. 273 ff. De Sanctis, "L'Iliade e i diretti della critica", *ibid.*, pp. 552 ff.

put the case rather more crudely, the critics are being refused their customary licence to condemn as un-Homeric or un-Achilleid or un-Odyssean, what it is their proper business to accept as "Homeric" at least to the extent that it occurs in this or that passage of one of the Homeric poems.

Another real step forward is the essay of Immisch, "On the internal development of Greek poetry; a contribution to an historical interpretation of poetry".[1] Previous critics had been too much inclined to regard the history of the Homeric poems as consisting essentially in the gradual disfigurement of an originally self-sufficient masterpiece—*Achilleid*, primitive *Iliad*, and what not—in a long process of transmission which was in the main from bad to worse. Immisch had been greatly impressed by the description, given twenty years earlier, by a Russian scholar, V. V. Radloff, of the popular poetry of the nomad Black Kirghiz tribes in Northern Turkestan.[2] Here, a large body of narrative tradition was preserved, as stories and not as poems, in the memory of every responsible member of the community. As the girl of Telmessos said, in Arrian's story about Gordius the Phrygian,[3] "We are all soothsayers here", so the Black Kirghiz, like Zoëga's Greek peoples, "all were that poet". Tell a Black Kirghiz, as they told Demodocus in the *Odyssey*, where you want him to begin, and he starts off chanting then and there, ἔνθεν ἑλὼν ὥς, . . . picking up the thread at that point. Ask him what chants he knows, and he replies, as the Sirens cried to Odysseus, "We know all things, even the whole tale of Troy".[4] Now, this communal poetry (*Gemeinschaftspoesie*) is something quite different from the *Volks-poesie*, the metrical folk-lore of Mediaeval Europe, where the lays or ballads or sagas are in traditional form as well as about traditional subjects; that stage, Immisch argued, comes very much later, and only when such a society has been somehow deranged and the survivors tax their memories for snatches of "what so-and-so said", and "how so-and-so put it" in the good old days. Obviously when that stage has been reached, there is room for patchwork and compilation, as when Topelius and Lönnroth went about Finland

[1] Johann Heinrich Otto Immisch, *Die innere Entwicklung des griechischen Epos*, 1904.
[2] *Proben der Volksliteratur der türkischen Stämme*, Vol. V (1885).
[3] *Anabasis* II, 3.
[4] θ 484 ff.; μ 189.

collecting what they could of the *Kalevala*, or Macpherson collected the tales about Fingal and Ossian in the Scottish Highlands. To go "lay-hunting" now, as Lachmann and his successors had been doing, in the Homeric poems as we have them, was for Immisch as fruitless as to attempt to reconstruct from Macpherson's *Ossian* what individual gaelic-speaking Highlanders told Macpherson. The eventual literary form, hexameter epic, *Hiawatha*-verses, Fitzgerald's *Omar Khayyám*, in which the results of such compilation are perpetuated and at long last written down, is the climax, not the decadence of a literary type. For generations, in such originally communal poetry, the commonsense and common judgment of a whole society has been engaged upon a common stock of events and ideas rather than of compositions. Certainly there were phrases, a repertory of memorable expressions, ever enriched, ever selected and revised. Certainly, too, there was shift of perspective, of taste, of political experience, of moral judgment, not necessarily for the worse provided the corporate life remained normally wholesome. One might expect, under favourable conditions, growing rationalism, growing delicacy of sentiment, vigour of fancy, intensity of romance. Where everyone is potential audience as well as potential poet, there is no question of interpolation, any more than of primitive kernel, in the sense assumed by current criticism of the Homeric poems. Obviously this aspect of the matter does not at all exclude editorial revision of such a body of communal poetry after the spell has been broken by some crisis and the product transferred to the custody of individual memories or individual manuscript. What it does eliminate is the "lay-hunting" after ready-made patches and snatches of traditional song or saga, which had been the customary procedure of Homeric criticism since Lachmann, and in a measure since Bentley and d'Aubignac. And once again it was a step towards a more scientific criticism of the poems and away from the discussion of discrepancies between the conjectural compositions of imaginary poets.

Among the many followers of Wolf, Lachmann and Kirchhoff, whose industrious analyses have explored every corner of the field, very few have succeeded in presenting their conclusions as a critical history of the poems. Among those few, two writers may be selected for closer examination, Gilbert Murray and Wilamowitz. Their works at this period illustrate respectively the broader and the narrower view of the critic's task, and each contains some aspects of subsidiary studies which have contributed appreciably to a fuller understanding of Homer.

Earlier in date, wider in treatment, but in some respects inevitably less convincing in retrospect, is Murray's *Rise of the Greek Epic*, the first edition of which was published in 1907. Thoroughly in the spirit of most English criticism is his insistence at the outset on the Homeric Problem as a single and special aspect of the interpretation of one of the supreme achievements of humanity, the Greek genius. More individual is his own special interest in the moral purpose which he finds in the Hellenic view of life as a rational struggle for betterment against older and ever imminent impulses of human nature, which collectively are barbarism and individually phases of ignorance, or rather of inexperience and irrationality. In this struggle, which he traces to its origins in the moral as well as political and material chaos of the historical collapse of Mycenaean civilization, older bonds of kinship or political obligation were ruptured with quite exceptional violence. Literally, in Aristotle's phrase, the City State came into existence "for the maintenance of life",[1] among waifs and adventurers accidentally jostled into neighbourhood and constrained to neighbourliness. Hence arose new conceptions of self-restraint and self-respect, the moral counterpart of a new social order based on mutual respect and mutual restraint. This enforced moral revaluation by the survivors from the dead past, when extended to their heritage of folk-memory and observance, effected a progressive "expurgation"—to use Murray's own phrase; traditional stories, which had originally reflected the morality of the decadence and the *débâcle*, were consciously revised as the new morality grew, though without ever wholly eliminating allusions to such barbarities as the use of poisoned arrows, human sacrifice, mutilation of dead enemies and so forth. Similar revision Murray conceives as having been almost unconsciously operative in regard to material culture also, as described in traditional narratives, resulting in the same incomplete and uneven modernization of references to armour, burial customs, marriage customs, construction of houses and sanctuaries and the like.

But in all this process of evolution, what was it that evolved? Analogy with ancient Hebrew literature, and also with old French

---

[1] γινομένη μὲν οὖν τοῦ ζῆν ἕνεκα, οὖσα δὲ τοῦ εὖ ζῆν (*Polit. A* 2. 1252. b. 30).

poems, such as *Roland* and *Saint Alexis,* leads to the conception of what Murray describes as a "traditional book", as the vehicle of transmission. Since writing was certainly in use in the Minoan-Mycenaean culture, it must be presumed, he argues, that literature existed, and that fragments of it were saved and treasured. Into the question what language was spoken before the *débâcle,* he does not enter at length; for him, "if the men of the migrations possessed a literature . . . it was much more nearly what the Greeks of the sixth and early fifth centuries meant by 'Homer', viz. the whole body of heroic tradition as embodied in hexameter verse". Three points in this conception, essentially that of Wilamowitz's essay of 1884, are worth noting: the tradition is in Greek; it is, as an aid to recitation from memory, not only metric and hexametric but also written; and it is all "Homeric" alike. The personal Homer is at all events not at the beginning of the growth of Epic. Examples are given of such "traditional books" at various periods, the private treasure of an individual collector and retailer of stories, never complete, always being interpolated, expanded, amended, as experience and imagination bade. Such in Greek traditions were the scrolls acquired by other individuals from the personal Homer. Comparison of Greek epic poems, considered as the result of such a process of transmission, with the no less composite Hebrew chronicles, such as the *Book of Judges,* illustrates the spontaneous freedom of imaginative and creative revision in early Greek literature, in marked contrast with naïve and respectful collocation of alternative versions almost unaltered in Hebrew scripture. The higher criticism of Hebrew literature, difficult as it often is, has therefore a far simpler problem to deal with than Homeric criticism. But Murray thought that he could detect early relics of traditions referring to events in peninsular Greece—Thessaly, Boeotia, Argolis—on the lines suggested by Dümmler and Bethe; a great conflation of heroic legends of divers origins, around historical incidents in the process of Aeolic colonization, which he regards as a very long and arduous one; and a third phase of similar conflation, when the poems in their Aeolic phase of recomposition became popularized further south and were supplemented by the rich heritage of Argolis and Laconia. It is in this phase, he thought, that we have the first glimpse of incidents which circulated among the more motley population of the Ionian cities, infused into this tradition by the literary corporation of the Children of Homer, who were engaged both in transmission and in revision. A last stage of transformation came, he suggests, through some transference of an older Pan-Ionian festival from Ionia to Delos, and from Delos to Athens, where it becomes the Peisistratid Panathenaea, for which an authorized version of the Homeric *corpus* of epic was not unnaturally required and provided.

It will be evident that in all this there is not much advance beyond the position reached by German criticism some while before. The only important novelties are the stress laid on moral as well as material revision, and the provision of a mechanism for this, by the acceptance of the possibility of such a "traditional book" established by the discovery not only of engraved script, but also of penmanship at Knossos. Throughout there is insistence on the possibility, and even the necessity, that poems such as the *Iliad* and *Odyssey* should come into existence through the superadded touches of a multitude of hands; the occasional emergence of a composer of exceptional skill or imagination is not excluded, but is clearly regarded as unnecessary. What takes its place is the strong social and moral impulse to hand down the common heritage not less but rather more and better, in literature as in the material world. As mediaeval craftsmen worked anonymously and concordantly on the fabric of a great church during centuries of changing style—adding and replacing with less respect for plan than for convenience, but dominated all by one usage and idea of workmanship—so, almost in Zoëga's phrase *questi populi Greci erano quell' Omero*: as Gaston Paris says of the *Chanson de Roland*—the name of its writer is *Legion*.

Another aspect of Murray's interpretation of Homer is characteristic both of his own contributions to Greek literary criticism in other fields, and of the period at which his *Rise of the Greek Epic* first appeared. The tendency to explain as *allegory*, that is to say, as meaning something different from what is said, was an old one among critics of the Homeric text, and a very convenient resource in dealing with difficult passages. While the Aryan hypothesis held the field, in the spacious days of the nineteenth century, it was inevitable that Achilles should in due course be sublimated into a Sun God, and the whole Trojan War into a diagram of the whole course of Nature. When, however, comparative mythology began to give place to comparative religion, or rather, perhaps we should say, to comparative ritual, in the hands of the new anthropological school of

Mannhardt and Wilcken, Usener and Durkheim, Tylor, Frazer and Jane Harrison, it was only to be expected that among the sources of Homeric episodes and personages, place should be found for the tree-spirits, the scapegoats, the sacred marriages, the grislyapparatus of totems and *tabus*, which were conceived as the stock-in-trade of Aegean religion until with the coming of the Olympian theology "the flood came and destroyed them all; and yet did not destroy them utterly, for there was a grim undertone of chthonic observance under that limpid flood water, which surged up now and again, clouding and defiling it". In another essay,[1] Murray developed this topic separately; there are aspects of Greek belief which are recognizable in Hesiod and become ubiquitous as we come to know more of the popular as distinct from the official practice of Olympian cults; they are clearly affiliated to the tree and pillar cults, animal symbolism and other symptoms of the prevalence of anthropological *Urdummheit* in the religion of Minoan Crete, as we see it in the sanctuaries and in the pictorial art of the palace period and its predecessors. How then, Murray asks, does it happen that these non-Olympian factors are so very nearly absent from the *Iliad* and *Odyssey*?

Murray's answer is the hypothesis of expurgation which has already been noted as central in his criticism of Homer. The *Urdummheit* was indeed there, in the chaos of the *débâcle*, rampant and unashamed; but it was there no longer as a system and rule of life, but as a festering, rotten mass of bad habits, anti-social, immoral, irreligious almost, in the eyes of the survivors who had been through that Slough of Despond. Nor had the Olympians, as their earlier votaries conceived them, turned out to be the secure guide of life which they may once have been in easier times; in the day of trouble they too had failed their worshippers, though not so utterly. Hence, as the new order took shape, much was suppressed and eliminated, because it was felt to be obsolete, in observance and in belief; and in poetry too, as in the material arts of this Hellenic renaissance, old stories and songs, as "nasty and brutish" as they were short, were transmuted and humanized into myths and legends of a new model. The cruelties of the primeval scapegoats and human victims became the horseplay of Odysseus over Thersites, and the *hieros gamos* became the *motif* of *contes gauloises*—Milesian tales, like the Διὸς

[1] *Five Stages of Greek Religion*, 1925.

208

ἀπάτη and the lay of Demodocus about the intrigue of Ares and Aphrodite; and the centre of interest shifted from the ritual drama of a dying god to the moralized human pathos of the tragedies of Hector and Achilles.

The other summary of current literary criticism to which I would direct attention at this stage, was contributed by Wilamowitz.[1] It is of importance, partly as an illustration of contemporary beliefs, partly also as an intermediate stage between his own original standpoint in 1884 and the very different outlook of his essay on the *Iliad* in 1916. A Trojan War, in the sense of a campaign of "all the Hellenes" against the Hellespontine fortress capital of a Thraco-Phrygian confederacy with outskirts in Macedon and Lycia, Wilamowitz refused to accept. Hissarlik is too small. One is tempted to ask, perhaps not historical questions about "contemptible little armies", but strictly strategical questions (since this is after all a question of strategy) about the relative size of places like Ypres or Verdun, in view of the magnitude of the issues. Wilamowitz further objected that the historic Ilion was founded during Lydian times, and that therefore the site was desolate during the centuries when the poems were being composed. But this is an argument in a circle, for it presumes that the poems were being composed only during the centuries when the site was desolate, and also that there was no folk-memory, poetical or otherwise, of the Sack, and before that of the fortifying and repeated repair of the Sixth City. On this point Leaf's virtual rejoinder, in his book entitled *Troy*, is in fact conclusive. More important, in respect of Wilamowitz's general defence of an evolutionary view of the poems, is the consideration that if, as he contended, there was no Trojan War historically, then someone must have invented it; and the less the traditional ground for such a story, the greater the imaginative genius of its inventor. With a great historical event in the background, piecemeal elaboration of the memory of it is perhaps conceivable; but if there was no Troy, how is an *Iliad* to be explained without a personal Homer? Wilamowitz followed Bethe in believing in the wholesale transposition of legends. On the plain of Troy neither Achilles and Diomedes, nor Hector and Andromache are "at home"; they have been contributed to the story by men of various origins, bringing their own local legends with them. But bringing them to whom, and contributing

[1] In *Kultur der Gegenwart*, ed. Paul Hinneberg, I, 8 (1905), pp. 4ff.

them to what story, if there was no Trojan War, and no personal Homer to collect them? Nor was there even, for Wilamowitz, the Peisistratid recension of the *Homeri libros confusos antea* which had been the alternative adopted by Wolf; for Wilamowitz still insisted that the poems as we have them were essentially of Ionian composition and of pre-Peisistratid antiquity. His insistence, however, on the justice of the popular verdict that, with all the faults which scholars find in it, the *Iliad*, and still more the *Odyssey*, is a masterpiece of great poetry, was beginning to force him to admit that somewhere in the long process of patchwork and redaction, a great mind had intervened. Somebody, sometime, had done something which reduced chaos to order—of a sort—and for Wilamowitz that somebody was Ionian, and that sometime was almost at the end of the process. In particular, he repudiated the notion that it was any use to try to characterize Homeric heroes, as one may characterize Hamlet or Faustus; for within the poems themselves "different poets conceived the same heroes differently".

Only a few months before the essay of Immisch which we were discussing just now, appeared the first of a series of studies by Dietrich Mülder which did much to put the whole theory of an Ionian Homer on a fresh and less problematic footing. Mülder was at no pains to conceal that he was trained in the methods of Kirchhoff and Wilamowitz; that he had practised "analysis" *secundum artem* until he found that it failed to give conclusive or even coherent results; and that as he found this to be the common experience of those who practised it, at all events in the sense that "their witness agreed not together", he determined to make the experiment of turning the analytical method against itself. In his first paper,[1] on the Cyclops episode in the *Odyssey*, he still spoke indeed of "expansion" and "working over" of an earlier composition; but he was already insisting, as a matter of critical method, that we must begin with the poems as we have them, not from a more or less problematical archetype; that we must ascertain in the first instance the method, the intention, and the literary and creative qualities of the poet who made the *Odyssey* what it is; and that only when we have defined and isolated this poet's work, is it permissible to apply the same strictly literary criticism to the sources which we can discover him to have used. In

[1] "Das Kyklopengedicht der Odyssee", *Hermes* 38 (1903), pp. 414ff.; see now Denys Page, *The Homeric Odyssey* (1955), pp. 1ff.

the Cyclops episode, for example, the widespread and common-place folk-tale of an encounter between an adventurer and a giant ogre has been individualized by the characterization of the country and of the primitive habits of a whole people of Round-Eyed folk, not positively monstrous, but outlandish; by prolonging and elab-orating the sojourn in the cave, in the light of the highly wrought conception of the hero's character which runs through the *Odyssey* and in some degree also through parts of the *Iliad*; above all, by combining with the giant and hero *motif*, that of the stratagem of punning anonymity—a stroke of genuine humour—by which Odysseus counters the Cyclops's call for help and achieves his escape. These are original conceptions of the creator of the episode as we have it; they are so intricately interwoven into the narrative that "patchwork", "expansion", or any kind of editorial manipulation of archetypal versions is out of the question. The whole story has been retold by a great narrative poet in his own way and in his own words.

Similar analysis of the twenty-second book of the *Iliad*[1] led Mülder to even more positive appreciation of the originality and command both of materials and of literary technique which distinguished the composer, rather than editor, of one of the central and (according to the whole analytical school) one of the oldest parts of the *Iliad*. The traditional account of the death of Hector is transfigured by the device by which the poet introduces his original conception of the pursuit round the walls of Troy, and by the pathos of Hector's deliberate return from a place of safety in spite of entreaties conceived in an almost elegiac tone. Incidentally he argued that even the *Making of the Armour* in Σ was never an independent poem, and that the loss of the original armour through the death of Patroclus was another inspiration of the poet, not a patchwork of earlier "lays". In view of these indications of original invention and mature pathos and romance in the very framework of the story, he insisted that the great poet must be placed at the end of the process of aggregation and assimilation of traditional elements, not at the beginning, at the *Achilleid* stage as conceived by Grote and his imitators. How late, then, must we look for the date of this man of genius? This question

---

[1] "Εκτορος ἀναίρεσις, *Rh. Mus.* LIX (1904), pp. 256ff. ('Ορκίων σύγχυσις appeared in *Neue Jahrbücher für das klass. Altertum* in the same year.)

Mülder answered by an instructive comparison[1] between the didactic passages which occur in many parts of the *Iliad*, especially in the mouth of Nestor, and the similarly didactic tone of much early elegiac poetry. The substance of the military advice formulates relatively modern practice, and contrasts it with the "good old days"; and this modern practice is distinctively Hellenic, of a not very early and already self-conscious phase in the development of the city-state *régime*. Some of the passages are recognizably topical, for example the references to the Cretan Idomeneus. In the rather paradoxical belief that these resemblances to elegiac poetry result from imitation of its tone, Mülder concluded that the great creative poet lived a little later than Tyrtaeus and Archilochus—an opinion in which he has found few to concur. It is, however, not an integral element in his argument, though it may provoke doubts as to the soundness of his literary judgment in other matters.

In another paper, also published in 1906 but written three years earlier,[2] Mülder outlined a general interpretation of the plot of the *Odyssey*, finding in it a conscious and sustained sequence of cause and effect in the career of a "hero" in the novelist's sense of the word. Into this scheme or plot, the poet has woven both adventures traditionally ascribed to the Odysseus who figures in certain parts of the *Iliad*, and also episodes not originally Odyssean but selected from current folk-lore and transmuted so as to elucidate the clearly conceived character of the versatile, much-enduring hero imagined by the poet; while the hero's character itself develops in detail, in response to the trials to which the poet chooses to expose him. Every poet, it is contended, is an "overworker" and "expander" in the sense that he will not and cannot leave his materials as he finds them; but what he composes is his own work, behind which it is only possible to detect themes and episodes, and vain to search for "lays" and a "kernel" with recognizable literary features. Some time before Mülder was in a position to recast into a book[3] his earlier studies and the numerous controversial reviews in which he had dealt with those who differed from his conclusions, his vigorous and novel application of the

[1] *Homer und die altionische Elegie*, 1906.
[2] "Die Phäakerdichtung der Odyssee", *Neue Jahrbücher für das klass. Altertum* XVII (1906), pp. 10ff. ("Analyse des zwölften und zehnten Buches der Odyssee" appeared in *Philologus* in the same year.)
[3] *Die Ilias und ihre Quellen*, 1910.

analytical method began to convert opponents and to find imitators. Cauer in 1909[1] accepted in essentials his insistence on an element of high poetic genius at a quite late date in the growth (as Cauer still held it to be) of the poems; even the motive of the *Wrath of Achilles* and the first book of the *Iliad* which enunciates it, is a "working part of a design", which was not primitive but, once invented, was employed deliberately to draw into one artistic whole a great number of varied and even incongruous materials. In France, about the same time, there was quite a little eruption of Homeric criticism, mostly of a purely literary kind, influenced but not dominated by Teutonic analyses. Michel Bréal, reviewing Robert's *Studien zur Ilias* in 1903, asked frankly what the Germans would have said if a Frenchman had published such nonsense; and he followed it up by a valuable essay[2] combining a moderately evolutionist view of the whole process of epic growth with the conviction that, for the poem to grow into such a work of art at all, there must have been a clearly perceptible plan or plot from a very early stage, to which additions or expansions conformed, however diverse their origins. In reviewing this book in 1907, the veteran archaeologist Georges Perrot confessed himself converted after long years to the notion of a single author. The language is homogeneous, an artificial medium perhaps, but the utterance of a single poet. He would, however, assign his single poet to the end of the ninth century, in accordance with ancient belief, and consequently he admitted that passages which betrayed the influence of customs or ideas of later date than this might have been inserted afterwards. The retrospect published in the same year by Maurice Croiset[3] of the stage reached by Homeric criticism generally at the close of the nineteenth century, was not by any means wholly favourable to the critics.

Very significant of this new trend in literary criticism is the third principal contribution of Wilamowitz to the subject, in his book on the *Iliad and Homer*,[4] a pendant, thirty-two years later, to his essay on the *Odyssey* in 1884 and, like it, amplified into a general survey of the Homeric Question as it appeared to him at that time. Many critical conclusions of earlier date he still refused to surrender. He

[1] In the second edition of *Grundfragen*.
[2] *Pour mieux connaître Homère*, 1906.
[3] *La Question d'Homère au début du 20me siècle*, 1907.
[4] *Die Ilias und Homer*, 1916, 2nd ed., 1920.

213

could see no trace of a vulgate text of the poems before the time of Zenodotus, only a chaos of discrepant manuscripts of which some were good ones. It was only gradually that the decisions of Aristarchus prevailed, and the great Alexandrians themselves *knew*, he believed, how precarious their hold on the real Homer was. Thanks to the rhapsodists of the fourth, fifth and sixth centuries, we can, however, have a fair notion of the Solonian text. Its dialect was a conventional and artificial one, in which poets, early and late alike, composed as well as they could, sometimes archaizing, sometimes not, as we may see from the less overworked text of Hesiod. But the rhapsodists themselves did not understand all that they recited; they accepted corruptions and contradictions as they found them, or explained them as best they might. Similarly, Wilamowitz had still no use for such comparison between Homer and other early literatures as had led astray Lachmann, and before him Wolf. Modern analysis, like the assimilation of epic to folk-poetry, "crumbles" the poems, through neglect of the evidence for design. This design, for him as for Mülder, can be recovered only by a new kind of analysis, which must begin with the latest additions and not attempt to dissect out an original core or kernel; and he submitted the results of his own analysis, of which it is sufficient to say that there is lacking any demonstration that the whole process was not rapid enough to have been comprised within the working life of a single composer. Within the *Iliad* as we have it, the ultimate units now recognizable by analysis are not originally separate lays, such as Lachmann supposed, but cantos of a "sequel of Songs and Rhapsodies", to revive Bentley's phrase, presupposing, both in the poets and in their audiences, acquaintance with a great *repertoire* of such narratives; and the *Iliad* was not the first nor the only attempt to present coherently larger masses of such material. The epic, as planned, is in our *Iliad*, but it is not identical with it. Unitarian critics have done well to insist on our poet's mastery of his material, but the materials themselves were already of a high order of epic technique; hence, among other things, arises the difficulty of dissecting them out. Our *Iliad* and *Odyssey* survived as they have, because they came into existence at the climax of this school of literary art. They superseded their forerunners, and they had no successors to supersede them. Of the poems of this epic decline, we know enough to recognize their limitations of scope and style. The reason for their degeneracy is also evident, in the competition of new literary forms—choric, lyric, dithyrambic, tragic; and eventually their place was taken by mere prose extracts and insipid parodies.

How the poet of the *Iliad* is conceived to have worked is described in a phrase, "The Muse told it all to him, and the Muses are the daughters of Memory".[1] What was at the disposal of Memory was of infinite variety, in content as in origin. Of real folk-memory about the colonization of the coasts of Asia Minor, he thinks there was little; not much, either, of events in old Greece before the migrations occurred. Of Evans's bilingual period he shows no knowledge at all. A real crisis, on the other hand, is discovered at the point where folk songs sung to the lyre passed out of vogue, and were replaced by the long resonant lines of hexameter verse, which by their characteristic and novel device of caesura were accommodated to unaccompanied recitation, and which consequently permitted the enhancement of vocal emphasis and dramatic gesture. The singer became the reciter, laid aside the lyre for the rod or laurel-spray, and allowed himself the new luxury of speech-making. This, it should be noticed, is a quite new point, and profoundly modifies earlier comparisons between the minstrels described in the poems as part of the retinue of Heroic chieftains and the verse-makers of the new hexametric *recitative*. For such a revolution in the art of presentation necessitated wholesale recomposition of the narratives themselves. Much in the same way, when epic itself was passing out of vogue, Stesichorus, and later still Pindar and Bacchylides, were similarly obliged to retranslate the old stories into their new metres. The creator of the new hexametric vehicle is for us all that we can know of a personal Homer. This is not very consistent with Wilamowitz's other contention, that Homer came at the climax of the hexametric literature and had predecessors in his own art, but let that pass. The last if not the greatest of the separatists[2] speaks to us out of maturer wisdom of a personal Homer, or more probably of two personal Homers, at the beginning and end of the style, dated somewhere between the completion of the colonizing movement across the Aegean and the Cimmerian inroads of the seventh century, which he correlates with internal changes in the Ionian cities and so with the growth of rival literary forms.

[1] p. 331.
[2] Or should one now say, "The greatest if not the last"?

Far more radical were the counter-criticisms of the few surviving representatives, such as Karl Rothe, of an older Unitarianism.[1] Its supporters have usually, and very naturally, underestimated the services rendered by evolutionary criticism and particularly by some of the most minute examples of analysis, in formulating the problems which any theory of single authorship must face, and in estimating the amount and variety of the traditional materials which in any case lay within the reach of an original and constructive master of imaginative poetry, at whatever period and in whatever local circumstances he may be conceived to have performed his work of creation. Yet in Rothe's later work he admitted that his personal Homer, whom he put (like most other German critics) very late within the period of formation, used earlier materials and did not merely make up his poems out of his head, though he still insisted that it is no longer possible to find out anything about them. And on the other hand, staunch unitarian though he was, he admitted both Attic interpolations, from some kind of Peisistratid recension, and also supplements to the poems as the personal Homer left them. Most significant of all as a symptom of a certain return to sanity on this side of the controversy too, was his admission that within the unitary poem there are signs of revision and development; as he quaintly but effectively put it, Homer supplemented himself. This is indeed a question which few of the modern critics of Homer have ever clearly answered. How much of the minuter or even of the more flagrant discrepancies in the poems as we have them necessarily require for their explanation a period of more than a single working lifetime? Look at the dramatic art and the metrical usage of Shakespeare in his earlier and in his later plays; look at what we might almost describe as the autobiography of Goethe's *Faust*, at the demonstrable overworking of Chapman's *Homer* and Fitzgerald's *Omar Khayyám*, at the slips of the pen, in spite of manuscript and even proof-readers, in *Pendennis* and *The Heart of Midlothian*.

More disconcerting still to the separatist or evolutionary school, was the inability of its exponents to arrive at any agreed analysis, even of the processes which may be supposed to have gone on in the

[1] *Die Bedeutung der Wiederholungen für die homerische Frage*, 1890; *Die Bedeutung der Widersprüche für die homerische Frage*, 1894; *Die Ilias als Dichtung*, 1910; *Die Odyssee als Dichtung*, 1914.

mind of a single composer active over a long term of years, still less
of the relations between early and late in the saecular reworkings of
a school of epic upon its traditional book or books. Is the first book
of the *Iliad*, for example, a late prologue, composed when the poem
was essentially complete in its complexity, or is it a lucky survival of
an immemorial lay about the *Wrath of Achilles*, when the *Wrath* was
itself a complete poem of only four or five books on the Alexandrian
scale which we still use? The methods habitually employed by
separatist critics rested indeed on highly subjective estimates and
distinctions; their witness agreed not together; and it was difficult
to avoid the conclusion that it was not by the traditional process of
"interpreting Homer by himself" that an ultimate decision was to be
reached as to who or what Homer himself was. Most devastating of
all, other critics of a later generation, conforming perhaps over-
zealously to the Teutonic principle that without analysis, personally
conducted, there is no hope of salvation for a critic of Homer,
repeated—let us hope because σχεδὸν πάντα ηὕρηται by this time—
the analysis of predecessors, some of them Teutonic themselves, and
found that they had misstated the facts. This provoked replies ex-
posing the lurid details from such scholars as Drerup, Shewan and
Scott,[1] and they did not themselves always avoid the sin of mis-
representation which they so rightly castigated. Indeed it looked as
though what had long been admitted in regard to Fick's distinction
between Aeolic and non-Aeolic sections, that the occurrences of the
distinctive symptoms were far too perplexingly distributed and
combined with other features from which, on the hypothesis in
question, they should stand apart, to be explained by any such
dichotomy, was demonstrable also about many other contrasts and
anomalies. In fact, in Alexandrian phrase, the principle of "analogy"
could be pressed too far, and if pressed strictly at all, led inevitably to
the crude hypothesis of wholesale interpolation to account for the
existence, still more for the precise distribution, of exceptions.
Critics were beginning, in their own school and period of criticism,
to pass from the phase represented in ancient Alexandria by Zenodotus to that of Aristarchus, with his wise insistence on that primary
criterion, "the usage of the poet", and his combination of linguistic

[1] Engelbert Drerup, *Das fünfte Buch der Ilias*, 1913; *Das Homerproblem
in der Gegenwart*, 1921. A. Shewan, *The Lay of Dolon*, 1911; *Homeric
Essays*, 1935. J. A. Scott, *The Unity of Homer*, 1921.

scholarship with an appreciation of external and circumstantial evidence, which set him constructing a map of the plain of Troy and enquiring into the usage, not only of the poet, but of the age and people which the poet professed to describe.

Meanwhile, yet another attempt, far more detailed and philosophical than its predecessors, was made to determine the historical and social conditions in which what in general terms may be described as an *Heroic Age* occurs at all. This is the contribution of H. M. Chadwick, professor of English at Cambridge, whose special competence lay in early Teutonic and especially in Anglo-Saxon studies, and whose book, *The Heroic Age*,[1] starts from analysis of the demonstrable growth of German and Anglo-Saxon epic, in the light of the known historical conditions of each principal phase; and applies these and analogous conclusions from the study of old French poetry and other schools of epic literature, to supplement our less copious information about the period within which it was by this time clear that the Homeric poems took their eventual shape. It was a real achievement of constructive history-writing to support by a wide generalization what Ridgeway, Murray and others had already appreciated as the central and crucial feature of the Heroic Age of Greece: namely, the collapse of an older order, in society at large as in the arts, before a series of aggressions by less cultured but more virile adventurers. Chadwick established, too, by comparison of the genealogical evidence in each instance, not only the main outlines of the consecutive phases of this process, but also the chronological *pace*, so to speak, at which one stage after another of the concomitant literary development was reached and left behind. Once again, the result was to suggest that the phase in which such personal themes as the ἀριστεῖαι (*prowesses*) of individual heroes, the personal wrongs of a Menelaus, an Achilles and an Odysseus in face of Paris, Agamemnon and the Wooers of Penelope, find literary memorial, is an early phase; that is to say, that the poet stands only very little removed in time from the hero (in the literary sense) of his poem; and that the political circumstances which permit such offences against an exceptionally sensitive code of personal honour, are found to coexist with phases of social disorganization or re-organization of religious beliefs and practices and of the art of war, which are at the same time transitory and yet assignable to their inevitable place in a

[1] 1912.

large historical sequence.[1] Within ten years of the appearance of Chadwick's book, there was a notable confirmation of this estimate of the Greek Heroic Age. Mention has already been made of the light thrown by Egyptian documents on the history of the shores of the Levant in the centuries from the fifteenth to the twelfth, and even occasionally later. The seventh city of Hissarlik had been recognized since 1902 as resulting from the arrival of new peoples from across the Hellespont; but the connecting link between events in north-western and south-eastern Asia Minor was brought to light only through the decipherment of the Hittite archives discovered by the German explorers of Boghazköy, the Cappadocian capital of the dynasty of Hattusil, the ally of Rameses II. This decipherment was a matter of twenty years' work and of much controversy which does not concern Homeric studies; but in 1922 E. O. Forrer announced its completion.[2] Naturally many scholars unfamiliar with this kind of decipherment waited for "further evidence" before adjusting their views of early Aegean history to new material of such a kind; and there no doubt was (and is) much to be revised in detail. But the main outlines seemed to be clear, and the concordance between Hittite documents and Greek tradition very close.[3]

[1] For the Homeric code of conduct, see now Fernand Robert, *Homère* (1950), and E. R. Dodds, *The Greeks and the Irrational* (1951).

[2] "Die Inschriften und Sprachen des Hatti-Reiches", *Zeitschrift der deutschen morgenländischen Gesellschaft* LXXVI (1922), pp. 174 ff.

[3] Another important contribution by H. M. and N. K. Chadwick was *The Growth of Literature*, I–III (1934–40). See also C. M. Bowra, *Heroic Poetry*, 1952. The blending of old and new, typical of compositions of this kind, is seen in the poetry of the Russian revolution, where the historical facts are known. The general tone is traditional, and so are some details. In the *Tale of Lenin* by Marfa Kryokova, Lenin

> ... took his warrior horse,
> Took his silken bridle,

and Chapaev, according to two other poets,

> ... could dive as a pike in the blue sea,
> Race as a grey wolf over the open plain,
> Fly as a hawk under the blue clouds.

How long will it be before these become submarine, tank and aeroplane? Weapons are both old and new; in a short poem the hero takes sharp sabre, heavy club, steel knife, and Maxim machine-gun—a nice extension of the epithet. This is close to the Homeric hero who throws great stones and uses bronze weapons, and yet fights in "modern" style with throwing

Let us now, as on previous occasions, summarize the main results of the revolution which took place in less than half a century after Schliemann set spade to Troy. The discovery that classical Hellenism was not the first civilization of Greek lands but had been preceded by the long rise and decline of the Minoan culture and of its Mainland offshoot, contradicted the assumption current up to 1871, that everything civilized, elaborate or refined in the Homeric poems must be late and must therefore either bring down the date of the poems themselves or rank as an accretion. Allusions to Sicily were typical of this change of standpoint. Unless demonstrated on other grounds to be "late", they might just as well be "early". Much of the poems' content had been shown to be consistent with the Mainland civilization of the pre-Hellenic period and with no other. The discoveries explained much that had been inexplicable, and pointed the way to the solution of many more seeming anomalies. For it could be seen that blurring in the narrative was caused by the combination of older and newer (but not always post-Mycenaean) equipment and practices. And if some datable objects were demonstrably Mycenaean, what was to be thought of the things which were undatable, either because they were common to all periods or because they were immaterial and left no visible traces? In particular, the Minoan-Mycenaean culture developed a naturalistic and eventually grandiose freehand art, whereas the nascent civilization of Hellas in the Early Iron Age only gradually emancipated itself under the tutelage of the mixed Oriental styles of the Syrian coast. Consequently it became an open

spears. It is a warning against looking for an historical period where old and new overlap. Sometimes tradition and fact are identified; *Das Kapital* is a "magic little book" which reveals a magic ring and a murderous woman with a gun is a fierce snake with poisonous bite. Sometimes the old is "expurgated"; Lenin rises in a formula traditional except for the omission of the morning prayer. Burial customs have a similar sanctity (Hdt. III, 38) and we can see why Mycenaean inhumations were dropped from the tradition; but omissions in Homer cannot usually be traced. These comparative studies are enlightening for the technique of Greek heroic poetry. Many Homeric inconsistencies are characteristic of an oral poet's concentration on today's recital and combination of effective detail from different versions—and incidentally uncharacteristic of an editor, who may be silly but is likely to be consistent. They also show how widely the use made of traditional material varies in different countries and centuries, and how outstanding was the poetic achievement of the composers of the *Iliad* and *Odyssey*.

question whether the naturalistic and vivid descriptions in the poems could refer to anything else than the Mycenaean culture. The further question remained, how did the poet know of that culture? Was he contemporary with it, or had he predecessors who were, or had he trustworthy historical tradition? Or was the whole of this class of resemblances a coincidence, and the realism of epic narrative testimony to the poet's creative genius, not to his date and surroundings?

Answers to these questions have reflected, sometimes unduly but always very naturally, the previous training as well as the personal predilections of the critics. Conservatives in literary criticism, such as most English scholars have been, were on the whole more easily impressed with the evidence for direct relations between the poems and the Late Bronze Age culture, because they were less committed to a late date for the poems in their present form. It was the champions of an "Ionian Homer", as we have seen, who were least of all disposed to admit that Mycenaean sites had anything relevant to offer them. Consequently, advances in archaeological research did little to change the course or restrain the adventures of literary analysis. At most they limited its scope by imposing chronological limits for a particular phase in the supposed growth of the poems, as (for instance) for a Thessalian *Achilleid*. They have even made easier the hypothesis of translation, by extending the limits of time permitted by the historical background and revealing crises or gradual changes of conditions which favoured literary development in the suggested sense. Literary criticism, on the other hand, being without instruments or method for ascertaining dates otherwise than from direct allusions to persons or events, was slow to shape its conclusions to limits imposed from another branch of study; and the prevalent disbelief in any coherent and articulate body of early tradition, uninterruptedly transmitted, was fostered at times by the insistence of some archaeologists on the completeness of the breach between Prehistoric and Hellenic.

This has been a long story; too long, I fear, and at times too complicated in its inevitable allusiveness, to be quite easy to follow. If it has any coherence at all, it is due not to the telling of it, but to the appeal of a great work of art and a great human document, an appeal alike to scholars and historians, to teachers of youth and men of the world. Homeric criticism, as we have tried to follow it across the centuries, changed its standpoint, its objectives and its methods, in response to large forces outside its own scope and control. Often it lost something by this response to the spirit of the time; but oftener, I think, it gained. For the touchstone of great literature, as of all great art, is its power not only to draw men out of themselves into the "realms of gold", but by its challenge to their predilections and prejudices to draw out from them the secrets of the heart; to reveal them, best of all to themselves; in any event, to reveal them as they were and as they worked to those that come after. And this magic of great literature does not fail. Studies such as those of which we have been trying to disengage the essentials, do not exhaust the significance of the Homeric poems. Today we think perhaps that we have mastered their meaning; tomorrow we shall see them as surely in another light, as we shall see the landscape and the buildings that we have known and loved all our lives. And of that there is no end, for those who shall come after as for those in whose steps it is our turn to tread; on the tree of knowledge,

οἵη περ φύλλων γενεή, τοίη δὲ καὶ ἀνδρῶν.

And she yieldeth her fruit every month.

Chapter Ten

JOHN LINTON MYRES

———————

SCHLIEMANN paid his first visit to Hissarlik in 1868. John Linton Myres was born in the next year, and "at Winchester he read Schliemann's *Troy* and was fired by Schliemann's example". In 1953 when Michael Ventris and John Chadwick showed how the records of Bronze Age Greece could be read, "he was among the first to congratulate and encourage the young authors".[1] It is usually only in the sciences that one man can live through two revolutions, and the rate of progress was possible for the historians of early Greece only because, like the scientists, they have been able to add to their evidence as well as reinterpret it. The work cannot be done in laboratory conditions. The excavator must take (and should publish) what he finds. Knowledge of the country, above and below ground, often takes him to the right place, and, when he knows his site, he can probe for the answers to precise questions. "There was, of course, a time when it seemed better to dig about anywhere than not to dig at all: the unknown was so vast. But those days are over. We begin to know not only what to seek next, but how and where to look for it, efficiently and economically."[2] It is, however, the method of the geologist, not of the physicist, and human remains have a habit of being more unpredictable than natural strata. The laboratory stage, analysis of metal or clay, preservation of perishable material and dating by scientific methods, comes later and is still in its beginning. "There is much scope, in archaeological research, for the

[1] T. J. Dunbabin, *Proceedings of the British Academy* XLI, pp. 349ff., where justice is done to his many-sided activities.
[2] Myres, p. vi.

special skill of the geologist, the chemist and the physicist."[1] Myres offered chemistry, physics and geology as well as classics for his New College scholarship, and he held a classical and a geological studentship simultaneously after his graduation. He came to archaeology well qualified to take part in its transformation from an astrological to an astronomical phase. The process has been described in earlier chapters, but with little suggestion that the author was himself concerned in it. Here an attempt will be made to fill that gap and carry the narrative onward from the date at which his notes stopped.

In his first two years in Greece he began to know the country and the people, and from then on the Aegean was as vividly alive for him in classical writers as it was when he was actually on its hills and seas. One of his most useful gifts was his power to see in his mind, and sketch on paper, places which he had not visited for half a century. His geographical sense was imaginative as well as practical. Undergraduates at Oxford in the 1920s had no excuse for one-dimensional thinking. E. M. Walker in lectures and tutorials was fulminating against theorists who sent armies over impassable mountains and holding up "dates and maps" as the fundamentals of ancient history (and for one undergraduate at least making them incredibly exciting); and Myres was bringing into the lecture room of the Ashmolean the colourful and smelly reality of the maps; "snow-flecked rock with lichens and mosses on the summits of Ida, Parnassus and Olympus; sand deserts within sound of the surf, around the Greater Quicksands".[2] If the audience was not sure whether he had said Patras or Patara, it mattered the less because "it is indeed remarkable how uniform is the plant-covering of Mediterranean lands, over more than two thousand miles from east to west".[3] A collection of Myres's essays on geography was published to mark his eighty-second birthday, and in reviewing it, J. O. Thomson comments, "If, re-read together, these essays seem sometimes to protest too much, it is largely because they have long since substantially won their case."[4] Certainly a great deal has been done. The reviewer himself has made a valuable study of Greek knowledge of the

---

[1] Myres, p. 264. (*A History of Technology* I and II (1954–6), edited by Charles Singer and others, shows what can be done on these lines.)

[2] *Ibid.*, p. 11.   [3] *Ibid.*, p. 7.

[4] *Geographical History in Greek Lands* (1953), reviewed in *JHS* LXXIV 1954), p. 210.

world in which they lived, but it would be useful to have a considerable expansion of his sensible eight pages on Homer.[1] A massive work on the Greek mainland by a contemporary of Myres, Alfred Philippson, was unfortunately only partially published at his death.[2] It is mainly geological, but no other book gives so good a picture of the country of North Greece; and for each district there is an Historical Appendix by Ernst Kirsten. The contrast between the two parts discloses the gulf which still lies between geographical observation and historical reconstruction, however well done. Much remains to be attempted, in working from what is securely established and supplying defects in the evidence; and literary critics have some justification if they sometimes choose to ignore the conclusions. The country itself is a stable factor; and Myres's appreciation of Robert Wood, and indeed his obvious prejudice in favour of English archaeologists, spring largely from his belief that they more readily saw the Homeric poems in their proper setting of mountain, plain and sea. It is a source of both strength and weakness; for it may be that Homer was the greatest of poets in this also, that he knew how to tell lies in the right way.[3]

The next few years were given to fieldwork, and some of his early articles were concerned with the second of Walker's fundamentals, chronology and the pottery by which the sequence of events can be elucidated. He made the identification of Kamares ware in Crete with sherds from Kahun which gave the earlier link between Minoan and Egyptian history mentioned on p. 157.[4] Other articles took him further east, to the distribution of pottery types in Anatolia.[5] It was

[1] *History of Ancient Geography* (1948).

[2] *Die griechischen Landschaften*, Bd. I–II (1950–6). See also H. Bengtson and V. Milojčić, *Grosser historischer Weltatlas*, I. *Vorgeschichte und Altertum* (1953).   [3] Aristotle, *Poetics*, 24.1460[a] 20.

[4] "On some polychrome pottery from Kamares, in Crete" (*Proceedings of the Society of Antiquaries* XV (1895), pp. 351 ff.

[5] "The early pot fabrics of Asia Minor" (*JRAI* XXXIII (1903), pp. 367 ff., cf. *ibid.* XXXII, pp. 248 ff. and *Man* I (1901); H. Frankfort, *Studies in Early Pottery of the Near East*. Late Bronze Age dates depend on the pottery sequence, systematically classified by Arne Furumark in *The Mycenaean Pottery* and *The Chronology of Mycenaean Pottery* (1941) and "The Mycenaean IIIC pottery and its relations to Cypriote fabrics", *Op. Arch.* III (1944), pp. 194 ff. Later finds have shown that his subdivisions are too rigid, and there are doubts about the absolute chronology; but the main framework is basic to all reconstructions.

a new subject with rapidly growing evidence; but his work is treated respectfully by Henri Frankfort in 1924, and some of his observations of enduring importance are characteristic; on the technique for introducing carbonaceous matter into clay, on climatological factors which produce fabrics and decoration, and on the co-existence of wheel-made and hand-made wares, illustrated from the contemporary pottery of Lebda in Tripoli. To quote Frankfort, "It may still be necessary to lay stress on the value of pottery in face of the unbelieving philologist or the ever-sceptical historian, and for their benefit I add, in Professor Myres's words: '. . . where broken pottery is cast out of a settlement, here it is allowed to lie and accumulate, layer over layer, later over earlier; so that the "sequence dating" derived from such a rubbish heap is as secure as the sequence of fossils in the sedimentary rocks and of the highest value as evidence for change of style, that is to say, of the notions, industrial and aesthetic, of successive generations of makers and breakers of pottery'. " Historians have been convinced; and it is fair to say that Frankfort went on with a warning to archaeologists. Myres met Arthur Evans in 1892 and worked with him briefly in Crete. The result of their friendship was far-reaching, for Evans never accepted "Late Helladic" as a separate culture worthy to stand beside "Late Minoan"; it "seemed to him to rest on a misconception of the crisis which brought Minoan culture on to the mainland—as he believed, by 'wholesale invasion from oversea', not by 'Minoanization' of a native people and dynasty".[1] Myres, too, became a philominoan, and this long affected his interpretation of Aegean history. Between his two loves, the civilized Minoan and the vigorous Hellen, there was only a decadent "Mainland Minoan", a title which denies him any honest pride in nationality. One of the very few corrections which Myres was able to make in the script of this book was to change "colonists" to "neighbours". It was not, however, in Crete that Myres found his most productive field of operations; the subject of his post-graduate research was "Oriental influences in Prehistoric Greece", and for this he turned to Cyprus, an island much troubled by sea raiders and tomb robbers. "The Cypriote peasantry have ever treated the relics of their ancestors with a levity and cupidity rare even in the Levant. Tomb-robbing was, and is, a nightly amusement, and European

[1] J. L. Myres, "Sir Arthur Evans" (*Proceedings of the British Academy* XXVII (1941), pp. 20–1).

residents have seldom seen reason to discourage this traffic, or forgo
their share of the spoils."[1] Even today, with adequate laws and a
well-organized Archaeological Service, it is difficult to prevent the
unscrupulous from finding a market and the well-meaning from
grubbing up the best pieces to take to the Museum. In the second
half of the nineteenth century, with the American, British and
French consuls among those who were bidding for the loot, General
Luigi Palma di Cesnola was chiefly remarkable for his success. Myres
judged him with dry tolerance: "With Cesnola's opportunities, an
archaeological genius had the chance to anticipate modern work by
a generation; it was a pity—but no fault of Cesnola—that the United
States Consul in Cyprus was not an archaeological genius."[2] At
least, the greater part of his collection could be identified. There was
less excuse for the British Museum expedition which excavated at
Enkomi in 1896, and whose report is wholly lacking in the information for dating the very important tombs they found.[3] Myres
excavated himself, but his chief work was salvage. His two Catalogues, of the Nicosia Museum and of the Cesnola Collection in
New York,[4] made sense of the rich material by classifying it in
relation to the finds from more orderly digging, and for the first time
provided a rational archaeological history of the island. There has
recently been an interesting reminder of this period. In 1903 a
"treasure", including a cloisonné sceptre surmounted by two birds,
was confiscated from three tomb robbers. Fifty years later G. H.
McFadden, by questioning the sole survivor of the gang, identified
the tomb and found that it was a cremation burial with much of its
content remaining, and one of the first burials found in Cyprus from
the period after the destruction of Troy.[5]

It is easy to see how strongly the current was setting. Since
Schliemann and Evans, the history of the Aegean reached further up
into the past from the first Olympiad than it stretched downward to
the fall of Constantinople. Much that had been obscure in Myres's

[1] J. L. Myres, *Handbook of the Cesnola Collection of Antiquities from
Cyprus in the Metropolitan Museum of Art*, 1914, p. xiii.

[2] *Ibid.*, p. xv.

[3] A. S. Murray, A. H. Smith, and H. B. Walters, *Excavations in Cyprus*
(1900).

[4] See note 1, and J. L. Myres and Max Ohnefalsch-Richter, *A Catalogue of the Cyprus Museum*, 1899.

[5] *AJA* 58 (1954), pp. 131 ff.

favourite author, Herodotus, began to have a new meaning, and, more surprisingly, despised writers such as Diodorus, Strabo, Pausanias and Apollodorus seemed to have their more fantastic stories confirmed by evidence of which they had no knowledge. The relevance to the Trojan War and the Pelasgian Theory was patent,[1] but that was only the beginning. In the Sather Lectures in 1927, Myres attempted to make a synthesis of all the evidence, old and new, for the whole period; "to restate an old problem in view of recent advances of knowledge; sometimes in the hope that a solution has at last been found; more often with the conviction that until this or that piece of exploration has been put in hand, no solution is possible. It is some gain to have even an obstacle defined."[2] From his historical reconstruction Homer emerges a Mycenaean, in language and content. The new evidence he expected has disproved some of his conclusions and supplied new arguments for others. The "method of enquiry" itself is more interesting; for the question how far tradition may legitimately be called in evidence is a living problem and a chief cause of irreconcilable disagreement among historians and critics.

Myres brought Indo-Europeans speaking *centum* languages into Anatolia and Greece about 1900 B.C. The eastern stream destroyed Troy II and became the dominant power in the Hittite state. In Greece it seems likely that the language was carried by *Urfirnis* peoples from the steppes, but they were given driving power by the arrival of a more vigorous stock from the North-West mountains, and it was these who were responsible for "Minyan" ware, developing it in Phocis and spreading it north to Thessaly and south to the north Peloponnese.[3] The southward movement met an expansion northward of Minoans from Crete, who from about 1800 B.C. exploited and colonized the mainland, establishing themselves earliest and most strongly in Argolis. Phoroneus, in the generation of 1760, is the first non-symbolic name in the Argive pedigree (which explains the early date). The Minoans then occupied Attica and Euboea and

---

[1] "A history of the Pelasgian Theory", *JHS* XXVII (1903), pp. 170 ff.; "The historical background of the Trojan War", *Klio* XIV (1915), pp. 447 ff. (with K. T. Frost).

[2] Myres, p.v.

[3] An evolutionary phase of "Minyan" was not found in the Peloponnese until much later. See p. 254 below.

later the South Peloponnese. The Ionic dialect developed in the regions most intimately in touch with the higher civilization of Crete. About 1400 the mainland Minoans attacked and destroyed their mother city, Knossos. Theseus is needed here, and the variant stories of his adventure preserved by Plutarch "include graphic details— the betrayal of the fleet, the surprise attack on the palace, the fight in the great gateway—which look like folk-memory". But genealogies fix him firmly in the generation of 1260, and we must perhaps be prepared for a virtual duplication of Theseus. The circumstances are not clear. A Minos who was nephew of Cadmus may have set up a new dynasty, but he cannot be disentangled from the later Minos who was grandfather of Idomeneus. Cadmus himself was a Minoan. He tried to restore the position by taking out new settlers to Thebes, where the Minoan palace had just been burnt. He taught his Greek subjects to write their own language in a barbarized version of Minoan script; most of the letters, according to Herodotus, were like the Ionian. The Minoans had already spread to the islands and coastlines of the eastern Aegean. Diodorus knew that, when the later settlers from the Aegean arrived, there were already in Rhodes civilized "Children of the Sun" whose documents "were washed away by the rain", a fate to which sun-dried tablets (like the Minoan) are peculiarly liable.[1] But whereas the Hittites, as they pushed east and south, came into conflict in Syria with Thothmes III and his Mittannian allies, Thothmes was on friendly terms, commercial and perhaps political, with a number of maritime states, Keftiu (somewhere north of Phoenicia), Asi in the Orontes valley (Greek Axios),[2] Alasya (Myres did not commit himself on the identification with Cyprus) and more distant islands. Their gifts include, along with other types, vessels similar to those found in Crete and on the Minoanized mainland, and this is easily explained by the Minoan settlements in the Levant. An echo of this relationship is found in the story of Epaphus in Egypt; Argive refugees were in Egypt since 1500, and some trouble over their return led to the "great killing" of Egyptian men by Argive women about 1450.

About 1400 a further change can be traced, coinciding with the

---

[1] A Minoan settlement at Trianda, earlier than the Mycenaean settlement at neighbouring Ialysos, can be fitted in here (A. Furumark, "The Settlement of Ialysus and Aegean Chronology", *Op. Arch.* VI (1950)).

[2] Dr. Schaeffer's excavations at Ras Shamra had not yet begun.

opening up of the way south by the destruction of Knossos. Heavy rain raised the level of Lake Copais (Deucalion's flood, generation of 1430). A few refugees came to Athens, led by Deucalion's son, Amphictyon. Most of them moved north, and, as Thucydides says, "Hellen and his sons grew strong in Phthia and other cities brought them in to their aid"; the country was distracted by the war with Knossos. The Cadmeians blocked their way southwards. Dorus and his sons were driven northward, and then were further split off from their southern kindred by a Minoan push into Thessaly at Iolkos, similar to the adventure of Cadmus. The Doric dialect thus developed in a "Minyan" region which had not been touched by Minoan influence, and therefore retained its primitive characteristics. Of the most immediately important branch, the Aeolids, some gained control of Orchomenos; others drifted west by the valley of the Spercheios into Aetolia and down into the west Peloponnese. There Sisyphus penetrated as far east as Corinth, and the movement perhaps displaced "Ion and his men" and sent them to "Ionicize" Attica in about 1300. For Herodotus knew that Athens had been Hellenized at some time, and had then learnt to speak Greek; and consequently in the distribution map of Minyan pottery, Myres stopped its greatest expansion at the frontiers of Attica. The pre-migration distribution of the Aeolic and Ionic dialects is thus explained. Meanwhile a new start was made in Argolis. Tiryns was "founded" by Proteus about 1350 and Mycenae by Perseus about 1300, and the walls remain as proof of it. These various dynasties had no political coherence. That they remained on fairly good terms with the Great Powers is shown by the continuing trade with Egypt and by the diplomatic exchanges between the Hittite kings and the kings of Ahhiyava, or Achaea, while hostility between Egyptians and Hittites continued. There were, however, signs of growing suspicion, and the Egyptians began to enlist the dangerous foreigners as mercenaries. But after the war in which the Egyptians defeated the Hittites at the Battle of Kadesh (1288 B.C.), Hattusil II and Rameses II were suddenly reconciled. They fixed their common frontier in the Lebanon, and the Hittite king paid a courtesy visit to Egypt in 1259. The reason was the growth of a danger threatening them both from a different quarter. For, about 1400, Indo-Europeans speaking a *satem* language, with Phrygian and Thracian affinities, had entered Anatolia and established themselves in the Troad under Dardanus. The Hittites knew of Asuva, in which was a city Taroisa;[1] and Homer knew of the Asian meadows on the river Caicus, and of two men called Asios, one Priam's brother-in-law, who fought on the river Sangarius, and the other from Arisbe. The first sign of trouble between Greece and the Hittites had arisen in this part of the world. In about 1330 Mursil complained that Tavagalavas son of Antaravas, an Ayavalas and a ruler of Ahhiyava, was attacking Laaspa, a place near Asuva; and this is the generation of Etevokleves son of Andrevas, who, if not an Aeolid himself, had at least set up an Aeolid in Orchomenos, and of a grandson of Aeolus who established himself in Lesbos.[2] In the generation of 1300, Perseus, "a 'Danaan' adventurer who had made good in the Levant, as the story of Andromeda and the crocodile shows", carried off a princess from the coast of Palestine. From the Anatolian side came some of the contingents in the Hittite army at the Battle of Kadesh, Ilians, Dardanians, Cilicians and so on, and the Shardana mercenaries of Egypt. The trouble was starting, and throughout the thirteenth century the pace was rapid.

In the generation of 1260 Laomedon built the walls of Troy. He was, as Homer tells us, "a horrible man", who (like the Hittites) interned his enemies in distant islands. His son Priam fought a great battle on the river Sangarius, helping the Phrygians against the Amazons, who are the clean-shaven Asiatics, contrasted with the full-bearded Armenoid invaders. In the same generation the "divine-born" kings established themselves in Greece and married into the older dynasties. Some, like Neleus and Tydeus, came from other parts of Greece and could trace their pedigrees further back there. Others were foreigners, as Pelops was in some sense a Phrygian, though not necessarily from Asia. These "men from nowhere" seem not to have brought their women with them. They would not be Greek-speaking, but they were too few to influence the language and learnt to speak Greek from their new subjects. It was they who became leaders among the kings. They had their wars in Greece. Argos eliminated Cadmeian Thebes in a struggle which lasted for two generations. Crete made an unsuccessful attempt to dominate Athens, perhaps for the second time; but this is the generation to which Theseus properly belongs. When Theseus was driven out, Menestheus for a time

[1] Asuva is now tentatively located in the Hermos and Kaikos valleys, but it had nothing to do with Troy, *AS* V (1955), p. 83.

[2] Etewokleweios in the Linear B tablets, *Documents*, p. 191.

became the ally or feudatory of Agamemnon. The connexion between the "Sea-power of Minos" and the Ahhiyava of Hittite records and of both with the Sea Raiders, is seen in the marriage of Atreus with Minos's daughter (or rather grand-daughter), Aërope. Minos, a generation earlier and in a more advanced position strategically, does the necessary preliminaries of clearing "Carians" out of Crete and the islands, establishing the Greek language where it was not commonly spoken yet (for in these days "all Crete was held by folk who spoke no Greek"), and colonizing advanced bases with the help of his brothers, Sarpedon and Rhadamanthys. His war-companions occupied Carpathus, and Aërope's brother, Althaemenes, took his people to Rhodes, where they were later ruled by an exiled son of Herakles, Tlepolemus. Then, as Myres cautiously put it, Attarissyas of Ahhiyava followed up the successes of Atreus's father-in-law by the raids on the coast of Asia Minor of which the Hittites complained in 1250, and attacked Alasya five years later. Cyprus in the next two generations passed rapidly out of the Minoan phase, and it was at this time that there was a seaboard power in the Peloponnese to take the dialect of Arcadia to Cyprus. With a land power in Anatolia and sea marauders led by their kinsmen in Greece, the stage was set for the land and sea raids on the Hittites and Egyptians. In 1221 the Akhaiwa-sha, Lykki, Shardana, Shakal-sha and Tursha in alliance with the Libyans raided the Delta in the reign of Merneptah. This is the generation in which the Argonauts not only voyaged in the Black Sea but also, according to Herodotus, fought in Libya and, according to Apollonius Rhodius, entered the Adriatic; in which Bellerophon fought the Solymoi, who lived where Sarpedon had settled, and was last heard of in the Aleian plain of Cilicia; in which Eumaeus was kidnapped from Syria and carried to Ithaca, and his nurse was carried off from Phoenicia by Taphians. There was a two-fold attack on Cilicia, when Calchas coming from the sea met Mopsus "leading his forces over Mount Taurus", and Amphilochus of Argos, as well as Calchas and Mopsus, founded cities and received honour in Cilicia and the country round. The power of the Hittites was shattered. The silence of their records after about 1200 is more eloquent than the boastings of Egypt. The years 1194–90 saw the renewal of the attack on Egypt by the Princes of the North; these were no isolated raids, but the concerted movement of whole peoples by land and sea. "The peoples of the north in their islands were in agitation, uprooted in the storm. . . . Not one held his place before them. Their chief powers were Pulisata, Zakkaru, Shakal-sha, Danuna and Uasha-sha; these lands were held together in a single league." And when the Egyptian records go on to tell of the spoil taken from them, they show that the scale of the Trojan War was not exaggerated. After the successes of Rameses III, the raiders were dispersed. The Pulisata went to Philistia, where their pottery shows their Aegean affinities and where in David's wars their champion Goliath was armed like a Cretan. Others carried the name of Sardes to Sardinia, the Tursha went to Etruria and the Shakal-sha to Sicily.[1] Then, perhaps because of the defeat, the allies quarrelled. There had been trouble earlier between Laomedon and Herakles. Now a much greater expedition was mounted by Agamemnon. The Athenians were half-hearted, the parts of Greece where Dorians were established kept aloof, Agamemnon's powerful friend in Cyprus excused himself with a gift, and the common people were nowhere enthusiastic; but from the rest of Greece the kings and their Companions were eager to support him. Then came the disastrous *Returns* to kingdoms disorganized by the rulers' long absence, Teucer's exile to Cyprian Salamis,[2] more trouble in Asia, where bearded invaders destroyed Carchemish and established themselves there, and danger on the seas, which Odysseus's plausible tales show to have been infested by pirates. The dynasties of the "divine-born" did not last long against a new danger from the north.

Myres suggested that the northern home of the Dorians could be traced by the Geometric pottery at Lianokladi in the upper Spercheios valley and at Boubousta on the Haliacmon, where it was found with late Mycenaean sherds. Under Aegimius in the thirteenth century (and therefore not because of the invasion of Macedonia in the twelfth), they had made an attempt to restore the "children of Herakles", Perseid exiles from Argos, and had been defeated by Atreus, who had used the opportunity to seize Mycenae. The Dorians had fallen back on Doris, where they remained outside Agamemnon's jurisdiction. A hundred years later, they forced their way south by the western route.

[1] And the Danuna to Cilicia, where they appear at Karatepe in the eighth century.

[2] The discovery that Myc. IIIC pottery made a sudden appearance at Enkomi gives much better evidence for Teucer than was available to Myres, who was here dealing with intractable material. See p. 275 below.

"Where there was prolonged opposition, as at Corinth, the precise position of the invaders' temporary camp outside the walls was still known in the fifth century. If there should turn out to be a misfit at Sparta between pedigrees and potsherds, the remedy is to look for the Laconian equivalent of the Solygeian Ridge." They surged into the Megarid from the south and threatened Athens; but Codrus successfully repulsed them, and Athens became a refuge for broken men. The political coherence of the "divine-born" dynasties had already brought Peloponnesian and Attic Greeks together. "The facilities for intercourse between Aeolic-speaking and Ionic-speaking people in 'Achaean' courts, markets and harbors, made possible the conflation of two more or less ready-made idioms into the *lingua franca* which is preserved in the Homeric poems." Meanwhile, when the Hittite power collapsed, the Phrygians took their place as a barrier between the Aegean and the aggressive empires of the east, and a related Thracian group lay between it and the Danube. Behind this double shield there was quiet from the end of the eleventh century until the rise of Cyrus, and it formed the "mould" into which was poured "the rich alloy of refugee colonization". The alloy was mixed in the crucible at a time and place when the memory of Mycenaean greatness and the Trojan War was still fresh, and the same cherished memories took shape in the Homeric epics of warfare and wanderings. Myres attributed little to the Dorians. The origin of cremation, iron fibulae and new weapons was found within the Aegean area. The Geometric style of pottery was as at home in Amyclae, the centre of resistance to the Dorians, as it was at Sparta. Mycenaean pottery differed from Minoan because of Minyan influences which gave it bold distinctive profiles and restricted hand-painted decoration to a single shoulder zone, the rest of the surface being "machine-finished by a sequence of plain bands, . . . a ceramic 'jazz', infectious, pervasive, soul-destroying, as all rhythmical vulgarities are". Fabric and paint remained the same, but with the loss of the *régimes,* decoration was no longer determined by "upper class" taste. Although no formative phase had yet been found in Attica, "the geographical distribution of its earliest manifestations points clearly away from the districts dominated by the Dorian and West Greek immigrants, and also away from the areas of refugee-settlement, Asiatic and insular. It points, as clearly, toward Attica, and—second only to this—to Boeotia and Argolis, which were less completely dominated by the newcomers than Laconia and most parts of the north country". Myres thought that, since the Attic Geometric style developed after the Ionian migration, any Geometric pottery in Ionia would have been taken there fully developed and would "throw light on the date when Attic geometrical notions began to spread oversea, as they are already seen to have spread overgulf into Argolia and overland into Boeotia". "The part which was played in a previous cycle of events by 'golden Mycenae' fell like Benjamin's lot to that state which politically found its 'place in the sun' last of all; namely Athens—or rather the united states of Attica." Because of this inheritance "even the 'coming of the Dorians', far-reaching in its social and political effects, turns out to have been essentially a domestic affair; a redistribution among tribes already Greek-speaking and recognized as members of an 'Hellenic family'."

It is a magnificent narrative, bold in conception and worked out in minute detail. The Greek Heroic Age is superimposed on the archaeological record, to take its place in the documented history of its neighbours. Myres was ahead of his evidence in deriving Geometric pottery from Mycenaean, and in crediting the conservation of tradition and the initiation of changes alike to the Athenians, not to either the Dorians or the Ionians. The intermediary stages which he noted as missing, have been found in Attica.[1] British excavations at Sparta in 1906–10[2] and at Mycenae in 1920–23,[3] had left an awkward chronological gap, which Myres bridged defiantly by keeping the Dorians waiting for two centuries in a temporary camp outside a Sparta which on the evidence was not yet there. The problem is not much nearer solution now, but his general view of the invasion as an upheaval within the Hellenic family has been strongly reinforced. The earlier centuries are unnecessarily complicated by his adherence to Evans's colonization theory, which left the individuality and achievement of Mycenaean Greece unexplained. As he expected, new evidence has called for new interpretations, especially on the dubious identification of some of the Hittite and Egyptian names. What matters most for Homer is whether he was justified in his use of the old evidence, the tradition of the Greeks themselves. It is

[1] See pp. 276 below.
[2] R. M. Dawkins, *The Sanctuary of Artemis Orthia at Sparta* (1929).
[3] A. J. B. Wace, *BSA* XXIV–XXV (1919–23).

obviously necessary to examine all the evidence for the dates of buildings. Is it legitimate to suggest, as G. E. Mylonas does, that Perseus built the first walls of Mycenae in 1350–30, that Atreus added the Lion Gate with its coat of arms in about 1250, and that Orestes in the twelfth century extended the fortifications to cover the water supply?[1] Are the legendary dates part of the evidence which ought to be considered? Myres sets out some excellent principles. "Homeric testimony by itself proves nothing but the opinion of a Greek poet, of early but uncertain date, as to the politics and strategy of bygone times." The sequence of events must be determined first independently on archaeological or historical evidence, and the tradition also put together from its sources. "If the result is coherent, it must be so for one of two reasons, either amazing ingenuity among the sixth-century chroniclers—in which event we have still to ask how they knew on what historical assumptions to proceed—or a living, accurate folk-memory of ancient times. And if the result coheres also with sources of information quite beyond the knowledge of those chroniclers, the conclusion seems unavoidable that Greek folk-memory was historically trustworthy; that it enables us to explore aspects of Greek antiquity for which we have not yet other evidence, and, in particular, to select the right localities wherein to look for such evidence." It was only when it appeared to him that the Greek "rough and ready calculation of dates by generations of men yields results which are conformable with archaeological evidence" that he claimed the right to extend the use of tradition to people and events for whom there was no external evidence. The first question clearly is whether the correspondence is well-established. For the earlier period (and Myres noted that tradition is less consistent then) it depends on the Trojan pedigree. Dörpfeld dated the destruction of Troy II to *c.* 2000 and the foundation of Troy VI to *c.* 1500, with which Myres's genealogical dates are in rough agreement. But in the American excavations of 1932–8, it became clear that Troy VI

---

[1] *Ancient Mycenae* (1957), pp. 39 and 182. A. J. B. Wace writes cautiously, "before the end of L.H.III B there was some disturbance in the Mycenaean world as shown by the destruction of the houses outside the walls of Mycenae. It has been suggested that this might have been caused by a civil war, perhaps between Atreus and Thyestes. Perhaps the rivalry between Eurystheus and the Pelopids, hinted at by Thucydides, was concerned in it" (*Goldman*, p. 134).

was founded as a fortified place at about the same time as the appearance of Minyan ware in Greece, "vaguely in the neighborhood of 1800 B.C.".[1] The dating of Dardanus to *c.* 1400 and of Laomedon to *c.* 1260 is much too late, and the generations must be stretched over about six hundred years instead of two. If the same is true of Greece, there is no need to put "Hellen and his sons" five hundred years after the Greek language had reached Greece, or to separate the end of the "sea power of Minos" from the fall of Knossos, or to make the burning of the palace of Thebes mark the beginning instead of the end of Cadmeian rule. The legendary past is compressed into a few generations, with greatly improved opportunities for meetings of famous men, as legend often is and as common sense demands. A story-teller does not want to say, "Then nothing much happened for two hundred years", or to spin out a line as sparse as the Roman worthies who fill the centuries between Aeneas and Romulus. Pedigrees (at least when they go back earlier than the thirteenth century) are worthless for absolute dating, and the appearance of heroes in the same story is not proof that they were originally contemporary, even in tradition.

This leads to a second qualification. Since legends were never completely systematized, synthetic "tradition" should be suspect. Since so many writers told so many stories, almost anything could be supported by their arbitrary combination. Two details quoted from the same lost work, the *Cypria* for instance, presumably belonged to the same version, though even then it may be dangerous to combine them. To deduce from Homer's mention of the robe which Paris brought from Sidon that Homer knew that Paris visited Sidon on his way from Greece to Troy, would probably be false. It would certainly be false to conclude from it that there was a tradition that Sidon was an island in the north Aegean. It is even more dangerous if the two statements met for the first time in a scholar's card-index. Strabo says that Zethos and Amphion lived at Eutresis before they went to Thebes. Stephanus of Byzantium says that they built the walls of Eutresis. Hetty Goldman combines them into a "tradition" that they built the walls of Eutresis before they went to Thebes, and concludes from it ("even if this tradition is not absolutely correct") that the Thebans were responsible for the building of the walls of Eutresis, in order to protect their road to Mycenae.[2] A third qualification

[1] See pp. 254 ff. below. [2] *Eutresis*, p. 69.

237

is that, in spite of the authority of Herodotus, we should not eliminate the cow from the story of Io and take the rest as history. The process as we see it is toward rationalization. There is no reason to suppose that an original prosaic abduction was first mythologized by poets and then rationalized back into its original form. If the Greeks knew that Perseus and Bellerophon were generals who campaigned in the Levant in accordance with a rational strategy, why did they bring in gorgons and chimaeras? When we go from footnotes to texts, we usually find that the story as told is quite different from the story as used for the history. It would in general be nearer the truth to keep the griffin and let the Arimaspian go. These are truisms; but the influence of Euhemerus is still strong.

Myres does not often indulge in crocodiles and Cadmeian Schools for backward Greeks. His argument usually is that at a particular time conditions were such as to make some country a reasonable place for Greek adventurers. And after all allowance has been made, there is plenty left. Tradition was tenacious of names attached to localities. The story of Mopsus in Cilicia is a good example, and probably Teucer in Salamis; both had local cult or family associations. Myres's claim that tradition has proved a good guide for excavators is well-founded. The greater legends have stood the test of archaeology well. Events of a kind that could have produced the legend have left their physical mark on the site. Most of them have been rejected at some time, and later found more reliable than the arguments used to refute them. The Ionian Migration is the latest suspect to be vindicated. The Dorian Invasion is on remand, and the strength of Greek tradition is a good argument in its favour, simply in the light of past experience. This is far from saying that because someone burnt Troy round about 1200 B.C. and did not stay to settle in the place, therefore we must believe that Agamemnon quarrelled with Achilles over a woman; but it is an argument for thinking that the people who burnt it came from Argolis. Again, the Aegean in the Bronze Age, and at no other time, was the sort of place in which the stories of the legends could have happened. Homer's version conceals this, for his war seems to be fought in an international vacuum. Some episodes came down with the stories. The misfortune of Periphetes is a certain example. The entertainment of Helen and Menelaus by a noble in Egyptian Thebes seems to be another. Theban priests boasted to all comers from Hecataeus to Germanicus of the horses and chariots of Pharaoh, but there was nothing for them to boast of in this story of private hospitality; Menelaus is one of the "tributaries" of the wall paintings in the fifteenth-century Viziers' tombs, seen from the Greek point of view. No doubt there are other episodes, less easily distinguished from later conditions and fictions. Complete scepticism is as irrational as credulity, and less fruitful, since it rejects a possible guidance. Moreover, however suspicious the Greek method of calculation was, whether it was based on invented or manipulated genealogies or on fraudulent Assyrian documents,[1] their dates for the destruction of Troy, the end of the Achaean dynasties and the Ionian Migration are no worse than their dates for Pheidon of Argos or the Lelantine War, and approximate, with a reasonable margin of error on both sides, to the dates reached on independent evidence. Eratosthenes and Dörpfeld have become so familiar that the oddity is perhaps forgotten. Why should a sixth-century genealogist or a learned Alexandrian hit on four or five hundred years before the first Olympiad, with so little to fill the centuries? As with earlier heroic chronology, shorter intervals would have had obvious advantages. Added to the political geography and organization of Greece, the strong substratum of Bronze Age fighting and architecture, and the indisputable memory of some artefacts, this is an impressive foundation for the conclusion, reached simultaneously by Myres and M. P. Nilsson,[2] that a great mass of material survived in tradition and so got into epic. For Myres, this made the poems Mycenaean, and his object was to close the gap by putting the poet as early as possible and bringing down the Mycenaean practices found in the poems to a date when they could overlap with new practices such as cremation and iron-working. Many critics have for this reason put Homer and an historic Homeric world in the tenth or ninth century, with the advantage that practically nothing is known about the period. But it is known that it completely lacked the wealth, unity and opportunity for foreign travel of the Mycenaean and Homeric worlds. For Nilsson, it turned the Homeric Question into "the problem of epic poetry and its origins, which may reach

---

[1] For a critical assessment see Sir John Forsdyke, *Greece before Homer: Ancient Chronology and Mythology* (1956), pp. 28 ff.

[2] *The Minoan-Mycenaean Religion and its Survival in Greek Religion* (1927), 2nd ed., 1950); cf. *The Mycenaean Origin of Greek Mythology* (1932).

much further back than the life of a man or a few generations".[1]
His concern therefore was to fill the gap, and his masterly summary
finds room for both evolutionary poetry and a unitarian poet. "It
may sound astonishing, but mythology was really out of date with
Homer. ... At the time when the Homeric poems were composed,
mythology on the one hand was rigidly binding as the subject-
matter of the poems, but on the other hand it was somewhat old-
fashioned and outworn. This state of things can only have come about
through a lengthy development, in which the myths were chanted
until the poets became somewhat tired of story-telling, and the
inspiration of a great poetical genius turned in another direction."
Homeric criticism, too, had turned in another direction. The
contribution of Mycenaean Greece to the contents of the poems did
not lose its importance. It is the only setting in which the stories
make sense, and to speak patronisingly of Schliemann's "pretty and
rare success story"[2] is to belittle a real renaissance in Homeric as well
as in historical scholarship. But there were things which were not
Mycenaean, but which were to be found in Geometric and Orientalizing art.[3] Neither group could be eliminated without destroying the
poems, and the suggestion that they ever co-existed in any historical
period was an hypothesis which lacked supporting evidence. They
had come together because each generation of poets had kept what
it liked of the past and added to it what it liked of the present.

This important advance was the result partly of Nilsson's specialized work on mythology, partly of more exact dating of archaeological material (though Myres rightly noted in a review[4] that he is less
completely at home with material objects than with legends) and
partly of contemporary work on metric, style and language. The idea
of a *Kunstsprache*, a poetic language distinct from any colloquial

[1] *Homer and Mycenae* (1933). The particular point is further developed
in "Der homerische Dichter in der homerischen Welt", *Die Antike* XIV
(1938), pp. 22 ff.

[2] M. I. Finley, *The World of Odysseus* (1956), p. 46.

[3] Frederik Poulsen, *Der Orient und die frühgriechische Kunst* (1912) and
K. Friis Johansen, *Les vases sicyoniens* (1923) had already appeared, but
compared with the Bronze Age, the period was little known. The years
that followed were productive: Emil Kunze, *Kretische Bronzereliefs* and
Humfry Payne, *Necrocorinthia* in 1931, Roland Hampe, *Frühe griechische
Sagenbilder in Böotien* in 1936, *Perachora* I in 1940.

[4] *Class. Rev.* XLVII (1933), p. 221.

speech, emerged from the work of many scholars, notably J. Wackernagel,[1] K. Meister[2] and A. Meillet,[3] and its evolution was explained by what E. R. Dodds describes as "perhaps the most important single discovery about Homer made during the past half-century"[4], Milman Parry's proof that Homer's style is typical of oral poetry.[5] Briefly, recitation by a combination of memory and improvisation is a strain on both poets and audiences. Poets therefore build up a vocabulary, not of words, but of phrases which fill the natural metrical divisions of the lines, less often of complete lines or longer passages, to express all the ideas they normally want to convey. This is most obvious in proper names; the poems contain, for instance, forty-six noun-epithet formulae for Achilles, without a single pair of the same metrical value. Metrical duplicates occur, but they are extremely rare because the poet did not burden his memory with unnecessary formulae. This principle of "epic economy" applies also to *spears*, *shields* and other common equipment, and to abstracts like *night* and *sea*.[6] The poet's task is lightened by having, for instance, nine metrically different ways of expressing the constantly needed meaning "with his spear", and the audience is both helped and pleased by the familiarity. It is not a rigid system limiting the poet's freedom of choice, as Parry emphasized in his later work, and it is no more plagiarism than the use of words which other poets have used before. Certain consequences are clear. The technique implies a long tradition of epic poetry before Homer, and (so far as it is safe to say that anything is accepted) that is generally accepted as proved. Dating passages by archaisms is ruled out, though in language the proportion of archaisms to neologisms is still called in evidence. A convenient formula could continue in use long after

[1] *Sprachliche Untersuchungen zu Homer* (1916).

[2] *Die homerische Kunstsprache* (1921).

[3] *Les origines indo-européennes des mètres grecs* (1923).

[4] In *Fifty Years of Classical Scholarship* (ed. M. Platnauer, 1954), p. 13.

[5] *L'épithète traditionelle dans Homère* (1928); *Les formules et la métrique d'Homère* (1928); "Studies in epic technique of oral verse-making", *Harvard Studies in Classical Philology* XLI (1930) and XLIII (1932); "The Homeric gloss", *Trans. of the American Philological Association* LIX (1928), pp. 233f.; "Enjambement in Homeric verse", *ibid.*, LXIV (1933), pp. 30ff.

[6] Gray, "Homeric epithets for things", *CQ* XLI (1947), pp. 109ff.

the thing it described had become obsolete. Descriptions of Mycenaean things are thus explained without the assumption that the poet had seen them, and they cease to be evidence for the date of the poems. Since the poet uses the metrically convenient formula, we may not build up a composite picture of a single hero's shield or helmet by collecting all the epithets applied to it, or base ethnological theories on the epithets of the heroes themselves. A helmet is ἀμφίφαλος because at some time during the development of the *Kunstsprache* this was a suitable epithet for a type of helmet, and a hero is yellow-haired if his name is an *ionic a minore* and a horse-driver if it is a spondee. But there must have been a time when the epithets were natural descriptions of familiar categories of things. Whether in a particular passage the poet may have chosen an individually appropriate epithet, remains an open question, but it would certainly be unwise to assume it. If a line is found in two different poems, it does not follow that one borrowed from the other, for two poets may have taken it independently from the common stock. This has catastrophic effects on the evidence of quotations in lyric poets as a *terminus ante quem*; the poet may be using a common epic formula.[1] It leads to the ridiculous position that, if one of the Geometric vases showing a shipwreck[2] had a line from the *Odyssey* painted on it, it would not be absolute proof that an *Odyssey*, still less our *Odyssey*, existed at the time. Poets would in general tend to reject what had become incomprehensible, to keep old formulae which applied equally well to the conditions of their own day, and to choose stories about peoples and places which still existed rather than about those which had disappeared. This may explain why there is so much in the poems which could either have come down from the Bronze Age or originated in the post-Mycenaean period; and it has two unwelcome consequences. It is not legitimate to use the common elements (such as parry-shields and ivory inlay) as proof that the poems belong mainly to either of the two periods, or to assume that the elements which cannot be dated at all (such as the constitutional position of a widowed queen or the legal rights of Thersites) belong to the one period rather than the other. Analytic arguments from internal inconsistencies lose most of their relevance. The poet is con-

[1] J. A. Davison, "Quotations and allusions in early Greek literature", *Eranos* LIII (1956), pp. 125 ff.
[2] Pl. 8. b, and R. Hampe, *Die Gleichnisse Homers*, fig. 7–11.

cerned with the effect of today's recitation. He need not fear that the hearers will refer back to what he said last week; and, since the day's recitation must be self-contained, circumstances must be explained when the plot needs them even if it breaks the chronological order. On the other hand, he cannot hope that the hearers will notice subtil references to previous recitations, and unitarian arguments from elaborate cross-referencing become even more suspect than they were.

Though oral composition carries no implication of single author-ship, its acceptance probably contributed to the belief in a personal Homer, in the various senses in which he is understood by W. Schadewaldt,[1] Maurice Bowra,[2] Renata von Scheliha,[3] Ernst Howald,[4] Karl Reinhardt,[5] A. Severyns[6] and many others. Most readers, like Wolf himself, have a conviction that each poem carries the stamp of a single mind, but that none the less the material is unmistakably traditional. Parry's discovery resolves the dilemma, and it has more weight than Robert Wood's very similar discovery, partly because it is proved, and partly because it coincides with the archaeological awareness. It remains doubtful whether "Homer" was wholly inside the tradition or whether he changed heroic poetry into true epic, perhaps helped in some way by the invention of writing. For most, the two poems had separate authors. For some, the poets reused well established "type" stories, as the *Wrath* is of the same type as the story of Meleager. For others, they created a new kind of epic and so transcended oral poetry. The meaning of the "original genius of Homer" in this new conception is discussed in a pene-trating study by Frederick M. Combellack.[7] "Where I should rather like to *know* as well as *feel* that Homer was highly original is in his manner, not his matter. In point of fact I do believe that the almost incredibly high degree of skill, the complete mastery of the material

[1] *Iliasstudien*, 1938; *Legende von Homer*, 1942; *Von Homers Welt und Werk*, 1944, 2nd ed., 1951.

[2] *Tradition and Design in the Iliad*, 1930; "The comparative study of Homer", *AJA* 54 (1950), pp. 184 ff.

[3] *Patroklos. Gedanken über Homers Dichtung und Gestalten*, 1943.

[4] *Der Dichter der Ilias*, 1946.

[5] *Von Werken und Formen*, 1948.

[6] *Homère*, I. *Le cadre historique*, II. *Le poète et son œuvre*, III. *L'artiste*, 1943–8.

[7] "Unitarians and Homeric originality", *American Journal of Philology* LXXI (1950), pp. 337 ff.

which the poems so often show, is Homer's own achievement. This is the 'originality' by which he so cruelly and so completely annihilated his predecessors and his contemporaries. He did not drive them from the field because he produced a work with a vast amount of new material, as though he was merely composing an improved new textbook in a scientific field burgeoning with multitudinous new facts. But even this originality in mastery over material can very seldom, if ever, be demonstrated in any strict sense of the word, because of our utter ignorance of Homer's surroundings and background."

Myres recognized that old and new were "combined in a Homeric World and a Homeric Age, which has become immortal mainly because it never existed outside Homer's vivid imagination".[1] A colonial society is likely to keep its "verbal furniture" although it makes a poor show in personal ornaments or household gear, so that the immaterial wealth of the Bronze Age may have survived through the poverty-stricken centuries which followed. But his single Homer, author of *Iliad* and *Odyssey*, was not degraded by being made one of many. He himself created his world, partly from inherited poetry, partly from heirlooms and casual discoveries, partly from eyewitness and travellers' tales. The repetitions are not the formless expedients of oral poetry, but deliberate artistry to create a pattern which is similar to the balanced symmetry of Geometric art and quite different from the frieze-structure of the Minoans.[2] This is a considerable concession to the "Ionian Homer". Moreover, Myres was much attracted by the bold suggestions of Émile Mireaux, who came to Homer from *La Chanson de Roland*.[3] Homer of Chios, in about 700 B.C., composed two short epics for festivals at the ends of the tin route which ran from the Black Sea through Euboea and Corcyra (Phaeacia) to Etruria. Two or three generations later a second great poet expanded them in patriotic support of Mytilene in her rivalry with Miletus and opposition to Gyges (Aegisthus). Mireaux is rich in interesting ideas, which are concealed by his extreme analytic method and the improbability of

[1] "Homeric Art', *BSA* XLV (1950), pp. 229 ff.

[2] Cf. "The last book of the *Iliad*" and "The pattern of the Odyssey", *JHS* LII (1932), pp. 264 ff. and LXXII (1952), pp. 1 ff.

[3] *Les poèmes homériques et l'histoire grecque*, I. *Homère de Chios et les routes de l'étain*, II. *L'Iliade, l'Odyssée et les rivalités coloniales*, 1948–9; summarized and discussed by Myres in *Greece and Rome* XX (1951), pp. 1 ff. and XXI (1952), pp. 1 ff.

his conclusions. Myres particularly liked his conception of the poet as an active force in a real world, and it encouraged him to look on the near side of the destruction of Mycenae; "it is a sound assumption that any great poem owes something to its background".

The full implications of oral poetry were however still unappreciated. Rhys Carpenter began from Milman Parry's "unanswerable and unassailable proof that the *Iliad* and *Odyssey* belong to the class of oral literature—composed in the mind and not on paper, retained in the memory and not in books, recited to audiences, heard and not read".[1] The first text was written in the old Attic alphabet, and therefore at Athens, not in Ionia. This could not be earlier than the renewal of trade with Egypt which made papyrus available, and was probably much later, since poets and reciters had no incentive to undertake the laborious task. "The Ionic orientation, literary patronage and cultural ambition of Peisistratos and his sons" make them "the only really likely sponsors of the undertaking". Hesiod on the other hand wrote his poetry, as his terse style shows. "If it was written down for posterity on sheets of lead, we are entitled to conclude that it was composed before Egyptian paper was introduced and hence most probably before Amasis favored Greek commercial penetration of Egypt in the second quarter of the sixth century"; the date suggested is the third quarter of the seventh century. *Iliad* and *Odyssey* must have been near the end of a long antecedent tradition of oral poetry in Greece, and we should expect to be led back into Mycenaean times or to folk tale and tribal lore which is even earlier; but Greek tradition put the Muses, not in Crete or Anatolia, but in the North, "in touch with the *European* elements of Greek speech and culture". When we examine the so-called Mycenaean element in Homer, we find that the sensational revelation of Schliemann and his successors is in fact a great illusion. Homeric narrative *refers* to Mycenaean culture, but only as the *Oresteia* does. Of the material culture of the Bronze Age, Homer knows nothing except a single helmet constructed of boars' teeth. Other epics, such as *Beowulf* and the *Song of Roland*, show complete indifference to chronology, scale, personalities and material background, and Homer is no exception. As for Troy, Demetrios of Skepsis and Charles Vellay were right in denying that it had any connexion with Hissarlik. "Nothing can be done to turn a five-acre stronghold into a broad-streeted town with

[1] *Folk Tale, Fiction and Saga in the Homeric Epics*, 1946.

palaces and temples on a lofty acropolis; nor can Hissarlik be moved further from the shore or made invisible from it; nor can Bunarbashi springs be made to flow beneath its walls." The poet or his predecessors put an imaginary city on Bunarbashi and turned the ruins on Hissarlik into the grave of Aisyetes; and, since it is possible to run round Hissarlik and not Bunarbashi, Achilles and Hector ran round Troy only in the sense in which one drives "around the town", backwards and forwards on a course between the Dardanian Gate and the springs. But the story of the abortive landing at Teuthrania proves that tradition was not sure that the objective was in the Troad, only that there had been a great and distant expedition. The Trojan War was really the Sea Raiders' attack on Egypt, and the truth lingered in the story of Helen in Egypt. Legend thinks nothing of changing a defeat into a victory. The name *Troia*, however, may be connected with E-truria, and explained by the Asiatic origin of the Etruscans. Achilles and all his family came from *Märchen*, with as little right to be with Achaean chiefs as Sigurd had to be with Burgundian kings. But the complex dramatic structure of the *Iliad* "goes far to confirm the suspicion that in the *Iliad* there has been a profound fictional disturbance and transformation of the traditional material of Saga and Folk Tale". The cultural epoch in which the fiction is set is "the so-called Oriental period of early classical civilization", and the mention of Phrygians and Amazons (who are Cimmerians), the existence of an Egyptian Thebes not yet sacked, the cult statue of Athene and the geography of the *Catalogue* suggest a date for its composition in the second quarter of the seventh century. The *Odyssey* is more closely dated to 630–20 B.C., because Odysseus's tale of a Cretan raid on Egypt closely resembles Herodotus's account of the Bronze Men of Psammetichus, and the position of Pharos a day's sail from Egypt proves that the Greeks still reckoned from the Bolbitinic mouth of the Nile, not the Canopic which they came to know after the foundation of Naucratis at the end of the seventh century. Knowledge of other places fit—Lotus Eaters in the Gulf of Sidra, Cyclopes in the island of Jerba off Tripoli, Laestrygonians in Bonifacio on Corsica, and vague ideas of what happened further west. But the content of the *Odyssey* is fairy tale, not saga, and takes us to the forest of European *Märchen* and the timeless folk tale of the bear's son. "If we excise from the *Odyssey* all that is borrowed from the heroic trappings of the Tale of Troy, we shall have a folk tale ingeniously converted into a novella, a story of quasi-contemporary human interest. And if we disregard all the folk-tale material ... we shall have a final residue of pure fiction, the poet's own formative contribution to his poem."

As an antidote against extremists who treat Homer as a war-correspondent (and it must be admitted that they still exist) it is salutary to insist on the importance of popular story and fiction; but this provocative book so combines credulity with scepticism that its object seems rather to shock than to convince. It confuses *origin* with *value* in a way that recalls the nineteenth-century treatment of drama; if Aristeas had anything to do with the sleeping bear, does that make Homer's Odysseus into the bear's son? It falls into the very errors which it castigates—only the Amazons are not close-shaven Hittites but Cimmerians; anything except what the poet says they are, as Myres said in a different connexion. It ignores the fact that Mycenaean and early classical enterprise spread over the same area, and that consequently it can no more be taken as evidence for the seventh century than for the thirteenth. It accepts evidence however fantastic which supports its thesis (for instance, Pausanias's early Hesiod written on lead (IX. xxxi. 4)—in the seventh century—and the connexion of Troy and Etruria), and ignores any which opposes it (for instance, Herodotus's statement (V. 58) that the Ionians called books διφθέραι and the evidence of the word βύβλινος that the Greeks got papyrus first through Phoenician intermediaries). "The archaeological arguments on which so much speculation is based contain a number of loose, vague and sometimes inaccurate statements, which give a misleading idea of the available evidence."[1] For instance, after conceding that "in Homer there is specific mention of bronze swords and bronze axes, hatchets and pruning hooks", he goes on "but otherwise there is not the slightest difference between the uses to which bronze is put in Homer and in normal classical practice". And the battleship is power-propelled, but otherwise there is not the slightest difference between the use to which it is put and the use of the trireme. Homer's warriors did *not* normally wear suits of bronze armour much like the accoutrement of the classical hoplite, and in fact, though it may be irrelevant, Aegean warriors of about 1200 B.C. *did* wear armour very like the Homeric; they did not have pairs of throwing spears, but Carpenter could not use them,

[1] H. L. Lorimer, *Class. Rev.* LXII (1948), pp. 14ff.

because neither did the hoplites. Homeric palaces are wholly unlike seventh-century houses. Although Homer does not mention inlay *on a sword*, he does know of inlay, and positive evidence here weighs more than negative. The boars' tusk helmet comes in fact in the *Doloneia*, and to most scholars proves traditional memory of the past rather than Homeric; our text is treated as oddly sacrosanct, considering the vicissitudes through which it is sent. But "Homer, der antiquarisch wenig, aber historisch wohl sehr viel mit der mykenischen Kultur zu tun hat",[1] knew much more about the world of his stories than this. When the Greece of the *Catalogue* is actually equated with the Greece of Pheidon of Argos, one is bound to ask if poor Pheidon is an adequate prototype of Agamemnon of Mycenae as leader of the united Achaeans. Troy is a long story. The case for Bunarbashi was soundly argued by Charles Vellay,[2] and Winifred Lamb replied temperately: "As most of the arguments advanced have been answered—or anticipated—by Leaf in *Strabo and the Troad*, I cannot do better than quote Leaf's statement that, as long as we do not accept the excessive estimate of Agamemnon's army in the *Catalogue*, 'an adequate force for the siege, or rather the masking, of a fortress at Hissarlik could easily find place along the sea shore from the lagoon to the Intepe with a depth of say 400 to 500 yards . . .'. To this I may add that should the course of the Skamander not tally with the Homeric evidence, a point which seems to me 'not proven', there are two more easterly courses wherein it may have had its bed. . . . Hissarlik, then, is definitely a town site, and one of considerable importance. . . . Its walls, though different in style to those of the mainland palaces, are no less impressive; its surviving buildings, though few, are distinctive. . . . Its area, which seems to M. Vellay inadequate, is practically the same as that of Gonia and not much smaller than that of Phylakopi: it seems to conform to the standard of the times, though I must confess that there is little material in the Aegean available for comparison owing to the scarcity of town-excavations."[3] Exaggeration of an expedition to the right place is more likely than memory of a great expedition to the wrong, and the natural explanation is that tradition knew of an

---

[1] G. Rodenwaldt, *Tiryns* II (1912), p. 204.

[2] *Les nouveaux aspects de la question de Troie* (1930) and articles in the short-lived *Revue des études homériques* I–V (1931–5).

[3] "The site of Troy", *Antiquity* VI (1932), pp. 71 ff.

attack on a Troy which stood on Hissarlik, and that poets staged the battlefield accordingly. "It is sad to see the Bunarbashi will-o'-the-wisp revived, even if only under the heading of fiction."[1] "Dr. Carpenter writes easily, as is his wont. His book is full of happy phrase, and vigorous comment, provocative and stimulating. It needs, and deserves, some revision; but it must have been as good fun to write as it is to read."[2] The lectures were deliberately kept "free of the elaborate dissections of the seminar and the heavier trappings of erudition, which—to mix the metaphor quite irremediably—are only too often the cheap coin of scholarship". Twelve years have passed since they were written, and a lot has happened. It would be unnecessary to spend so long on the book, if it were not that it was typical of a new approach, and that it is still frequently quoted as the final authority, not for much that is valuable in it, but for its unsupported and eminently quotable general conclusions.

The old question whether a single poet wrote the two poems, and the later question whether the poems give a true picture of Greece at the time of the destruction of Troy, were now replaced by others. How long did the tradition of oral poetry last? And what happened to the poems between its end and their first appearance in writing? "Bearing in mind the recent insistence of linguistic and literary critics, especially Meillet and the lamented Milman Parry, on the antiquity of the hexameter and the obscurity of its origin, and on the remarkably strong element of tradition in the language to which the constant use of formulae testifies ... the Homeric scholar must consider not only the earliest form of the *Wrath of Achilles*, but the origin of heroic poetry in Greece, which must far antedate that of the Tale of Troy; the Homeric archaeologist must ask himself whether it is not to be carried back far beyond the actual attack by which the city perished in the opening years of the twelfth century." Hilda Lockhart Lorimer provided "a fresh collection of the archaeological evidence, vastly increased since Helbig's day", which she considered the first requisite of future research, in *Homer and the Monuments* in 1950. The first hundred pages give a compact history of the Aegean down to the end of the Geometric period. The last seventy-five contain a temperate statement of the conclusions reached. The *Iliad* as we have it has a unity to which the *Embassy*, the *Games* and the

[1] H. L. Lorimer, *loc. cit.*

[2] J. L. Myres, *American Journal of Philology* LXIX (1948), pp. 205 ff.

Ransoming of Hector are integral. It cannot have been composed after the introduction of hoplite warfare. From these two premises taken together, it follows that it was substantially the work of one great poet not later than the end of the eighth century—substantially, because interpolations long and short are recognized. The *Odyssey* has the same kind of unity and from the knowledge it shows of the Aegean and of Phoenician activity there, cannot be earlier than the last third of the eighth century. Since the *Odyssey* is by a different poet, later but not much later than the poet of the *Iliad*, dates tentatively suggested are the third quarter of the eighth century for the *Iliad* and the turn of the eighth and seventh centuries for the *Odyssey*. Confirmation is found in the interpolations, which can be dated "with a high degree of probability, sometimes with virtual certainty" to the seventh century, except for the two Athenian interpolations of the sixth century, the *Presentation of the Robe* and the Salamis-Athens entry in the *Catalogue*. The material which the poets used originated in the Bronze Age, but less of the material culture survived than had been supposed by Reichel. Too much interpolation is admitted to satisfy a unitarian like Bowra. Too decisive an influence on our text is left to the eighth-century poets for Dodds. But the real value of the book is independent of the conclusions, sane and well-argued though they are. It lies in the central 350 pages of close discussion of armour and fighting, dress, architecture and funeral customs, and the dispassionate discussion of the relation between the archaeological and Homeric evidence for them. Very little is missed, down to 1947 when the script went to the printers, and new material was being inserted well after what seemed the last possible moment. Since then, fresh evidence has accumulated, but *Homer and the Monuments* remains the framework into which it can be fitted. The author had collected the material in Oxford while teaching for the Homeric Archaeology Special Subject in Honour Moderations and after her retirement. She wrote affectionately of "Sir John Myres, who encouraged me to pursue the study begun in Greece and who has always been ready to put at my disposal his vast stores of learning and to exercise a criticism both stimulating and kind". Myres thought the book over-cautious in its assessment of some of the evidence. For him the poet's own additions were still "the major interpolations, all just earlier than the adoption of hoplite armour, but later than the revival of intercourse with the East". But he went far towards being convinced by its fundamental conclusions. "Both poems are thus presented as falling within one lifetime. At most the major additions are of the years following 'Homer's' death, when his pupils inherited, edited and wrote down what he had left. But 'epic tradition', as the great poet received it in the age of Western colonization, came down from before the Ionian migration, in some sort of guild, with a Mycenaean legacy. This is perhaps as near to historical truth as it is possible to go. Others have filled in details, and will continue to do so. But Miss Lorimer has not only contributed by masterly handling—not of the monuments only—to a real advance, but has greatly facilitated the task of her successors."[1]

Belief that such an advance is possible, generous help to all students, endless fertility in proliferating ideas, and an all-embracing curiosity, were characteristic of Myres in all his work. "This was first suggested by Sir John Myres in 1895" is a typical footnote in the most unlikely contexts. Enjoyment of words and pattern, practical interest in how things were made and what places looked like and an eye for detail as part of a whole were the gifts which served him best in Homeric studies. He was the least typical of scholars, yet the changes in his opinion of the Homeric question ran parallel to the developments of the half-century; and some of his latest work, on the Minoan script, belongs to the next chapter.

[1] J. L. Myres in *Antiquity* XXV (1951), pp. 69 ff.

Chapter Eleven

THE LAST DECADE

---

*H*OMER AND THE MONUMENTS shows signs of the strain and isolation of wartime, but the period during which Homeric studies necessarily lay fallow was a good opportunity for such a work of consolidation. Since the countries round the Aegean have been reopened to the excavator, discoveries have poured in almost as fast as they did in the amazing years after 1893, when "a book even three years old must be behind the times".[1] Renewed excavations, even on such much-explored sites as Troy and Mycenae, have been remarkably rewarding, with the promise of more to come; new sites are being opened up with the advantage of accumulated experience on virgin soil; and in particular the enthusiasm and friendly co-operation of Turkish archaeologists have made a beginning in the great area between Greece and Mesopotamia which has long been the most serious gap in our knowledge of early civilization. The results are still for the most part contained in preliminary reports and articles, and many of the most important excavations are still going on; but it is already obvious that there is growing evidence for interrelation in space and continuity in time. Aegean daggers at Stonehenge[2] and Iberian tholos tombs in Greece[3] must be considered, whether or not they are accepted, and connexions between Beycesultan in the Maeander valley and the Bronze Age Aegean are established and must somehow

---

[1] J. I. Manatt, *The Mycenaean Age*, p. xiv.

[2] R. J. C. Atkinson, *Stonehenge* (1956), pp. 84–5.

[3] Myres in *Antiquity* XXVII (1953), pp. 3 ff., and Stuart Piggott, *ibid.*, pp. 137 ff.

be explained.[1] On many of the sites written records have been found, and as the number of scripts and languages which are (more or less) intelligible increases, the *corpus* of published documents grows.[2] From annals with names and regnal years, hymns, epics and cosmographies, trade accounts and regulations of administration and religion, information can be obtained which turns prehistory into history. If contemporary records are the test, the Hittites of the fourteenth and thirteenth centuries are now less genuinely "prehistoric" than the Greeks before the Persian Wars. The literary evidence poses a new problem. Historians are used to handling documents supplemented by archaeological evidence, but these documents need philologists rather than historians. Archaeologists who try to use them are as baffled by their lack of philological *expertise* as the philologists are when they try to use the archaeologists' results in the interpretation of the documents. Shortly before his death, Myres told me that he regretted that he had never had time to become a philologist. Since in both fields scholars realize that their own results are curiously misleading without experience in their methods, the ideal would be the combination of both disciplines in one historian, but such a giant has not yet arisen. Hope seems to lie rather in the fruitful co-operation of archaeologists and philologists. Both the difficulties and the potential value of such a double approach are explored by Hugh Hencken in his *Indo-European languages and archaeology*,[3] which he describes as "an experiment in treating simultaneously the evidence of language and the evidence of archaeology to see if and how they may be brought to bear on common problems". It is significant that of the 129 entries in his useful bibliography, 81 were published since the end of the war and 124 were not available to A. Meillet in 1922, when he wrote his *Introduction à l'étude comparative des langues indo-européennes*. Hencken emphasizes the danger of arguing from culture to language or from either to race. "In Mexico a small band of invaders equipped with gunpowder and horses was able to impose its religion and to a considerable extent its language on peoples of highly developed cultures. On the other hand, conquering armies like the post-Roman

[1] *AS* VI (1956), pp. 118ff.
[2] An excellent selection is given in J. B. Prichard, *Ancient Near Eastern Texts relating to the Old Testament*, 2nd ed. 1955.
[3] *American Anthropologist*, Memoir No. 84, 1955.

invaders of France, Spain and Italy, who moved into the areas of more highly civilized peoples, quickly adopted the language, religion and culture of their subjects and were soon lost among them." The doubt infects the successive cultural changes in Greece, with their suggestion of new settlers coming from an origin which is still quite unknown, but the diffusion of these cultures belongs to the period which is now emerging from the mists of illiteracy. This book would be incomplete without some attempt to assess the effect of these changes on Homeric studies, but it is made tentatively and with full realization of its provisional character.

The arrival of Greek-speakers is the natural starting point, but its date is still disputed.[1] The beginning of the second millennium seemed at one time certain and is still most probable. There was a wide destruction of the Early Helladic settlements, and at Korakou, where the stratification was first properly observed, developed wheel-made "Minyan" and matt-painted wares occurred immediately above the burnt level.[2] At about the same time, newcomers with horses and wheel-made Minyan ware founded the Sixth Settlement of Troy,[3] and further east invaders appeared in the Halys bend where, some centuries later, they became the dominant power in the Hittite kingdom.[4] The last group certainly brought with them Indo-European languages, and they used a monochrome pottery of metallic-looking shapes as well as painted "Cappadocian" ware.[5] The natural conclusion was that three streams of more or less related peoples were responsible for the changes. There have recently been complications. The excavations which the American School of Archaeology is now conducting at Lerna,[6] have shown that there was unbroken development there from Neolithic to Late Helladic. The destruction took place during Early Helladic times, and Middle Helladic pottery appears gradually and without signs of violence. This strengthens the evidence against a universal catastrophe which

[1] F. Schachermeyr, "Das Problem der griechischen Nationalität", *Relazioni X Congresso Internat. di Sc. Storiche, Roma*, 1955, VI, pp.153ff.; now also J. Mellaart in *AJA* 62 (1958), pp. 9ff. for a different view.

[2] C. W. Blegen, *Korakou* (1921), pp. 124ff.

[3] C. W. Blegen, *Troy* III (1953), pp. 5ff.

[4] O. R. Gurney, *The Hittites* (2nd ed., 1954).

[5] H. Bossert, *Altanatolien* 626–59, 367–80, 388–96.

[6] Latest report by John L. Caskey, *Hesperia* 26 (1957), pp. 142ff.; cf. *ibid.* 25 (1956), p. 173.

had been observed previously on other sites; at Tiryns, for example, H. Dragendorff had reported no break in the pottery series, although this was later attributed to confused stratification.[1] It must now be accepted that a transitional period, without the distinctive wares of either Early or Middle Helladic, was followed first by hand-made Minyan, then by wheel-made Minyan, and finally by matt-painted wares. During these evolutionary phases, Korakou apparently was uninhabited. The destruction was thus less universal and less simultaneous than was thought, and more survived from the earlier period. There were, however, changes in burial customs, cult and building techniques. The desertion of many Early Helladic cities in favour of smaller strongholds, almost all inland, suggests a more rural population and a loss of interest in trade. But the strongest argument for the arrival of the Greeks at this date is a more general one. From now onward two divergent influences can be traced in the Aegean. They might be called indigenous and intrusive or Aegean and Indo-European, but it is perhaps safer to call them Minoan and Helladic. It is likely that each was composite. There may have been Indo-European, or at least alien, arrivals in the mainland earlier; certainly Early Helladic elements persisted, and the highly civilized population, shown especially by a veritable palace (the House of the Tiles) and other fine buildings at Lerna, had a lasting influence. On the other hand, there were certainly immigrations to Crete which did not reach the mainland. But in the Early Bronze Age there is no sharp cleavage within the area, and it is reasonable to suppose that to this period belong the placenames common to Asia, the Cyclades, Crete and the Mainland, which are usually thought to be pre-Greek. From the beginning of the Middle Bronze Age the whole character of the two cultures is different. However strongly Minoan influences impressed themselves on the Mainland, they were absorbed and transmuted. This is particularly clear in the constant transformation of borrowed *motifs* by mainland potters who preferred formal and disciplined pattern.

Relations between newcomers and natives in the three areas were very different. The Hittites took their name and much of their culture, including their ceramic tradition, from their more civilized predecessors. At an early date, they adopted the cuneiform script of

[1] *Ath. Mitt.* XXXVIII (1913), pp. 341f.; Kurt Müller, *Tiryns* III (1930), p. 204.

Mesopotamia.[1] Their social organization, however, was unlike anything found in Asia Minor before them, and its resemblances to the earliest Greek society that we know is close enough to suggest some affinity between the two peoples.[2] By the time that they emerge into history, they have absorbed so much that their original characteristics are obscured. Excavations in the lowest levels at their capital, Boghazköy, where German archaeologists resumed work in 1952 after an interval of thirteen years, will give more information about the earliest period.[3] The founders of Troy VI, on the contrary, borrowed practically nothing. Even in the earliest levels, there is nothing to show that any of the previous inhabitants survived, except some fragments of wares "which in technique seem to attach themselves to the pottery of Troy V".[4] Not a single letter scratched on stone or sherd has been found, and on the present evidence, Troy remained illiterate in the middle of a literate world. The possibility that they wrote on perishable material cannot be ignored, but the result for us is that they are still a "prehistoric" people, whose language and organization are unknown. Minyan pottery is the most obvious link between them and the Middle Helladic people, since the resemblance seems too close to have resulted from independent borrowing; but what the connexion was remains obscure. Troy VI prospered greatly until it was destroyed by an earthquake at the end of the fourteenth century. For its period of greatness, we have the thorough re-examination of the site by the University of Cincinnati to supplement Dörpfeld's sound consolidation of Schliemann's inspired but destructive beginning. After the earthquake, rebuilding was on a meaner scale, but there was no break in culture or change of population until the city (Troy VIIa) was burnt by some enemy about a century later. The enemy did not occupy the city they had destroyed, for the impoverished squatters on the site continued to make the same types of pottery. This period of reoccupation is the first stage of Troy VIIb. After it the site was abandoned until the arrival of new

---

[1] *AS* III (1953), p. 9. One group used a hieroglyphic script, which was recently deciphered with the help of a Phoenician bilingual inscription, R. D. Barnett, "Karatepe, the key to the Hittite hieroglyphs", *ibid.*, pp. 53 ff.

[2] L. R. Palmer, *Achaeans and Indo-Europeans* (1955).

[3] *AS* V (1955), pp. 14–16.

[4] C. W. Blegen, *op. cit.*, pp. 12–13.

occupants is shown by the appearance of "knobbed ware" of a barbaric type, and this change (in the second stage of Troy VIIb) marks the real end of the city founded nearly a thousand years earlier. The knobbed-ware people seem to have amalgamated with the Troadic, and "we reach the Eighth Settlement during the life of which, passing through a Geometric and an Orientalizing phase, and falling more and more under Greek influence, Troy finally becomes thoroughly Hellenized".[1] If Hector's Troy has any historical reality, it must therefore be Troy VIIa, and from the stratification after the destruction, there should be evidence to show how much of the burnt city would have been visible, both when the Greeks arrived in Asia Minor and when Greek influences in Troy VIII prove that they had knowledge of the site. The next volume of the American report will thus be the most important for Homeric studies, and it would be foolish to try to anticipate it. The excavators have, however, given the general outline which has been summarized here.[2] For Homer, the chief question is how far the description of the city and its history in Greek tradition is confirmed. Though Homer's Troy was old compared with the Achaean dynasties, it was obviously too young for the reality, and there is nothing to suggest a time when the Trojans lived in Dardania, because Ilion was not yet founded ἐν πεδίῳ. Homer's Troy fell in a private quarrel; Troy VIIa was destroyed in a general catastrophe, in which the Hittite Empire disintegrated, the cities on the coast of Cilicia and Syria were sacked, and the Delta invaded by land and sea. Both differences concentrate the interest, in a way normal in legend, as in fiction. The main events are the same in history and legend; a great and powerful city on the shores of the Hellespont is destroyed once, not by an army of ordinary men, and later (round about 1200 B.C.) attacked and burnt by an enemy who immediately abandons it. "From its very beginning the Sixth Settlement already possessed the character of a royal stronghold",[3] with room only for the palace (scooped away to make room for later foundations, but certainly on the acropolis) and the houses that

---

[1] C. W. Blegen, "New evidence for dating the settlements at Troy", *BSA* XXXVII (1936–7), p. 11. This volume of the *Annual*, presented to Myres in honour of his seventieth birthday, was not published until 1940.

[2] C. W. Blegen, *op. cit.*; J. L. Caskey, "Notes on Trojan chronology", *AJA* LII (1948), pp. 119 ff., with references to preliminary reports.

[3] C. W. Blegen, *Troy* III, p. 12.

served it. But in Troy VIIa little houses were crammed into every open space and a notable feature of the period is the building of cellars, well stocked with storage jars. The stronghold was, as far as its restricted area allowed, turned into a fortified city; and since this is hard, archaeological fact, it is worth noticing that Homer's Trojans were less than a tenth of the attacking Greeks (B 123ff.). The impressive walls, faced with smooth stone, the four remaining gates, enfiladed and defended by buttresses and towers, are easy to identify in the *Iliad*, but they are not peculiar to Troy; other cities also were fortified. They have, however, two peculiarities. The broad ramparts had a steep batter and were surmounted by a parapet which formed with them an angle or "elbow". "Even if the chinks were filled with clay in ancient times, it must have been possible for enterprising attackers with ease to swarm up the sloping face of the wall. But when they reached the top of the battered portion, they encountered a much more troublesome, not to say insuperable, obstacle; for before them rose the vertical upper part of the wall."[1] Patroklos himself got no further (Π 702). Again, in the *Iliad* the wall had a most vulnerable part (Z 433), explained in later literature by the inferiority of human builders compared with Apollo and Poseidon. The walls of Troy VI were replaced, section by section, by increasingly magnificent stonework, but the rebuilding was not completed. By some unexplained folly, the inhabitants left one section of the inferior old wall on the west, bonding it in as a permanent part of the new circuit, and turned their attention to building towers on the southeast side.[2] Neither feature would be obvious once the walls had fallen into disrepair, and Greek knowledge of them is difficult to explain unless tradition included memory of *these* walls, not of walls in general. Moreover εὐτείχεος in Homer is not a general epithet of cities, but is attached to the particular city, occurring only in two phrases which describe the capture of Troy.[3] Within the walls, there were "spacious, free-standing houses that were laid out at intervals on a series of broad concentric terraces, which rose on successive steps toward the midpont of the citadel. . . . At least four gateways provided access to the citadel, and from these entrances roadways led up to the central area."[4] The epithet εὐρυάγυια is used nine times of

[1] C. W. Blegen, *Troy* III, p. 87.   [2] *Ibid.*, pp. 102–4, 109–13.
[3] A 169 = Θ 241 and B 113 = 288 = E 716 = I 20.
[4] C. W. Blegen, *op. cit.*, pp. 6 and 10.

Troy; it is used once in the *Iliad* of Mycenae, and in the *Odyssey* once of Athens and once of cities generally. Compare this with εὐκτίμενος, which is used 33 times with 20 different nouns, and again we seem to have a traditional epithet of Troy, very occasionally transferred to other places. "Broadwayed" is right for Troy VI but not a notably good description of a Mycenaean fortress and wholly inapplicable to later πόλεις before the Hellenistic age of town-planning. The simple, isolated houses[1] compare with the complex Mycenaean palaces as the houses of Priam and his sons compare with the palace of Odysseus, but this cannot be pressed, since the palace of Troy is lost. The house of Paris, built by the best architect, is of polished stone (Z 244, 313). In Troy VI in the best houses (there are considerable variations) "the skilful technique and the patient labour devoted . . . to the shaping, dressing and fitting of hard stone" actually led Schliemann to disregard the little that he found of this level, because they were "built in so regular and fine a style of masonry that he was convinced they must be ascribed to Greek times".[2] The Lion Gate and the Treasury of Atreus have fine ashlar facing, but it does not seem to have been characteristic of Mycenaean houses and it certainly was not of early Hellenic houses; again the feature picked out is an exceptional one. Buildings inside the city cannot have been recognizable after the burning, and it strains credulity to believe that so many points of resemblance are accidental. It is noticeable that the description suits Troy VI and the events suit Troy VIIa; the real city had lost its greatest prosperity even before the enemy came to destroy it. It looks as though tradition had again concentrated history. The events would be preserved in the story. The description may have been preserved because such a city, like the palace plan, had no successor to supersede it as a suitable residence for a great king; there is no reason to doubt that the poets thought of it as more of a *polis*, or that they provided it with its Greek-seeming temples. Where the tradition was preserved is a problem. It cannot have been at Miletus, the only place in Asia Minor where a continuous tradition of Greek poetry is even conceivable, because the memory of Mycenaean Miletus had been wholly lost, and it seems most likely that it was one of many stories told in

[1] F. Schachermeyr compares them with the Middle Helladic houses at Eutresis, *RE* XXII, 2, p. 1493.
[2] C. W. Blegen, *op. cit.*, pp. 3 and 323.

the Greek oral poetry of the mainland and gained in popularity after the migrations because of its local interest.

Continuity in Greece itself, which had been assumed to account for the survival of Bronze Age memories, has become an established fact from the Middle Bronze Age onward. At Mycenae in 1952 I. Pappademetriou discovered a new Grave Circle, an event not so revolutionary but almost as surprising and important as Schliemann's discovery of the first.[1] It is in its original state, undisturbed by later Mycenaean planning, and to that extent is unique; and where it resembles Schliemann's Circle, it gives an opportunity to watch burial groups and stratification in a way that could never have occurred to Schliemann. Historically, its importance is immense. A. J. B. Wace, in his excavations before and after the war,[2] showed that in Middle Helladic times only the summit was fortified, and a cemetery stretched over the soft rock of the hillside where the Lion Gate and the Cyclopean Walls stand today. Pappademetriou's Circle (B) was built in this cemetery as a special (and certainly royal) burial place. The surrounding wall was thick and rough. The earliest graves go back perhaps half a century before Schliemann's circle (A) and are single cist graves like those in the rest of the cemetery; evidence for dating is not yet published, but at least one such cist grave (A') is earlier than the Shaft Grave (A) which encroached on it. The latest graves overlap in time with some of those in Circle A, which must therefore have been laid out, also in the cemetery, while Circle B was still in use. The graves in Circle B were covered by small mounds, with grave stelai, some of which were found in place. The stelai are both plain and figured, but the chariots shown on several of the stelai from Circle A do not appear. The graves in Circle B contain one to four bodies, and though the richest have swords, gold masks and ornaments like those found in Circle A, precious metals are less abundant. They are, however, rich in fine Middle Helladic pottery. About half a century after the latest burial in Circle A, a Shaft Grave in Circle B was cleared and extended, the bones of the previous occupant piously buried, and an elaborate built under-

[1] G. E. Mylonas, *Ancient Mycenae* (1957), Chapter VI, contains a preliminary account, with good illustrations.

[2] A. J. B. Wace, *Mycenae* (1949) and reports in *BSA* XLV, XLVIII–LI (1950–6). Wace has died since this was written, *iam senior, sed cruda deo viridisque senectus.*

ground tomb constructed in it. This fraternity in death shows that, if there were any new arrivals, they were fully accepted among the old. Change took place gradually, with no sign of violence. The strongest influence comes from Crete, shown in Minoan weapon types in Circle B and transforming Middle Helladic pottery into "Mycenaean" in Circle A. Amber came from the north, apparently down the west coast, since it is particularly copious at Kakovatos. They had already been in touch with Troy VI, where Minyan and matt-painted sherds were found in early levels, and it may have been from Troy, or from the Hittites, or from the Egyptians, as Schachermeyr thinks,[1] that they learnt to domesticate horses. All this could be the natural development of growing prosperity and wider dealings with the outside world.

Mycenae is no longer exceptional in passing through these transitional and early stages. In Argolis there is the same gradual change at Lerna and the same types of burials—Middle Helladic cist graves, similar graves with two bodies, enlarged cist graves, and two Shaft Graves. In Eleusis a cemetery was in continuous use from the Middle Helladic period, and Mylonas thinks that development can definitely be traced from small to large cist graves, and so to Shaft Graves.[2] The graves are almost certainly those which were shown to Pausanias (I. xxxix. 2) as the place where Theseus buried "the men who marched against Thebes".[3] Even as far north as Iolkos, a Late Helladic I palace has been found immediately above the Middle Helladic buildings; the preliminary report notes with satisfaction that a vase with a ship on it was found in the Middle Helladic levels.[4] In Messenia, the finds from this early period are even more unusual. A tholos tomb was found to contain practically nothing except Middle Helladic pottery;[5] it must therefore have been built in the Middle Helladic period, and is something like a century earlier than

[1] *Anthropos* XLVI (1951), pp. 705 ff. He thinks the kings of Mycenae got their wealth by plundering Crete and by helping in the expulsion of the Hyksos from Egypt. But it now seems likely that their prosperity began a little earlier.

[2] *Proceedings of the American Philosophical Society* XCIX (1955), pp. 57 ff.

[3] Reports in *Ergon* 1954–6.

[4] *Ibid.* 1957, pp. 43 ff.

[5] C. W. Blegen, "An early tholos tomb in Western Messenia", *Hesperia* XXIII (1954), pp. 158 ff.

the appearance of the tomb type elsewhere in Greece. The Greek Archaeological Service has excavated a large number of tholos tombs with princely grave goods—inlaid dagger blades, seals and ornaments very like those from the Shaft Graves at Mycenae but belonging to the period of the pillaged Mycenae tholoi; and a building which contained a store of L.H.I pottery with "two matt-painted vases purely Middle Helladic in technique".[1] These all come from the neighbourhood of Messenian Pylos, and prove that even at this early date its rulers were comparable to the kings of Mycenae and no slower in accepting new ideas. The changes begin in the palaces and take some time to spread to smaller towns. Middle Helladic pottery went on being made, and mainland taste gave the new style the characteristics which distinguish it from Minoan. But the rulers themselves must have been in close touch with one another for the new fashions to appear so widely in Greece at much the same time.

This is the Greece of the seventeenth and sixteenth centuries, three hundred years before Troy VIIa was burnt. It happens that the only representations of the body-shield in action, not merely used as an ornament or carried by a static figure,[2] come from the Shaft Graves and we must use them to illustrate the death of Periphetes. There is, however, no evidence that the shield was superseded until the end of the thirteenth century,[3] and the memory of it need not come from so remote a period as this. The vivacity of the art is a temptation, but there is no need to complicate the issue by looking to it for parallels to Homeric themes which are equally at home in less remote centuries. Men have at all times protected their flocks and herds from wild beasts, and the appearance of the scene on a mutilated stele from Grave Circle B is an interesting link in a series which reaches from Akkadian seals to Geometric Greek bronzes, rather than an apt parallel to the similar scene on the Shield of Achilles.[4] So, too, a

[1] Sp. Marinatos, "Excavations near Pylos, 1956", *Antiquity* XXXI (1957), pp. 97ff.

[2] For example, a figure on a Myc. IIIC ivory plaque from Delos carries an 8-shield made of two complete circles, like an upended bicycle, proof that it was not in use at the time (*BCH* LXXI–LXXII (1947–8), Pl. XXV).

[3] See pp. 179ff. above.

[4] G. E. Mylonas, *op. cit.*, p. 137. Cf. H. Frankfort, *Stratified Cylinder Seals*, no. 658; F. Matz, *Geschichte der griechischen Kunst* I, Pl. 32b; R. Hampe, *Frühe griechische Sagenbilder*, Pl. 24–5; K. F. Johansen, *Les vases sicyoniens*, Pl. XXIX, 2; cf. Pl. 7 here.

striking head cut on an amethyst from the grave under the same stele is only doubtfully "reminiscent of the long-haired Achaeans"; for apart from the discrepancy of date, his shock of hair is short compared with the curling locks of his contemporaries in Crete, with whom it would be natural to compare him. The pleasant joke of attributing gall-stones to "a rich and perhaps truly 'Homeric hero' diet", would not call for comment, if it were not such a good example of a common willingness to find Homeric parallels in the common lot of humanity.[1]

For the century after the Shaft Graves, the time of the early tholos tombs at Mycenae, an outstanding problem was the relations between Crete and the Mainland. It had long been recognized that from about the middle of the fifteenth century Knossos diverged from the rest of the island. While in other cities pottery styles developed without much change, at Knossos an individual style with mainland features appeared, and the dynasty which ruled in the palace there showed a more warlike spirit. The other cities of Crete were destroyed in circumstances which suggested that Knossos was trying to establish control over the centre of the island.[2] Soldiers of this time found in graves near Knossos were laid out with swords and spears and all the solemn apparatus of military honours.[3] This lasted until about 1400 B.C., when the palace was surprised by an enemy and destroyed in a violent fire. After this disaster, the city never recovered its former greatness. The course of events could be followed, but the reasons for them were obscure. Now a new fact has to be taken into account, from material supplied originally by archaeologists but interpreted by others.

Evans had recognized writing on seal-stones and on one tablet in Herakleion Museum; and he went to Knossos largely in search of Minoan literacy. In 1900 he found one deposit of pictographs, which

[1] G. E. Mylonas, *op. cit.*, pp. 139 and 157; it is unkind to choose these examples when there are so many to hand, but "the newest song is always sweetest".

[2] This is not certain. The latest pottery reported is: Ay.Triadha, L.M.IB; Gournia, Pseira, Mochlos, Palaikastro, L.M.IB–II; Mallia, Phaistos, Tylissos, Nirou Khani, L.M.II; Knossos L.M.IIIA.1. This suggests a successive destruction of the cities throughout the second half of the fifteenth century, but they may all have been destroyed in the same catastrophe.

[3] M. S. F. Hood and P. de Jong, *BSA* XLVII (1952), pp. 243ff.; cf. LI, pp. 81ff.

he published promptly,[1] and masses of linear inscriptions on sun-dried tablets, burnt hard by the fire which destroyed the palace. An earlier script was found in the excavation of Ay.Triadha in 1902–12,[2] and called Linear A, the Knossian script becoming Linear B. Evans published a synopsis of signs and the most complete tablets in volume IV of the *Palace of Minos* in 1935, but a *corpus* of the two or three thousand friable and chaotic fragments was a formidable under-taking. When he died in 1941, little was ready except photographs and technical plans for printing, with a number of alternative arrange-ments of the signs, and Myres took over the task of completing it. But in 1939 C. W. Blegen had found another royal archive at Mes-senian Pylos, with the complication that the Linear B script, which had been assumed to denote a non-Greek language, was found at a time and place in which Greek was generally believed to have been spoken. Work on the scripts was now going on independently in three countries; many scholars, of whom Johannes Sundwall and Alice E. Kober were the most conservative, were forming their own theories and working methods on the evidence of isolated *graffiti* and tablets and selections published from the main finds; and no one had access to the whole material. Co-operation had not been remarkable, and it was with no expectation of success that Alice Kober asked Myres if she could see his material; but she was welcomed with open-handed generosity. It was a fortunate meeting, for their gifts were complementary. "What Myres could give was wide-ranging theories —bold, but stopping well short of wholesale attempts at translation. It is good to have this: no student will neglect the lively pages dis-cussing sign by sign, nor those on the Palace Archives".[3] Alice Kober also suspected decipherments, but she was as sceptical of *all* theory as she was unshakable on fact.[4] Her demonstration of inflexion in the tablets was fundamental to the final solution. It was one thing Myres could not believe, but he accepted her systematic

---

[1] *Scripta Minoa* I, *The Hieroglyphic and Primitive Linear Scripts* (1909). Pictographs from Mallia were published by F. Chapouthier in 1930, but the linear scripts were really a separate problem.

[2] Published by G. Pugliese Carratelli, "Le Inscrizioni preelleniche di Haghia Triada in Creta e della Grecia peninsulare", *Mon. Ant. dei Lincei*, XL (1945), pp. 422ff.

[3] Sterling Dow, "Minoan Writing", *AJA* 58 (1954), p. 86, in a useful summary.

[4] See "The Minoan Scripts: fact and theory", *AJA* 52 (1948), pp. 82ff.

classification of the tablets by commodity ideograms. She died in 1950 at the age of forty-three, in the year when conditions began to improve. A number of specialists contributed to a *Mid-Century Report*, and as the repair of bomb damage made Herakleion Museum accessible, Emmett L. Bennett, the expert in the Pylos tablets, checked some of the transcripts and references for Myres. In the next year, the Spanish journal *Minos* was started, to publish articles and to record the contributions which more and more scholars were making to the subject. The material already found was published, the Pylos tablets in 1951,[1] and the Linear B tablets from Knossos in 1952,[2] and a few months later it was augmented by several hundreds of tablets from Pylos and a small group, important as the first found outside palace archives and the first (except one) from Mycenae.[3] The evidence was now abundant, but the difficulty of reading documents in an unknown script and language, and (except for the helpful ideograms) of unknown content, remained. Michael Ventris had composed the questions for the *Mid-Century Report* and given his own answers to them. From 1951 he began to send to anyone interested *Work Notes on Minoan Languages Research*. He was an architect by profession, and an amateur of the scripts ever since, at fourteen, he heard Evans lecture at the Jubilee Exhibition of the British School of Archaeology at Athens. His belief, first expressed when he was eighteen,[4] was that Minoan and Etruscan were "both variants of a single 'Pelasgian' language", but his methods were independent of any assumption. In 1952 he suddenly realized "that the unexpected Greek solution was inescapable. . . . It was at this stage that Myres put Ventris in touch with John Chadwick, who had been working independently on Linear B in Oxford for six years and whose cryptographic flair and specialist knowledge of the Greek dialects have been invaluable."[5] "Evidence for Greek dialect in the

[1] *The Pylos Tablets: A Preliminary Transcription*; replaced by *The Pylos Tablets: Texts of the Inscriptions Found 1939–54* (1955). See also *A Minoan Linear B Index* (1953).

[2] Arthur J. Evans, *Scripta Minoa* II, edited and supplemented by John L. Myres. E. L. Bennett, *Corrections to Scripta Minoa II* (1952) is concerned with identification of tablets.

[3] E. L. Bennett, "The Mycenae Tablets", *Proc. of the American Philosophical Society* XCVII (1953), pp. 422ff.

[4] "Introducing the Minoan Language", *AJA* 44 (1940), pp. 494ff.

[5] *Documents*, pp. 22–4.

Mycenaean archives" appeared a year later,[1] and its reception by "linguists and archaeologists was immeasurably more favourable than might have been expected, considering the enormous number of ill-considered attempts which had been prematurely publicized over the past fifty years".[2] When it was found that tablets unknown to the authors were amenable to their rules,[3] the solution was accepted in principle. Seminars were set up in Uppsala, Paris and London, and a new field of Greek studies came into being. Ventris and Chadwick continued their collaboration in *Documents in Mycenaean Greek: 300 selected tablets from Knossos, Pylos and Mycenae, with introduction, commentary and vocabulary*. It is a great beginning, which Ventris himself would soon have left behind, but in September 1956, when he was thirty-four and just before the book was published, he was killed in a motor accident.

The aggressive rulers of Knossos in the late fifteenth century had their archives kept in Greek, and were therefore mainland conquerors who had seized the city in the middle of the century; it was probably under them that Linear A was adapted for the purpose. The surviving tablets belong to the years of the destruction, about 1400 B.C. There is nothing to show who overthrew them; but since the result of the destruction was too lasting for it to have been a mere raid and there is no sign of a Minoan revival afterwards to suggest a native uprising, the probability is that they were attacked by a rival Greek power. In tradition there was no doubt that Idomeneus was of the same nationality as the mainland kings. The Mycenae and Pylos tablets are about two centuries later. Script and dialect, and (so far as they are known) contents and names show the same close resemblances as the material civilization. The script changed so little over the two centuries, that it seems likely that it was used by professional scribes and that literacy was not widespread. The next written Greek belongs to the second half of the eighth century and is in the Phoenician alphabet. There was no language barrier to prevent the telling and retelling of stories continuously through the four or five intervening centuries. These conclusions are independent of the content, much of which is, as would be expected, obscure. The Greek is half a millennium older than anything with which it can be

---

[1] *JHS* LXXIII (1953), pp. 84 ff.   [2] *Documents*, pp. 22–4.
[3] C. W. Blegen, "An inscribed tablet from Pylos", *Geras G. P. Oikonomos*, 1953, pp. 59 ff.

compared, the syllabary is ill-suited to writing Greek, the tablets are often fragmentary, and their contents are account-book entries of a technical character, with a high proportion of personal names. Even for its users, a system which did not note final consonants or, generally, the first of double consonants, cannot have been satisfactory, since the same combination of signs may stand for a great variety of sounds, and case-endings are frequently indistinguishable. Yet it is only the solver of a crossword who hesitates whether *bow* is *arc* or *bob*, and *John owes Henry* is ambiguous only if the word order is variable. The scribes were working in a familiar context (unknown to us), and seem to have set out their items with businesslike regularity. The free word order of poetry would be more troublesome, if the Greeks attempted to record it in writing as their neighbours did. Written or oral, the poetry would be to the tablets what Chaucer's description of the Merchant's dress was to the merchant's own ledgers. "Chair, ebony, with (back?) decorated with gold birds, and foot-stool, inlaid with ivory (rosettes? pomegranates?)" would in poetry come in an act of courtesy, as it does in Homer: "Her then she made to sit on a chair, silver-studded, beautiful, with patterns on it, and there was a foot-stool for her feet"; and "Corslet, 1: (Plates? rows of scales?)—large, 20; small, 10; on the helmet, 4; cheek-pieces, 2", would come in an arming scene or battle. "Secondly he put his corslet round his chest . . . on it there were ten (bands? rows of scales?) of (dark blue paste?) and twelve of gold and twenty of tin. . . . And on his head he set his (two-horned? made of two plates?) helmet, with four (plates? bosses?), with a horsehair crest."[1] Here is the origin of Milman Parry's formulae, when on archaeological evidence they had their beginning in the Bronze Age. *Oimoi*, *kyanos*, *amphiphalos* and *tetraphaleros* were probably as obscure to the poet of the *Iliad* as they are to us, and the nature of the formulae,

---

[1] *Documents*, pp. 343 and 379, cf. L. R. Palmer, *Minos* V (1957), pp. 58 ff.; 389 ff., cf. τ 55 ff., and Λ 19 ff. On the whole subject, see: Sir Maurice Bowra, *Homer and his Forerunners* (1955); T. B. L. Webster, "Homer and the Mycenaean Tablets", *Antiquity* XXIX (1955), pp. 10 ff., "Early and late in Homeric diction", *Eranos* LIV (1956), pp. 34 ff., and "On the track of Mycenaean poetry", *Classica et Mediaevalia* XVII (1956), pp. 149 ff.; L. J. D. Richardson, "Further observations on Homer and the Mycenaean Tablets", *Hermathena* LXXXVI (1955), pp. 50 ff.; Roland Hampe, "Die homerische Welt im Lichte der neuesten Ausgrabungen", *Gymnasium* LXIII (1956), pp. 25–56.

with their verbal association of noun and epithet, creates a strong probability that the poetry was oral throughout. New formulae would go on being made as long as there was a living oral tradition, and old formulae would be adapted to new conditions. The Mycenaeans were themselves makers of fine metalwork; the phrases which assume that treasures were made by Sidonians and carried by Phoenicians, or made by gods and handed down as heirlooms, must belong to the post-Mycenaean period. Since Mycenaean poetry is completely unknown, its form and content are open to free conjecture from the survivals in Homer and in Greek tradition generally. It certainly included battle scenes, but there is nothing to show whether they came in panegyrics of living kings or in stories about heroes of the past.[1] The few fairly certain Mycenaean names in Homer tend to be thickest in routine fighting of Pylians, Cretans and Thessalians, in genealogies, and in court officials,[2] which suggests poetry celebrating the ruling dynasties. Periphetes, the only man from Mycenae except Agamemnon in the *Iliad* and the only man to be killed for incompetent handling of a body-shield, also has a father with a Mycenaean name, Kopreus, who held the position of King's Messenger and was inferior in status to a fighting man. "Hesiodic" catalogues, in and out of Homer, may well contain some of the oldest material.[3] Another possible subject is the mythology of the Eastern countries with which the Mycenaeans had dealings; if so, such hideous tales as the attack of Kronos on his father were distasteful to the Ionians, for their appearance in Homer is slight compared with their Hesiodic elaboration. It is, however, equally possible that they reached the Greeks later, along with Orientalizing art.[4] Stories of magic, of epiphanies of gods and goddesses, and of the supernatural powers of kings, are probable but unprovable. The differences between Minoan Cretans and Helladic Mainlanders are so great that we should not assume that they had a common religion or mythology;[5] but it is

[1] Sir Maurice Bowra, *Heroic Poetry* (1952), pp. 9ff.

[2] Gray, "Mycenaean names in Homer", to appear in *JHS* LXXVIII (1958).

[3] As was suggested by K. Marót, in "La Béotie et son caractère hésiodique", *Act. Ant. Hung.* I, 3–4 (1953), pp. 261ff.

[4] T. B. L. Webster, "Homer and Eastern poetry", *Minos* IV (1956), pp. 104ff.; T. J. Dunbabin, *The Greeks and their Eastern Neighbours* (1957), pp. 56f.

[5] Luisa Banti, "Myth in pre-classical art", *AJA* 58 (1954), pp. 307ff.

reasonable to suppose that Minoan ideas had a considerable influence on their artistically receptive neighbours, and so have found their way into Greek language and Greek thought.

For the civilization which spread over the Mediterranean between the destruction of Knossos and the destruction of Mycenae, any term is question-begging. The artistic *koine* makes it impossible to be sure from which manufacturing centre goods or influences spread. "Late Helladic" is non-committal for the mainland, but hardly applicable to Rhodes, Melos or Miletus. "Achaean" carries suggestions of Homeric "divine-born" dynasties which may or may not be justified. "Mycenaean" may suggest an equally misleading origin or political domination for Pylos or Athens, but at least the tradition which made Mycenae the leading state could not have arisen after its destruction, and it is supported by the position of the great fortified citadel at the centre of a network of strongholds and roads. Mycenaeans in the cultural sense traded or settled from Syria to Sicily.[1] Egypt was open to them until the reign of Akhenaton, and the Myc. IIIA pottery from his short-lived capital at Amarna is the most certain synchronism for dating the succession of pottery styles. There is no evidence of peaceful relations between Egypt and the Aegean after Rameses II had restored the military power which was eclipsed by Akhenaton's preoccupation with religious reforms and the confusion which followed his death. Mycenaeans traded with Troy VI–VIIa, and had free access to Cyprus, Syria and Palestine, and to Cilicia when it was dominated by the Hittites. Western Anatolia was controlled by two independent powers, apparently Asuva in the Kaikos and Hermos valleys and Arzawa in the Maiander valley, hostile alike to Troadic, Hittite and Mycenaean influences; and here the Mycenaeans held only one outpost at Miletus and a settlement at Colophon. From the absence of surface finds, the south-west corner of Asia Minor was practically uninhabited at this time. It is generally accepted that the Kings of Ahhiyava, with whom the Hittite kings had diplomatic relations, were Mycenaeans, but their kingdom is put in a variety of places. It seems unlikely that any except the central power of the mainland, with Miletus as its outpost, Millavanda, would be admitted to the quasi-equality which the Hittite kings accorded to

[1] T. J. Dunbabin, "Minos and Daidalos in Sicily", *BSR* n.s. III (1948), pp. 1 ff.; L. Bernabò Brea and M. Cavalier, *Civilta preistoriche delle isole e del territorio di Milazzo*, 1956.

Ahhiyava, but Rhodes is often suggested, both as the power with which the Hittites dealt and as the chief trading centre of the Levant.[1] Of all this, the Greeks knew nothing. They had some stories of private adventurers, such as Bellerophon, which we may recognize as probably originating in this period, but they had no coherent picture of the great powers or of expansion in the Heroic Age east of Rhodes. Even the Milesians were non-Greek speaking, and Teucer did not go to Cyprus until after the Trojan War. In contrast with this ignorance, their knowledge of Greece was good. The east Peloponnese was occupied by the Kingdom of the Atridae; in the south-west was the equally wealthy Kingdom of Pylos, unknown before the excavations which began in 1939.[2] Since no fortifications have been found, it seems unlikely that it rivalled the military strength of Argolis, but it has produced the finest palace so far found. The painted plaster floor, the frescoed walls, the archive room, the bathroom and lighting, and the courtyard in which animals would not have found grazing, are unlike anything in Homer; Ithaca is not a fair comparison, but the luxury of Nestor and Menelaus, which impressed Telemachus after the simplicity of his own home, and the still greater magnificence of Alcinous, showed themselves in a different way. The Palace, as the archives prove, was the administrative and military centre for the district round.[3] The society was feudal in the sense that it was based on an elaborate system of land tenure. At the head was the *wanax*, with the largest *temenos*, and under him a *lawagetas* and other officials, with smaller *temene*. The land was divided between public and private ownership, but individuals who had freehold in the latter might also possess leaseholds in either. The *basilees* were local officials, responsible for the local levies, but representatives of the king, the *hequetai*, seem to have served with them. Records were kept of supplies issued, and of contributions paid or due; of workers, free or slave, some

[1] F. H. Stubbings, *Mycenaean Pottery from the Levant* (1951); also three Penguin books, O. R. Gurney, *The Hittites*, Sir Leonard Woolley, *A Forgotten Kingdom*, and Seton Lloyd, *Early Anatolia*; and the reports of the Beycesultan excavation, especially James Mellaart in *AS* V (1955), pp. 52 ff.

[2] Latest report in *AJA* 61 (1957), pp. 129 ff.

[3] This summary is kept general and short, to avoid as far as possible the considerable literature of controversy, See *Documents*, pp. 119 ff. and bibliographies in *Minos* for later work.

attached to the king or the commander of the host; of the posting of guards; of sacrifices and ceremonies; and, in minute detail, of land ownership and tenancy. There was considerable division of labour in pasturage, metal, stone and wood working and other essential and luxury crafts, personal service and the professions of herald, messenger, priest and priestess, but since there is no special class of farmers, presumably every freeman worked a piece of land. Zeus, Here and Dia, Poseidon, Hermes, Artemis and Athene, Enyalios and Paiaon (but not Ares or Apollo), Dionysus and lesser divinities such as Eleuthia and the Winds, all receive offerings, either at Pylos or at Knossos or at both. On the relevance of this to the Homeric poems opinion is sharply divided. Homeric society is obviously much simpler. The family of Odysseus has humble friends in its servants and equal rivals in its nobles. "The difference between the two societies", writes M. I. Finley, "was in structure, not merely in scale or dimension. . . . It is a grave error in historical method to assume, as if it were an axiom, that the two societies were essentially or even significantly alike solely because their respective ruling classes spoke Greek dialects and had some gods with similar names."[1] Finley's own axiom is that, with minor exceptions, the background of the poems is coherent; he puts the poets in the seventh century, and since the background is neither Mycenaean nor seventh century, he dates it to the ninth or tenth century. It is worth considering, however, whether "Homeric" society is not simply the poets' idea (inherited from their immediate predecessors but modified by their own experience) of what society was like when the events they are describing took place. In the *Iliad* Agamemnon, ἄναξ ἄνδρων, Lord of all Argos and many islands, wielder of a Zeus-given sceptre, surrounded by kings and their Companions who are a class apart from the common people, is "essentially" not unlike the *wanax* and, what is more important, he is essential to the plot. But most of the time he behaves as though he were *primus inter pares*, obliged to persuade and not command, surrendering his sceptre to the speaker who has the floor, even to some extent expected to consult the will of the army. We know nothing about the constitutional position of a king in the poet's own day;[2] but there is a good probability that this is how he had to behave, and that the poet equated him with the

[1] *The World of Odysseus* (1956), pp. 160–1.

[2] A. Andrewes, *Probouleusis*, 1954.

vanished ἄναξ required by the story, by the fiction that, where all were βασιλεῖς, Agamemnon was somehow βασιλεύτατος. The position in the *Odyssey* is more complex, since we do not know the laws of succession in either period. But it is certainly possible that the poet accepted Penelope's position without understanding it, for the excellent reason that without it there would have been no story. There are details which seem more like the Greece of the tablets than the cities of Ionia—the giving of a "gift" in lieu of personal service, the honours paid by the Lycians to their king and chief officer, the *temenos* offered to Meleager and the cities offered to Achilles;[1] but these are not essential to the poems. Generally, when the plot allows it, the direct rule, illiteracy and homeliness of society in the *Odyssey* at least, is post-Mycenaean. Before we can date more closely, we need to know how the eighth century differed from the ninth or tenth.

Memory of the greatness of Pylos is particularly good evidence of the accuracy of Greek tradition, because no impressive ruins seem to have remained visible. Elsewhere excavations since the war have not substantially changed earlier opinions about the great centres of legend. The fortress of Gla in Lake Copais may definitely be added to Thebes and Orchomenos as Mycenaean, since renewed excavation has found Myc. III pottery. Four gates and some houses have been cleared, and evidence found of a violent destruction, but details are still awaited.[2] Enough Mycenaean pottery has been found in Ithaca to suit Odysseus's small kingdom, though the story may owe some of its popularity to its considerable importance for trade to the west down to Geometric times.[3] Attica is a special problem which will be considered later. In Thessaly, Peirithoos and Jason have long been well provided, and a palace has now been found at Iolkos with three building periods, Myc. I, Myc. II–IIIA and Myc. IIIB; the latest palace was burnt about 1200 B.C.[4] No city of any date has been

---

[1] *N* 669 and *Ψ* 295ff; *M* 310ff.; *I* 574ff.; *I* 149ff. See also M. I. Finley, "Homer and Mycenae: property and tenure" (*Historia* VI (1957), pp. 133ff.). It is true that Homer does not say that the kings of Sicyon and Corinth had a *feudal* obligation to the king of Mycenae, but *any* obligation is inconceivable except in the Bronze Age.

[2] *Ergon* 1956, pp. 34f., and 1957, pp. 32f.

[3] *BSA* XLIV (1949), pp. 307ff., and XLVII (1952), pp. 227ff.

[4] *Ergon* 1957, pp. 43ff.

found in the Spercheios valley for Peleus. Mycenaean tombs and a settlement have been found at Pharsalus, and the claim which the city made, as capital of Achaea Phthiotis, to be the Homeric Phthia has been revived.[1] T. W. Allen called it an "admirable specimen of heraldic history".[2] The Pharsalian nobles annexed Achilles from the Malian fishermen. "Here we have a plain motive, and we see what it was able to accomplish. It could not touch the text of Homer, but, partly by ignoring it, partly by interpretation, secured itself a place in the Homeric world." The objections which Allen saw remain, that Phthia was a district, that it did not cross Othrys, and that Achilles's river is Spercheios, not Peneus. The resemblance between Mycenaean Greece and the Greece of legend is close on the strictest interpretation; an interesting new development is the acceptance of the *Catalogue* as an historical document correct in every detail. Viktor Burr suggested that it came from a Mycenaean muster list which gave one commander, the cities from which the troops came, and the number of ships; Homer added other leaders and the poetic colour.[3] At that time only a Ugarit muster list was known, but some of the Pylos tablets also enumerate forces for guard duty.[4] The case needs careful examination. If names of unknown cities in the *Catalogue* are given to nameless sites, the number of identifications is impressive. But if only places which can be identified with certainty are considered, the proportion with Mycenaean remains is much smaller. Moreover, there are difficulties in the balance of power in the *Catalogue*. Thessaly, including the Spercheios valley, contributes 280 ships, roughly a quarter of the total; about another quarter comes from Central Greece, and only just over a third from the Peloponnese, an odd distribution of the armed forces of Mycenaean Greece at any time. In Thessaly, three inland kingdoms along the Peneus send 92 ships from their coastless fastnesses, and six jostle for room along the coast, with Eumelos in Iolkos sending only 11 ships compared with 177 from the other five. New sites are being

[1] *Ergon* 1956, pp. 46f.

[2] *The Homeric Catalogue of Ships* (1921), pp. 119f.

[3] *Neon Katalogos* (*Klio Beiheft zur neuen Folge*, 36, 1944); cf. A. Heubeck, *Gnomon* XXI (1949), pp. 197ff., F. Focke, *Gymnasium* LVII (1950), pp. 256ff., K. Marót, "La Béotie et son caractère hésiodique", *Act. Ant. Hung.* I, 3–4, pp. 261ff., and George Huxley, *BICS* 3 (1956), pp. 19ff.

[4] *Documents*, pp. 183ff.

found,[1] but Iolkos was the centre and the rest of the country less Mycenaeanized. A handful of Mycenaean sherds in a Bronze Age level does not make a Mycenaean city, or Troy would have to be included in the confederacy of Agamemnon. In Central Greece, Orchomenos is crushed into a corner of Lake Copais, with only one city and no access to the sea. In the Peloponnese, Mycenae is cut off from the Gulf of Argos, and hangs on the very edge of a kingdom which faces to the Isthmus and extends along the north coast toward Patras; Achaia also is yielding burials,[2] but strategically Mycenae depended on Argolis. The largest individual contributions come from the states which are most important in legend, in the rest of the *Iliad*, and in Mycenaean Greece, but their frontiers have been distorted to make room for others. Changes of this kind were likely to be made in the centuries of oral transmission between the fall of Mycenae and the earliest date at which the *Catalogue* can have been included in the *Iliad*.

"Knossos, a great city, where reigned nine-year Minos, familiar friend of Zeus", and the stories of its power, should belong to the time before its destruction; the idea of kingship it implies is foreign to the rest of Homer. The palace at Thebes was burnt about the middle of the fourteenth century, while Myc. IIIA pottery was in use, and the one royal tomb at Orchomenos probably belongs to about the same time. In the same century the great walls of the cities in the Argolid and probably of Athens were built.[3] It has been suggested that the defences were excessive for any force likely to be mounted against them, and that they were built to display strength, not to protect weakness; but danger can never have been very remote. Attacks on fortified cities are often shown in the pictorial records of the Pharaohs, and on a silver vessel from Grave Circle A, on frescos at Mycenae, and perhaps on frescos at Pylos.[4] What particular attack was feared is not known; but the fall of Knossos was a recent warning, and in the end the walls proved too weak. For about a century, however, fine houses spread fearlessly outside the walls of Mycenae and probably in the open country round. Then Mycenae,

---

[1] *BCH* LXXX. i. (1956), pp. 309 ff.

[2] e.g. *ibid.*, p. 291, *Ergon* 1957, pp. 88 ff.

[3] A. J. B. Wace, *Mycenae*; G. E. Mylonas, *Ancient Mycenae*, pp. 32 ff.

[4] H. Bossert, *Altsyrien* 908, 942, 944; *Altkreta*³ 42, 77; *AJA* 60 (1956), p. 95.

Tiryns and Athens all strengthened and extended their walls and brought their water supplies under cover.[1] The Athenians did this the most competently, by building nine flights of steps down a deep shaft to a fountain actually within the walls, and at the same time they blocked their postern gate. Although the excessive use of timber suggests haste against an imminent danger, some of the inhabitants were not deterred from building little houses outside the walls on the north-east slope, over the path and stairs to the blocked postern. Still in the period of Myc. IIIB pottery, all the houses outside the walls at Mycenae were plundered and burnt, and they were not rebuilt; this is the fire in which the tablets were baked hard. It seems to be shortly after this that Troy VIIa was attacked and burnt, since no imported pottery later than Myc. IIIB was found before the destruction. At the very end of Myc. IIIB the houses outside the walls of Athens were hurriedly evacuated and left un-occupied, and Iolkos and the Mycenaean settlements in Chalcidice were destroyed. When the Myc. IIIC style had just developed, the palace at Pylos was sacked and burnt; the archives record arrangements made to patrol the coast, so that the attack was expected from the sea.[2] After the destruction of Troy, Enkomi (the Bronze Age predecessor of Cyprian Salamis) was occupied by people who made Myc. IIIC pottery.[3] These are the years of the disappearance of the Hittite Empire and the land and sea raids on Egypt. Yet the Athenians now let their internal water supply go out of use, and for several generations not only fortresses like Mycenae and Athens, but open towns like Korakou and Asine, continued to exist, though with diminished prosperity. But before the end of the twelfth century, Mycenae was burnt, and Athens was the only Mycenaean city to escape.

Athens was more important throughout the whole Bronze Age than was once thought. Eleusis may have been independent, but the

[1] A. J. B. Wace, "The last days of Mycenae", *Goldman*, pp. 126ff.; O. Broneer, "Athens in the Late Bronze Age", *Antiquity* XXX (1956), pp. 9ff. Troy VIIa was apparently destroyed a little before rather than a little after 1200 B.C.

[2] For the relative date of the destruction of Troy VIIa and of Pylos, see C. W. Blegen in *AJA* 61 (1957), p. 133. The order of events within Myc. IIIB is uncertain.

[3] J. du Plat Taylor, "Late Cypriot III in the light of recent excavations", *Palestine Exploration Quarterly* 1956, pp. 22ff.

whole of Attica was thickly inhabited, to judge from the rich cemeteries reported yearly by the Greek Archaeological Service.[1] Athens itself has been too continuously built over to be a good site for early periods; but fine Chamber Tombs found in the American excavations of the agora show that it shared fully in the prosperity of the period, and its strong walls mark it out as the dominant city of the country.[2] After the fall of Mycenae, the importance of Athens is paramount. In excavations begun by the German Archaeological Institute in 1926, there was found a cemetery which continued in use from Submycenaean times onward without a break.[3] The pottery in the earliest graves is a debased Mycenaean, poorer in quality and more formalized in decoration. It then improves in quality, some Mycenaean shapes disappear and others become sturdier, and the compass-drawn concentric circles and mathematical precision of the severe Protogeometric style is evolved. In the pottery of later graves, the process continues to Attic Geometric and so to Protoattic, with no sharp break at any point.[4] With the development of the pottery, other changes took place. Cremation replaced inhumation at the transition from Submycenaean to Protogeometric and remained virtually universal till full Geometric. The graves are poor in metal, but iron became normal for weapons within the Protogeometric period. Many but not all the women in Submycenaean graves had at their shoulders the long, straight pins which fastened the "Doric" dress.[5] The first reaction to these discoveries was (characteristically) a conviction that the Greeks were wrong in saying that the Dorians did not penetrate into Attica; clearly some of them did, for here were their graves. The excavators in their first publication explained the

---

[1] See especially reports in *Ergon* on a cemetery at Perati, near Porto Raphti, with gold and silver, bronze swords and mirrors, Egyptian beads, a Syro-Hittite seal, etc; and for earlier finds, F. H. Stubbings, "The Mycenaean pottery of Attica", *BSA* XLII (1947), pp. 1 ff.

[2] By Homer A. Thompson. See I. T. Hill, *The Ancient City of Athens*, 1953.

[3] W. Kraiker and K. Kübler, *Kerameikos* I (1939); IV (1943); V. i. (1954).

[4] The series can be followed: Emily D. Townsend, "A Mycenaean Chamber Tomb under the Temple of Ares", *Hesperia* XXIV (1955), pp. 187 ff.; V. R. d'A. Desborough, *Protogeometric Pottery* (1952); K. Kübler, *Kerameikos* V. i.; J. M. Cook, "Protoattic pottery", *BSA* XXXV (1934–5), pp. 165 ff. J. D. Beazley, *The Development of Attic Black-figure* (1951).   [5] Cf. Paul Jacobsthal, *Greek Pins* (1956).

changes as "the first effect of the new Dorian institutions", and found in Geometric pottery "the clearest expression of Dorian discipline and austerity".[1] In *Homer and the Monuments* the graves are still taken to show "small infiltrations of the Dorian stock".[2] But if so, the Dorians failed to produce the same changes in their own countries. Study of Protogeometric pottery from all parts of the Greek world proved that it was not only evolved in Athens, but that it spread from Athens, sometimes with a considerable time lag. "From the fact that signs of a change in the method of burial were already visible in sub-Mycenaean, and from the fact that the new style used in its development the old shapes and decorations to a great extent, it is perhaps unlikely that there was any significant change in the population. . . . The rest of Greece, unaware that the life of Spring had been reborn in Athens, slept on awhile".[3] The places which first show signs of being woken up are those, such as Ithaca, Thessaly and Crete, where a lively Bronze Age tradition persisted.[4] Formalization was a mainland principle of decoration throughout. Moreover, the beginning of other changes can be traced within the Bronze Age. The cut-and-thrust sword, now translated into steel, was well established in Myc. III in bronze. Two iron knives have been found in the Myc. III cemetery at Perati, and four adult cremations (with a fifth not yet confirmed) among the normal inhumations. Two early cremations have also been found near Pylos,[5] and the tradition that the Neleids took refuge in Athens makes this distribution significant for the post-Mycenaean cremations in Attica. It is possible that a dress pinned on the shoulder had survived, outside court circles, from Middle Helladic fashions; for straight pins, found in several M.H. burials, were lying at the shoulders of a woman in one grave, and pins with rock-crystal heads in Grave Circle B are thought to have been used in this way.[6] The last link in the chain from Mycenae to Homer was found at Smyrna.

[1] *Kerameikos* I, pp. 173 and 177.   [2] p. 341.

[3] Desborough, *op. cit.*, pp. 298f.

[4] In Thessaly there was a break in the pottery tradition, with a return to hand-made ware, but the tholos tomb type persisted, and considerable Protogeometric remains are reported above the palace at Iolkos, *Ergon*, 1957, pp. 43ff. In Ithaca and Crete pottery shows fusion of old and new.

[5] *Ergon*, 1957, pp. 89ff.

[6] *AJA* 30 (1934), p. 408, cf. 29 (1933), p. 539. G. E. Mylonas, *Ancient Mycenae*, pp. 144ff.

It had become fashionable to say that the traditional Greek date for the Ionian Migration was much too early.[1] No pottery earlier than developed Geometric had been found in Anatolia, except at a Protogeometric settlement at Asarlik which did not survive, and there was too little history to fill too many centuries; the movement was not the latest of the migrations but the earliest of the colonizations. An Anglo-Turkish expedition under Ekrem Akurgal and J. M. Cook dug from 1948 to 1952 at the old city of Smyrna, destroyed by Alyattes about 600 B.C. Under the spacious seventh-century city there were Geometric houses, going back to about the middle of the ninth century, and below them several occupation levels with local monochrome ware and Protogeometric pottery. The early period "seems to have covered a considerable space of time; in its forms and development the pottery corresponds closely to Attic Protogeometric. . . . The Protogeometric must go well back into the tenth century but probably not earlier".[2]

The difficulty is to find the Dorians at all. Myres had already abandoned the dramatic old story of vigorous northerners with iron leaf-shaped swords, slashing their way through the bronze rapiers of effete Mycenaeans; burning their dead to the horror of their inhuming enemies, and drinking to their victories out of Geometric cups, amid the applause of wives who fastened their Doric dresses with pins or fibulae. Like destroying ghosts the Dorians left no sign of their arrival, and when, much later, the great Dorian cities emerge, they share in the common culture which had never been interrupted in Attica. Connexions between Central Europe and the Aegean can be traced sporadically at all periods, and recent evidence has suggested that the north was not always the receiver.[3] V. Milojčić finds in them evidence for one invasion (the Philistines) at the end of the thirteenth century, causing the destruction of the Mycenaean centres, a second (the Dorians) at the transition from

[1] First suggested by J. H. Jonkees, "The date of the Ionian Migration", *Studia Vollgraff* (1948), pp. 71 ff.

[2] J. M. Cook, *JHS* LXXII (1952), p. 104. The absolute dating of Protogeometric is disputed. It depends on whether a settlement near Haifa, in which two sherds were found, was destroyed by Shishak I or about two generations later. Desborough, *op. cit.*, pp. 182 and 294; W. F. Albright and A. J. B. Wace, *Goldman*, pp. 163 and 134f.

[3] V. G. Childe, "Notes on the Chronology of the Hungarian Bronze Age", *Act. arch. acad. Scient. Hung.* VII (1956), pp. 291 ff.

Submycenaean to Protogeometric, and a third period of northern influence within the Geometric period, about 800 B.C.[1] It is, however, a difficulty that such northern elements as can be traced are not concentrated at these dates, and might as easily be the result of peaceful interchanges as of invasions. Although there was destruction at the end of Myc. IIIB, the civilization lasted on through the Myc. IIIC period, with nothing except a more efficient armament to suggest newcomers, and the positive evidence for continuity from Submycenaean to Protogeometric is strong. F. Schachermeyr attributes the destruction to the sea raiders who were loose in the Mediterranean at the time of Rameses III; they created a desolation into which barbarians moved southward at the beginning of the Protogeometric period.[2] This is attractive, as the population might have withdrawn before raids on the south-east coast to Arcadia and Achaia; but it is difficult to see how coastal settlements like Asine and Korakou could have survived so long, or why Athens escaped in the final disaster; Attica is vulnerable to attack from the sea but lies off the route of invaders from the north.[3] Still more drastically M. Andronikos eliminates the invasion altogether.[4] If a small tribe of North-West Greeks whom we call Dorians migrated within the frontiers of Greece, their movement was secondary and accidental. The real cause was that the aristocracies, weakened by feudal wars and loss of oversea connexions, were overthrown by their subjects. This can be seen at Athens, since the self-sacrifice of Kodros is an incredible tale to explain the expulsion of the kings from their palace on the Acropolis and its dedication to Athene and Demeter, the goddesses of artisans and farmers. The "innovations" are in fact revivals of Early and Middle Helladic ways which had never been abandoned by the common people. A. J. B. Wace also insists on this continuity, not only at Athens but in the Peloponnese. Pottery of the "Granary Class" was found at Mycenae both before and after the

[1] "Die dorische Wanderung im Lichte der vorgeschichtlichen Funde", *AA* 1948–9, pp. 12ff. and "Einige 'mitteleuropäische' Fremdlinge auf Kreta", *Jahrbuch des römisch-germanischen Zentralmuseums, Mainz*, II (1955), pp. 153ff.

[2] *Relazioni del X Congresso Internazionali di Scienze Storiche* VI (1955), pp. 653ff.

[3] A. Philippson, *Die griechischen Landschaften* I, iii (1952), pp. 755f.

[4] "The 'Dorian Invasion' and archaeology", *Hellenika* XIII (1954), pp. 221ff. (in Greek).

destruction and forms a connecting link between the two periods. There was a "Dorian Invasion", eighty years after the Fall of Troy, but it was also the *Return of the Heracleidae*, and "the opening of the Iron Age did not bring about a cultural revolution. These events produced only a political change, which of course had its effects on culture, but did not fundamentally change its character. All that came after was as Greek as what had gone before."[1] Something more violent, however, is needed to account for the main fact, that the countries from Boeotia to the Peloponnese which had been the heart of Mycenaean civilization were virtually obliterated. It is true that the meagre evidence from the Peloponnese known to Desborough has been increased by one Protogeometric grave at Mycenae, belonging perhaps to the second half of the tenth century.[2] The country was not wholly unpopulated for two hundred years. But something pretty drastic must have happened to prevent successful rebels or new dynasties from establishing themselves in the old strongholds or building new ones, and to cause the shift of population, prosperity and initiative to Athens, and later to the regions which had been peripheral in Mycenaean times. Attempts to know better than the Greeks have been so frequently proved wrong that it is unwise to reject tradition on a matter of such large importance. They brought Thessalians, Boeotians and Dorians all from the north—and the Thessalians at least left hand-made pots as evidence of their existence. On the other hand, it is barely credible that "the Dorian peoples were for the most part nomadic peoples using only domestic pottery and so primitive in cultural development that they had little to provide for the spade",[3] or, if they were, that the earlier population did not continue its old activities on however humble a scale. Cities of refuge or baronial manors may be discovered in the future; at present the problem is unsolved.

The distribution of dialects in classical Greece is at least still evidence for some movement of peoples, though the generally accepted account of their development has recently been challenged.[4]

[1] *Op. cit.*, p. 135.

[2] *BSA* XLIX (1954), pp. 259f. Also now from Argos, details not available, *Arch. Reports* 1956 (*Suppl. JHS* 77), p. 9.

[3] N. G. L. Hammond, "Prehistoric Epirus and the Dorian Invasion", *BSA* XXXII (1931–2), p. 170.

[4] Ernst Risch, "Die Gliederung der griechischen Dialekte in neuer Sicht", *Mus. Helv.* 12 (1955), pp. 61ff.; John Chadwick, "The Greek dialects and Greek prehistory", *Greece and Rome* III (1956), pp. 38ff.

The dialect of the Linear B tablets is, of course, unadulterated pre-conquest, and specifically should be the ancestor of Arcado-Cypriote. The grouping *Myc.Arc.–Cyp.Ion.Lesbian* δίδωσι, *Dor.N.W.Gk. Boeot.E.Thess.* δίδωτι is therefore what would be expected. It is less convenient that the independent labio-velar in Mycenaean qe-to-ro-po- should correspond to *Ion.Att.Dor.* τετράποδ-, *Larissa* πετρο [ετηρίς], or to find a grouping *Myc.E.Thess.Lesb.* ρο, *Ion. Dor.N.W.Gk.* ρα/αρ. Moreover Mycenaean Greek seems free from dialectic variations, though until tablets are found in Attica or some area thought to have been Ionian, this means little. The question arises, whether it is reasonable to suppose that dialects and races were unalterably fixed by about 2000 B.C. and thereafter could only mix. Analogies show that dialects are more fluid than this; differences can disappear, so that a single language comes into existence, or appear, so that a language breaks up into dialects. With the Linear B tablets added to other evidence, it may be possible to divide dialectic variations into (1) those which existed before *c.* 1200, (2) those which appeared between the destruction of Mycenae and the migrations, and (3) those which are post-migration. The conclusion reached is that no distinctive mark of Ionic is certainly earlier than the fall of Mycenae; that when Lesbian differs from E. Thessalian, the Lesbian form is younger and sometimes agrees with Ionic; that no difference between Old Aeolic (represented by E. Thessalian) and Doric–N. W. Greek is certainly earlier than the fall of Mycenae; that when Doric–N. W. Greek differ from E. Thessalian, they often agree with Ionic; and that the forms distinctive of Doric mostly belong to the middle group. The theory put forward is that in the second millennium there was one North Greek and one South Greek dialect. In East Thessaly, which was isolated and provincial, Old North Greek was preserved in its most archaic form; Doric developed and acquired its characteristic form in contact with other dialects in the middle period; Lesbian developed after the migrations in contact with Ionic. In the same way, Old South Greek in Arcadia and in Cyprus kept its archaic character, whereas Ionic developed in contact with other dialects. Consequently, resemblances between Homeric Greek and Arcadian can be explained either as archaisms or as Old Ionicisms, and we need no longer suppose that the Dorians stayed in the backwoods (of Illyria or anywhere else) for about a thousand years, and yet arrived speaking a dialect so like those they found in

Greece that the long independent development seems impossible. This interpretation has not yet been subjected to the criticisms of philologists. The epic dialect as we know it is a synthesis of variant forms, but obsolete forms could have been retained along with the modern ones, as old formulae were, and for the same reason—their metrical convenience. If the theory is right, it changes the archaeologist's problem without making it easier. Immigrants into the Peloponnese from such civilized parts as North Greece south of Thessaly were less likely to come as destroyers and more likely to leave recognizable pots about. Again, the problem is unsolved.

The Greek settlers in Asia Minor would take with them stories about ancestors who were not too remote to seem historical, but who none the less had lived in a different and better world. It is easy to imagine that the drab poverty of the present made them live much in the past; they would exaggerate, but they would not want to forget. "From this sense of departed glory and the imaginations it bred the Dark Age gave to the Greeks the conception of a heroic past."[1] The simplicity of their lives would give them little to replace the possessions of their heroes, though some might lapse because they were incomprehensible. But there are still about five centuries before we reach Peisistratos. It is a period much less written about than the spectacular efflorescence of Mycenae. The eighth and seventh centuries, in which the slow growth gained momentum from the rediscovery of the world, are the subject of six lectures by T. J. Dunbabin, excellently edited after his tragic death by John Boardman.[2] So far as we know, a long period of illiteracy lay between. No Mycenaean tablets later than c. 1200 have yet been found; the earliest inscriptions in the Phoenician alphabet belong to the second half of the eighth century, and they already show considerable facility in writing.[3] The Phoenician alphabets from which the earliest Greek letters are derived belong to the ninth and eighth centuries, and the early eighth century is a probable time for the borrowing. Contact had to be made with the East first. It is surprising that the art of writing was not remembered, at least in Athens. In Cyprus there is no evidence of literacy between the twelfth and the seventh centuries,

[1] Sir Maurice Bowra, *Homer and his Forerunners* (1955), p. 28.
[2] *The Greeks and their Eastern Neighbours*, Society for the Promotion of Hellenic Studies, Supplementary Paper No. 8, 1957.
[3] *Ibid.*, pp. 59 ff. See Pl. 8. a.

and yet Cypriote syllabaries in the Bronze Age and the classical period had some signs in common. It is possible that the Greeks went on using Mycenaean script, and, unlike the Cypriotes, abandoned it completely as soon as they met the more convenient alphabetic system. Wace suggests that there may have been an overlap, and if the Dorian invasion was no more than a political disturbance, complete loss of literacy is inconceivable. One Protogeometric or Early Geometric pot with a Linear B sign on it would be decisive, whereas the negative cannot be proved. But the negative evidence piles up, and the Greeks' own belief that the heroes were illiterate is more natural if writing was known to be a recent invention. If, as has been suggested, writing was a specialized skill in the Mycenaean Age, it may well have vanished with the palaces and the centralized administration which made it necessary.[1] A recruiting officer in 1919 was surprised at the amount of illiteracy produced by only four years of disturbed schooling.

By the eighth century the map of Greece has taken its classical shape, with a concentration of power once again in the Peloponnese but with different centres—Sparta, Argos, Corinth and Olympia. The end of the virtual isolation of the Aegean is shown both by the hybrid monsters and other eastern *motifs* which appear on vases and by the presence of foreign goods on Greek sites. At Perachora in Corinthia there were hardly any except local votives in the temple of Hera Akraia, which was perhaps built in the ninth century but was in use until the third quarter of the eighth, but in the temple of Hera Limeneia, although it was built about the middle of the eighth century, scarabs, faience, amber and ivories were common even in the earliest levels.[2] It is the same all over Greece; there are occasional imports in the ninth and early eighth centuries and a rapid increase thereafter. Before the middle of the eighth century (the earliest part has been washed away), there was a Greek settlement at the mouth of the Orontes, modern Al Mina and almost certainly the Posideion of Herodotus (III. 91), and there may have been others in Cilicia. The pottery found there is mainly Cycladic and Rhodian, until its activities were temporarily interrupted by the conquests of Sargon of Assyria at the end of the century and Corinthian pottery appears

[1] Sterling Dow, "Minoan Writing", *AJA* 58 (1954), pp. 120ff.

[2] Humfry Payne, *Perachora* I (1940), p. 34. *Perachora* II is expected shortly.

after the break. But before that, it traded with the Kingdom of Van and the small states which preserved the traditions of the Hittites until they were swallowed up by Assyria, and bronzes from these countries have been found in all the main centres of Greece.[1] The Phoenicians were another small people who flourished during the eclipse of the great powers. "After the uncritical acceptance of Phoenicians everywhere, opinion swung to the other extreme and denied any commercial importance or artistic merit to the Phoenicians and regarded the many ancient references to them as a sort of φοινικικὸν ψεῦδος. More recent study has done much to rehabilitate Phoenician art".[2] There is no evidence of Greeks in Phoenicia, but they met them as traders in the east and as rivals in the west. There must have been close contact when the alphabet was borrowed; and the Greeks set their own stamp on what they borrowed, in art as in writing. Traders and craftsmen might have been expected to make their way down the river valleys of Anatolia to the cities on the coast; but the country is difficult and the hills were inhabited by backward tribes. The material from Smyrna and Emporio in Chios[3] is not yet published. The German excavations at Miletus were renewed in 1955, and a preliminary report says that in the earliest Bronze Age level the pottery was foreign to the Aegean and probably mainly Anatolian, but included some M.M.III–L.M.I sherds and either L.M.I or L.H.I; from L.H.I Miletus was predominantly Mycenaean. Above the Bronze Age levels, Protogeometric and Geometric settlements were found.[4] The publication of this material will be of decisive importance. On present evidence it seems that Ionia lay off the sea route from east to west which ran through Rhodes and the Cyclades, and was late rather than early in responding to the new influences. Such conservatism would foster a tradition of heroic poetry which clung to the memories of the past. It is, however, a constant difficulty that for Geometric Greece the earliest and fullest evidence is Attic. "At this time Athens led the Greek world and, in general, the art of other regions of the Greek world is interesting and forward-looking in so far as it follows the lead of Athens."[5]

[1] Sir Leonard Woolley, *A Forgotten Kingdom*; T. J. Dunbabin, *op. cit.*, p. 25ff.

[2] *Ibid.*, p. 36.

[3] *Archaeological Reports*, p. 35ff. (*Suppl.* to *JHS* 76 (1956)).

[4] *AS* VII (1957), p. 24.   [5] T. J. Dunbabin, *op. cit.*, p. 44.

The Athenians were the first to paint men and animals and whole scenes of action on their vases, and it is from Late Geometric Attic pottery that we get most of the evidence for comparing with the Homeric poems. The funeral vases show the dead man stretched on his bier, sometimes drawn on a cart, surrounded by mourners and animals for sacrifice. Processions of armed men on foot and in chariots pass in his honour, and there are chariot races and funeral games, with tripods and other prizes. All that is needed for an Homeric funeral is there, except the burning of the body; and cremation, which the Athenians no longer practised, went on until the end of the Geometric period east of the Aegean. Chariots appear in battle-scenes, and warriors have pairs of throwing spears and parry-shields (Pl. 5. a and 6. c.). The fighting is so Homeric that T. B. L. Webster has suggested that they are illustrations of legends, not contemporary battles.[1] He argues that some of the groups, such as a man with a centaur, are certainly mythical, and that others correspond in general and in detail with Homeric descriptions of battles, funerals, dances and so on. He suggests that the Dipylon or Hourglass shield was taken from the 8-shield on Mycenaean works of art which had been preserved, as an ivory carving with a warrior is known to have been put in the foundation deposit of an eighth-century temple on Delos,[2] and that it marks the scene as heroic, as it certainly does in the post-Geometric period. The elaborate funerals are, he thinks, appropriate to kings or heroes, but not to common men. The funerals, however, are the difficulty, since it hardly seems possible that the dead man on the vase is not the same as the dead man buried under it; the family might give him a simulacrum of a fine funeral even if it could not afford the reality. The Dipylon shield differs both from the real 8-shield and from its representations in Myc. III art. On vases its wasp waist is absurd, though no more so than the triangular men with matchstick legs, but a little model[3] looks like a genuine shield, and may have been in use, in life as in art, at the same time as the round shield. Whatever the subjects, the realistic detail must be drawn from life, and the close correspondence with the equally realistic narrative of Homer justifies us in assuming that life at Athens and in Ionia was not very dissimilar.

Some of the eighth-century scenes, however, are undoubtedly

[1] "Homer and Attic Geometric vases", *BSA* L (1955), pp. 38 ff.
[2] See p. 262 above.　　　　　　[3] *Monuments*, Pl. VII, 2–4.

mythical, and many may be. In the seventh century, heroic scenes become very common, on Corinthian and Argive as well as on Attic vases.[1] At about the same time, there are several other important changes. At the very end of the Geometric period hero cults were established for Agamemnon at Mycenae and for Menelaus at Sparta, and votive offerings began to be deposited in Mycenaean tombs.[2] Lines of poetry are written on Late Geometric vases. A new kind of poetry which does not belong to the oral tradition begins with Hesiod and Archilochus. And no elements later than about 700 B.C. are assimilated into the Homeric poems.

Oral poetry is not necessarily killed by the beginning of a written literature, and Homeric epic undoubtedly continued to be oral in the sense that down to the fifth century it continued to be heard, not read. But no one would believe that it was "popular" poetry appealing to illiterate audiences and ignored by the educated. It was absorbed by the earliest writers and given a new twist. The inscription on a Geometric cup from Ischia challenges comparison with the cup of Nestor because whoever drinks of it shall not lack the pleasures of Aphrodite,[3] and an inscribed jug from Athens is the prize for the one of the dancers who ἀταλώτατα παίζει.[4] An heroic theme is given a personal and erotic turn, in the manner of lyric. At a time of stagnation oral poetry may remain nostalgically conservative; but the Homeric tradition was sensitive to all that was new in the Geometric period, and the seventh and sixth centuries were full of even more stimulating changes. The hoplite was a magnificent figure, and from the early seventh century painters visualized the hero in hoplite panoply. They sometimes gave him an archaic hourglass-shaped shield, but he held it at a slant as though it were buckled to his arm like a hoplite shield (Pl. 5. b.). This is only one stage further from fact than the change which gave him a pair of throwing spears instead

[1] T. J. Dunbabin, *op. cit.*, pp. 77ff. lists 62 earlier than *c*. 650 B.C. Homer does not put mythological scenes on works of art; the Shield of Achilles, for instance, differs markedly in this from the Hesiodic *Shield of Heracles*. This is another argument for a date before the end of the eighth century.

[2] J. M. Cook, "The cult of Agamemnon at Mycenae", *Geras Antoniou Keramopoulou* (1953), pp. 112ff.

[3] *Röm. Mitt.* LX–LXI (1953–4), p. 42, Pl. 14–16, 1. Here Pl. 8. a.

[4] *IG* I, 492 a. The verses on an oinochoe from Ithaca seem to have epic echoes but the point is obscure, *BSA* XLIII (1948), pp. 81ff.

of the Mycenaean thrusting spear; but epic tradition, which had fully accepted the first change, completely rejected the second. This is the most obvious proof that the fluid tradition froze by about 700 B.C., but the same is true of the poems as a whole. No ancient work was wholly immune from corruption and interpolation, as the textual history of Greek plays shows. There are a few more or less certain later lines and passages, though far fewer than would have been expected even if there had been an eighth-century text of *Iliad* and *Odyssey*. The important thing is that the blazon or allegorical figure or panegyric of Athens or philosophical concept of divine morals is never assimilated into the tradition. The *Doloneia* by its differences shows what has not happened to the rest. Neologisms are numerous and of a quite different quality; the character of the heroes is degraded; the bow of Odysseus is intruded from the *Odyssey*, as it is not in the *Games*; there is antiquarianism which has preserved the uniquely interesting but inappropriate boars' tusk helmet, striving after variety, and false archaism; the time sequence is interrupted, and Odysseus's stomach is overloaded. The large inconsistencies elsewhere (the point at which the *Catalogue*, the description of the Greek wall, the *Teichoskopia*, and the parting of Hector from Andromache are introduced, the two assemblies of the gods, the odd behaviour of Penelope and so on) are of a kind normal in oral poetry; they make an immediate effect, they introduce good details out of contradictory versions, they enable the recitation to be made long or short, and (in Homer) they avoid the need to go back in time to tell what happened in the meantime. Even (but this is heresy), even Achilles's forgetfulness of the *Embassy* is perhaps not wholly inexplicable.

An unbroken history is a more probable background for a continuous tradition of heroic poetry than a series of periods divided by catastrophes. Greek pots and Greek language can now be traced from Mycenae and Pylos to Ionia, though they both look different when they get there. One result of this is that customs normal in one period sometimes appear exceptionally in others, and this has thrown some unjustified doubt on their use in evidence. Among the countless Mycenaean inhumation burials, there are now two rich cremations from Pylos, one from Prosymna and four or five from Attica.[1] This helps to explain why cremation suddenly appeared in Attica at the end of Submycenaean, but it does not alter the fact that inhumation

[1] p. 277 above.

was the normal Mycenaean practice and cremation the universal Homeric practice; the funeral of Patroklos is not an oddity. A single Mycenaean rider does not alter the fact that the Mycenaeans normally used chariots and that in the poems riding is not heroic.[1] Although a lamp has been found in a Protogeometric grave, the lamp of Athene is still one of a number of exceptional things in the *moving of the arms*.[2] The *argumentum ex silentio* is rightly suspect when there is not much evidence to go on; a late date for the Ionian migration never had proper archaeological foundation, and cautious writers always noted that it might be disproved by excavation. But epic deals essentially with what is typical, and, when the positive evidence is abundant, a few exceptions do not stultify the conclusions drawn from it. It is hard fact that Homeric men lived in a world which is realistic in the sense that there is little in it which did not have a real counterpart at some time (the contrast with the silver bows and living tripods of the gods is instructive), but unrealistic in that things which never existed together are comfortably combined within it; and that this process of digestion did not continue after the end of the Geometric period. To make the Homeric world wholly Mycenaean or wholly Ionian, or to put it in some hypothetic halfway period between, or to say that it is fiction, except in the sense that the poems are works of art, is to sacrifice the firm ground established by Milman Parry and generations of archaeologists.

There is, in spite of considerable differences of emphasis, some agreement that this is how the poems came into existence. Controversy has turned on to their fate after they had taken some kind of shape. G. M. Bolling's attempt to establish the Athenian *Iliad* may be taken as the starting point.[3] His assumptions that the Alexandrians

---

[1] M. S. F. Hood, "A Mycenaean cavalryman", *BSA* XLVIII (1953), pp. 84ff.

[2] *Archaeological Reports* (*Suppl.* to *JHS* LXXVI (1956), p. 40 and Pl. I.E.) See also R. Pfeiffer, "Die goldene Lampe der Athene", *Studi italiani di filologia classica*, XXVII–XXVIII (1956), pp. 426ff.

[3] "The archetype of our *Iliad* and *Odyssey*", "The latest expansions of the *Iliad*", "The latest expansions of the *Odyssey*" and "Vulgate Homeric papyri", *Amer. Journ. of Philology* 35 (1914), pp. 125ff., 37 (1916), pp. 1ff. and 452ff., and 42 (1921), pp. 253ff.; "On the interpolation of certain Homeric formulas", *Class. Phil.* 17 (1922), pp. 213ff; *The External Evidence for Interpolation in Homer*, 1925; *The Athetized Lines of the Iliad*, 1944; *Ilias Atheniensium: the Athenian Iliad of the Sixth Century*, 1950.

obelized only when they had manuscript authority, that corruption
was always by addition and never by omission, and that consequently the Athenian text could be established by omitting everything that had ever been questioned or omitted, seem to oversimplify
a complex problem, and detailed study of pre-Alexandrian papyri[1]
and Platonic quotations[2] have shown considerable variations in the
pre-Alexandrian texts. The influence of the Athenian text on our
version is undoubted; its absolute primacy has perhaps been too
readily accepted; and its origin remains a mystery. In an epic diction
which developed over some five hundred years and was transmitted
for about as long before it reached Alexandria, it should be possible
to trace elements of different date. G. P. Shipp applied the analytic
method statistically, and reached the conclusion that "neologisms"
are more frequent in the *Iliad* in similes and other non-narrative
passages of all kinds.[3] The traditional language was more likely to be
adequate for routine descriptions of fighting, feasting or travelling,
but it is a difficulty that in the poem passages of various kinds run
into each other. M. Leumann attacked the question in a more
qualitative way, and argued that the poet sometimes misunderstood
himself, and therefore could not be the same poet.[4] A good example
is κύμβαχος; a supposed original which described a blow on the
helmet followed by αὐτὰρ ὁ κύμβαχος ... was taken by the poet of
E 586 to mean "and he fell head over heels" and by the poet of *O* 536
to mean "and the helmet fell". Another is more dubious; in *Π* 471
κεῖτο παρήορος means "the trace-horse lay"; in *H* 156 (story of
Nestor's youth) ἔκειτο παρήορος means "he lay sprawling" and in
Θ 80ff. (Nestor in danger) someone cuts παρηορίας; "we are forced
to the conclusion that the whole sequence of Nestor scenes in
H–Θ was composed by a poet who knew the trace-horse scenes of the
Patrocleia without knowing or understanding the word παρήορος".
But this would mean that the same poet in one place knew the word
παρήορος but not what it meant, and in another knew about trace-
horses and the word παρηορίαι but not the word παρήορος, and this
seems less probable than that the word was used simultaneously in

[1] G. Jachmann, "Vom frühalexandrinischen Homertext", *Nachr.
Ak. Göttingen Phil.-hist. Kl.* (1949), pp. 167ff.
[2] J. Labarbe, *L'Homère de Platon*, 1949.
[3] *Studies in the Language of Homer*, 1953.
[4] *Homerische Wörter*, 1950.

two meanings.[1] The accumulated examples are impressive, and show that there was a tendency to use a word in the same place in the line even when the meaning was different; but misunderstanding of the word is not the only explanation of this. If there is misunderstanding, the poet may be using a word out of a long passage which he has borrowed from a predecessor, and the question arises, when did the development end? The one datable sequence ends with an eighth-century inscription (ἀταλάφρων-ἀταλώτατα); and the Linear B inscriptions now give a long perspective for the stratification of language, much as Schliemann's discoveries did for the stratification of history. Linear B philology is still too insecure for firm conclusions, but an experiment has been made by T. B. L. Webster.[2]

Textual and philological arguments, however, are linked to the larger question how such long oral poems could have been handed down at all. For "a great epic poem launched on the stream of still-living oral popular poetry without the anchor of writing must of necessity be 'sung to pieces' and in plain words atomized by improvising rhapsodes".[3] And one suggestion is that the pieces were put together again in Athens. Rhys Carpenter drew this conclusion in 1946,[4] and Reinhold Merkelbach undertook a thorough rehabilitation of the ancient evidence for it in 1952;[5] both thought their views heretical, but the Peisistratean Recension is on the way to becoming orthodoxy. Merkelbach says that the fourth-century idea of Attic interpolation in the *Catalogue* could have arisen only when there was a generally accepted tradition of an Attic recension, and that the issue between Dieuchidas of Megara and the Athenians was whether Solon or Peisistratus was responsible for it. But the Megarians could not confute the Athenian claim to Salamis by producing a rival text. Therefore the Athenian recension was the only recension. He concedes that there may have been a written version before it reached

---

[1] These are the examples quoted by L. R. Palmer in *Fifty Years of Classical Scholarship* (ed. M. Platnauer), pp. 23f.; a small point worth noting is that ταλαύρινος is said (Leumann, p. 200) to be too civilized an epithet for Ares; yet a Mycenaean god and goddess can be all shield (M. P. Nilsson, *Minoan-Mycenaean Religion*[2], fig. 156, 158) and Ares has the old equipment of shield with helmet and spear.

[2] *Eranos* LIV (1956), pp. 34ff.

[3] E. Drerup, *Homerische Poetik* I, p. 77.   [4] See p. 245 above.

[5] "Die pisistratische Redaktion der homerischen Gedichte", *Rhein. Mus.* 95 (1952), pp. 23ff.

Attica; but this would not be enough to protect the text, least of all against interpolation of episodes, and the Homeric text was amazingly free from such major interpolations. Therefore the selection from a number of current epic poems must have been made at Athens. The evidence is ambivalent; it might be argued instead that appeal to Homer, on the arbitration over Salamis, on the Athenian claim to Sigeum (Hdt. V. 94), and in the Persian Wars (Hdt. VIII. 161 and IX. 27. 4), could not have been made if everyone had known that the text was made recently in Athens. Athens declined in the eighth century, and in the seventh she had definitely lost her lead,[1] and did not recover it until after the Persian Wars. It is a curious fact that her importance in the Mycenaean period fully justified her claim to heroic importance, and that throughout the Protogeometric and most of the Geometric period she ought to have had no difficulty in gaining a place in the Trojan War. Her unimportance in Homer, in spite of her early connexions with Ionia, is a puzzle. But in the sixth century she was not likely to pirate Homer unchallenged. The whole story has a very spurious sound; but even if accepted, it would prove inter-polation, not recension. Next there are vague references to someone (Solon, Hipparchus or Pericles) who introduced musical competitions at the Panathenaic festival and insisted that Homer be recited in the proper order. Again, even if true, they do not prove that before this was done, there was no recognized order. For the full story of Pei-sistratean compilation, there is no authority before Cicero, and it is inconceivable that Herodotus, who tells all he knows about Homer, should have missed a story so suitable for praise of Solon or blame of Peisistratus. "Of the theory (of the Pergamene Homerists?) that Peisistratus *primus Homeri libros confusos antea sic disposuisse dicitur ut nunc habemus,* the fourth-century and older Hellenism knew nothing, and modern scholars should at last stop bolstering up the hypothesis of an Athenian archetype of our text of Homer (credible in itself) on alleged 'evidence' from ancient writers."[2] A more

[1] A. Andrewes, *The Greek Tyrants* (1956), p. 83; cf. J. K. Brock, *Fortetsa: Early Greek Tombs near Knossos* (1957), p. 218, for the dwindling of Athen-ian trade to Crete in the eighth century and the increase of Corinthian trade in the seventh century.

[2] F. Jacoby, *F. Gr. Hist.* (1955), 485 F 6, note. See also J. A. Davison. "Peisistratus and Homer", *Trans. of the Amer. Philological Ass.* LXXXVI (1955), pp. 1 ff.

reliable measure of Athenian influence is the Atticisms in our text. They are numerous where an Attic form could be substituted without affecting the metre, but J. Wackernagel proposed to attribute to Athenians only Γ 152–3, H 470, Ψ 226 and τ 520, with B 759–70 and Λ 470–1 accepted as late.[1] Since Greeks had a strong sense of the appropriate dialect, this cannot be used as an argument against extensive Athenian rewriting, but it is certainly not evidence for it. The literary influence of Athens, not necessarily exercised in Athens and probably after the Persian Wars, would be enough to produce the Athenian colour.

The real argument for a sixth-century Athenian recension (and it is a strong one) is the great improbability of a written text of such long poems at an earlier date. Writing is likely to be used first for laws and contracts. The expense and labour of writing the *Iliad* and *Odyssey* would be great, and poets used to oral composition would need a strong incentive to force the effort on them. The Panathenaic festival, with its regular recitations, is the first known occasion which supplied such an incentive. There is in fact a flat contradiction: a written text of the poems is impossible before the sixth century; but if the poems had been orally transmitted they would have assimilated new material during the seventh and sixth centuries. The compromise that they were memorized and repeated with little alteration satisfies no one, because it is alien to the methods of oral poetry. If a single written text, preserved by the Homeridae (about whom we know practically nothing) or for a festival at the Panionion (about which we know nothing),[2] is really impossible, we must suppose that for some reason the convention of the heroic world was so firmly fixed that poets and improvisers confined themselves to it and shut their eyes to the seductions of a new world. It seems possible for a generation, but hardly for longer. On the other hand, the written text was not a physical impossibility. The alphabet was there, and trade with the Phoenicians could have brought papyrus, if the local supply of skins was inadequate. No other people first used writing to paint or scratch lines of light poetry on their pots, and the Greeks may also have been exceptions in its early use for preserving their great heroic poems. The coincidence between the earliest writing and the closing of the epic tradition is striking.

[1] *Sprachliche Untersuchungen zu Homer* (1916), p. 159.
[2] H. T. Wade-Gery, *The Poet of the Iliad* (1952), pp. 19 ff.

Little has been said of the issue between analysts and unitarians, because it has recently been well summarized by E. R. Dodds.[1] For him "between the more moderate spokesmen of the two schools the difference is now largely one of terminology: what the analysts call nuclei or prototypes, the unitarians call sources; what the analysts call expansions, the unitarians call interpolations." It has been the hope of reasonable men before. According to H. L. Lorimer in 1925, Gilbert Murray said that he had used similar arguments to Leaf and Allen, and that they were both very angry. The question how far each poem, in spite of its diversity of material, bears the stamp of a single mind will continue to raise up devotees for and against, and it is difficult to imagine any new evidence which can be brought to its solution. But there are other questions which cut across the analyst and unitarian division. When and where did the poems become so fixed that additions must be called interpolations? If it was not till Peisistratean Athens or Ptolemaic Alexandria, they must be judged by different literary standards and largely discounted as historical documents; but it is not necessary to be a unitarian to believe that the couplet which superimposes a gorgoneion on Agamemnon's shield is alien to the *Iliad* as a whole. Is the Homeric world Mycenaean with a few anachronisms, or eighth century with a few garbled survivals, or something intermediary, or a synthesis of them all, or a fictional world of the imagination? Fundamentalists, who may be analysts, are now more concerned to look for the bench on which Telemachos sat than for the tree under which Homer slept, and sceptics, who are often unitarians, concentrate more on the geography of Ithaca than on the authorship of the *Odyssey*. Such questions as these may be answered by fresh evidence, especially by new discoveries of tablets and by excavation on post-Mycenaean and post-migration sites. Certainly the last part of the *Lexikon des frühgriechischen Epos* will differ in its archaeological and philological material from the two which have appeared.[2] The danger perhaps is that Homeric preconceptions will have too much influence on interpretation; for, as Myres said, every kind of evidence should be interpreted by its own appropriate method.

[1] *Fifty Years of Classical Scholarship* (ed. M. Platnauer), pp. 1 ff.
[2] Edited by Bruno Snell; the first part appeared in 1955.

INDEX